The Metabolife® Story

The Rape of Cinderella

Michael J. Ellis
Former CEO and Co-Founder
Metabolife® International, Inc.

MJ ELLIS Publishing

For further information, please visit:
www.themjellisgroup.com

Book design by Arbor Books, Inc.
www.arborbooks.com

Printed in the United States of America

The Metabolife® Story: The Rape of Cinderella
Michael J. Ellis

1. Title 2. Author 3. Memoir/Business/Health

Library of Congress Control Number: 2008911210

ISBN 10: 0-9822402-0-1
ISBN 13: 978-0-9822402-0-5

To my children,
Christian, Joseph (Mikey), Nicholas, and Isabella (Bunny),
all of whom unknowingly saved my life during the hardest times.
Thank you.

In honor of my father, Joseph Ellis, Sr. (1921-1990), my best friend.

To my mother, Carmen Ellis. You're the best, Mom.

To all the Metabolife employees, distributors,
and customers who put their trust
and faith in me and Metabolife.

To my oldest son, Christian Ellis.
Christian, without you, this book
never would have been possible. Thank you.

Special thanks to Monica Ellis
for enduring all the stress and challenges,
and for being a wonderful person
and outstanding mother to our children.

Table of Contents

This book was written from the perspective of its author. As such, some of the legal and historical accuracy is subject to the author's own memory. It should be considered a primer of the events surrounding Metabolife International, Inc.—a kind of high-level overview of everything that has happened to the author and why (in his own opinion). A great deal of material supporting the accuracy of this story can be found at www.themjellisgroup.com for your review.

While much of the material in this book is presented as if it were the author's reflections on a single deposition, some of the content was drawn from multiple depositions.

Finally, it should be noted that, at times, the story is not told in chronological order. Since this is such a complex account of events, it was determined that separating each chapter into its conceptual, rather than chronological, context made the most sense. The result is a story that occasionally jumps from one year to another (and back again).

At Least if You Believe Everything You Read on the Internet

Make no mistake; I'm a bad, bad person.[1] I have a dark, dark history. I'm the kind of man with a death on his hands. The kind of man with a history of illegal drug activity.[2] And the kind of man who refuses to apologize or even take blame for anything he's ever done.

So who am I? For starters, I'm the inventor of Metabolife 356, one of the most profitable and wildly popular weight loss supplements ever unleashed on the public. I'm also one of three founders of Metabolife International, Inc., one of the most successful dietary supplement companies in history. That much is certain.

And to those who would care to write about me, my gains were ill gotten, my product…deadly. In fact, I'm directly responsible for the thousands upon thousands of serious health problems suffered by my customers.[3] All because I concocted and released a product under the knowledge that it would adversely affect the health of

---

[1] http://www.signonsandiego.com/uniontrib/20040723/news_1n23metabo.html.

[2] http://www.yourlawyer.com/articles/read/8666.

[3] http://oversight.house.gov/Documents/20040827102309-56026.pdf.

anyone who took it—a product so deplorably dangerous that the Food and Drug Administration, in all its benevolence, eventually had to step in and put a stop to it.[4] And you know what? I knew *exactly* what I was doing.[5] I just didn't care about the consequences. Could you really blame me? There was just so much *money* to be made.[6]

Just in case that's not enough to get you going, I should also mention that I'm a tax fraud. A *colossal* tax fraud. My partners and I accomplished this feat by offering significant political kickbacks and siphoning record amounts of money into secret offshore accounts. Oh, and it's rumored that we had more than just a passing concern in the suicide death of our former accountant, Mike Compton.[7] And the best part is that, despite all of this, despite the fact that my company and I were charged with nearly a hundred million dollars in tax evasion, we essentially got away with pleading to defrauding the government of just over $300,000.[8]

You shouldn't be surprised, reader. I'm a bad, bad person. The kind of man who would cultivate a history of gun-related trouble. A history so colorful that I would even be indicted on substantial weapons charges.[9] The kind of gun-toting lunatic who would get himself so deep into federal crime that he'd have no choice but to effectively destroy his company and all those who depended on it for income by copping to a plea of lying to the FDA.

So I'm a corrupt businessman. I'm the inventor and peddler of a violently harmful product. I'm a drug dealer. I'm a tax fraud. A gun nut. And a liar of the highest regard. Yes, reader, I'm all of those things and more.

At least if you believe everything you read on the Internet…

---

4 http://www.fda.gov/oc/initiatives/ephedra/february2004/.
5 http://www.usatoday.com/news/health/2002-08-15-ephedra_x.htm.
6 http://www.signonsandiego.com/news/business/20030720-9999_mz1b20metabo.html.
7 http://www.signonsandiego.com/news/business/20031202-9999_1b2metabolif.html.
8 http://www.signonsandiego.com/news/business/20051006-9999-1b6metabo.html.
9 http://www.ergogenics.org/metabolife5.html.

Chapter 1

Superman Never Makes It to the Beach, Or "Prepping for a Deposition"

Steve Mansfield. A brilliant and creative former U.S. attorney? Yes. A pain in the ass at that particular moment? Yes. Can I blame him? No. I mean, I was supposed to be in there learning about how to conduct myself during a deposition for an FDA-backed lawsuit being leveled against my company. And there I was, only caring about finding the right moment to run a gag or tell a joke. You know, to lighten the mood.

The year was 2000—the retail turn-of-the-century, the average American locked in a weight-loss battle, our diet pill, known as Metabolife 356, flying off the shelves—and me and three of my attorneys were sitting around in Bill Low's corner office in the giant, conservative, shimmering-cheese-wedge skyscraper that was Higgs, Fletcher & Mack, LLP. "San Diego's law firm since 1939," I think is their motto.

Anyway, Bill had the standard lawyer's office and the view to prove it. He sat to my right—tall in front of his window, looking intently at Steve from the leather captain's chair he kept parked behind the big mahogany desk that stood between him and the rest of us. He's good-looking with narrow eyes, Bill is, with his strong jaw and slightly receding hairline. His thick brown mustache he wears in that well-groomed painter's brush style. Bill's a no-nonsense kind of guy—the kind of guy who, if you ask him a question, doesn't speculate on the answer. He just tells you, "I don't know. I'll find out." The kind of guy who researches everything. I mean, by the time all this legal fallout for Metabolife was over, he knew more about ephedrine than I did.

So counting Garry Pay, another of my legal team, there we all were: everyone but me looking a little too uptight. Professional, but uptight. Especially Steve. And really, to be honest, it was all starting to wear on me. You could cut the tension in the air with a knife. So what I did was, I only half-listened to Steve while I mulled over the details of a great joke I'd heard recently. The one about Superman. *How did that one go?*

"They're going to try to set traps in there," Steve said, sounding a little nervous. "If they tell you something you don't understand, then tell them you don't understand. You understand?"

I smiled distantly, but still ignored the question. Instead of answering, I took a gold pen off Bill's desk and passed the time by fidgeting with it. Turning it over from hand to hand, twirling it around. Casually, I scanned the desk for a piece of paper I could draw on. Doodling is a favorite pastime of mine. Helps me keep my head straight.

The reason Steve started glaring at me just then—and probably the reason he felt the need to talk to me about traps in the first place—was because I wasn't just any witness going in for deposition. I was the CEO of Metabolife International, Inc. And CEOs tend to make terrible witnesses. So naturally, my attorneys, Steve and Garry especially, seemed anxious about putting me in the deposition box.

I guess this latest round of indifference on my part did it for Steve, because he finally went silent. For a long while, I could feel him staring at the top of my head. "Mike," he said, sounding like maybe he was speaking to a dog he half expected to piss on his shoes, "are you even listening? This is important."

I stopped fidgeting and glanced up at Steve, who sat in the

plush chair across from me. My eyes stayed on him just long enough to notice his frustrated expression and the graying hair that he kept in perfect lawyer-shape on top of his head.

I nodded impatiently.

"What are you going to tell Frantz if you don't understand a question?"

I leaned back in my chair, feeling its front legs graze my shoes as they picked up off the ground. "I don't know," I said, nonchalant. "I guess I'll just tell him to get fucked."

All three of my attorneys stopped breathing.

"Mike," Bill said. "C'mon."

"What am I gonna do?" I said incredulously. "If I don't understand something, I'm going to tell him I don't understand."

I watched as Steve looked back down at his notepad. He nodded like a grade school teacher satisfied with a student's answer. But by the time he started in with his next deposition briefing, I'd long since stopped listening. I mean, I knew that in twenty minutes or so, I'd be getting thoroughly rat-fucked, so what did it all matter? Why not think about Superman going to the beach?

"Remember to pause after questions," Steve said. "We'll need time to object and—"

"Hey, Bill," I said, interrupting Steve. "You ever hear the one about Superman going to the beach?"

Bill's eyes told me he was agitated, but to his credit, he smiled slightly. "I don't know," he said.

I let my chair rock back down to the floor so that all four legs were touching. I stared at the twirling pen in my hand as I continued: "Superman wants to go to the beach, right? But he doesn't want to go alone. So he says, 'I know! I'll go see what Batman and Robin are up to.'"

Garry, sitting in the guest chair to my left, leaned in slowly to listen. His discomfort was obvious.

I didn't break stride: "But he gets to Batman's place and Batman says, 'No, buddy, I can't. I'm a little busy taking care of Joker. And Robin's got homework.'"

Bill smiled his impatient half-moon smile.

"So Superman says, 'I know! I'll go talk to Spiderman.' But Spidey's all tied up with Mary Jane, if you know what I mean. Superman's starting to think that maybe he'll have to go to the beach alone, right?"

I looked up at Steve, who was doing that thing he does when he's pretending not to listen: He stares at the notes he's made on the yellow legal pad on his lap. Steve is a meticulous note-taker. He would take pages and pages of notes during this deposition, I knew. I'd seen him do it many times before.

"But on his way to the beach," I said, louder this time, just in case Steve couldn't hear me through his note-studying, "Superman remembers the Green Hornet. *Let's see what Green Hornet is up to*, he thinks. But Hornet isn't home. His Chrysler's not in the garage."

I look up at my three attorneys. At this point, none of them even seemed to be paying attention. A war of attrition, I guess. I stared incredulously at Garry Pay. Surely, *one* of my attorneys would want to hear the punch line—dirty or otherwise. But Pay shook his head, too. At about 6′5″ and 340 pounds, Garry had kind of a Baby Huey thing going on—only difference being that he wasn't a giant, yellow, diaper-wearing duck. He might not have had the pear shape or the deer-in-the-headlights eyes, but he definitely had that kind of demeanor. Young guy. Nicest guy. Anyway, being that he's a Mormon, I guess I shouldn't have been surprised that he didn't want to hear the dirty ending to my joke.[10]

"Man, you guys need to loosen up," I said, chuffing frustration through my nostrils.

---

[10] Some background on Garry Pay (other than being a Mormon): former football player at BYU. A center, I think. He was good enough there to get drafted by the Chiefs, who he played with for two years. I'd met Pay a few years prior at an association meeting, back before he'd even thought about taking the bar exam, let alone passing it. He worked then for a company called Enrich International, a network marketing firm. But by the time we reached deposition day, Pay was a good regulatory attorney with Patton Boggs in Colorado. He made an excellent member of Metabolife's increasingly enormous legal team. But still, he was always looking for obstacles when most people looked for solutions. Didn't matter what came up in conversation; didn't matter how Steve figured we could circumvent all the likely traps; Pay had an obstacle for us.

No response.

"Fine then. You don't want to have any fun, we won't have any fun. What've you got for me?"

Just then, Ken Dix—another of my attorneys—poked his head into the room.[11] A vain man, that Dix. The kind of guy who wore expensive suits and paid for obvious hair-plugs just to cover his own perceived inadequacies. He looked us over from face to face, then left without saying a word.

I glanced at Bill, who shrugged.

Taking advantage of the lull in conversation, Steve got up, setting his legal pad behind him on the seat of his chair. "Excuse me," he said. He made for the door, obviously going to take a leak.

I thrust my hands to either side. "Wait a minute," I said. "I was just getting into this deposition shit."

Steve ignored the comment and pushed through the door.

Bill cleared his throat. I went back to playing with his gold pen.

"I know that what Steve's telling you is obvious," he said. "I know you already know it. But the deposition notice says specifically that Frantz plans to introduce the video as evidence. So it's important that you don't say anything you don't mean to say. And be aware of body language."

Sure, I was listening. But that didn't mean that my eye hadn't finally caught something to doodle on: Steve's discarded legal pad. I leaned forward and pulled it onto my lap.

Bill continued as if nothing was out of the ordinary. I guess he assumed that I was using Steve's pad to take notes. "He's going to try to paint a picture of you that isn't exactly favorable. He'll try to

---

[11] Actually, I probably shouldn't call Ken Dix "another of my attorneys." Really, he was one of Metabolife's. And I can't say as I'd ever much liked him, either. Why? Because he would panic at the drop of a hat. He was opinionated. Vindictive. Envious. And he was the kind of so-so attorney who would hand out privileged information like candy on Halloween. I remember hearing from a former employer of his that this particular ineptitude had once cost them a lot of money.

Later on down the line, Ken would fuck Metabolife and wind up drawing severance pay. I remember catching his eye one time in the airport after that. He literally turned and ran away, shuffling like a speedwalker as he looked back over his shoulder to make sure I wasn't chasing him.

make you out to be some kind of career criminal who knew his product was dangerous and still put it on the market."

My attorney made an important point, here. You don't win cases on facts; you win them on perception. The lead personal injury (PI) attorney in this case—a toad of a man named Jim Frantz—would be trying to depict me as a convicted drug dealer. He would surely draw connections between Ephedrine and methamphetamine—even where there were none in the case of my product. He would do all that he could to tell the viewer of this taped deposition that, while I might have gotten out of drug dealing, I was still firmly rooted in legal drugs.

But right then, I wasn't fully listening to Bill. I had more important things to do.

I flipped to about the tenth page on Steve's legal pad. I did this for a couple of reasons. First, there wasn't enough room to draw on the top page (my attorney had covered it in his notes). And second, I knew that he would eventually reach this page during the deposition—and that fact would make for some prime comedy.

So I started drawing. I stuck my tongue out slightly as I polished up the top half of my drawing: the back of a man's head and shoulders. This doodle would be big enough to take up the whole page.

Steve wasn't strange when it came to his work habits.[12] Most of the attorneys I've met in my long string of legal battles fall into one of two categories: either they work their asses off or they do the opposite of work their asses off. The reason that they can exist in either of these ways is that they've basically created their own industry. In other words, the legal world is so complex, so convoluted, that you now *need* an attorney for everything from defending yourself against trumped up lawsuits to filing paperwork at the office. Lawyers just help you get through the fog. A fog that they

---

[12] See, here's the thing about Steve. Yes, he was a brilliant and creative former U.S. attorney, but it seemed sometimes like the law was all he thought about. Who could blame him? He's a capable lawyer and his wife's a superior court judge. And today, his fortitude—and probably his exceptional work with Metabolife—has landed him a partnership at Akin, Gump, Strauss, Hauer & Feld, LLP.

created. Throw in the fear that gets propagated by the justice system and you can't help but want to hire a whole team of lawyers. That's the ultimate job security, right there.

So they might be a necessity. But that doesn't mean that you don't have to keep them loose. Keep them on their toes.

I set down my pen and held my drawing at eye-level. I'd just finished the perfect rendering of a bare-assed man bending over, shooting the moon. I showed it to Bill, who stopped talking for a moment to shake his head and chuckle. Then, I flipped the pages back so the top page was showing and replaced the pad on Steve's chair. The pen I tossed onto Bill's desk.

The second I leaned back in my chair, I heard the doorknob being worked. Ken Dix poked his head in again. He curled his lips back anxiously as he spoke.

"They're ready for us in there," he said.

As Ken slid out, Steve slid in. He charged straight for his legal pad, none the wiser.

As the last to stand, I fell in behind Pay and Mansfield, Bill Low bringing up the rear. We all filed out of Bill's office together—and as we did, I was struck by the notion that all of my attorneys looked like executioners leading a man to his death.

Chapter 2

Profile of a "Dealer"

Pay had broken his personal record in the forty-yard dash on the way down the hallway, so by the time Steve and Bill filed in to the conference room, doing their best impression of hard-assed lawyers, he was probably already seated at the table. I took my time going inside. Ken Dix, who'd apparently stopped to get a drink from the fountain, brushed past without a word. Meanwhile, I stood outside the doorframe, just out of sight, hunched over a familiar circular can: my Skoal smokeless tobacco. Scooping out a small pinch of the chalky brown dip, I loaded up my lower lip. This would carry me for at least an hour or two.

I took a deep breath and entered the conference room. Immediately, my demeanor changed from joking mode to deposition mode. My heart rate jacked to the point where I could feel it in my throat. I was nervous as hell, but I did my best not to show it. *Don't let them see you sweat,* I thought.

Still, I knew that the stakes would be higher in this room. Here I was, representing the most successful weight loss company in history, the creator of Metabolife 356, by far the most affordable, safe, and effective diet pill on the market. But if I said something wrong—or even mildly inaccurate—it could wind up placing the entire company and all of its employees at risk. Just the slightest turn of phrase could hand Metabolife over to these rat bastard PI attorneys. Then everyone would be out of a job.

Nobody had noticed me yet because everybody was too busy trying to look important or intimidating. So I took the moment of anonymity to worry about the dip in my mouth. I realized quickly that nobody would ever notice it. There just wasn't enough in there to create that weird bump in my lower lip. I ran my palm over it, just to be sure.

No, I thought. *I'm fine.* My head, too, was fine, despite the anxiety. I knew that this was because I'd remembered to take two Metabolife tablets before coming into the office that morning. Metabolife always kept me focused and alert. More than ever, that fact would come in handy on this day.

As I snapped back to the reality of the impending deposition, I watched as another of my legal team, Dave Allen, stood from his place at the table and walked in my direction. He extended his hand for shaking. A man with a round face and fair complexion, Dave was one of those lawyers who just looked like a nice guy. Like a guy you might want to have a beer with after work. But don't let the blue eyes and the careful part in his thick red-brown hair fool you; when it comes to being a lawyer, this guy's a bulldog. And sharp as they come.

"Hi, Mike," he said. He wore a wildly colored tie with his conservative suit, I noticed. Yellow and red on kind of a smoky gray.

Bill swooped in from my left before I could reply. "Remember to pause before you answer. We'll need time to object, if we have to."

I nodded slowly, my eyebrows raised as I examined the room. The conference room. The place where I'd get deep fried. It seemed simple enough. A rectangular conference table in the middle. Lawyers and staffers of all stock and stature shuffled around it. Behind the empty seat nearest me—in the center of the long end of the rectangle—was a screen like the ones they use as backdrops at the DMV. Only in this case, the screen was gray. I laughed inwardly at its washed-out color, realizing its underlying purpose: just another subtle element in the plaintiff's attorneys' attempt to portray me in a negative light. I'd look ghostly and sickly on the deposition tape. Like a man facing his death.

The wall opposite the doorway, on the other side of the conference table, was not a wall at all. Floor to ceiling windows. Outside, the view of San Diego's business district was drenched in the bright sunlight of what looked like a nice day. So it was bright outside. And it was bright in the room. This entire collection of light, I knew, would be shining directly into my eyes. I wouldn't be able to see the opposing counsel. Plus, my pupils would constrict when they wanted to dilate—which would make me look and feel even more uncomfortable in front of the camera.

I noticed, also, that beside the camera, they'd set up a series of lights. These would serve a dual purpose. They'd light the way for the camera and also shine directly in my face. In the end, this would make things feel like an old-fashioned police interrogation.

Examination over, I looked back at Allen, but he seemed to have run out of words. He patted me on the shoulder, gave a reassuring nod, and headed back to his seat at the far right corner of the conference table. My eyes panned down to the far left corner, where they settled on a woman who I figured to be the stenographer. She made a note on a legal pad to her right, just then. Across from my seat, the business chair, a man who appeared to be the camera guy fiddled with tapes.

So apart from these three—and Pay, who could not have been more intent on riddling out his notes—everyone else was shuffling around. The PI attorneys, two men who'd be doing their best to make me look like an asshole, conferred quietly on the other side of the table. Frantz and Keegan. I'm not exaggerating when I say that I could smell Frantz's cheap cologne all the way from where I was standing. In fact, it seemed to fill the entire room.

Anyway, I figured if I was going to fry, I might as well get the job started. So I took my seat in front of the washed-out-gray screen and flattened my tie. I remember feeling glad to have worn the dark blue tie because it wouldn't clash with the background too badly and make me look like some kind of alien on camera. You have to worry about these kinds of things. My attorneys thought so, anyway.

I blinked into the camera lens, which was pointed squarely in my face. Such a cold eye. And I'd get to stare into it for an entire day.

As if taking a cue from me, everyone else found their seats.

The camera guy immediately hit the button and started the recording. "Good morning," he said, speaking sidelong into the camera. "This is the videotaped deposition of Michael J. Ellis taken at 401 West A Street, twenty-sixth floor, San Diego, California, on Wednesday, May 24, 2000, in the matter of Potier versus Metabolife, case number GIC 731141. My name is Terry Taylor of Kelly and Company. The deposition is now commencing at 10:12 a.m. The court reporter today is Shelley Schniepp of Peterson & Associates."

Shelley looked up briefly and smiled, showing her teeth. Her hands moved rapidly over the weird keyboards stenographers use.

Terry continued without missing a beat. "Would all persons present please identify themselves, beginning with the witness?"

My heart fluttered. I placed my hands on the table, then immediately removed them when I remembered that you're not supposed to do that sort of thing. It makes you look nervous or fidgety on camera. "Michael J. Ellis," I said blandly.

Allen jumped right in after me. "David Allen," he said. "Akin, Gump, Strauss, Hauer & Feld on behalf of Metabolife International, Inc."

That's a mouthful, I remember thinking.

Just to my left at the table and just off-camera sat Bill Low. He always dressed well and kept himself looking clean cut. Today was no different. "William Low on behalf of Metabolife International, Inc."

William, I remember thinking.

Then it was Mansfield's turn. He sat to my right, also just off-camera. He wore bright suspenders and a tie that day. If he'd been wearing a belt, too, I would've been worried. To keep your pants up with suspenders is strange enough, but to feel that you need a belt, too? A man like that's got serious security issues.[13] Anyway, like he always does, Steve got right to the point: "Steve Mansfield from Akin, Gump on behalf of Metabolife."

To the right of Mansfield sat Ken Dix. He seemed entranced by his cuticles, which he picked nervously. Maybe he lacked confidence. I don't know. Maybe he was actually aware of the possibility that the other attorneys in the room were better than him. "William K. Dix," he said, never looking up from his fingernails. "Vice president, general counsel, Metabolife."

Vice president, I remember thinking. Then, I shuddered inwardly.

Garry Pay sat at the end of the table, also to my right. When it came his turn to speak, he laid his hand flat on his legal pad and leaned forward. "Garry Pay, assistant general counsel, Metabolife."

To Garry's right sat a woman I didn't recognize. She had dark brown hair with heavy bangs in the front. Pale skin. Soft but unremarkable features. She seemed rather cold. But then, so did everyone in the room, at that moment. "Lisa King," she said. "Walsworth, Franklin, Bevins, and McCall, for Chemins Company." Chemins had been brought in on the lawsuit, as they were the manufacturer of Metabolife.

To Lisa's right, next to Dave Allen, was another woman I didn't recognize. She had blond hair and either hazel or green eyes; I don't remember. Attractive. Long, slender nose and carefully plucked eyebrows. "Tawnya Boulan on behalf of Herbalife International America," she said.[14]

---

[13] Actually, Steve doesn't have any kind of security issue. He's an excellent attorney who always keeps a level head. In fact, both he and Bill have this way of making a guy feel comfortable, even when he's under unreasonable amounts of heat. Probably has to do with their excellent command of the language. They talk slowly and precisely and reason things out. If you're going to rate attorneys, there's really no comparison.

[14] Herbalife. The other organization being filed against in the lawsuit. See, the plaintiffs in this case were claiming injury due to the fact that they had taken Metabolife in conjunction with Herbalife, another dietary supplement and network marketing firm. This company had developed the Formula One Nutritional Milkshake, so they were in the hot seat with us and Chemins. So here we all were: three companies with their feet in the fire.

And now we'd come to Keegan and Frantz, attorneys at law. If I'd invited ten total strangers into the room and asked them to pick the two personal injury attorneys out of the group, nine out of ten would have gotten it right. Keegan sat between Boulan and the camera. Skinny guy. The only one of the two ambulance chasers who looked fit enough to actually catch the ambulance. Glasses. He reeked of sweaty excitement—Metabolife being his first big case, I'm thinking. His expression throughout the deposition was priceless: like a guy who might drool all over the table at any moment.

"Patrick Keegan," he said, "Krause and Kalfayan, attorneys for plaintiff, Yolanda Perez." He enunciated each syllable. Almost like he was trying to sound smarter than he actually is. When he said "Kalfayan," for example, he sounded a little like the lion from *The Wizard of Oz.*

Then there was Frantz. Standing as tall as Napoleon. You could just tell that he'd been holding his breath in anticipation of his turn to speak. There's no way around it: Frantz had a jowly face. Goofy smile. He kept his hair slicked back in that near-greaser style. Chubby guy. Chubby enough to need Metabolife. I'll give him this: He dressed himself well. But then, how good can you look when you have the face of a toad? And as a quick sniff of the air reminded me, he capped it all off with what smelled like the entire bottle of his obviously cheap cologne.

"Jim Frantz," he said with an air of exaggerated importance, "attorney for Julie Cunningham-Potier, plaintiff."

Introductions now behind us, the videographer instructed the court reporter to swear me in, which she did coldly and efficiently. I found myself wondering, *And why don't they swear in the attorneys?* I mean, if there was anyone in that room set to do some lying, it would be the lying rat attorneys seated all around me.

But in any case, we were off: Frantz kicking in with the standard opening questions about how to spell my name. I watched my attorneys take notes on my answers. Like, what, they didn't already know how to spell 'Ellis'?

"Have you ever had your deposition taken before?" Frantz asked.

"Yes, sir," I said. Earlier, I'd decided that it would be a good idea to call Frantz "sir" whenever I could, though it made my skin crawl to do it. Here was a man who would be asking me questions designed to make me look like an irresponsible and careless person, and I had to call him "sir."[15]

"How many times?"

"I'm not quite sure." I suppressed the smile that boiled up within me. With all these frivolous lawsuits, I'd been in this hot seat so often. "I would guess between six and twelve times."

The lead attorney for the plaintiff then explained the ground rules for a deposition, which I found kind of funny since I'd just explained to him that I'd already done this six to twelve times. Still, I answered his questions carefully and thanked him when he was finished explaining. If I hadn't been so nervous, I would've been bored already.

Then, Frantz shifted gears, returning to the deposition line of questioning. It all seemed so unnecessary—like we were already wasting time—but see, PI attorneys always share information. In the hours and days that would follow, I knew I would be asked a number of questions that would seem completely random, if not entirely irrelevant to this particular suit. But when you have multiple lawsuits levied against you, you're basically fighting all of them at once. Throw in the Food and Drug Administration (FDA) and everything gets even more convoluted and difficult. The FDA is like the Borg from *Star Trek*. You can fire back at them, but the moment you do, they adapt to your attack and come back at you with something new.

"Back to the divorce proceeding within which you gave a deposition," Frantz continued. "Who was that friend?"

Allen piped in. "Objection; relevance," he said toward the

---

[15] But the question is, why was he trying to paint me in such a negative light? I have a theory about the answer: Because no matter how many times these PI attorneys and/or the Food and Drug Administration tried to "prove" that Metabolife was an unsafe product, they couldn't. There was just too much science showing that our product was unfathomably safe. So the next best thing, I guess, is to suggest that the founders of the company peddling said product are untrustworthy bastards.

camera. Then, he flashed a glance at me before taking down more notes. "You can answer."

"That was for a friend of mine," I said. "Michael Blevins. His divorce proceedings."

I had a feeling that Frantz would dwell on this particular deposition because he would want to establish my relationship with Mike Blevins. But since his way of getting down to the point was roundabout at best and just plain stupid at worst, I'll just come right out and say it:

I first met Mike Blevins when I was thirteen or fourteen years old. So that's forty-one years now that we've been friends. See, growing up, Blevins had been dealt a bad lot in life. At sixteen, he'd been cast to the wind by his mother and father. His father, Bob, an irrational drug abuser who hated Mike for some reason, took his wife and youngest child up to San Francisco, leaving his oldest son behind in San Diego. His mother, Joni, never wanted to leave her son, but she had no choice. Bob was a violent man.

When Mike turned eighteen, Joni would come back down to San Diego and reunite with her son, but not before two years of being forced to abandon him. Mike would forgive his mother, but for a time, he'd had to deal with living in his old Volkswagen bus, which he'd parked in front of my parents' house.

My mom would help take care of him. She would do his laundry, feed him, and clean for him whenever she could. Eventually, Blevins moved into his own place—a garage apartment that cost him thirty dollars a month. I remember going over there often with my mom and hanging out with Blevins while she picked up his laundry, cleaned, and just generally mothered him around.

So that's the point about Blevins and me. From the beginning, we were closer than friends. More like brothers. And being his brother, I have to say that he's a great human being—one of the greatest human beings—despite what has happened to him in his life. Over the years, he's proven himself as nothing short of an exceptionally hard worker. And a bright, intelligent one, too. Did he make mistakes? Yes. But that didn't mean he didn't have an excellent perception of right and wrong—or a strong desire to avoid doing wrong by anyone. The reason Frantz brought up my old friend wasn't just because of his checkered past, though. It was because he ran the distributor operations for Metabolife.

Clearing my throat, I reached for a glass of water, careful to slide my hand in on the surface of the table. I didn't want my hand to shake, see, because the shaking would show the camera how nervous I still was. Keeping it pressed to the table would prevent any unwanted signals.

With the fact that I knew a man named Blevins more or less out of the way, Frantz changed subjects wildly again. He began to appear as if he thought that jumping around from topic to topic might be sufficient technique to bait me into a trap, catch me in a lie. One thing he obviously forgot: I'm not an idiot. But Frantz's ultimate goal was obviously to make me look like a loose cannon who cares very little for the value of human life. And given such a goal, the best place to start digging would be my career as a police officer.

"Did you ever provide any deposition testimony," Frantz said, pausing for effect, I guess, "or any testimony in conjunction with any matter that you were involved with at the National City Police Department wherein you…there was a claim made against you by someone?"

I proceeded slowly for a few reasons. First, I wanted to give my lawyers time to object—which they didn't. Second, Frantz was so awkward in speech that I often had to replay everything he'd just said in my head, just so I could be sure I understood him. And third, this was a sore and potentially damaging subject; I wanted to tread lightly.

"Yes," I said.

"When was that, roughly, that you provided testimony in respect to that?"

"I believe 1980."

"What was the 1980 incident about?"

"Objection," Allen barked. "Relevance." He then nodded to me, which I assumed meant I could answer.

"It had to do with a police shooting I was involved in," I said as nonchalantly as possible.

"Just to understand, was there some sort of a civil claim filed by the person that was shot?"

"Objection," Allen said. "Relevance."

"Yes," I said.

"Were you the shooter in the incident?"

"Objection; relevance."

"Yes."

"Were the hearings in respect to that in terms of hearings within the police department?"

I paused for a long time, unsure of what Frantz even meant. Allen used the pause to object yet again.

"Counsel," Keegan said, pinching the bridge of his nose, "I don't want to interrupt the flow of the questioning, but I'm sure you're aware that relevancy objections aren't necessary since relevancy objections aren't waived if they're not given at the time of the deposition."

"I also know this video is intended to be played at trial," Allen said, sounding as if he was talking down to Keegan already.

I found it difficult not to laugh.

"I don't think I've ever shared with you my intentions at any time," Frantz interjected.

I watched as Allen looked over at Bill incredulously. "It's in the *notice*," he said.

"Well," Frantz said slowly, like a toddler who's caught in a lie and has to buy time to think up an excuse. "I've never shared with you whether I intend to play this video at trial. Whether I do or I don't is irrelevant anyways."

"Let's just make it clear," Allen said, thrusting his hand out for emphasis. "In the notice of deposition, it specifically says that that's your intent."

I zoned out for a minute, wondering how it is that two grown men, two trained lawyers, could sound so much like children arguing on a playground. After another ten minutes or so of bickering—and once they'd managed to determine that Frantz was, in fact, an imbecile regarding his own deposition notice—the sharks in the room all agreed on setting up a continuing objection from my bulldog of a lawyer. This way, Allen wouldn't have to keep chiming in on this line of questioning.

Frantz's expression seemed to smooth over to relief as he continued. "Did you ever testify at a hearing at the National City Police Department in respect to the 1980 shooting incident?"

I remember 1980...

An investigation was conducted in my honor—the kind of investigation no reasonable cop wants to be a part of. Recently, in the line of duty, I'd shot and permanently disabled a young man in his twenties. A man named Villa. Since the shooting had come during the pursuit of a suspect, I felt and continue to feel that it was clean. But my own feelings can't halt an investigation.

I don't recall much from the inquiry other than the outcome. It would be determined that the shooting was justified, that I'd committed no improper act in pursuing and subduing the suspect. A civil action would be filed following the hearing, but as it was brought against the NCPD for issuing hollow-point bullets, I really don't recall how it went.

Frantz broke me from my thoughts of those painful days by—honestly—asking me where and when I was born. I answered in a confused sort of way. We then covered my high school years, my brothers, my relationship with my mother. I seriously began to think that Frantz was gearing up to ask me out on a date.

I glanced over at Garry Pay, who would've looked like he might pass out from exhaustion if his hand wasn't tracing a pen carefully over his notepad.

For a good hour, maybe more, Frantz and I discussed my educational background: high school, a brief stint at Southwestern, and the sheriff's academy at Miramar. Frantz took special interest in whether I'd received training in the identifying or creation of illegal street drugs, specifically methamphetamine. In any case, he seemed particularly fascinated by the concept of a two-day drug course at police school.

"Did you receive some sort of certificate for that course?" he asked.

"Yes," I said.

"What was that you received?"

I felt like rolling my eyes, but held off. "A certificate."

"That you attended the course and as a result of attending the course, you received the certificate?"

I waited for my attorneys to jump in. Something—anything—to get this guy to speed things up. We get it already. But that's the thing about depositions. There's this urge to just start talking. To just spill out the whole truth in story format without having to wait for questions. But you can't. Depositions aren't designed to reveal the truth. They're designed to paint a picture of some *version* of the truth. It's all a gotcha game. If Frantz won the day, his version of the truth would show up on video; and his version considered me a liar and a killer and a drug dealer and a dishonest businessman. Of course, I'm none of those things—so I had to make sure that Frantz didn't win the day.

Incidentally, I got some reprieve from the monotony when I looked over at Mansfield. He'd just turned a page in his legal pad. Instantly, his face went beet red. He leaned forward and covered his notebook with his chest, shielding it from view of the others with his elbows. He glared at me.

I caught a glimpse of my artwork before he managed to get it covered. I must say, that was one accurate brown-eye.

It took every ounce of my willpower not to laugh into the camera and probably every ounce of Mansfield's not to tear my head off from the embarrassment. But laughing was out of the question. Emotion of any kind is out of the question on a deposition tape.[16]

As soon as Mansfield calmed down and I got back to focusing on the matter at hand, we took a short break—just long enough to change out and replace my plug of Skoal.

By the time we returned, Frantz had finally decided to come off

---

[16] I'd felt from the very beginning that keeping cold and calculated wouldn't be a good idea—I mean, people don't like people who don't show emotion—but those are the rules of a deposition. At least, those are the rules according to all the good attorneys at Akin, Gump.

the drug course certificate line. Instead, we spent more time than I care to think about discussing my career history—everything from picking tomatoes to working in my father's clothing store to more of my time with the NCPD. Then, we covered more careers: my time as a chauffer, a commercial real estate agent, the purveyor of a failed home security firm, and a fraud investigator for an insurance company. We discussed the end of one marriage and the start of another, my history of entirely legal campaign contributions, more about my ongoing friendship with Mike Blevins. And then, finally, he hit me with the line we'd all been waiting for:

"Were you convicted of a drug offense?"

"Yes," I said as calmly as possible.

"Was that a felony conviction?"

"Yes."

This obviously excited Frantz, because he began stumbling over his words. "When did you learn that you first…first learned that you may be…you were suspected of…let me take that back." He paused for what felt like a long time. "Did you ever manufacture methamphetamine?"

It's 1988. I'm walking behind Mike Blevins, who shuffles slowly because he's carrying a box full of equipment. I have a similar box in my hand.

We're heading from the van down the long, tree-lined driveway to an old house in Rancho Santa Fe—an old house I'd recently leased under my name. It's a single-level home constructed in a 1950s style. Its rooms are large, its paint a stark white, and its flooring linoleum and old carpet. The back is lined with sliding glass doors, which open to a pool in the backyard. The yard is picturesque, as it carves into the edge of a lemon and orange orchard. It's an affluent area of San Diego, this Rancho Santa Fe. And expensive—despite what the outdated appliances and spiders and cockroaches running around everywhere might suggest. You pay for your neighborhood, I guess.

But Blevins had suggested that we pay the extra. "We'll draw less suspicion in a nice neighborhood," he'd said.

So anyway, we get up to the house and Blevins sets his box down on the stoop. He looks exhausted and incredibly wired with stress as he runs a hand through his sandy-blond hair. He stands about 6'4", so he's a big man. But despite his tough exterior, it's clear from when you first meet him that he's a sensitive and caring guy. The kind of guy liked by almost everyone.

After dusting off his hands, Blevins unlocks the door. We carry our boxes inside and set them in the living room. Blevins switches on the light.

For a long while, we wait. Neither of us can think of anything to say because we're both so weirded out and nervous by what we're doing. I don't know about Blevins, but I still can't believe we're doing it at all. Here we are, waiting for a cook, a man who'd agreed to come out and help us make our product, courtesy of Blevins' father, Bob. The cook? A guy named Brian.

Then, finally, we hear the doorknob work its way to unlatched. Brian steps inside. He's tall and broad. Taller even than Blevins and much bigger than me. A good-looking kid. And in great shape. From the moment I lay eyes on him, I can tell he's a little on the stupid side. He just has that look about him—like everything in life is a mystery.

Brian glances nervously from window to window. "Hey," he says.

"Took you long enough," Blevins says.

I just shake my head, unable to speak because I'm more nervous than I've ever been.

"We got that burner like you said you needed," Blevins offers.

The burner Blevins had purchased from a storefront suggested by Brian himself. Our setup had disappointed the cook upon first meeting. In fact, Brian had claimed that we didn't have anything close to what he'd need in order to cook up our product. So Blevins had gone out with his dad's dishonest seed money and purchased a burner to Brian's exact specifications. Yes, Blevins' dad was a drug dealer. A lowlife of the highest regard. And there we were, taking his money. Helping boost his operation.

"So where's it at?" Brian asks.

Blevins points to the box nearest him.

"Well, let's just hurry the fuck up," Brian says anxiously. He rifles through the box and fishes out the burner. My heart skips about eight beats as I watch him pull out a knife and clip the head off the plug, exposing the wire inside.

"What're you doing?" I ask.

"Don't worry about it."

I can't believe my eyes. There doesn't seem to be any logical reason for what Brian's doing. He's prodding the wires around, looking like he's trying to get them into position before jamming the bare wires into the outlet. He then tries switching on the burner, looking remarkably surprised when it doesn't work.

Blevins glances over at me in desperation. I shoot him a look that says, "Not my fault, man. This is *your* guy."

It takes Brian nearly two hours to get the wires into a position where it works. Blevins and I pass the time by continuing to move boxes full of equipment into the house—all requested by our intrepid cook. The minute we finish, Blevins gets a call on his cell phone, which looks like a small suitcase. He'd carry that ridiculous thing around by its shoulder strap everywhere he went. When he presses the receiver to his face, he looks like a WWII soldier calling back to the sergeant for more mortar fire.

I watch as his expression changes from hopeful to frustrated to completely nervous. His forehead looks sweaty as he replaces the giant phone on its giant hook.

"Landlord," he says. "We got another notice."

Brian and I groan.

This means that we'll have to re-pack all of our things and hide them behind a wall of boxes and furniture. See, the landlords I'd rented from were in the process of trying to sell the house to a new owner. So pretty regularly, we'd get these notices that they intended to show the house. Whenever one arrived, we knew it meant we would have to cover the evidence.

"Fuck," Brian says. "I just got this burner working."

Frantz passed a document around the table to me. It took a while because each of my lawyers on the left side of the table had to examine it first. Two little pieces of paper stapled together. When my eyes fell on the top sheet, my heart sank. My drug indictment. The plaintiff attorney really hammed it up, just then. "Is there anything in there that is incorrect, to your knowledge?" he asked.

"Objection," Allen said coldly. "Instruct the witness not to answer on several grounds: one, relevancy. Two, not likely to lead to admissible evidence. Three, as you recall, this is an indictment and you're asking him whether or not allegations in an indictment are correct, which would not be within this witness' knowledge because it applies to more than just this witness."

At that, Frantz got all huffy on us. "Well," he said, "don't coach the witness, please."

"Excuse me?" Allen asked, glaring around from face to face as if he couldn't believe what he was hearing.

"You're coaching the witness and that's inappropriate."

Allen smirked condescendingly. "I went to Mr. Frantz's school of objections during the deposition of Ms. Perez."

Frantz, for his part, ignored the jab. "Mr. Ellis," he asked me, "did you manufacture methamphetamine on or about October 28, 1988?"

It's Labor Day weekend, 1988. Brian's just returned from the kitchen with our first batch of product. Even though Blevins and I know almost nothing about meth, we can tell immediately that something isn't right. We'd both done our research and had seen pictures of it. I had my drug course certificate from the NCPD, after all.

"Hey, isn't that supposed to be white?" I ask.

Brian looks completely oblivious to my meaning. "Yeah," he says. "Why?"

"It's pink, Brian," Blevins says.

"Oh…yeah…I guess it is."

"Great," Blevins says, sounding about as frustrated as I'd ever heard him sound. "This is shit."

"It's not shit," Brian pleads. "I just let it cook a little long, I guess. It'll be fine."

"Brian, it's shit."

I shake my head, aggravated.

Brian offers a blank stare.

"I'll take it up to my dad, then," Blevins says with a sigh. "See what he thinks."

I remember picturing Bob Blevins' likely reaction: silent fury. Bob was an odd and dishonest man. Average in height. Not fat or thin. What hair he had left was a salty gray. A former professional prizefighter with the face to prove it. His ears: cauliflowered. His nose: bashed in. His forehead: wrinkled with age and abuse. His hands: mangled, tough, and scarred. He might have been kind of quiet, but that was only because he let his clothing do the talking; he'd wear patterned sport coats over his bright polyester shirts— which he wouldn't even tuck in to his ridiculous slacks.

Anyway, our suspicions would be confirmed several days later when Blevins returned from Sacramento, where he'd delivered a sample to his dad. Here's how the conversation went, as is my understanding:

Bob Blevins: "This shit's terrible."

Mike Blevins: "You've got to be kidding me."

Bob Blevins: "Terrible. What the hell are you three doing down there, anyway? I can't sell this."

Mike Blevins: "Well, we didn't know. Brian's supposed to be the one who knows what he's doing."

Apparently, Brian had no fucking clue what he was doing. We'd learn this the hard way over the next forty-five days (the time it would take him to produce about seventeen pounds of product). As far as I know, none of it was any good.

And that would be the worst forty-five days of my life.

↩√↪

Frantz took his jolly time getting around to his next question and I found myself wishing for another break. If nothing else, I just needed to change out my dip. This stuff had long since past its prime. I knew, though, that I couldn't ask for a break, because it would make me look sinister or untrustworthy in front of the camera, like I had the need to hide something—or maybe just wanted some time to sort out a false story with my lawyers.

But Frantz marched on. "Mr. Ellis, you pled guilty to a felony count of unlawful use of a communication facility to facilitate a drug trafficking offense; is that correct?"

Frantz might have misspoken—it was a communication device, not a facility—but that didn't make him any less right about my guilty plea…

↩√↪

It's the winter of 1991 and I'm standing in court. Above me, towering on the bench, is a judge named Rhoades. So far, Rhoades has proven himself to be a no-nonsense kind of guy. A good man. Very fair. He has the look of a judge about him, too. Late fifties. Heavyset with kind of a round face and a strong brow.

I'm here in this standard, big, open, busy, loud courtroom with my attorney, Jan Ronis, a guy I'd known since we were kids. Ronis is good-looking, well dressed, and boasts a pretty decent history of defending people involved in drug-related offenses. I'd always respected Jan, but never thought I'd have needed his services. He proved himself as a capable litigator from the very beginning, though, putting in the obligatory efforts to have evidence dismissed due to an illegal search. A lost cause.

Everything around us seems organized in a disorganized sort of way—and that includes the U.S. attorney trying our case. He's looking entirely ready to move on. Almost as if he's bored. My attention is snapped away from his yawn as I hear the booming voice of Judge Rhoades.

"Michael Ellis," he says, "you are hereby sentenced to five years of probation." He says a whole lot more after that, but I'm so stunned and relieved at the same time that I don't hear any of it. No jail time. But *five years* of probation? For leasing a house?

Rhoades then bangs his gavel and I'm ushered out along with Jan.

⌒✦⌒

"So, Mr. Ellis," Frantz said with the slightest smirk. "You pled guilty to a felony count of unlawful use of a communication facility to facilitate a drug trafficking offense. Is that correct?"

I looked the PI attorney straight in the eye as I answered. "That's correct."

But that's not the whole story…

Chapter 3

Profile of Two Dumbasses

In these depositions, you wish you could tell the whole truth all at once, but you can't. You're forced to follow the sometimes cloudy path of questioning. But with personal recollections, you don't have that problem. So about my sordid past before Metabolife, here's the truth as I see it.

And I guess the best place to start would be my friendship with Mike Blevins...

It's 1976 and I've just put in my formal application to the National City Police Department. I'd tried plenty of other careers—including a long stint working for my father in his clothing stores—but in '76, I was completely unemployed. No income. Fortunately, Craig Bradshaw, a detective friend of mine, had a solution for me. The fateful call, I remember, went something like this:

"Hey, buddy," he said. "I thought of something that might help you with your little cash flow problem."

My ears perked up. For a detective, this Bradshaw sure was perceptive. Here I am with absolutely no job and even less money. Flailing. "Yeah?" I said hesitantly. "What's that?"

"Why don't you come work with me?"

I paused for a moment. "Like, as a detective?"

"Oh, hell no. You're not nearly smart enough for that."

We both laughed.

"I mean at the NCPD. You could drive around in a squad car or something. Not even *you* could screw that up."

"Gee, Bradshaw, thanks for the vote of confidence."

"Seriously, man. Put in an application. I'll recommend you."

So it seemed reasonable. The National City Police Department. I figured I wouldn't be anything like the other applicants. They would surely be the kinds of guys who'd dreamt of being cops their whole lives, while I was the kind of guy who just needed some income and figured a job with a gun might be interesting. But still, it was worth a shot. Only trouble was that, around that time, *Police Story* had just entered triumphantly into its fourth year on TV. So everyone and their brother wanted to join the force. Three hundred applicants during my cycle. And only three openings.

But thanks to Bradshaw's recommendation—and some rigorous training at the sheriff's academy at Miramar College—I got in.

Two years in at the NCPD and I find myself in full-force cop mode. Blevins, meanwhile, seems like he's up to no good. I'm not sure what he was doing for a living at the time, but I do know that he had this Porsche he used to drive around like it was his job to drive a Porsche.[17] Anyway, he pulls up to my driveway right as I'm getting home from work. I'm walking inside when I hear the familiar howl of his car. I turn to see him rolling down the window, sunglasses glinting, face beaming.

"Hey, Mikey," he says—he was always calling me Mikey. "Let's go down to Tijuana."

I grin, exhausted. "When?"

"Right now." He pushes his sunglasses onto his head and winks a blue eye at me.

---

[17] It was funny watching Blevins squeeze in and out of that thing because, as I mentioned, he's about 6'4". Between his blondish hair, strong build, sensitivity, and expensive car, he did pretty well with the ladies in '76.

I shake my head. "Now?"

Blevins nods emphatically. "Right fucking now."

I shrug and hop in the tight passenger seat. We roar for the border.

Once in Mexico, we do what we always do: speed around in the Porsche like a couple of bastards, hopping from bar to bar, drinking our faces off. We drink so much on this occasion that I don't recall a whole lot about the events as they pass. But I do remember a few things:

I remember realizing at some point that I'm still carrying my off-duty police gun (a Colt .45 auto), which proves pretty stupid considering we're in Mexico, where getting caught with a gun would land me some time in one of those hellish Mexican prisons. I also remember picking up a guy who claimed to be a cab driver. Why? Because we figure he's a local and would know where we could find all the good bars. I remember the guy just riding around with us for the rest of the night. Poor bastard had to cram himself behind the seats of Blevins' Porsche.

So we go from bar to bar, bar to bar—all under the recommendation of this strange cabby. And then the night peaks...

"Pull over, Blevins," I say drunkenly. "Gotta take a piss."

Blevins does as he's asked, his broad shoulders slumping as he hunches over the wheel. "Where?" he says, pulling up to an alley before I can even answer.

"Right here's fine," I say. I plow out through the door, looking for the first dark corner in which to piss. It presents itself on the street near what appears to be yet another bar.

I start pissing. "Hey," I say back over my shoulder. "This place looks good. We should try it."

Before the answer comes from Blevins and the cabby, I feel a tap on my shoulder. It's a mustachioed man in uniform. Wide-brimmed hat. Clearly a Tijuana cop.

"Yeah?" I say.

The officer must not speak English, because he motions to the fact that I'm pissing on the wall of a bar. I look down at my own stream of urine as if noticing it for the first time. Using my free hand, I fish around in my shirt pocket for my NCPD badge. I produce it, saying nothing. Then, I finish pissing, zip up, and hop back into the car. Not a word to the cop, who turns, looking stunned, and watches us squeal away in the Porsche, laughing and yelling into the night.

I look over at Blevins, whose Roman nose stands in profile to the full moon. "Holy shit," he says. "I can't believe you just did that."

"Had to urinate," I say.

The cabby laughs, which I find funny because I still don't know for sure if he speaks enough English to understand me.

"Good thing you're strange enough to stun that cop," Blevins says.

"Why?"

"Because if you weren't, you'd have spent at least one night in Mexican jail."

I chuckle.

"You know what they do to gringos in there."

The cabby makes a weird grunting noise and we all burst with laughter.

Pretty much everything after that is a complete and total fog.

It's 1980. One of my last years with the NCPD—a job I would never come to miss. Do I like cops? I don't know. Do I respect cops? Yes. I respect them because I'd learned the hard way that they're basically asked to be the perfect human beings in an imperfect world. And that's just not right. See, sometimes you have to make life-changing decisions in a fraction of a second. Much of the time, making the right decision can be an impossible proposition.

So I'm living in National City at the same time I've been assigned to tool around in my patrol car there. Corner of Eighth and R. The other cops I work with are good people, and I enjoy the neighborhood despite its rough exterior. Something like seventy percent of the population is under some form of government subsidy, which creates an environment that borders on "gangbanger warzone."

But the night that I first start to question my decision to become a cop is the night that I'm working as a training officer. I've got a rookie named Terry Sullivan with me and I'm running him through the ins and outs of driving through gangland in a squad car. Sullivan's got dark hair and looks to be in his early twenties, which means he's both ignorant and eager at the same time. A nice guy. One who would later become a lieutenant in the force.

"So you're a reserve, I hear," I say.

Sullivan nods.

"You got another job?"

"Yep. I work at the supermarket."

I chuckle. "So you bag groceries during the week and criminals on the weekends."

Sullivan returns the chuckle. "You got it."

"What brings you to the NCPD?"

The rookie sighs. "I guess I just wanted the chance to help people. I've wanted to be a cop for a long time."

I smile and nod. Seems reasonable.

We're on National Avenue. Casually eating slices as we sit by the front window at a pizza place called Napoleon's. Saturday night. As I swallow down a fresh bite, I inform the rookie that on Saturdays, the low-riders always cruise down Highland Avenue at a steady pace. It usually meant gang activity, but I say it with a proud sort of smile because I like the Mexicans in that neighborhood. Regardless, the point I want to impart to Sullivan is that it's Saturday night and that Saturday nights tend to get rough.

"See," I say, washing things down with my Diet Coke, "each neighborhood has its own gang. But then, on Saturdays, other gangs come in from other cities, too."

Sullivan looks rapt.

"They all clash in parks and alleyways."

Then, fate intervenes. Just as I finish the comment, the rookie and I get that familiar call over the awkward two-ways we've got attached to our gun belts. Gang fight on Highland. Always a gang fight on Highland.

"We're on it," I say as I depress the button on the two-way.

Sullivan and I pull together our half-eaten slices and all our trash and just dump everything into the can as we head out. One of the hazards of being a cop: You're always getting interrupted during meals. We then hop into the squad car and go tearing off.

"Just keep your head on straight," I say. "Fights usually scatter when we show up in the car, anyway."

Sullivan nods, looking either nervous or excited. I'm not sure which. My own heart starts racing as we make the halfway point to Highland.

But here, we turn onto Fourth Avenue. A residential area. All the houses around us are low-income, most being detached homes, many looking dilapidated. Shadows of their former selves. The yards are unkempt—tall, splotchy grass, barren gardens, and withering trees. Up ahead, right in the middle of an intersection, I see a raucous fight—all limbs and fists flying everywhere. This fight is completely unrelated to the one we've been called to police. But that's National City. Fights break out everywhere.

I steal a quick glance at the rookie, who looks confused. Up ahead, a group of guys with that unmistakable gangbanger look holds down another guy. Sullivan and I both watch in horror as one of the thugs makes a motion like he's stabbing the guy on the ground.

"Here we go, rookie," I say.

He makes to get out of the car, but I extend my hand, signaling for him to hold tight. I flip a switch from the massive array of buttons and switches on the dash. The spotlight beside the rearview flashes on, beaming over the huddle of fighters.

"Alright," I say. "Now!"

We both leap from the car. Before my feet even hit the ground, the gangbangers scatter. Several of them pick up the victim and toss him into a car, which wheels up out of nowhere.

"Hey," Sullivan yells feebly.

But the car takes off, leaving only two of the suspects behind. My blood boils as I realize that these are the two who'd done the stabbing.

"Hey," I say. Equally feebly.

The two men take off. Sullivan and I pursue.

I find myself ignoring one of the attackers. Ignoring my rookie. The second banger is my target. Why? Because he's still carrying what appears to be a knife in his hand.

"Stop!" I yell.

He doesn't stop. He makes a hard and unexpected left from the street and onto the sidewalk. It's dark despite the streetlights and we're tearing down the sidewalk between all these rundown homes and the street. Old-style, '50s-era California construction. All wooden, unkempt yards, cars in the driveway, barking dogs, rancid smells. Still, over the howl of the dogs, I can hear the suspect breathing as I sprint at full speed.

"Stop!" I yell again.

He doesn't stop, but I'm gaining on him. I can hear my rookie and the other suspect running behind me. I'm right on top of my guy now—so close that I can see the colors and fibers of his clothes.

I reach out to grab him by the shoulder, but just as I do, something tells me to turn around and look back. Craning my neck, I see the other attacker. He's come up behind me and makes to lunge. I glance down. He's got a screwdriver in his hand and it's headed straight for my kidney. A stick and run.

I turn as the suspect thrusts forward. The impact of our shoulders brings me to a tumbling stop, but the attacker's momentum carries him forward. Without hesitation, he continues on. I spin around to check on my rookie, who barrels past in pursuit.

"Sullivan, no!" I yell over my shoulder. "Get away from the guy!"

Sullivan either doesn't hear or doesn't listen.

I turn back toward the pursuit. The banger I was originally pursuing is long gone, but through the darkness, I can still see the man with the screwdriver and Sullivan. "Freeze!" I scream. "Stop or I'll shoot." I draw my gun.

Neither man stops, so I take a few quick strides forward. I hear Sullivan repeat my words.

"Freeze!" he yells. "Or we'll shoot."

Finally, the banger with the screwdriver slows. I'm standing about a hundred feet away—ninety-nine feet, according to the investigation that would follow. The suspect turns at the waist slowly—Sullivan, still jogging, nearly on him now. But he doesn't seem to notice the banger's hand. As he turns, he makes as if he'll stab my rookie. My heart stops.

Here's the life or death moment. The right choice that every perfect cop in an imperfect world is supposed to make. I can't let the rookie catch him. At the same time, I know that if we let this guy make it to Highland Avenue, all hell will break loose. Sullivan, any other officers on the scene, and countless other bystanders would be in danger. There would be hundreds of people out there on Highland and we'd all be fucked.

The suspect spins to his left, brandishing his screwdriver. Without hesitation, I fire. In one split second—in one impossibly long moment—all our lives change. The bullet tears into the suspect's side. He drops to the ground in an awkward heap.

Relief washes over me. *Good,* I think, *I stopped him. Sullivan's safe.* But the feeling is short lived. *Oh shit,* I realize. Terror rushes up my spine in a sudden crushing wave. The world begins to take on a strange, dreamlike quality. Everything goes hazy and dark. *I've just shot a man.* Only I'm not sure how badly I've hurt him. So I make the ninety-nine-foot run to the scene more out of horrified curiosity than anything. All the while, I know I have to keep my head straight for the sake of Sullivan.

I refuse to look at anything but my rookie. "If he moves," I say to Sullivan, "shoot him."

My rookie nods, drawing his gun and looking nervous. Stunned. He stands there at 6'1", holding the gun with two quivering hands.

My adrenaline—pumping so ferociously during the chase and its aftermath—finally rolls back. I look down at the suspect and shudder. Every ounce of me goes numb when I notice the purple blood oozing from the young man's mouth. He's small and Hispanic, his soft face running paler by the second. Such frail humanity.

I can't take the sight that I've created. I have to turn my attention to something else, but the only thing I can think to do is to look in the direction of the other suspect. He's long gone. Off to Highland Avenue.

Keeping an eye on Sullivan, who still seems plenty nervous, I depress the button on my two-way. Slowly, I tell the dispatcher that there'd been a shooting.

"Ambulance on the way," she responds.

Hours seem to pass. The suspect isn't moving. Sullivan's still standing over him, but I take a quick seat on the curb. Dogs bark in the distance, but it's eerily silent otherwise. Not another person in sight. All the lights in all the windows have been put out. And it feels as if thousands of eyes have trained on me.

"It'll be alright," I mumble to myself. "It'll be alright."

And then I feel a gentle hand on my shoulder. I look up to see Assistant Chief Cliff Reid, the first man to arrive on the scene. He immediately glances over to the rookie. Then, the suspect. Then, back at me. Strangely, he nods.

"You say there was another man?" he asks.

"Yeah," I say. "The one I was pursuing. He got away."

He nods again. "I'm gonna go take a look around," he says. "See what I can find."

For a long while, Reid surveys the neighborhood. Other investigators bustle around, some of them questioning Sullivan, others prodding me. The paramedics arrive and the suspect is carted away.

Reid returns. "Dang, man," he says. "Everywhere I go, there's a knife or a club or a weapon or something on the ground."

I do what I can to smile, but it's difficult.

"I guess once the shot went out," Reid continues, "everyone dropped their shit and ran."

"Must have thought I was shooting at them," I say darkly.

Reid laughs. I don't join him. Here I am, trying to get hold on how drastically one moment can change your life.

I remember pulling up to the station that night. Everything seemed darker. The place was a three-story building with kind of a strange architectural arrangement. National Avenue stood above it, but when turning off of National, the road to the entry level of the station actually traveled downward. The first floor, the one where we conducted our police business, lay underground, next to an embankment, while the top two floors—those housing the city's office and mayor's office—beckoned to the darkness of National City.

There was a long counter that greeted anyone who walked through the front door. To the left sat the dispatcher's desk. The desk was enclosed, but it featured a sliding glass window that could be opened to the lobby. It always annoyed all of us to have to get buzzed through the short, swinging door next to the counter, but safety first, right?

As I got buzzed through the door, I noticed that apart from a few dispatchers and a couple of scattered officers, the station was essentially empty. Typical for a Saturday night—everyone out in the field. Sergeant Charlie Furr caught my eye, as he appeared to be the only person of authority at the station. He waved solemnly as he entered his office.

I turned to my rookie, who followed diligently behind. "You wait here," I said.

He gave me a glassy-eyed look, but seemed to agree. I was glad not to argue because I just wanted to take care of business. And I knew that it would be a good idea to isolate myself from Sullivan. This way, the rookie could tell his side of the story without my having to worry about whether it had been clouded with my own. I wanted the investigators to get the whole truth—and my rookie seemed like the only guy in position to do that without bias.

Leaving Sullivan's side, I went straight up to Furr's office and knocked on the door.

"Come in," came the reply.

I swung the door open, my eyes settling immediately upon Furr, who hit me with a funny kind of expression. I took my .357 service revolver from its holster and turned it over, handing it to the sergeant.

"You'll want this, Sarge," I said. "It's evidence."

Furr took the weapon from me, shaking his head solemnly. Clearly, he'd already heard the news. I'm sure everyone in the station, in the field or otherwise, had heard by now.

"Well, Mike," he said. "You gotta do what you gotta do."

"Well…" I said, pausing for a long time. "This is the right thing to do. Just take it."

He clasped my gun sidelong in both hands, the strange look never leaving his face. It was almost like he didn't know whether to cry or start swinging his fists at whoever passed by. Either way, he was clearly uncomfortable.

At that moment, Lieutenant Fowler entered without knocking. We all called him "Steely Blue Eyes" because he had the most intense blue eyes. He furrowed his brow as he shined them on me. "Mike," he said, "before we start talking about all this, why don't you and Sullivan wait until you have counsel?"

I gave him a blank stare.

"I don't wanna violate your constitutional rights."

I nodded.

"Until then, you should just plead the fifth if anyone asks you any questions."

This would be the first time I'd been told by anyone to plead the fifth. It wouldn't be the last.

I thanked Fowler and left the office. Back in the bullpen, I saw Reid, who must have arrived during my conversation with Furr and Fowler. He appeared to be waiting for me.

From Reid, I would learn that the suspect I'd shot was a twenty-year-old named Villa. By then, it was also clear that the hollow-point bullet from my PD-issued .357 magnum had done way more damage than I'd hoped. The bullet had entered just below Villa's neck, exploding from the impact of striking his scapula. Fragments slid down to his spinal cord, severing it.

"Will he live?" I asked desperately.

"We don't know," Reid said, shaking his head.[18]

Fowler came up behind me and placed a comforting hand on my shoulder. Reid, meanwhile, took on a rather military tone and posture.

"Mike," he said curtly, "are you going back out?"

I lost all my wind for a moment. "I don't have a gun."

"Would you like me to get you one?"[19]

Fowler appeared stunned as he came up beside me. "Chief, I don't think that's wise." He paused briefly, looking me over. "I think Mike should just go home."

It would be around midnight before I would get home that evening. My wife, Susan—like she always did—had waited up for me. I felt

---

[18] Eventually, the news would come through that Villa had been paralyzed from the waist down. He turned out to be a gangbanger, but that didn't make me feel justified in doing what I'd done. Not even when they found drugs in Villa's car did I feel right about it all.

In the weeks that would follow, several members of the PD would find crude signs in the neighborhood offering a ten-thousand-dollar bounty in exchange for the murder of Mike Ellis. An investigation would uncover that the signs had been posted by a few of the gangbangers from Villa's hometown of Calexico. Fortunately, I was well known in the area, and the attitude of the local gangbangers seemed to be, "If Ellis shot him, he deserved it." That obviously wasn't much solace.

[19] I remember feeling devastated by Reid's words but, looking back, I think that he was just trying to help. See, Reid was an old-school, long-time, stand-up cop kind of guy. And he probably just wanted to let me know that everything would be alright. That he had great confidence in me as a person and as a cop. I guess the sentiment just didn't come out right. Either that or he didn't know how affected I was by all that had just gone down. See, cops don't cry in front of other cops. Not in this perfect world.

overwhelmed the moment I laid eyes on her.

"What's wrong, honey?" she asked as she stood up from the couch.

My wife was five feet tall. She always claimed to be five feet and a quarter inch, and I never begrudged her that extra quarter. She was (and is) an attractive Sicilian girl with long hair and a small frame. I'd met her at Southwestern College. We would later divorce, but even to this day, we've remained the best of friends. Like a brother and sister, almost.

"I shot a man today, Suzie," I said. It made me feel no better to admit to something like that.

Immediately, my wife took me in her slender arms and pressed her face to my chest. We both began to cry. And though we were crying together, I couldn't help but feel utterly alone and completely shattered. Like nothing would ever be the same again for as long as I lived.

My father was the one person that I wanted to speak with on that night, but I couldn't because he was in the hospital at the time. Fighting for his life after open-heart surgery. Induced to paralysis with medication. For that conversation, I would have to wait until the following morning. I'm not sure he could even hear me, though, considering the state he was in.

That would be the morning, standing there over my father's motionless, hospital-gowned body, when I would first realize that I had to leave the PD.

"Dad," I said softly, "you were right. I'm no cop."

He breathed slowly from his tube, unable even to nod in reply.

"I can't handle this kind of responsibility," I said.

Soon after, I was exonerated from any wrongdoing. The shooting was deemed justified.

A year later, once I'd left the PD, I washed my hands of the salaried lifestyle. My marriage to Suzie would end in 1987. And our divorce would be a smooth one, as far as divorces go.

For the better part of the '80s, my dad and I embarked upon a few entrepreneurial ventures that wound up failing. We tried an alarm company; I worked for my grandfather's warehouse; I got into being a chauffer; Dad and I opened up a few video arcades. None of it wound up making either of us any real money.

Blevins, meanwhile, was facing a different kind of trouble: family trouble. Specifically, family health trouble. His mother had fallen terribly ill.

By 1988, I'd taken a job in real estate. So had Blevins. He did all he could in those days to make money to support himself and his ailing mother. His work kept him so busy that he looked like a totally different person. Gaunt. Run down. Always agitated. The degree to which he'd changed was alarming. But who could blame him? Every dime he made went to his mother's care, and it still wasn't enough.

My memories of Joni, Blevins' mom, will always be positive. She was a wonderful, warm-hearted, and caring woman when healthy. Unfortunately, she'd made one poor decision—the one that led her to marrying her dirtbag husband. And that decision virtually drove her to alcoholism, which in turn facilitated her willingness to serve as her husband's punching bag, which probably in turn led to her medical issues. It's likely harder to avoid a stroke when you've been cracked in the head a few too many times.

Regardless of her mistakes, Blevins had dedicated his entire life to helping his mother return to health. And that included regular visits to check up on her. I recall one visit in particular. It sticks out in my mind because Blevins had just gotten a letter from the hospital. His latest bill. Staggering. A number that he knew very well he'd never be able to afford.[20]

So there we were at Blevins' sister's house, Blevins kneeling down next to his mother's bed. Joni was completely indolent at the time. The strokes had caused her so much damage that she couldn't recognize her own son. By then, she couldn't even speak.

---

[20] Corners had already been cut—for example, Blevins' sister had taken Joni in when the cost of private care got to be too high—and with this latest bill, my best friend found himself with his back to the wall.

She would just lay in bed with her mouth lolling and her eyes wandering. But Blevins knelt, ready to confess that he couldn't afford to take care of her anymore. I stood behind silently—there for moral support.

My best friend folded his hands and placed them on the side of his mother's bed, burying his head into them as if praying. "Ma," he said slowly. Then, he went silent for a long while, his shoulders heaving as if crying.

I looked over at Blevins' sister, who had placed her hand over her mouth. Tears lined her eyes.

Suddenly, my friend began to speak again—only his tone was different this time. More confident and resilient than before. "Don't worry, Ma," he said. "We'll get you taken care of."

Then, he stood and looked back at me, his eyes bloodshot and moist. "I'll figure something out," he added.

His mother cooed, but could not reply.

Blevins and I were living together in a condo in the University Town Center area. The neighborhood was decidedly middle-class, with its wide, paved streets lined with improbably tall trees that bled into the green, green grass. Condos everywhere. Yuppies everywhere. Our place had two bedrooms, but was attached to a building arranged in an upstairs-downstairs kind of setup—we'd enter from the second floor, which housed the kitchen and living room, then would have to go down the stairs to get to the bedrooms.

I was sitting on the couch and watching TV in the standard, white-walled living room when Blevins came in, looking all bleary-eyed. He immediately plopped down next to me.

"What's going on, bud?" I said. "You look like hell."

Blevins stared at the floor, bags under his eyes, clearly stressed. His shoulders might have been slack, but his tone was serious as a heart attack. "Mike," he said. "I'm broke."

Naïvely, I didn't pick up on the gravity of it all. "Mikey," I said, smiling, "we're both broke."

"I'm serious," my friend replied, sounding hurt. "I can't afford to support Mom anymore. I can't cover those bills."

"What about the money you're earning from the—"

"I'm spending every dime I make on her."

His sudden frustration startled me. For a while, I couldn't think of what to say. "So what should we do?" I finally asked.

Blevins spoke slowly, seeming to choose his words carefully. "My dad says he's got an opportunity for me. He's going to line me up with some people who can help me make money fast. All I need is a place to set up shop." My friend looked shifty. Nervous. Over and over again, he frantically ran his hands up and down his thighs.[21]

"What kind of opportunity?" I asked.

Blevins sighed, resigned to his fate. "Drugs."

I leaned forward, startled. "Drugs?"

"Meth."

"Meth?" I said emphatically.

"Meth."

I stood and paced away from my friend, unable to believe what I was hearing. Then, something terrible occurred to me. "Wait a minute," I said, sort of speaking to the wall. "What are you even telling me this for?"

Blevins took a long while to collect his thoughts. "Like I said...I need a place to set up."

"Which means what, exactly?"

"I need to lease a house."

Instantly, it dawned on me. "And you don't have the credit to do that yourself."

Blevins shook his head. "No," he said meekly.

"And so you need me to do it for you."

"Yes."

---

[21] Later, I would learn that Mike had actually gone to his dad in the hopes of borrowing some money. Bob Blevins had refused him on account of the fact that the money would be used to help his ex-wife. Instead, the asshole offered his son an "opportunity."

I sighed, trapped. Obviously, I felt uneasy about the situation, as I'd never done anything even remotely like this in my life. But how could I say no, knowing who and what the money would be for?

"Listen, bud," Blevins offered, "we'll only be doing this for a short time. We'll just make the money we need to make to cover Mom's expenses. Then we're out."

The sincerity in my friend's eyes was unmistakable. He obviously hated the idea of making meth almost as much as he hated the idea of working with his father. But at the time—even though neither of us knew a damn thing about the drug world—there just didn't seem to be any other way. And without my signature on a lease, there wouldn't be *any* way.

"So where are you going to get the materials you need to…you know…make the stuff?" I asked him, looking back over my shoulder.

"My dad's got it all lined up," Blevins said.

"Do you know what you're doing? Like, how to make it?"

Blevins threw his hands up defensively. "What? Fuck no. What do I know about meth? Dad's got a guy he's gonna bring in."

"You trust him?"

"I don't *know* him."

I cocked an eyebrow. "Who is this guy?"

"Guy named Brian."

"He any good?"

"I think so. How the hell would I know?"

I couldn't help but worry. How could I even consider becoming a career criminal? Dealing meth? It all sounded so ludicrous.

"Tell me again…" I said, turning to look my friend square in the eye. "How long do we have to do this?"

"In and out," Blevins assured me. "Just a short time and we're out. We're done once Mom's covered."

I should have listened to my gut right there. I knew it was a terrible idea getting in on this. But we couldn't just sit back and let Joni die. So I agreed. We shook hands slowly and uncomfortably on that day. To save a woman we both loved, we would enter into the dumbest arrangement either of us could even imagine. It would spiral far beyond our control and get bigger than we could ever have anticipated. But we had to go through with it. The alternative was just too terrible to even consider.

In short order, Blevins found a house in a nice neighborhood in Rancho Santa Fe. We figured we would attract less suspicion if we searched the nicer areas, and Rancho Santa Fe offered the perfect little place. Resigned to my complicity, I signed on the dotted line, and little did I know at the time that my involvement would eventually be far more than I could have ever anticipated.

Bob's cook, Brian, turned out to be an idiot. I don't even know how many times he nearly blew up the house. Apparently, many of the ingredients used to make meth are highly flammable. On top of all that, we constantly had to set up and tear down the operation because the owners were trying to sell the house. Everything had to be hidden every time they showed the place to prospective buyers.

It was all like living in some stupid dream.

Then, we couldn't even make any drugs. Not any good drugs, anyway. Brian would make a pound or so, it would turn out the wrong color, and then we'd send it up to Blevins' dad, who would tell us it was trash.

So in the end, Blevins never made much money for his mother. Everything he brought in he wound up spending on the equipment he had to buy from a connection recommended by Brian. I took in a little cash—$17,000 for the seventeen pounds we made—but that all wound up being split between the rent on our ultra-nice rental home and all the other expenses that came along with constantly moving things around.

But that wasn't even the worst of it. Eventually, it got clearer and clearer that Bob Blevins was setting us up. My friend would come home with these stories about how strange things were at the site where he'd picked up some flask or burner. Brian's connection.

"Mikey," I said, "that sounds like a federal storefront."

"What do you mean?" Blevins said, his halfhearted smile quickly fading.

"I mean you're buying your equipment from some government front. You're being set up."

Blevins stood speechless.

That was it for me. Forty-five days of hell and we had nothing to show for it. We had no money, no product, a terrible cook, and to top it all off, Joni's health was declining rapidly.

"Mikey," I said, "I'm done, man. This has gotten so much bigger than I thought it would."

I looked at my oldest and dearest friend and realized that the expression on his face was actually that of relief. Whatever stress I'd been feeling, I'm sure he'd felt tenfold. Mike's the kind of guy who knows right from wrong. He's also the kind of guy who takes responsibility for his own actions. But here he was, involving me in something that I wanted no part in—he'd enlisted a former cop, a guy who used to put away drug dealers, to facilitate his meth operation. I know it killed him inside.

"Actually," he said, nodding almost gratefully, "you're right. I can't do this anymore, either."

I clapped my hand on my old friend's shoulder. "We'll just have to find another way to help your mom out."

Too little, too late. Two events came crumbling down on us at virtually the same time we decided to close up shop. The first was that Joni Blevins died. So our feeble attempt to funnel money into her care had failed miserably. But you know what? Joni never knew what her son was doing. The other crippling event reared its ugly head when I went back to the house in Rancho Santa Fe to pick up our dismantled equipment—which we'd stored in the garage until we could figure out what to do with. With Blevins up in San Francisco at the time, we were still kind of waffling about it all. Should we give it to his dad? Take it to the dump? Destroy it? But as I stood now in the garage, sorting through the equipment, it became clear that things had been moved, tossed around, taken. My heart sank as I realized what had happened: Our garage had been raided. Brian's federal storefront connection had brought the hammer down on us.

So I hopped the next plane to San Francisco, where I filled Blevins in on the details. Without much hesitation, we both came to the conclusion that it would be best to surrender ourselves to the courts.

To be honest, it was a relief when we decided to turn ourselves in. We'd done a terrible thing in making that meth. And we knew we had to pay the price. Neither of us was happy with the outcome, obviously, but it was time to pay the piper for what we'd done.

I'm standing in front of Judge Irma Gonzalez of my own accord. She's young, kind, and unintimidating. And you know what? Despite myself, I couldn't help but find her oddly attractive.

It's a busy day in the courtroom. Horrible day. People clamor and converse all around, waiting for their turns at the chopping block.

I turn back and see my father. It strikes me then that in the soft light of the courtroom, he looks a little like Ben Cartwright from *Bonanza*. Always a scrapper, my father, even as a child. At 5′6″, he stands shorter than me, and with his slight frame, he doesn't exactly carve an intimidating presence. Add to that the fact that he'd recently been diagnosed with terminal cancer and he gets even frailer.

Given his recent medical struggles—and the bills that come along with that sort of thing—it's killing me that he's here to do what he intends to do. He's offered to put up his condo as bond despite his overwhelming embarrassment at the situation and disappointment with me. Here, indeed, is the kind of guy who stands behind you no matter what.

But he nods once at me, signaling that it's time for me to pay attention to the judge.

"Do you understand the charges to which you are pleading today?" Judge Gonzalez says.

"I do," I say meekly.

"And how do you plead?"

My attorney nudges me and nods.

"Not guilty, your honor."[22]

Before I can even get my bearings, I'm being carted off to central booking. Dad posts the deed to his condo. They shuffle me through fingerprinting and picture taking. One U.S. marshal takes my picture for the file while another asks me if I have any scars or tattoos.

"I've got scars on my shoulders," I say. "And a couple on my side from a kidney stone operation."

"Any other scars?" he asks.

"Well," I say slowly. "I'm circumcised."

The marshal chuckles, unable to help himself. "Well, okay then."

Nineteen-ninety. By now, we'd discovered that it was Blevins' dad who'd brought the heat down on us. He'd been caught selling drugs and had turned state's evidence on his own son just so he could get a more favorable sentence. So thanks to Bob Blevins, forty-five days of hell is all that we'd gotten out of the whole thing. That and five years of probation for me and six years of jail time for Blevins.

I'll never forget the day I drove my best friend to prison. On the way up, we stayed at some cheap hotel run by Native Americans. A sleazy, sleepy, filthy hotel. The place was so cheap that the pictures on the wall were those paint-by-numbers things you give to kids. So

---

22 While we'd come in to surrender ourselves, attorneys always tell you to plead not guilty until they have a chance to examine the case. But it seemed ridiculous here. Blevins and I knew we were guilty as hell and would just be pleading out later, anyway.

Blevins and I got some felt pens and added our own little art to the pictures. Crude stuff.

When we'd finished, we broke out the cards and played gin, all the while sitting around and talking about how badly we'd fucked up. Here's a man on his way to prison, Blevins, and he's letting his sarcastic sense of humor shine. A hard worker. Bright. Intelligent. Caring, despite his tough exterior. And now a felon.

I shuddered when I realized that I was a felon, too.

"I never should have trusted that son of a bitch," Blevins said.

"That rat bastard fucked us, didn't he?" I asked.

Blevins gritted his teeth, dealing out the next hand. "Yes, he did, my friend. And I'm sorry."

For a while, we let the cards do the talking for us.

"You know," Blevins offered, "the worst part about all this is that I'm never going to be able to get a good job again. Who'll hire a drug felon?"

I shrugged and did my best to keep the mood light. "Mikey," I said, "we're brothers, you and I. You go away…six years is a long time. But when you get out, I'll have something for us to work on."

I still tear up when I think about that day. Blevins was a guy who had no chance to make it in life. Abandoned by his parents at sixteen years old. And here he was, sitting across the shitty little hotel room table from me, doling out cards for gin, swearing to everything he'd ever known that he would never break the law again.

And you know what? He hasn't.

Chapter 4

Ancient Product

After I got grilled pretty thoroughly by Frantz on the topic of methamphetamine, we took a lunch break. En route to Bill Low's office, it occurred to me that I felt just about hungrier than I'd ever been. Being a deponent exhausts the body, causes the stomach to rumble in more ways than one. So we all shuffled through the door in Low's office, nobody saying much of anything. I followed behind Garry Pay, whose frame has always dwarfed me. I mean *really* dwarfed me. With the sun shining in from Low's windows up ahead, I felt like I was tailing some giant, earthbound eclipse.

We all took our seats and Ken Dix fired up the question about what we were going to eat. Somebody recommended a sandwich shop nearby, so we ordered from there. In no time, the delivery guy showed up. Low paid him, but I knew that that meant Metabolife had just paid him.

Wasting no time, I unwrapped my sandwich. What unfurled from the wrapper was this ridiculous cheesy freaking thing. I shook my head and smiled. Good thing I was hungry because this sandwich looked like Blevins' descriptions of prison food.

I shot a glance over at Steve Mansfield, who'd just finished choking down a bite of his own sandwich. "You're doing really well, Mike," he said. "Really well."

Dix chimed in, his mouth full of sandwich. "Yeah," he mumbled. "*Really* well."

I nodded and took a drink of the Diet Coke Low had handed me. All of my attorneys appeared thoroughly relieved. And content, chewing on their free sandwiches.

Then, I remembered something. "Hey, Steve," I said.

Steve looked up from under his brow, his hands pouring over his meal.

"I saw you falling all over your notes during those questions about my drug course," I said. "What was that all about?"

Mansfield just shook his head, smiling reluctantly.

I grinned as we shared our little inside joke. "Nice brown-eye," I said.

Dix's head popped up. "What? What are you talking about?"

I chuckled for a moment with Mansfield, who still seemed to be shaking off the gag. "Nothing," I said. "Steve just thinks I'm paying him the big bucks to make crude drawings in his notepad."

Dix looked lost. Pay and Low, meanwhile, had already learned enough about me to know to just let it die. Pay had finished his sandwich and now seemed to be concentrating all of his efforts on sucking down his drink. Low sat silently on his own little planet behind his desk.

So we took our time at lunch. About an hour later, we'd all finished eating and briefing, so we started the short walk back to the conference room. Just before we stepped through the door, I fell behind my attorneys so I could put a little more Skoal in my lip. Just a pinch. It wouldn't last me long, but I couldn't really go in there without it. It would help settle my nerves. Give me something familiar to latch onto in a room where I'd be wracking my brain, answering questions, and cooking under the fierce white light of the camera.

Plug inserted, I filed back into the deposition room behind my huddle of attorneys. The room, by that point, seemed to smell like Frantz's cologne even when he wasn't in there. And then, on cue, the squat little PI attorney came in from the hallway and brushed past me, making a beeline for his seat beside the camera. He stopped for a second to talk to Keegan, who looked pretty satisfied with himself.

I remember wondering whether Frantz and Keegan had eaten.[23] Frantz must have, because he looked all cheerful. Like he was winning a war.

The midday sun shined now through the windows across from my seat. This, I knew, would make the afternoon's questioning even more tiresome. But I took my seat, wanting to get this whole ordeal over as soon as possible. After a minute or two of shuffling around, everyone else followed.

The videographer stood, fiddling with some buttons on his camera before speaking. "This is the beginning of tape number two in the continuing deposition of Michael J. Ellis. It's still Wednesday, May 24, 2000."

Funny. With all these questions, it didn't feel like Wednesday anymore. Felt more like we'd talked our way right into Sunday.

Frantz seemed to have a special swagger about him after filling his gut with lunch. "Do you know Rochell Baba?" he asked, throwing his head back like a rooster.

"No, sir," I said. The troubling part was that I had no idea who Frantz was talking about. The good part was that I'd been out of his presence long enough to be able to call him "sir" again without feeling like I needed to throw up in my mouth.

My confusion wouldn't clear up any time soon. Frantz would continue to drop a whole slew of names, few of them really recognizable to me and none of them seeming in any way relevant to the case against Metabolife. As I listened and answered, it started to seem as though he was beginning to confuse even himself. The expression on his face: priceless. It looked as if he and Keegan had

---

[23] Metabolife sure as hell wasn't going to buy their cheesy sandwiches for them—otherwise, I'd have had to order them from Black Flag.

done what he assumed to be a whole lot of preparation during the breakthat he figured he was really going to knock me out of the park. But as soon as it became clear that he was still an idiot, research or no, he appeared to lose steam.

Then, through the sharp camera and daylight, I make out just the slightest glimmer of hope as it entered his beady eye. Frantically, he rifled through a file and produced a document. As he passed it my way, I saw that it looked like just two sheets stapled together. When Low handed it to me, I squinted and looked it over. My eyes had trouble focusing without my glasses, but it appeared to be a copy of my indictment on the meth charges.

"May I get my glasses?" I asked my inquisitor.

My inquisitor answered cheerfully. "You betcha."

I fetched my glasses from the corner of the table nearest Garry Pay. He glanced at me only briefly as I grabbed them up. Then, he immediately went back to scribbling his notes.

I pushed the glasses over my nose. Yep, it was my indictment.

Frantz immediately hit me with a series of questions designed to get to the heart of my conviction. He was definitely trying to make me seem like some kind of career dealer. I found myself not answering any of the questions, though, because Allen kept objecting and telling me not to answer.

So when the "career dealer" line failed, Frantz shifted gears. For the first time in this half-day-long deposition, we were finally getting into a topic that seemed relevant.

"When did you get into the nutritional business?" the PI attorney asked as he casually rubbed the bridge of his nose. "What year?"

"I believe around 1991."

"What training have you had in herbalism? Let me ask you this: What is herbalism?"

I looked to my attorneys for guidance on what Frantz might mean by "herbalism." Mansfield shrugged, so I was on my own.

"I don't know that there is such a word," I said.

"So, to your knowledge, there may or may not be even such a word; is that correct?"[24]

I strained to keep my face absent of any frustration. "There might be."

"What training have you had in the area of herbs?" Frantz asked. "Formal training, if there is any that you can get?"

"Such as an institution or something like that?" I asked.

"Correct."

"None."

"Was there a reason you got into the herb business?"

I mulled that one over for a while. Here I'd been told that Frantz wouldn't be asking any "why" questions because they're dangerous for a plaintiff's deposition. And here he was asking another one.

"That's kind of…I don't know how to answer that."

Frantz appeared to struggle with the task of rephrasing. "Was there…what prompted you to get involved with the herb business?"

"Okay." Now I had my bearings. "Actually, my father prompted me to do that."

Frantz's face lightened up about six shades. "How did your father do that?"

"My father thought that I should take a formula that I designed for him and take it to market to make people feel better."

"When did your father tell you this?"

"In the '90s. Nineteen-ninety."

Through the light, I could see Frantz as he began waving his hand around in a vague circle. "Did he just tell you one day? Tell me how this conversation arose."

"My father was dying of cancer and I designed a product for him to make him feel better, improve the quality of his life. He liked it so much that he continuously told me that I should try to market the product."

---

[24] I couldn't even believe this guy. These questions were getting harder and harder to answer. Not because they were biting or even difficult, but because they were the opposite. Increasingly, I began to think that this was all just a waste of everyone's time.

I'm not sure if Frantz was expecting a softer answer or if he was just thoroughly unprepared. I had the impression that just about everyone who knew about Metabolife knew that it was originally developed to help my father. Either way, he tripped over his next few questions and seemed to be downplaying the cancer issue. By the time he'd brought me back around to where he apparently wanted me, he started firing on all two cylinders again.

"Did you design the product yourself?"

"Yes," I said slowly.

"What product is it that you first designed?"

"Well, it didn't have a name. It was a product involving putting specific herbs together with the intention of making him feel better."

"Well, when you say you put specific...you put specific herbs together, you did it yourself?"

"Yes."

"Where did you get information on what herbs to put together with what herbs?"

"Well, literature." I chided myself inwardly. I'd been around Frantz long enough now that I'd even started to talk like him. "I purchased several books and I read those books on traditional Chinese medicine."

"So you self-taught yourself?"

"Yes, sir."

"Is that correct?"

I furrowed my brow, a little confused as to why I was suddenly getting the third degree. I answered more emphatically this time. "Yes."

"So you bought these books and then you...after reading the books and looking at some literature...what are the names of the books?"

"I don't recall."

"You don't remember?" He sounded even smugger than usual on that one.

"It was ten years ago."[25]

"What did you...how did you make it?"

I felt like chuckling, but I knew I couldn't. Those were some strange days, making that tea.

Nineteen-ninety. By then, my father, Joseph, had been fighting cancer for many years. Bladder cancer, kidney cancer, and eventually bone cancer. My dad was born in Lebanon, but had grown up in Mexico because the U.S. had closed up its borders when he was on his way to the States with his family. In any case, all of his friends were Mexican. And they all believed in holistic medicine. So they had been bringing Dad all kinds of weird concoctions like dried rattlesnake—all of them just hoping to cure his cancer.

Meanwhile, I was like most Americans back then; I thought herbal remedies were phony. I thought wellness came from a pill, not from a plant. So it all started with my research into the things that Dad's friends were giving him. I really just wanted to make sure that their so-called remedies weren't going to make him worse. But after a while, it occurred to me that herbal medicine really *is* medicine. Not only did it have a five-thousand-year track record of success in Eastern cultures, but most Western medicines were derived from herbs, as well.

So I started reading into it a little more. Based on my research, I found some herbs that I thought would help my dad enjoy a little more energy—give him the strength and wellness he would need to spend some time with his family during his last days. I mean, my son Christian was about eight years old then, so Dad just needed more energy to play.

---

[25] We went on to waste a half-hour on whether I could actually remember the titles of books I'd read a decade prior, whether I knew where I might have stored them, and whether I kept records on precisely what herbs I used to create my first herbal tea. It felt like I had to tell Frantz about six times that this original tea was not, in fact, Metabolife; it was merely my first attempt to make something to help my father feel better. Still, he kept prodding.

Once I'd come across an array of herbs that I thought might help, my next step was to find a store that sold them. I found that store on El Cajon Boulevard in San Diego. The Herbal Shoppe was very small and very holistic; everything inside—including the friendly shopkeepers—was warm and earthy. I would later learn that the Herbal Shoppe had gone out of business. Not because the owners didn't care, but because that's just not the kind of business that survives very long. At least not on El Cajon Boulevard.

I'd always found the staff to be very helpful. Whenever I had questions about an herb, they'd fill me in with as much detail as they could. When they didn't know what I was talking about, they'd point me in the direction of some literature that might help.

Based on my research and their recommendations, I'd gather up the herbs I needed. Then, I'd take them home, put them in a pot of boiling water, and make myself some tea.

Those early efforts had been terrible. Most of the time, I'd just wind up with a stomachache. So I would go to the Herbal Shoppe and let them know that my teas had been a failure.

I remember one such day in particular. The shopkeeper on that day was a tall young man in glasses and a colorful bandana. He never got too worked up about anything. And he gave me my first real insight into how to make yourself an Eastern remedy.

"That ginseng gave me a little energy, I guess," I said, "but mostly I just got a stomach-ache."

"How did you make it?" the shopkeeper asked in a friendly sort of way.

"I boiled it into a tea."

"No." He smiled patiently. "I mean, what did you make it with?"

I shrugged. "I don't know. Ginseng. Just boiled some water."

"Well, there's your problem. You didn't balance it out, man."

"Balance it out?" I cocked an eyebrow, confused.

The shopkeeper would go on to explain to me that there are a few central tenants to holistic medicine based specifically on Chinese yin and yang precepts. The Chinese believe that everything in nature has two opposing and yet complementary component parts. These two component parts work together to create a balance, or a harmony. For every yin—or cool element—there must be a yang—or warm element. According to the Chinese, this dual nature exists in everything that can be found on the Earth. It also exists within us all. To the practitioner of holistic medicine, illness is essentially either the absence of one balancing force or the dominance of another. As I learned on that day at the Herbal Shoppe, this is true of herbal teas, as well. You can't boil up a tea with solely warming elements without expecting it to throw your body off balance. My ginseng concoction was too warm—and so I got a stomach-ache.

"You need to add a few cooling herbs to balance out your tea," the shopkeeper explained. "If you do that, you'll get what you're looking for."

I nodded pensively and walked over to the array of bins on the far left wall of the shop. As my new friend continued to fill me in on yin and yang, I scanned the bins for an herb that had recently caught my attention during my reading. I had learned that, for five thousand years, it had been used by the Chinese as a bronchial dilator, but that it also had properties that might bring energy to the sick. Naturally, I was eager to try it, as I still hadn't found anything to help my dad.

In a minute or two, my eyes came across what I was looking for. It sat in an undisturbed pile within its dusty wooden bin, looking very much like chopped bamboo, only significantly smaller. It was coarse and woody, skinny as toothpicks, but with little knots and crags everywhere. Bamboo chunks reduced to the thousandths. The bin's label was damaged slightly, curling over itself, so I had to smooth it out to make sure I was reading it correctly.

I turned to the shopkeeper. "What can you tell me about *ma huang*?"

⌒*ℳ*⌒

After beating around the bush for some time, Frantz finally arrived at a point. From the look on his face, it appeared as if he believed this to be the first nail in my coffin.

"What is it that you recall today in terms of the ingredients that you used the day that you felt good, you got the feeling that you had endeavored for?"

The only thing I felt at that moment? Confusion. Like maybe I needed an herbal tea. I couldn't for the life of me fully understand the wording of the question, but I answered it as best I could. "When I added ma huang to the product."

Frantz suddenly lit up like a kid at Christmas. For a second, I lost his face in the light of the camera. The sun beat its path across the San Diego skyline behind him. My retinas screamed for me to train them elsewhere. So I did. I concentrated on the table in front of my accusers.

"So the first time you added ma huang to the product was about the ninetieth day or roughly, whatever three-month period, after you first started experimenting?"

"It could have been. I'm not sure."

Frantz nodded in affirmation of his own line. "What did you feel like that time that you added the ma huang roughly ninety days after you started the experimentation with the herbs?"

"I felt better," I said. "I felt more alert. I felt a feeling of clear in wind, breath. I felt a little more energy."

Ephedrine, one of the active compounds that can be derived from ma huang, is a remarkable compound, even in its natural state. The sense of wellness it brings is even deeper than what I could describe on that first day of deposition.

Frantz was obviously excited. So excited that his questions got even less intelligible than usual. "Did you measure how much ma huang you had put in that tea that day that you made it when you felt good, you felt more alert, you felt more energy?"

"I don't think I used any sophisticated measuring equipment, but when I think back, I know I didn't put a lot in."

"So you don't know how many milligrams of ma huang you had in the first cup of tea that made you feel more alert and more energetic?"

"No, I do not."

"As far as—was there any caffeine you put into that first…that one batch that made you more alert, more energetic?"

"No, I did not."

"So strictly ma huang? What else did you add to it?"

"I don't remember the other cooling herbs, but I put cooling herbs into it."

"Cooling herbs?"

"Cooling, yes."

"What are cooling herbs?"

I went on to explain to everyone's favorite PI attorney the tenants of traditional Chinese medicine. As he pieced things together in his slow head, connected the dots frantically, Frantz did what he could to make the concept of cooling herbs sound lethal.

"Do you have any cooling herbs in the Metabolife 356?"

"Yes," I said blandly.

"Which ones are the cooling herbs?"

I scanned my brain for the Metabolife label, which I'd seen more times than I can count. "You would have the spirulina."

"Spirulina?"

"Uh-huh."

"What else?"

"You will have the pollens." I faltered. There were too many herbs to remember offhand. "If I can look at a label, I would probably be able to go down it better for you."

I listened for the sound of Frantz shuffling through his papers. He didn't disappoint. As I looked up, I noticed that his hands were trembling. Finally, he produced a single-sheet document, looking it over for a minute.

"I'm going to hand you—it says 'Metabolife 356' on it and…actually, there's no label on this one, though."

I glanced over at Allen just in time to see him roll his eyes. "Jim," he said, "I think it's on the back."

Frantz turned the paper over and nodded curtly. "Let's just mark it since we're going to use it." He scribbled a note on the sheet and then passed it down the row to me.

"It appears to be a likeness of the Metabolife 356 bottle," I said.

"Looking at exhibit three, does it refresh your recollection as to some additional cooling herbs that are in the Metabolife 356 product?"

I remember thinking, *It refreshes a lot more than that.* Looking at that label at that moment, it seemed as if everything about developing the product and starting our company came flooding back to me.

⌒⅄⌒

I stood in a small one-bedroom loft in a complex in Chula Vista. My apartment. Lower-middle-class is how I would describe both the place and the neighborhood. It all felt very plain—all white walls and linoleum flooring. Very *apartment.* But I couldn't complain. The rent was low.

So there I was: banging around in my tiny, narrow, isolated kitchen, just trying to boil a ma huang tea on the gas stove. And as the water came to a boil, I thought about Brian and his burner. This brought a pained smile to my lips.

Then, it hit me: a stench like no other. My nostrils roiled as I cupped my nose with my hand. Instantly, the whole apartment went stank. Unbearable stank. Nuclear grade stank. I probably should have been cooking fish heads and rice along with it, because my place instantly started to smell like the rankest outdoor markets in southern Beijing.

My tea. An herbal remedy that smelled like a sweaty foot that had just wiped an ass. There wasn't enough money in the world to make me want to drink that shit.

I eyed up the sink. It would take care of business. I could just pour the nasty concoction down the drain and wash my hands of it—wash my hands of this entire holistic experiment.

But then I remembered my dad. Remembered that I had no choice; that I *had* to drink it. I *had* to find something that would help him.

So I strained my concoction and poured it into a cup, trying not to breathe as I brought it to my lips.

It hit my tongue and I immediately spit it out. "Oh, shit!" I yelled.

I couldn't put enough sugar in that awful tea to make it taste good. But still, I swallowed it down.

At the time, I didn't know that the act of boiling the ma huang was what released the extracts or alkaloids within it—the elements that would make me feel the way I would soon come to feel. I didn't know anything about ephedrine back then. But not ten minutes after choking down that tea, I began to get a sense of wellness. I could breathe better. I had more energy. Even before I could reason it all out, I knew I was on to something.

Dad's going to love this, I thought.

Chapter 5

Fathers and Mothers

People often ask how it is that my product became about weight loss in the first place. The simple answer is that it happened by accident. When I first developed what would one day become Metabolife 356, I had no idea that it would help people to lose weight. In fact, I came to it during the search for something completely different…

I'm in my father's house and it's 1990. My father, meanwhile, sits on the couch in his underwear. The TV runs to my right. Dad brings a cigarette to his lips. He'll smoke at least three more while I'm here, I know. In those days, due to his failing health, I was calling Dad a few times a day and visiting at least once. But on this day in particular, I have an additional motive for coming over: Dad had told me over the phone that he'd tried my ma huang tea.

My father was never a complainer about his condition, but for the first time in a long time, he looks comfortable and energetic.

"So," I say casually, "you look good."

"I *feel* good," Dad says with a curt little nod.

"So the ma huang…"

Dad interrupts me. "You know that stuff tasted terrible, though."

"I know," I say, chuckling. "Did you put the sugar in it like I said?"

Dad exhales through his smiling teeth what must have been a long drag of his cigarette. "There's not enough sugar in this *house* to make that stuff taste good."

I laugh again.

It feels good to enjoy the moment, but the moment won't last. Before my laughter even dies, Dad's face begins to contort in discomfort.

"Hold on," he says, getting up.

By this day, Dad's condition has worsened to the point where his prostate's basically ruined. His urinary process is a mess. And because of it, he's always having to get up to piss. Much of the time, he doesn't even know when the piss is coming, either. He'll just go in his pants, not realizing it until he feels the warmth on his leg. It's obviously embarrassing for him, but he takes it in stride. But sometimes it means having to stop whatever he's doing to find the nearest place to relieve himself.

In a minute or two, Dad returns to the couch, a fresh, unlit cigarette in his hand. He pats his free hand over the couch cushion next to him, feeling for his lighter. When he finds it, he lights the smoke.

"So you feel like you have more energy, then?" I ask him.

"Yes, more energy," he says. "I feel…good." He leans closer, looking conspiratorially over his shoulder. "And you know something? That stuff actually made me kind of horny for a while."

I lean back and bark with laughter. "Boner tea."

"I'm serious, Mike," he says, cocking his eyebrows. "You should make that stuff into a pill. It'd be like a boner *pill*."[26]

"That's not really what I was going for when I gave you that stuff," I say.

---

[26] Of course, at the time, there was no such thing as Viagra. A boner pill that actually worked would have sold off the shelves.

"But you *have* something here, son," Dad says adamantly. "I feel fantastic. There's *value* in this. People will *buy* it."

I shake my head, thinking deeply. Glad of my father's improving levels of energy. Naïve to what I was sitting on at the time.

It would take more than a few conversations like this one to sway me into pursuing Dad's line of thinking. But between Dad's urgings and the advice of a chemist friend I'd met at the gym, it occurred to me that I could take this little tea of mine to an expert and get some help on making it better. Given that the formula still tasted like fresh hell, I figured it could always be improved—or at least maybe someone could teach me how to make it into a tablet instead of a drink. Plus, if I talked to a person in the business, I might be able to get a few tips on how to manufacture my apparently effective product.[27]

In search of these answers, I get out the phone book and look for a company that might be able to help me. I find one in an herbal manufacturer named Vita Tech. The address suggests that they're near L.A., but as Jim Frantz would find out the hard way during a deposition more than ten years later, I have no idea where exactly. Regardless, I set up an appointment with an employee of the firm.

Dad manages to talk me into tagging along on the road trip up to Vita Tech despite my protests regarding his weakened condition. I allow him to come with me only on the condition that he drinks a healthy portion of my ma huang tea before we leave. He proves more than ready to follow through on that one.

So on the following day, I'm in the car with my father and we're tooling around what I guess was Orange County. Hopelessly lost. All I know is that we're very near L.A.—and I know this because the traffic is thick and there's smog everywhere.

---

[27] For all I knew at the time, there were already fifty companies selling a formula just like mine. But I actually would have welcomed that idea. Would have considered it good news. At least if there were already people out there selling what I'd stumbled across, they'd be able to tell me why ma huang could make a dying man stronger, why a plant could give a healthy man a sense of alertness, clear-headedness, and a general feeling of euphoria.

"You're sure it's around here?" my father asks.

"No, Dad," I say, sounding a little more frustrated than I would've liked. "I'm not sure."

In the distance, I see what looks like a busy retail district. But as soon as I take the turn onto the street, it's clear that it's all residential.

"So we're lost," Dad says.

I remain silent for a while, gathering my patience. And my confidence. "We'll find it," I eventually say. "It's around here somewhere."

We reach the next intersection—one of those enormous, L.A.-original, six-way numbers where each street contributes about three lanes of traffic to the hellish nightmare that results in the middle. As we sit at the traffic light, waiting for what feels like six hours, I find myself so busy looking around for any sign of Vita Tech that I don't notice my father's uncomfortable expression and shifty legs.

"It's green," Dad says.

I ease out into the middle of the giant intersection. We'll be turning left.

"Pull over," Dad says suddenly.

I glance forward to inspect our situation. We're in the absolute middle of the intersection. And since we're turning left, we have to yield to the improbably long line of cars coming through from the other side.

"I can't pull over," I say. "We're in the middle of an intersection."

"I gotta go," Dad says frantically.

I shrug my shoulders sympathetically. "What can I do?"

Dad leans into the passenger door, feeling for the handle. "I gotta go now."

I watch as my father steps out of the car, right into the intersection. There must be a hundred cars all around us.

Dad drops his fly and lets loose.

Tears come to my eyes as I pour over the tragedy of it all. Here's Dad, unable to control himself, the cancer having ravaged him. During his latest prostate surgery, the doctors gave him a prosthetic.

And as he waves the thing at traffic, it looks like he's got a big boner. A woody in the most literal sense.

But how can I not laugh when the chorus of honking begins all around us?

Dad finishes pissing in record time and then drops back down into the passenger seat. He's chuckling.

"When you gotta go, you gotta go," he says.

We did find Vita Tech on that day, but not without a whole lot of driving around. In any case, after a series of meetings, we were able to consult with their representatives and revise and upgrade the formula for a product I originally called Nepogen, the product that would eventually become Metabolife 356.

So with product now in hand, I knew that my next step would be to ensure that it was safe enough to sell to the masses. To that end, I hoped to conduct more research and more safety studies than any herbal supplement company had ever conducted before. Why? Because I needed to be certain that none of my customers would ever get hurt taking my product. And besides, it's difficult to get a person to buy a pill from a total stranger unless they know it's safe.

Over the next four years, in my efforts to learn as much about the safety study process as I could, I discovered that fully funded and exacted safety studies are fairly rare in the herbal supplement industry. But I didn't like the idea of following the leader on safety. I wanted my company to be different. Guaranteed safe. So in 1994, I contacted Jim Cameron of Chemins Company, a large and successful private manufacturer of herbal and OTC products.[28]

I had known Jim for a while at that point, and he couldn't have been any younger than seventy or seventy-one at the time I first

---

[28] Full disclosure: At the time, Cameron and Chemins found themselves in a little trouble with the Food and Drug Administration over a product called Formula One. The FDA, using the Texas Department of Health as a forum, was making claims that the active ingredients of Formula One weren't "safe."

contacted him about safety studies. He had the full head of white hair to back up the guess, anyway. Thin and fit for his age. Honest, trusting, and loyal as the day is long. Between him and his wife, Diane, the wonderful woman who worked alongside him at Chemins, I'm confident that you couldn't find a pair of people on the entire planet who better understood the process of manufacturing herbal products. And like most people in their line of work, they really *believed* in natural ingredients.

Eventually, Jim agreed to fund a safety study for my product. He had two conditions: 1) It would have to be a joint study that included Formula One and 2) I would be the one to line up the scientists for the project.

My end of the bargain came together in fairly short order. Michael Scott, a man from a research consulting firm called ST&T Consultants (Science, Technology, & Toxicology), offered to set up extensive animal testing on our two products, Formula One and Nepogen. Through Scott's company, we were able to arrange a series of tests to be conducted on rats and beagles. Given that most studies in the U.S. cause animal rights issues, Scott suggested that we go abroad for the venture.[29]

ST&T brought in a doctor named Wayne Snodgrass to write up the protocol and directives for the study. With Snodgrass at the helm of the research, the scientists at two major Asian universities would conduct what are called LD-50 studies. This involved giving a control group of animals a regular dosage of the product. From there, they would continue dosing them more and more and more, increasing the dosage over pre-established periods of time.

Now, ultimately, everything is toxic at a certain level. If you drink a gallon of water in ten minutes, you'll die. If you eat a quarter-pound of salt, you'll die. Even fruit and vegetables are poisonous if you eat enough of them. So the scientists knew that at some point, fifty percent of the animals would die from an overdose

---

[29] I wasn't crazy about the idea of hurting rats and beagles, either, but I knew it would be necessary if we were ever going to prove the safety of our two products.

of Nepogen—and this would determine the average point of lethal toxicity for the product.[30]

In the end, fifty percent of the animals in the study would have died from cardiac arrest due to the consumption of unreasonable levels of Nepogen. The fifty percent of the animals that survived were allowed to recover for twenty-four hours before ultimately being put to rest as well.

For our study, the subjects that didn't die from toxic levels of the product—even after having their bellies stuffed with Nepogen for days on end—presented absolutely no ill effects on their organs and tissue. So every fiber of their bodies was found to have recovered from a lethal dose in a mere twenty-four hours.

Meanwhile, from the subjects that did die, we could now determine what would amount to a lethal dose of Nepogen. If you take the active ingredients in Nepogen and compare them to the active ingredients in Metabolife 356, the equivalent lethal dose for a healthy adult would have been four ninety-count bottles. Try fitting that in your own stomach.

So the results came back even better than anyone could have imagined. My product—the one that would eventually become Metabolife 356—proved to be one of the safest that ST&T had ever studied.

A year or so later, my improbably safe product has already failed as an energy supplement. With plenty of help from scientists and industry experts—and a few tweaks to the formulation—I've decided to rename and reformat Nepogen into something that might sell a little better.

I'm standing in my brother Joe's real estate office. I'd call it a

---

[30] Incidentally, the scientists revealed to us that Nepogen was formulated in such a way that they actually had to force-feed most of the animals in order to reach the lethal toxicity level. Literally, they couldn't fit enough of it into their stomachs.

"C-rated" building. It rests all nonchalant on a two-lane road in a touristy kind of area. Spanish looking, I'd say. There's a little school nearby, but otherwise, we're knee-deep in tourist shops and money traps. The building itself is rather strange, given the sheer diversity of the businesses that share it. Next door to our real estate and network marketing company, we have an accounting firm. On the floor below us: a palm reader.

Just inside our front door, there's a reception area, though we don't very often have anyone sitting behind the counter. Beyond the counter, to the left and to the right, we've set up private offices. Straight back behind the counter is the conference room, which we've arranged to house my network marketing efforts. This is where I'll do the bulk of the distributor recruiting in the days and weeks to come. My brother had loaned his dining room set in order to furnish the conference room. And while it's nice to have a place to sit and spread out, the old furniture looks pretty ridiculous in there.

By this point, I'd come up with a name for my new weight loss product, taken care of the packaging, and was beginning to make plans on how to sell it.[31] So in this way, this strange little building, for all its quirks, would bear witness to the birth of Metabolife.

But none of that really mattered unless I could find a way to get my hands on a little seed money…

I'm standing in one of the private offices with Jim Weaver, an FBI agent friend of mine. I'd told him about all the things I'd been working on and he'd come in to see what all the commotion was about.

Weaver's a good man. We'd become friends after my arrest in '88.[32] I'd say that Weaver is about six feet tall. Blondish hair and blue eyes. Fit. A great sense of humor and a remarkable amount of

---

[31]   I should mention that my first employee, Melody, was instrumental in creating the artwork and logos for the label. Melody did an amazing job and was always a pleasure to work with.

[32]   He was the case agent who arrested me. How many criminals become friends with the cop who arrested them and vice versa?

sincerity. From what I understand, he's a highly experienced and well-respected senior agent.

My friend seems to be enjoying my makeshift little setup. Basically, he's standing behind the "counter" in my administrative office. I use the term "counter" liberally here, given that my "counter" is a piece of plywood resting over a couple of chairs. Ridiculous or not, this is the table I use to package the product and hand it off to the distributors. Not that I'd had any distributors to that point, but still.

Weaver finds the humor in it all. "So you think people will come in to this office and buy this stuff from you?" he asks.

"Yeah," I say, oblivious to his meaning.

Weaver's all teeth. "And then they'll actually go out and sell it?"

"Hopefully, yeah."

"Amazing."

I fidget with one of the bottles on the table, sort of shaking it by turning it over on its end and then back again, listening to the sound of the tablets crashing around within. "Listen, Jim," I say. "I just need fifteen grand."

"For *what?*" Weaver asks, beside himself, still grinning from ear to ear.

"To get this thing started."

My old friend laughs.

"Look, dummy," I say, only a little miffed, "this stuff's gonna work. It's a weight loss pill that actually does what it says it does. I'd get a loan if I could. But I'm an ex-felon. Who's going to trust me?"

Weaver continues laughing. "No way am I giving you fifteen grand to sell that stupid fat-pill."

I shake my head and smile with my eyes. "You won't have that stupid grin on your face when it works."

Years later, Jim would tell me that turning down my offer was the dumbest move he ever made. His wife still teases him about it.

So anyway, even though I've been rebuffed by Jim Weaver, I'm not about to give up. I believe in my product and know that there are a few other avenues I can pursue. So I start with the most logical: a new friend of mine named Bob Bradley. Bob had just gone through a rather ugly divorce, so I figure he'll be up for trying something new. He's proven himself a successful entrepreneur, anyway, so that usually equates to a certain sense of adventure. Only Bob, he's always been a pragmatic man…

We're standing in the garage of Bob's generally upper-middle-class house—a nice four-bedroom place in a single family, detached-home neighborhood in Tierrasanta. Bob's set up a weight room in here and I've lately made a habit out of coming over to work out and talk about my business ideas. We were milling around between sets when I hit him with my latest:

"I don't know anything about network marketing," I say. "But I think it'll work for Metabolife."

Bob nods pensively. "I don't know, Mike," he says. "Network marketing? Like Amway?"

I smile knowingly. "I was thinking we could do it more like the Mormons do it."

Bob nods pensively again, ignoring the joke. "What makes you think it would work for this pill?"

I explain to my new friend that I'd met a guy at an association gathering who was a huge proponent of network marketing—particularly in how it applied to dietary supplements. "He thinks Metabolife would be a natural fit," I say.

Bob walks over to the bench press in the corner, repeating his theme for the day: "I don't know, Mike."

I've learned enough about the viability of my product by now to get frustrated about the wariness and disbelief of all my friends. I might be the kind of businessman who runs about a mile a minute, but Bob's a cautious guy. This caution would keep me and the company level for a lot of years to come. Still, I'd had about enough of it for one day.

But true to form, just as I'm about ready to give up and move on to something else, Bob eventually comes around. "Okay then," he says, offering his hand for shaking.

Shocked at the unexpected turnaround, I clasp my new business partner's hand. "But listen," I say as soon as I've collected myself. "If we're going to do this, I want you to understand that we'll have to make Blevins an equal partner once he's released."

Bob smiles guardedly. "You sure he'll be alright?"

"Absolutely," I say. "And besides, I promised him a job for when he gets out. Promised him I'd set something up that we could both work on."

"I don't know," Bob says slowly. "He's in prison."

"Bob, this isn't up for debate. He has to be involved."

My friend sighs. "Why not? What's one more felon on the company board?"

I laugh and we shake hands again.[33]

Once we had the company leadership picture worked out, I would explain to Bob that I didn't like the structure of traditional network marketing because the focus has always been on the act of getting as many distributors as possible. Plus, the pay plan is all wrong. People at the bottom levels just don't see any rewards for their efforts. So in my mind, if we would be running with this sales model, it would mean tweaking the pay plan, making it easier. And as I would tell Bob, I wanted to be product-driven rather than distributor-driven.

"What do you mean?" he would ask. "You don't want to focus on getting as many distributors as possible?"

"No, I'm interested in getting distributors," I would say. "I just want to make sure we give them a product they can actually sell. A product they can make money from."

I still laugh when I think about what I said that day. As excited

---

[33] In the hours and days to come, Bob would agree to fund the project as long as he could run accounting while I ran everything else. Spearheading the financial side of things would obviously appeal to my new business partner because he's always been good at organizing. A small details kind of guy. One who can build infrastructure with the best of them. I mean, here we're talking about a man who had taken his father's small towing company and turned it into a thriving business by incorporating an auction operation. He would run car auctions and his company would take a portion of the profits on every car sold. Tremendously profitable. Hence the nice house with the well-outfitted garage-gym.

as I was about what we had, how could I have ever known then? How could I know that with the right people in place, Metabolife 356 would be more than up to the task?

It's just before closing time on August 1 of 1995, the first day after Metabolife officially opened its doors as an herbal supplement company. I'm standing behind my makeshift plywood counter, assembling a package of product for the man who'd been my first distributor of Nepogen. Running shrink-wrap around a bundle of bottles of Metabolife 356, assembling the sales literature, laminating a card with a distributor number on it, that sort of thing.

Isaac McLemore.

Here's a man I'm excited to have back—even though the first time he'd bought product from me (Nepogen, at the time), his check bounced. Here's why I'm excited: 1) He's the first distributor to come through the doors of Metabolife's ridiculous office and 2) His enthusiasm is contagious.

"Only twelve bottles?" he asks me. "I'll have those sold before you even get home tonight."

I nod appreciatively. "How you going to pay for this?"

Isaac fishes around in his pockets. "I'm gonna write you a check."

"Okay," I say with a wry smile. "Just don't let this one bounce."

The distributor goes wide-eyed. "What you talking about?"

"Your last check bounced," I explain. "If I'm going to get you in on Metabolife, I need to know you'll cover the check this time."

Isaac looks crestfallen. "I'm truly sorry, Mike. I didn't know." Then, he brightens up a little. "You know I'll make good on that first check. And I'm serious about selling these bottles quick."

He stands there all bleary-eyed—a combination of worry about his bounced check and anxiousness about the chance to make it right. All 6'3″ of Isaac McLemore. I've never known a better salesman or a more loyal friend. Late forties. African-American. He's a character, that Isaac. If he saw an angle, he'd go up to a homeless man and recruit him to distribute Metabolife. Then, he'd go and recruit Donald Trump. Greatest recruiter and network marketer I've ever met. But how did he do it? Because he's likeable, has a magnetic personality, and carries so much presence about him.

Anyway, on the day he first arrived to buy Metabolife 356, I knew very little about Isaac, save for the bounced check. Still, I hand the materials over. "That's all the stuff you'll need right there," I say. "You know what you're doing?"

"Please," Isaac says, all blasé. "You're gonna be seeing a lot more of me. I'll have all of San Diego popping these pills before noon tomorrow."

"So you know about network marketing?"

Isaac beams. "Do I know about network marketing?" He pauses for effect. "Do I know about network marketing? Please. Everything I've ever done was with network marketing. I'm gonna be the best distributor Metabolife ever had."

I chuckle cathartically. "You're the *only* distributor Metabolife's ever had."

From that day forward, Isaac would come in on a daily basis to buy product and check in to see where I was with my network marketing model. I always had questions for him and he always had answers.

It would be an understatement to say that I would be right to trust him. In fact, as I look back at things today, I know that my company never would have gotten off the ground without him. Not only would he prove to be a tremendous salesman, but he would teach me just about everything I know about network marketing. And you know what? He did make good on that original check.

Mother's Day, 1996. Metabolife had seen very little success to that point, even though we'd been around for nearly a year. My new wife, Monica, and I were making enough to scrape by, but not enough to provide for our family in the way we'd always dreamed. We were living in Rancho San Diego, out in El Cajon. Renting a small, single-family detached home worth maybe $120,000. A mostly white neighborhood of schoolteachers and military personnel.

By then, Monica and I had two children: a four-year-old named Joseph, who we called "Mikey," and a two-year-old named Nicholas.

I was fretting on that Mother's Day because I knew I had to do something special for my wife—I mean, she'd been so accepting and understanding about what I'd been trying to accomplish all year. Only trouble was that I didn't have any money to spend.

Monica would turn twenty-nine that year. Cute as a button with long brown hair and brown eyes. Beautiful. Great body, even after having two children. And I loved her dearly. Despite my struggles with business, she seemed to believe that I knew what I was doing. We might not have had any money coming in, but give her credit: She let me have my shot at all this. And we both paid the price for it in the early days.

To help make ends meet, I'd been working insurance fraud cases and serving as a chauffeur whenever I got the opportunity. Monica, meanwhile, would take the bulk of the responsibility with the kids. She would also help out as a receptionist at Metabolife from time to time.

Anyway, Monica must have noticed that I'd been fretting all morning.

"So what have you got planned for me today?" she asked.

"I was thinking we'd go back to South Bay," I said anxiously.

"Chula Vista? The river?"

I nodded.

"That sounds great," she said, beaming. "The boys will love it!"

That was one of those moments when you feel your love for someone wash over you—when you get all warm and numb at your core and feel it radiate out to your toes and fingertips. We couldn't afford anything beyond buying a pack of hotdogs and taking the kids to the river. And here I was, married to a woman who didn't mind. In fact, she *loved* these simpler things in life.

So we packed our stuff, got the boys dressed and ready, and headed down to the Sweetwater River area.

"We're gonna catch ku-ku-ku—" Mike stuttered from the back seat of the car.

"Kukas," I said, finishing his sentence.

"Yeah! We're gonna catch kukas, Daddy?"

I turned to smile at my son. "Yep. A whole bunch of them."

Mikey cheered. Nicholas, always one to imitate his older brother, followed suit.

Monica giggled and reached back to check the security of the boys' car seats.

We arrived at the river on what proved to be a beautiful morning. On the hill up ahead rested the Bonita Shopping Center. But otherwise, everything else about the area was peaceful and serene. Blue sky overlooked the lushly green grass, the fields dotted with little ponds and streams everywhere. Gazing down into the valley, I could see a large channel that looked as if it had been constructed by the Army Corps of Engineers. Our destination.

The kids were excited before we even got out of the car—Nicholas to walk around in the grass near his mother and Mikey to wade out into the riverbed in his shoes and catch crayfish, which we'd called "kukas" since he'd been old enough to talk. So with Nicholas climbing all over Monica, who lounged in the sun, and Mikey bouncing all around me, I prepared the crayfishing lure. This involved opening a pack of hotdogs and tying one of them to the shoestring I'd brought along in my pocket.

The second I handed the string over to Mikey, he skipped off into the water, shoes and all, a look of sheer intention on his face as he dropped his bait below the surface. A few seconds later, he pulled the string back out of the stream. There, gripping the hotdog, were a couple of crayfish. Mikey squealed with delight.

"Kukas!" he said.

Beaming with pride, I noticed something missing from the

equation. "Oh, wait, buddy," I said, heading toward the water. "You forgot your bucket."

I grabbed the bucket from the shore and handed it to Mikey, who had already scraped the first crayfish off his hotdog and had dunked it back into the stream. When he had it securely in hand, I went back to sit down on the shoreline.

I glanced back at my wife, who could not have looked more content. Even Nicholas seemed entranced by what his brother and I were doing. He would just stare, rapt, for almost the entire trip.

Mikey, meanwhile, had another dog full of crayfish on the line. He scraped the lot of them into the bucket I'd just brought over.

"You getting some good ones there, buddy?" I asked.

Mikey never took his eyes off the water as he dropped the hotdog back down. "Uh-huh," he said.

We would spend a good portion of that day by the stream. Then, that night, we would go home and boil up our catch. Such simple living.

But our poverty didn't bother my wife in the slightest. See, money had never been an issue for Monica. Her main concern was her family and our kids—and as long as we could provide for them with a healthy home environment, she seemed happy. She put up with my long hours, she worked for Metabolife when she could (when Mikey was in school and Nicholas at daycare), and she even trusted me in the early days when I had to pay Melody with a credit card. From the very beginning, Monica saw this as our future. Did she understand all of it? No. But she had faith in me. Even when it seemed our little company would never make it.

And at the end of the day, Monica still told me that it was her best Mother's Day ever. How can a man help but love a woman like that?

Chapter 6

Moral Obligations

Here's the thing about Isaac McLemore: He's a guy you can trust. Just like with that bounced check, he always made good on things. And usually in short order. This should give you an idea: I not only trusted Isaac enough to essentially be the face of my product in the field, I trusted him enough to teach my son Christian how to make a living. Christian would quickly learn some of the most valuable lessons of his life from his slightly strange new mentor. Take, for example, the day he learned that as a salesman, you have to be willing to use all the resources you have at hand.

Isaac had just gotten a call informing him that his dad had died. Even though he never cared much for the old man, it represented a big day for him and my son, since the two of them had to go and pick up the inheritance. My best distributor was excited because he figured he could get some use out of the only thing his father had left behind.

En route to the location, Christian rode in the passenger seat of Isaac's beater, as usual. He was and is a good-looking kid. Very intelligent. Witty. Everyone, no matter where they are in life, seems to like him. And as he sat there in his business suit—a smart gray to match Isaac's—he looked every bit the exceptional salesman he would one day become.

"So we're going to be riding around in a limo?" he asked, wide-eyed.

Isaac made the turn onto the next street, similarly wide-eyed. "A limo," he said excitedly.

"Your dad left it to you?"

Isaac laughed halfheartedly. "Yeah, probably the only thing he ever gave me…only thing was worth a damn, anyway."

Shortly, the two of them pulled up to the spot where they'd been told they would find the limo. The place looked like a police impound lot. High fences with razor wire, a guard gate, a sign-in procedure, all that.

The elderly man at the gate was so old and run down that he could barely walk, but he still managed to lead Isaac and my son out to the impound lot. Slowly. Anticipation ran high.

Christian tells me that when the limo finally came into view, he had to bite his lip to keep himself from laughing. Turns out, the thing was something straight out of the Bates Motel. The Bates Motel airport shuttle, maybe. It looked like hell. Rust spots everywhere. A slightly cracked windshield. The hood so dented and wrenched in that it actually touched the top of the engine. And when they opened up the doors, it smelled like piss inside.

"Yeah," the old gatekeeper said slowly. "Some vagrant must have come along and pissed in it. Still runs, though."

Isaac shot a quick, appraising glance at Christian, who was still trying hard not to laugh.

"Thank you, sir," he said to the old man. "Where do I sign for it?"

The gatekeeper presented a form attached to a clipboard, which Isaac took and quickly signed. Then, he grabbed the keys dangled before him, motioned for my son to hop in, and sputtered off.

So there they were: my best distributor and my son, tooling along El Cajon Boulevard in the Bates limo, no air conditioning, both of them wearing suits. No less than a hundred degrees outside. They must have been sweating like pigs. And I can't even imagine the smell.

Still, like anything else, Isaac didn't let it get to him. They weren't even a mile down the road before he stopped, got out, and started pandering to some lady working at the Wienerschnitzel across the street. And here's the moment my son first learned what selling really is: Isaac managed to sign up as a distributor some hotdog stand employee. Right there at her place of business. So he's sweating, he's in a suit, he's just stepped out of the driver's seat of the most ridiculous limo any of us had ever seen, and he's *selling*.

But that was Isaac. Didn't matter. He could sell you anything. The only hurdle between him and a sale was the one that involved getting you to listen. To clear that hurdle, he had a particularly effective sales tool: He'd pin a hundred-dollar bill to the front of his suit jacket. So picture Isaac hopping out of the limo and running up to people, grinning, that hundred flapping suggestively in the wind, a bottle of Metabolife in his hand.

I like to imagine Isaac with that hundred-dollar bill, chasing a fat woman outside of some ghetto Wal-Mart—a woman just trying to get to her car with her shopping cart. He's doing whatever he can to get her attention and it's all she can do to shuffle away from this tall, pushy black man trying to talk to her.

"Ma'am," he would say, pointing to the hundred, "if I don't tell you about Metabolife today, I'll give you this hundred-dollar bill."

That would've gotten her attention. Her *full* attention.

And Isaac would soak it up like late-morning sunshine. "What if I told you this product could help you lose weight while you sleep?"[34]

---

[34] Today, this little vision always makes me feel all warm inside, but back then, I remember being more than just a little concerned. See, I had to remind Isaac that, to most of our potential customers (to say nothing of my broke ass), a hundred dollars was a lot of money.

"You've gotta change that to a twenty," I would say.

"What?" he would ask. "Why?"

"Think about the neighborhoods you're walking around in, man. You'll get robbed."

"Oh, yeah," he said, smiling that magnetic smile. "You're right. I'll make it a twenty, then."

Christian tells me that most of the time on those long days—no matter how much money Isaac pinned to his jacket—the vast majority of people would just tell them to go fuck themselves, anyway. More often than not, Isaac would at least get the prospects over to the limo to take a look at the product. But then, the whole system was probably screwed from the beginning. Who would buy a bottle of pills from some strange black man—especially when they came from the piss-smelling back seat of a limo?

From what I hear, Isaac was like a carnival barker. "Step right up, folks." Everywhere they went, it was, "How you doing, sir? Let me tell you about Metabolife."

But in sales, you can only take something like that so far. Isaac, the king of network marketing, knew this. He knew that if he wanted to succeed, he had to get as many people under him as possible, all of them selling in the name of his own distributorship. It was just a matter of recruiting the *right* people…

Isaac definitely had the enthusiasm and know-how to recruit anybody he wanted. Maybe it was his background as a basketball player. I don't know. But as he saw it, as a practicing psychologist, he also had the perfect pool of potential distributors to draw from: his own clients. He would talk to a patient suffering from depression and say, "Hey, you know what your problem is, man? You need to make more money." Couples counseling? "You guys just need to get more money coming in." Drug addict? "You should try focusing your attention on something new." A cross-dressing schizophrenic? "Here, let me tell you about Metabolife."

And you know what? They all agreed. Readily. They all signed up as distributors.

In that first year, thanks mostly to Isaac, we had a whole army of people with emotional issues out selling Metabolife. They might not have sold much in the early days, but at least these otherwise troubled people were out doing something for themselves. And, eventually, things would improve for every one of them, too.

Over the months that followed, Metabolife began to gain ground. See, the product actually did what it advertised: help people lose weight without having to change anything about their lifestyle. So it was obviously only a matter of time before sales began picking up steam. With our success building, Isaac continued to recruit distributors, almost all of whom managed to sell at least a few bottles of Metabolife. From there, repeat customers quickly became a reality. And I couldn't believe it, but it started to look like maybe we had a business that would work. We were still hemorrhaging money at the time, but at least we were finally moving bottles.

Naturally, I was charged up. With every passing week, my wife and I spent more and more time in front of that plywood desk, laminating distributor cards and shrink-wrapping cases of product. Morale ran high.

Bob, meanwhile, didn't see things that way. Tensions had begun to build between him and me. It got to the point where it was a rare occasion to see him in the office. Can I blame him? No. He had other, more profitable companies to attend to. But he couldn't begrudge me the opportunity to give him hell whenever he actually showed his face at the office.

I remember one such day in particular. Bob had been out for nearly a week when I saw him walk in. So I threw all normal niceties aside and yelled from my spot in the conference room over to the front door. "Hey, Billy Bob!" I called. "Good to see you finally."

Despite the distance, I could see Bob cringe. He stood darkening the doorway, looking back at me like I'd just spit on his mother.

"I asked you not to call me that," he yelled back from across the office.

"Oh, sorry, Bob," I said. "Cosmic Cowboy, then?"

"Damn it, Mike."

I laughed to myself as Bob stormed into his private office. The last thing I heard before he shut the door behind him was the sound of his briefcase dropping hard on his desk.

Monica turned around to face me from her spot at the reception counter. Her beautiful brown eyes squinted into mock anger. "You shouldn't give him such a hard time, you know."

"Yeah," I said, shaking my head. "Well...he'll be alright."

"I mean, his job has to be boring."

I grinned. "Oh, you think so, honey?"

"I know so," my wife said coyly, a little half-smile taking shape.

"How do you know that?"

"Because *my* job is boring and I'm the one answering the phones."

I decided to feign ignorance. "So?"

"So if I'm not getting any calls, we're not making any money. If we're not making any money, Billy Bob's got no money to manage."

I laughed. "I'm gonna tell him you called him that."

My wife and I always kept up a nice flirtatious rapport, but that didn't make her any less right. Even with sales picking up, we needed more money or we weren't going to make it. And with network marketing on a shoestring budget, there's only one way to make more money: recruit more distributors.

That's why the call that came in later that day was so serendipitous. Here's how I remember it:

I'm excited about the call because I know who it's from before he's even allowed on the line. The door's shut on my office for once and I've got the yellow overhead lights humming. The receiver of the phone pressed to my ear and I'm waiting for the voice of an old friend.

"This is Blevins," comes the voice.

"Hey, bud!" I holler. "How're things in the clink?"

Blevins ignores the jibe. "Mikey! Good to hear your voice, man."

"You watching your backside?"

My oldest friend laughs.

I go on to fill Blevins in on the state of the Metabolife project. I explain to him that things would be going a whole lot better if we had more distributors in place.

"You know, Mikey," he says, "why don't you let me take a crack at it?"

"At what?" I ask naïvely.

"At selling this stuff."

I chuckle softly. "You're kidding."

"No…why?"

"I hate to break this to you, but you're in prison, bud."

"So what? I could recruit distributors. There's all kinds of guys in here need to make money. Captured audience."

"It's bad enough Isaac's getting me all these mental patients," I say, laughing. "Now you're going to get me convicts."

"No," Blevins says matter-of-factly. "Just their families."

We kind of joked about it then, but Blevins wasn't really kidding. Over the days and weeks that would follow, he'd make it his personal mission to bring in every single person in the facility. Every day, he'd work on the project by recruiting prisoners to call their people on the outside. Then, as soon as he had his family or friends on the line, the prisoner would pass the phone to Blevins, who would close the deal. And we'd have ourselves a new registered distributor.

After maybe a month of this, I would get the most surprising call:

When I picked up the receiver, I heard the familiar voice of the female operator pipe through the line. "Will you accept a collect call from federal prison?"

My heart skipped. "Yes."

The phone beeped and blipped for a while. And then: "Hello?"

"Hey, bud," I said. "Good to hear from you."

Blevins replied in the usual fashion. "Hey, Mikey." Then, he added a fateful twist. "Listen, I was wondering where I need to send these applications for distributorships."

I sat in stunned silence for a second. "How many you get?"

"A few."

Blevins had more than a few. He'd recruited an army of prisoners' families and friends, all of them selling under the distributorships of the guys on the inside.

Imagine buying a pill from the back of a man's limo. Now, imagine signing up to be a distributor for a product after picking up the phone and hearing, "Will you accept a collect call from federal prison?" Somehow, despite this obvious handicap, Blevins pulled it off.

As stunned as I was about the numbers he'd pulled in, I knew I had to pay Blevins for his trouble. I couldn't mail him money on the inside, so I set aside an account for him. Each month, I'd put a hundred dollars in. Only things were so bad back then that I couldn't always afford that hundred. Whenever I was short, my mom would help me out. She'd send me a check for a hundred and I'd deposit it in Mike's name.

"It's for Mike?" she would ask. And that's all she needed to know.[35]

Anyway, after finishing up the call with Blevins, I headed out of my office, passing by the conference room on my way down the hall. Inside was Isaac. He stood next to the wall while three other people—Christian and two others who I assumed to be distributor recruits—sat around the dining room style "conference" table.

As I stopped to watch, Isaac began banging his head against the wall. "This is your life right now," he said to the recruits.

The recruits nodded.

My top distributor continued to bang his head on the wall. "This is what you're doing every day out there on the streets."

"Yeah, you're right," one of the recruits said.

Isaac finally stopped banging his head. "Why not make something of yourself?" he asked energetically. "And why not make a little money in the process?"

Just as I turned to leave, a wide smile on my face, Isaac noticed me.

"Hey, Mike!" he yelled through the door. "Why don't you come in here and tell us about Metabolife?"

---

[35] See, Mom was already sending money orders to Blevins on a pretty regular basis. To get any of the basic comforts in prison, you need money to buy things at the commissary. And Mom didn't want Blevins washing his hair with bar soap. So she sent whatever she could.

So I went in and sold the recruits a few cases of the product. Many of these people would either give up or just use the product themselves, I knew, but a sale was a sale. And besides, most of the people we brought in seemed concerned only with the camaraderie promised by working with Isaac. He made it fun to be a part of Metabolife, even in the early days.

But before the two new recruits could even shuffle out the door and into the big world with their new cases of Metabolife, Isaac put his hand on my shoulder, kind of barring them from leaving.

"Hey, listen," he said casually. "I've got some people coming in later and we're gonna sign 'em up."

"How many?" I asked.

"Eight."

I raised my eyebrows in alarm, bobbing my head around the recruits so I could survey our little conference room. We could maybe fit six people comfortably around the table. Eight would be pushing it. "We can't do that here," I said.

"What do you mean?"

"Well, there's not enough room in here."

Isaac cast his big eyes to the new recruits. "You see that?" he said. "We got so many people who want to sell Metabolife, we can't even fit 'em in the office anymore."

The recruits smiled and nodded. Then, Isaac dropped his arm from my shoulder and allowed them to leave. Christian shook his head in awe.

"So how are we gonna do this?" I asked as soon as the three of us were alone.

"I know a place," Isaac said. "I'll tell 'em to meet us there."

A couple of hours later, Isaac, eight prospective recruits, and I sit around one of the biggest tables at a restaurant called Coco's. Dinner rush. Pretty standard diner fare. Not exactly high-end. The plush booths feature far too much wear on the plastic upholstery. Sticky tables. Cheesy lighting. Semi-open kitchen area. A cash register up front. The waiters don't seem to want to be here. And it's so busy at the moment that our own waiter looks harried. Maybe even a little pissed.

We've been stashed in a back room, I guess, because our crew looks so unreasonably motley that they're worried we might start hassling other guests. Probably accounts for the fact that we've got the room to ourselves, too. In any case, I glance from eye to eye at the people Isaac's brought in and find myself understanding exactly why they might have wanted to quarantine us. More of Isaac's clients, I assume. They all look like they're right out of the mental hospital.

As I take it all in, the gangly, curt waiter swoops in from my right. This is the third time he's swooped in. At least.

"Are you ready to order now?" he asks again.

I take another appraising look at my company. Every last one of them has cast his eyes away. We're in a diner and it's clear that none of them want to buy anything. They've all ordered waters and nobody's planning on paying for any food. If the waiter didn't look pissed before, he certainly does now. He looks like a man who's just eaten a hot chili.

"We're still looking at the menu," Isaac offers.

I have a hard time making contact with the waiter's prying eyes. Finally, he sighs, gives up, and stalks off.

Now alone in the room again, we spend the better part of an hour talking about Metabolife, Isaac leading the way on the marketing part with me stepping in on the product information. During this time, the waiter would come back on three more occasions, sounding more exasperated with each passing request for our orders. I guess he finally got the picture that we planned to freeload, because on his next visit, he comes with manager in tow.

The manager's red face contorts into rage. Barking mad before he even gets down to any real barking.

"Are you guys going to order anything or what?" he asks tersely.

Keeping with the unspoken strategy, everyone sort of avoids his eyes.

"That's it," he says, clearly steamed as he gives us the thumb. "Get out."

Immediately, Isaac's on his feet, throwing game his way. I watch as he attempts to calm the manager down in the only way he knows how.

"No, listen," he says. "You're a salesman." He motions grandly at the table and everyone sitting around it. "This is a *sales meeting*. Network marketing."

The manager tries to turn away, but Isaac won't let him. He keeps himself in front of the man with admirable bobs and weaves.

"All these guys are going out into the field to sell a product called Metabolife," he adds. "And they're going to make a ton of money, aren't they?"

"Yeah," a few of the recruits say casually.

Isaac shakes off their lack of enthusiasm and turns his attention back to the manager. "And if you let us stay," he says, his eyes getting wide, "I'll sign them all up under *you*. You know how network marketing works, right?"

So here we are getting booted out of a restaurant and Isaac's trying to recruit the manager. And you know what? He gets the guy to sign up. The manager actually came around and signed the distributor forms.

But that's Isaac McLemore: the best damn salesman who ever lived. Without him—to say nothing of Blevins' efforts from prison—we never would have made it. Those two guys carried the company for a long time. And soon, I'd have both of them working on Metabolife from the outside.

As I mentioned, when I dropped Mike Blevins off at prison, I told him that I'd be there to pick him up on the day of his release.

I'm a man of my word.

The four- or five-hour drive up to Boron Prison from San Diego went quickly because I was so excited to get my old friend back. The place was just as I'd remembered it. I found it just off the old 395 Freeway, in the middle of the high desert in an area the locals called the Four Corners—the Four Corners being crammed with truck stops, cheap motels, and old residential areas. The prison camp itself settled a mile or two outside of Boron proper, in an area where Borax soap was once mined and processed. Old construction. And from what I understood at the time, no air conditioning. Always hot inside in the summer and cold in the winter.

I sat in my car, thinking about the sheer level of this hell as I waited for my friend to be released to the world again. Six years. Two thousand, one hundred and ninety days. The enormity of a number like that baffled me. I honestly couldn't imagine spending any time in prison, let alone the greater half of a decade.

And just as I'd worked my mind into a total storm of anticipation, Blevins appeared through the doors, grinning a little hesitantly as his eyes settled on the van I'd driven up in. He looked much healthier than when he'd gone in. Ripped as hell and in great shape. Later, I would learn that his remarkable conditioning had come from a combination of working in the kitchen (which meant healthier food than most of the other prisoners), walking sixteen miles a day, and strength training during most of the daylight hours, but at first glance, I couldn't help but be surprised.

As he got up alongside the van, I stepped out and immediately hugged my old friend. Earlier, I'd guessed that the moment would be overwhelmingly happy, but instead, something strange came over me. For the first time in all the time I'd known Blevins, I couldn't think of anything to say. We hadn't seen each other in six years and I couldn't even speak.

As we eased out of the hug, Blevins seemed at a loss, too. In fact, if anything, he must have felt more tongue-tied than I did.

"Good to see you, bud," I offered.

Blevins' eyes couldn't seem to get enough of his surroundings. He looked overwhelmed. "Yeah," he said weakly.

A long, uncomfortable silence followed.

"Nice day," Blevins finally said.

I ran my hand over my mat of black hair. "Yeah."

Even as we piled into the van and headed down the long road to San Diego, things went on in much the same way for at least a half-hour. Eventually, we got to the point where we could talk to each other just like old times, but I quickly learned that this would be one of the greatest struggles of my best friend's life: getting re-acclimated to the outside world.[36]

So after a long and somewhat uncomfortable ride home, I dropped Blevins off at the halfway house he'd been ordered into in downtown San Diego. The place was a flophouse. Terrible. Run down. The moment we laid eyes on it, we knew we'd made the right decision to petition the courts to have Blevins come and work with me.

"Don't worry, buddy," I said. "With what we've got going on at Metabolife, we'll get you out of here in no time."

"Yeah," he said softly as he exited the van. "No time."

And as I watched him amble toward the flophouse, I felt my energy for the project renew. Multiply. Overwhelm me with purpose. Like a bird taking flight.

Even with Blevins injecting new life into the company, we still had a few more months of struggling to deal with. It came to us at one point that part of the reason we weren't getting off the ground was that we were still operating out of a real estate office in a ridiculous building. Basically, we had no space and even less credibility.

So Blevins and I, now two of a three-headed team of primary shareholders, petitioned Bob for the funding to move into a new space. Once Bob agreed, we had the green light.

---

[36] He hadn't been in for that long, but this was 1996. Plenty of things had changed. Watching Blevins during our only stop en route to San Diego, for example—at an Arco AM/PM convenience store—reminded me of having pet birds as a kid. You can take a bird out of the cage, but that doesn't mean it knows what to do with itself once it's out. Usually, it just bobs its head around, nervous about its new and unexpected vulnerability. That feeling of being confined for so long—and having that confinement suddenly replaced by freedom and mobility—there's just no way to describe that level of anxiety.

Now, this all happened in November of '96, so the slumping economy actually worked in our favor. Bob and I were able to find a cheap place that we thought might fall within our price range. It wasn't the best area of town, but not the worst, either. A little east of I-5 in the Pacific Beach area: 5070 Santa Fe Street.

Just to be certain that we could afford it, I ran the numbers. The conclusion I came to was that we would need to sell seven cases of Metabolife per day in order to pay for the increase in rent.

"Can we swing that?" Bob asked.

"Absolutely," I said, not quite as confident in my mind as I sounded in voice.

So we signed the lease and started moving our stuff.

While it felt great to have more space, we knew going in that we would have to make a few improvements to the building if it was going to be workable. Originally, the place featured five offices, a kitchen, a conference room, and a garage-style rolling door in the back that opened up to a small loading dock. There was a reception area, as well, and I remember smiling as I thought about my wife sitting behind the counter, brightening the place up in her luminous way.

Before we could even begin improving the space, though, we knew we needed to make it feel a little more like our own. To this end, we enlisted an acquaintance of Bob's, a guy named Al Heflin, to create a storefront sign for us.

"You see that, boys?" Blevins said as we all stood outside the building, staring up at the beautiful new sign we'd hung over the front door. "We're now a legitimate business." He slapped Bob and me on our backs as we sighed and took it all in. For the first time, it felt like we'd arrived.

Coincidentally, the money would start to agree with us. We sold our seven cases a day. And in the coming year, we'd begin to sell a lot more than that. In fact, we'd soon reach the critical mass that allowed us to turn a profit and start paying our distributors.

The day we cut Isaac his first check was a particular milestone for all of us. I don't remember how much it was for, but it couldn't have been much. Still, Isaac had been working his ass off 24/7. At the time, he was selling a hundred bottles a day to military base retail sites. Passing out cases from the back of his ridiculous limo.

To my surprise, Isaac started crying when I handed him his first check.

Startled, I put a hand on his heaving shoulder. "What the fuck's wrong with you?" I asked lightheartedly.

Isaac shook his head as he wiped the tears from his eyes. "Nothing," he said. "It's just that this is the first time in network marketing I ever got paid."

I chuckled and slapped him on the back. "Let's just hope it's not the last time."

Isaac beamed down at me. My own grinning champion of Metabolife. He'd worked his ass off for us and was finally getting paid. And it had brought him to tears.

At that moment, I came to understand a greater responsibility than I'd ever realized before: that I had an obligation to those people who would help me fulfill my original dream. A deep obligation. A moral obligation.

See, for a man to have a dream, that's one thing. But to have other people working hard on your dream, that's something almost unfathomably bigger. These great people, these distributors all across the board, were spending their entire working lives on Metabolife—on making the business thrive. How could I not want to treat them fairly? How could I not want to treat them *more than* fairly?

So I decided right then and there as I watched Isaac wipe away his tears that I would always stand behind my distributors; I would make sure that they were all taken care of, no matter what.

Chapter 7

Radio Metabolife®

By 1996, we would adopt a new corporate strategy—one that would ensure that hundreds and eventually thousands of other distributors would be crying tears of joy just like Isaac's. This all coincided with a period when it seemed like we were finally turning a corner as a company and a product. In San Diego, at least, most people had actually *heard of* Metabolife.

So we now had ourselves some decent product recognition. On top of that, our regular customers were losing weight by the train-load. People would come down to the office every day to sing our praises; people who'd tried and failed with every diet fad, every workout, every technique prescribed by their doctors; people who'd begun to doubt that they were even *capable* of losing weight in the first place. But there was Metabolife: giving hope to the hopeless and delivering results to the people most in need.

We heard from men with stories about losing more than a hundred pounds in two years. We had women coming down to the office carrying their old pants—pants that looked like they would've fit an aircraft carrier compared to what these women looked like now. One lady burst into Mike Blevins' office in tears because she'd tried everything to lose weight. Everything. And nothing had worked. But thanks to our product, she'd already lost 175 pounds and had plans to lose a little more.

That was the thing about Metabolife 356. It worked. Exceptionally well. For almost *everybody*.

So thanks to our track record of results and our growing level of recognition, we'd entered that phase of being a "cool" product. I mean, tell someone you're an Amway distributor and they run; tell them you're with Metabolife, and they listen. People were *excited* about what we were offering. And this obviously translated into a fair deal of success in our little corner of the world.

Given similar circumstances, almost every successful company carries a singular goal: expansion. For us, expansion meant delivering the story of Metabolife to the masses—to go big and mainstream—but at the same time, we knew that we would have to do it in such a way that we wouldn't lose that distinction of being "cool." We were still a small, up-and-coming company, but would the efficacy of our product alone be enough to help us stay "cool"?

This was only part of what worried me on that fateful Sunday night in 1996. My other great concern: the fate of my entire company now rested in the unsteady hands of a radio campaign…

I lay in bed next to my wife, completely unable to sleep. Monica, meanwhile, slept soundly—and had been for an hour or two. A half-hour passed as I stared up at the ceiling with my arms folded behind my head, trying to count the imperfections in the plaster. Then, an hour. Finally, I'd had it.

"Honey," I cooed, "are you awake?"

Monica groaned, but did not wake up.

So I shook her gently. "Honey?"

No response.

I sighed in frustration, rolling over to my shoulder. Too nervous to sleep. Too busy fretting over the fact that the following morning would most likely make or break the entire company. Too worried about the realization that the whole strategy had been my idea in the first place. At 6 a.m. on Monday, thanks to Z-90 in San Diego, Metabolife would reach out to its target market through its first-ever radio campaign, a campaign we were calling the "Weight Loss Challenge." Live. Unscripted. No do-overs.[37]

For the challenge, we'd already gathered thirty people—some of them radio talent and some of them radio listeners—and recorded their weights. Each participant was instructed to take Metabolife for the week that followed, being careful not to change a thing about their diets or exercise habits.

"Just take Metabolife according to the package instructions," we told them. "That's it."

The idea, then, was that every Monday morning for a month, we would weigh the participants to demonstrate the number of pounds they lost during the previous week.

Would this sell product? Absolutely. But what if we went on the air and found that nobody had lost any weight? Devastation. As a company, we'd be ruined.

So I fretted on in the darkness, no one to talk to.

"Honey?" I said again.

Another groan. Monica just wouldn't wake. She's beautiful when she sleeps. Very calming. But not calming enough on this night.

"Monica," I said, "I need to talk to you." I felt wretched waking her up, but I couldn't help myself. I was just so nervous.

Finally, my wife began to stir. "What is it?" she asked groggily. She turned to check the clock. "It's 3 a.m."

"What about the distributors?"

Monica made an unintelligible noise. "Distributors?"

"We at least have to make their money back."

I was referring, of course, to the other—and maybe most

---

[37] I'd chosen Z-90 because it played hip-hop music, and I believed at the time that the kinds of people who listen to that particular genre are also the kinds of people who keep an open mind when it comes to new ideas. And Metabolife—a weight loss supplement that actually did as it advertised—was certainly a new idea.

significant—reason I couldn't sleep that Sunday night. If the campaign failed, we wouldn't have just destroyed our company; we'd have ruined about twenty honest and hardworking people, as well. See, with Metabolife still so new and essentially profitless, the Weight Loss Challenge had been possible only because, under my advice, our twenty distributors had agreed to pool their money together to pay for it. A $6,000 campaign. No small number for any of us. In return, the distributors would be getting an equal one-twentieth share of whatever money we made, but still. Would we make enough to cover their investment? Probably. But a whole lot was riding on the weight loss of thirty total strangers.

"You will," Monica said sleepily.

"But what if they forgot to take their Metabolife?"

My wife sat up, her eyes still half shut and her tongue still apparently asleep. "What if who forgotta take their Metalobife?"

"The listeners," I said. "The radio…the people from the Weight Loss Challenge…"

"Oh." Monica lay back down. "They didn't forget." Almost immediately, she began to breathe softly and slowly again. She was out.

I remember thinking, *Oh, gee, thanks, Monica.* A part of me already knew that the listeners wouldn't forget. But what if they *did*? What if they actually *gained* weight on the air? Where would we be then?

I'm down at Z-90, standing in the packed radio booth used for a morning show the station calls "Mark in the Mañana." It's a standard booth divided in half by soundproof glass. On our side of the glass, we've got a long table set up with radio microphones, all of them pointed in our direction. On the other side, there's a room full of the standard high-tech equipment used to mix and transmit radio shows. The giant mechanical units boast arrays of dials and buttons I couldn't possibly understand. Normally, Mark's producer would be sitting in front of these machines, but since he's in the mic room with us, I guess he's been replaced by his understudy.

In addition to Mark's producer, I'm in with Mark himself and eight of his morning-show listeners. All eight of the listeners are varying degrees of overweight—and as our intensive screening process proved, not completely crazy with emotional or destructive self-image issues. None of them were hoping to lose a hundred pounds in three weeks or anything like that. Just a few vanity pounds.

I can see the sales rep, Irene, through the window that divides the mic room from the hallway. A woman in her thirties with kind of fake-looking blond hair, Irene believed wholeheartedly in holistic medicine. Very spiritual. The kind of person who would take off once a year to some ashram where they did crystal healings or some shit like that. In any case, Irene had worked with Blevins and me in setting up the Weight Loss Challenge. She'd done a great job for us, especially considering the fact that this was no standard ad campaign. [38]

The idea had been to get three disc jockeys from the peak hours of the day—Mark in the Mañana and then the two DJs from the afternoon and early evening shows—to compete against one another in our Weight Loss Challenge. Each of the DJs would assemble his own team of nine listeners (Mark had eight because his producer wanted to get in on the action), subject to our screening process. At the start of the first week, the participants would weigh themselves live on the air. Then, for the week that followed, they would all take Metabolife. We'd cap it off by another live weigh-in on the following Monday. And at the end of the month-long competition, the team that lost the most weight would win prizes.

Given that we needed three major DJs, plenty of the station's valuable time, and would be running a rather unique campaign to

---

[38] And she would eventually come to marry Mike Blevins. The marriage wouldn't end well, but that's a different story altogether.

begin with, Irene really had to go to bat for us with the station's executives. I smiled at her through the glass because here we stood on the first weigh-in day. Irene had put herself on the line right along with us—and now came the moment of truth…

She gives me the thumbs up just before we go on the air.

As his producer and his eight teammates sort of mill around the microphone table, Mark speaks smoothly and calmly over the airwaves. "Good morning, San Diego," he says. "We're here with Mike Ellis of Metabolife, getting ready for the weigh-in for our week-long Weight Loss Challenge."

The contestants hoot and cheer.

"Team Mark," he continues, "have you been taking your Metabolife all week?"

"You know it, Mark," one of the contestants says.

"Yeah," says another. "Absolutely."

"And do you think you've seen any results?"

"Oh, yeah," one of them pipes in. "I been feeling all kinds of energy. I feel good, you know?"

"I haven't been as hungry, neither," says another.

"So there you have it," Mark says confidently. "We've got a scale set up here in the booth and we're gonna weigh in this morning and see where we stand. I got a good feeling about this, guys. We're gonna win."

More hooting and cheering.

Mark then turns to me. "Mike, you wanna tell us how this works?"

"Well," I say shakily, my heart racing, "we'll have each of you step on the scale and we'll figure out how much weight you've lost since last week. Then we'll add up all the weight and compare it to the afternoon and early-evening teams. Then we have prizes for the winners at the end of the four-week challenge."

"Very good," Mark says. "Who's up first?"

"Mary," the producer offers.

"Alright, Mary," Mark says, "let's see what you got. You been taking your Metabolife this week?"

Mary claps her hands once. "Oh, yeah, Mark," she says, grinning infectiously.

"Alright then, Mary. Step on the scale."

Mary does as she's asked. Hollering erupts from the other contestants as Mark announces her weight.

"So Mary's lost four pounds," I say, feeling all the tension pour out of me instantly. *It worked!*

More hooting and hollering from the other contestants.

Mary explains to the listeners that she'd been eating all week. "Just like I always do," she says. "It's amazing."

"Now why is that, Mike?" Mark asks me. "How is it that Mary could eat whatever she wanted and still lose weight?"

"That's just how Metabolife works," I say simply. "Because it's formulated to boost your metabolism, it actually works better when you eat."

"It works *better?*" the DJ asks incredulously.

"That's right, Mark."

Even though I'm not down at the Metabolife offices, I can actually *feel* those phones starting to light up. I imagine our twenty distributors—all of them having volunteered to serve as operators and take calls for the duration of the campaign—scrambling to answer all the phones we've set up.

The rest of the time in the booth flashes by so quickly that I barely have time to register it all. Contestant after contestant gets up on that scale.

Second person: three pounds.

Third person: two pounds.

Fourth person: five pounds.

We get through nine of the contestants before it's Mark's turn to step up to the scale. I hold my breath for this one because I know Mark himself is critical to the campaign. His listeners won't quite buy into the hype we're generating if the man they tune in to hear every morning doesn't show them a little progress.

I look him over as he waits for the scale to register. Dark hair.

Hispanic. Mid-twenties. Most DJs have the perfect face and body for radio, but not Mark. Mark's actually good-looking and has a fairly normal build. I imagine it's his soft-spoken but hip-hop personality that endears him to his listeners.

As I wait for him to announce his weight, a recent memory flashes into my head. Mark's birthday had come up at some point during the first week of the campaign, so we'd invited him down to the Metabolife office to celebrate. As a gag, we'd gotten him an inflatable doll that looked just like Burt Reynolds. It was funny at the time, but what was even funnier is what we did with it.

Mark had left the doll at the office. So one day, we got some duct tape and fastened the thing to the back end of a truck belonging to one of our employees, a great guy named David Beady (and, fortunately, one who could take a joke). The doll was naked, so we taped one of its hands to its crotch, leaving the other hand waving in the air. Because David had backed his truck into a parking spot near the front door—so the tailgate was very near the bushes by the wall—we knew that he wouldn't be able to see the doll when he left the office after work.

Around closing time, we watched from the windows as David walked right past the doll, climbed into the driver's seat, and drove away. We all rolled on the ground with laughter when we saw the doll's free hand wave in the wind as David's truck pulled out of the lot.

Later, we would learn that the gag had more life to it, too. David would be idling at an intersection when a carload of pretty young girls would pull up next to him, all smiles.

David would later confess to thinking, *God, I must really look good today.*

I guess he didn't even notice the doll when he stopped to fill up at the gas station on the way home. It wasn't until he got home that someone clued him in on his ridiculous tailgater.

So anyway, back at the station, Mark announces his own weight and I do the math.

"Two pounds," I say, exhaling a little too audibly.

"Two pounds!" Mark hollers. "I lost two pounds! And I didn't change *anything* about what I did or ate."

The contestants hoot and cheer.

"I even ate a lot of pizza over the weekend," Mark adds. "That's amazing."

More cheers.

"So, Mike," Mark says, "how did we do all together?"

"Collectively, you've lost..." I pause for dramatic effect. "Thirty-eight pounds this week."

"Thirty-eight pounds! For real?"

"Thirty-eight."

Mark turns to the contestants and starts doling out high-fives. "That's right, morning team. Thirty-eight pounds. We gonna win this thing."

I smile at Mark and motion about whether it's okay for me to leave. When he nods, I take off, immediately picking up my cell phone to try calling back to the Metabolife offices. But I have trouble getting through to Bob because things are so frantic.

"Bob, how'd we do?" I ask when I finally get something other than a busy signal.

"I can't believe it," he says. "The phones are going crazy."

"Are they keeping up?"

"Who?"

"The distributors."

"Yeah..." Bob says, sounding a little beside himself. "Yeah, they're doing a great job. They're making money."

I explode with laughter. "Is my wife down there?"

"She's punching in these credit card numbers by hand. You should see her go."

I can hardly contain myself. "Tell everybody I said 'great job,'" I say. "I'll be down as soon as I can."

I rush down to the offices. On the way, I listen to Mark in the Mañana:

A caller asking how they can get in on the contest.

A skeptical caller asking Mark if he really didn't change anything about his lifestyle.

A caller claiming to be a longtime customer of Metabolife. "I lost thirty-five pounds in the year after I had my baby," she says.

"It's *working!*" I yell out the window as I make the turn onto the freeway.

⤳⫯⟜⟩

In the days and weeks that would follow, we had nothing short of a frenzy on our hands. I would monitor the campaign on my radio, calling the radio stations pretty regularly whenever I felt like the DJs hadn't mentioned the contest or Metabolife often enough. Whenever I did this, the station's producers would have one of the Weight Loss Challenge contestants call in and talk about their progress.

Orders kept rolling in.

But it wasn't all sunshine and roses. We would occasionally have trouble with the talent. I remember that one of the guys weighed somewhere near 230 pounds. During one weigh-in, he'd actually gained weight. Fortunately, I was there to diffuse the situation.

"Two-hundred thirty-two pounds," the producer said.

"I actually gained weight," the DJ offered.

"Yeah, two pounds," I said.

The DJ laughed. "Hey, I can't help myself. I was out last night partying. Had some pizza. I guess I forgot to take it."

I joined in on the laughter. "That's the thing with Metabolife," I said sarcastically. "It's a lot of work. All you have to do is remember to take it."

"Yeah," the producer said. "That *is* a lot of work for some people."

"For some people," I said.

"For some people," the DJ repeated, chuckling at himself.

Forgetful talent aside, by the end of the four-week campaign, the average weight loss per contestant was seven or eight pounds.

So collectively, the thirty participants in the Weight Loss Challenge had shed 240 pounds.

We might have seen the results of the product coming, but the response from the customers was bigger than we ever could have guessed. People were driving all the way from South Bay to the offices in Pacific Beach to buy it. It got to the point where we had to have a few of the distributors open a location at a gas station near the radio station in Chula Vista. The new location would have long, chaotic lines of customers waiting outside every day.

With the success of the Z-90 campaign, we knew we had something going for us. And that meant branching out. San Diego isn't a big market, but if it worked in San Diego, it would work elsewhere. But where to go?

At the same time, Blevins, Bradley, and I were locked in a fight over the most appropriate price for the product. I thought it should be $49.95 and they would only go as high as $34.95. So we knew we would need a test market to see which number would be the right one. We didn't want to go up to L.A. because if we were wrong about the price, we would bomb out in one of the biggest markets in the nation. So it seemed logical to see how we would fare at $34.95 in Middle America.

Why Sioux City, Iowa? Because one of our best distributors lived there. Ron Sanculi.

Summer had come down hard on Iowa that year and here I had to get off the plane on the tarmac. It was hot and humid as hell. Even before my foot hit the ground, sweat poured from my brow. And for some reason, it really smelled outside, too.

Ron was waiting for me on the tarmac as I came down from the plane. All 5'7" and 150 pounds of him. Fit, that Sanculi. Half-Filipino, half-Polish, and looking kind of Puerto Rican. He had a mustache done up in that Pancho Villa style. Dark, average length hair. The proud father of the cutest kids (ages scattered all over the board from twelve on up to twenty) and the proud husband of the greatest wife, RaeLynn.

Ron was kind of a food nut, I guess, since he owned a grocery store and marketed this salsa he called the Mad Butcher Salsa. It was a great-tasting Mexican salsa—especially considering the fact that Ron was Filipino. But, lately, it had been Metabolife that had dominated his entrepreneurial focus—so much so that he'd agreed to make his city the guinea pig for our $34.95 price tag.

"Welcome to sunny Sioux City," he said as I walked up to him on the tarmac.

"Yeah, Ronny," I said, chuckling. "Sunny is right."

We shook hands and Ron turned to lead the way through the airport and out to his car. I swear, the smell of farmland never left my nostrils. Even in the airport, it reeked of shit.

When we got into Ron's car, I noticed that he rolled the windows down. No air conditioning. And even as we took off, it didn't get any cooler from where I was sitting. So it's hot, humid, and it smells like a cow farm outside.

"How can you live here?" I asked.

Ron shrugged his shoulders. "Why?" he asked, grinning.

"It's hot, it's humid, and it stinks," I said. "Ron, you live in a fart."

The distributor laughed.

"How can you live here?"

"You get used to it," he said jovially. "You should see the winters."

So the first thing we did in Sioux City was the main thing you do during Midwestern summers, I guess: We assembled in Ron's backyard and fired up the barbeque. We were on the back porch as I watched Ron cooking the meat over the fire. There were bugs flying everywhere. On the deck, on Ron's face, swarming in the air, landing on the meat and getting charred into the surface.

Now I'm from San Diego, where we don't have bugs. I wasn't used to this sort of thing. I remember thinking, *Man, half the meat on there is bugs.* I considered passing on the meal before I realized that the little bastards were cooked anyway. *What could it hurt?* I thought.

And so we ate.

The next morning, we got up early so we could get down to the radio station before the morning show. I sat alone in the living room, wearing shorts and a tank top, mouth breathing because it was still so damn hot. Silence. I figured everyone else in the family was asleep as I waited for Ron to finish getting ready.

Anyway, as I sat and waited, I began to hear this faint sound coming from outside. A strange sound. Unnatural. Nothing like the usual farmland stock. The noise grew louder as I got up from the couch and went over to stand beside the front window.

PING! Whack! PING! Whack!

Curious, I pulled back the curtain and peered outside.

There, outlined by the rising sun, I saw one of Ron's sons. He held a golf club in his hand. A driver. And just as he caught my eye, he reeled back to hit another golf ball.

PING!

I watched the ball in flight, bolting away toward the horizon. When it landed, I realized the source of the other noise. Down the hill from the Sanculis' yard rested an old farmhouse. Ron's son was hitting golf balls off the house with spectacular force.

Whack!

I remember thinking, *What in the hell is this crazy kid doing?*

PING! Whack!

PING! Whack!

I shook my head and sat back down on the couch, exhausted already from all the sweating I'd been doing just standing there. For a while, I just sat there listening to the strange noises. Then, as quickly as they'd come, they were gone.

But the peaceful, sweaty silence wouldn't last long. Suddenly, there came a pounding on Ron's front door. A frantic and aggressive pounding.

I got up and answered the call, swinging the door open to see this short, Okie-looking old guy standing on the stoop. He looked pissed.

"What the hell's going on?" he barked.

"What?" I asked. "What do you mean?"

"Your kid's hitting golf balls into the side of my house!"

Feigning ignorance, I went back to the front window and gazed outside. The kid had already taken off like a striped-ass ape. "Hey, man, I'm a guest here," I said. "I don't live here."

Turned out that the neighbor was a nice guy. We laughed about it later. And if I recall correctly, he would later become a distributor of Metabolife, as well.

But that's Middle America, man. Bugs and heat and golf balls and farmhouses.

Anyway, after he'd barked sufficiently at his son, Ron and I made our way down to the station, where we set up a Weight Loss Challenge to mirror the one we'd just completed in San Diego. Over the next month, the challenge would go well. But damned if we didn't make nearly as much money at the $34.95 price point.

So I went back to meet with my partners in San Diego. We all sat around in our slightly more comfortable conference room, mulling over the potential reasons we didn't make as much money in the Midwest as we'd hoped.

"Iowa's just not ready for Metabolife, I guess," Bob offered.

"No, listen," I said emphatically. "It's not that Iowa doesn't want Metabolife. It's that Iowa doesn't want it at $34.95."

Bob shook his head. "But who would pay $49.95 for a bottle of weight loss pills?"

I knew this was the answer. I mean, how could Iowa just not identify with a weight loss product? They had people there who wanted to lose weight just like in Southern California. "Look, $49.95 is the right price."

"What makes you so sure, Mikey?" Blevins asked.

I sighed. "It's real simple. When you're talking about buying a weight loss product, you're talking about people who've wanted to lose weight their whole lives. They've tried everything. Nothing's worked."

"So maybe in Iowa they don't like the idea of pills," Bob said, continuing his line.

"That's not it, Bob. It's that our price point doesn't suggest that we've got the solution they've been looking for."

Blevins began to nod knowingly. Bob, meanwhile, didn't seem to be on the train yet.

"Is the solution they've been searching their whole lives for going to cost only $29.95?" I asked him. "Are they going to throw their money away on something as cheap as $34.95?"

Bob shook his head again. "I don't understand."

I raised my eyebrows for emphasis. "They'll pay fifty bucks because something that costs fifty bucks will *actually work*."

There I got him. He started nodding in rhythm with Blevins.

"Just let me try it at $49.95," I said, casting my hands out in a show of desperation.

"Okay, then," Bob said.

"Let's do it," Blevins added.

With our new strategy in place, we knew it was time to enter the big show. So Blevins and I went up to KOST Radio in L.A., where we found the reception to our idea for a Weight Loss Challenge to be lukewarm at best. The station didn't seem to want to commit to something so time-consuming, expensive, and difficult to manage—and we still didn't really have the cash flow to cover L.A. radio prices, anyway.

So as a counter, we suggested a campaign that called for the two peak-hour DJ teams to take the product for a month and then talk about the results live on the air. On a regular basis, they would be asked to tell their listeners about how Metabolife 356 made them feel, what kind of weight they were losing, and all that.

We thought it was a good idea, but the execs at KOST didn't

seem too sure about it all. Fortunately, we had Jan Rice in our corner. Jan might have been a new advertising sales rep at the station, but that didn't change the fact that she was absolutely instrumental. She demonstrated enough faith in Metabolife to get the others at the station to come around and let us do our campaign. Actually, it probably helped that we were her first clients, because the brass likely figured they could let the rookie take the heat if things went belly up.

So thanks to Jan's unwavering support, the campaign was on. The first weigh-in would be on the following Monday morning.

For me, this meant another sleepless Sunday night…

Why couldn't I sleep this time? I didn't have a group of thirty people to count on, after all. But that's exactly why I was worried. I knew now that the Weight Loss Challenge worked. And this wasn't a Weight Loss Challenge. This time, we would be counting on two DJs to show the listeners results. Who knew if they'd be motivated enough to take it regularly? Who knew what they would even say on the following morning?

On top of all that, we'd be telling our story to the masses in L.A. If it didn't work, we'd lose out on one of the biggest markets in the entire country.

But then what if it *did* work? Would we have enough staff in place to keep up with the demand we'd get out of such a massive city?

The idea of falling short on manpower really hit a rough note for me that night. I spent several hours tossing and turning over this funny feeling I had about Bob. In preparation for the campaign, I'd asked him to complete an extremely important task. But he hadn't been in to the office all week. Was it possible that he hadn't done what I'd asked him to do?

So I found myself gently shaking my wife awake again. "Honey?" I said softly. "Are you awake?"

Monica groaned, but did not wake.

"We don't have any SOPs," I said to myself.

SOPs. Standard operating procedures. Given our success in San Diego and Iowa, we'd hired a few operators to take the calls for the orders coming in from L.A. No more distributors punching in credit card numbers. Because we had new staff and new prospects for the volume of our orders, I knew we would need two things to support a successful KOST Radio campaign. The first was a credit card account that would allow us to take orders over the phone without actually having to physically swipe the cards being used. And the second was detailed SOPs that would guide our new operators and shippers. If we had hundreds or even thousands of orders coming in, these people would have to know exactly what they were doing to take those orders. Otherwise, we'd get backed up, lose orders, and shatter consumer confidence.

Bob had assured Blevins and me that he'd nailed down the billing end of things with our bank and with the credit card companies, so I knew we'd be okay on that end of things. But I suspected that he hadn't taken the SOP task seriously enough. I couldn't blame him. He had other businesses to run. But this thing was going to explode. I could feel it.

So if Bob hadn't completed the SOPs, what were we supposed to tell the operators? The shippers? There would be no flow-chart to guide our staff through the moment of taking an order, to the entry of that order, to the billing of that order, to the shipping of that order.

I looked down at Monica, sleeping so peacefully next to me. I thought about how she'd signed on to take orders and do whatever she could to help make this campaign go off without a hitch. I thought about her brother, Steve, who'd volunteered to work for free in our makeshift shipping department. How could I leave them out to dry like that?

Besides, since L.A. radio time is so expensive, we'd invested virtually all of our money on this one campaign. If we screwed something up, we'd be out of business.

So I got up and went down to the office. As it turned out, my feeling had been correct. Bob didn't complete the SOPs. So it would be a long and sleepless night preparing that stuff. And it would end on a frantic note.

When our first spot went live on the "Mark and Kim in the Morning" show, the phone bank in the office exploded. Call after call. Our operators, following their fresh SOPs, couldn't ring up the credit cards fast enough. They had to type everything in by hand. Then, they would take addresses and get the info down to the shipping department on foot. I can only imagine what Monica's brother Steve's day must have been like down in shipping, but he did a great job for us.

I stood just outside the shipping area, talking to Blevins—who was down there trying to help as much as he could. We were both about as ecstatic as we'd ever been.

"I told you, bud," I said, a big, shit-eating grin plastered on my face. "We're gonna make it."

Blevins couldn't seem to stop laughing. "I can't believe it."

"Forty-nine ninety-five!" I yelled.

"Forty-nine ninety-five!"[39]

But the joy would be short-lived. Not only had Bob failed to create the SOPs, he also hadn't set us up with the kind of credit card account apparently required to do such a large volume of business. In order to take credit card orders over the phone, you need what is called a direct response mail order account. But we were set up with a standard credit card account—one that would allow us to take orders from people coming on site to actually swipe their credit cards through the readers.

---

[39] That day, we learned a couple of things. First, always prepare. Scratch that. Always *over*-prepare. Second, price is important when it comes to sales and the way the consumer perceives a product. Perception is everything. If they see that it's expensive—if it hurts just a little to buy it—then they're all the more likely to invest. They have to see the value right there on the label.

There's a magic number (and I don't know why this is the case, but it is) that makes people want to do business with you for the long term. That number is 600—as in $600 per year. Once a customer has spent $600 with you, they're a customer virtually for life. And $49.95 per bottle for a month's supply got us up to that magic annual number.

Only we weren't getting cards to swipe; we were typing in the numbers passed to us over the phone. So this triggered a fraud alert down at Bank of America.

The bank seized our accounts before we could even get the product out the door. So there we were, with tens of thousands of dollars in orders and no way to fulfill them. Unless we got some money freed up, we would lose all kinds of business. Enough business to crumble the company.

Fortunately, Bob made good on his mistake. In fact, he saved our asses by loaning us money from his other businesses. We now had the cash flow we would need to get things moving again. He kept us afloat financially for the several months it took for the bank to realize that we weren't actually frauds and release our money to us. After that, we obtained the right accounts with new credit services. And we were done with Bank of America.

Disregarding the bank-related meltdown, we'd turned a $5,000 profit in one day. A big number for us. And with milestones like these, you've just got to celebrate.

Bradley, Blevins, and I were all standing outside the Metabolife office, milling around in the parking lot, bullshitting and staring up at the dusk-ridden sky. All smiles.

"Boys," I said, "we did a net of five grand in one day."

Blevins howled happily.

I extended my hands to either side, palms up. "You know what that means," I said.

Bob looked down at the hand I'd presented him like I'd just finished wiping my ass with it. "No," he said. "I don't know what that means."

"We've gotta do a ring around the rosies."

Blevins laughed.

"I'm not gonna do that," Bob said. "That's stupid."

"C'mon, Bob," I said. "We made five grand today. You don't have to worry about looking gay."

"Yeah, Bob," Blevins chimed in. "You already look gay anyway."

At that, Bob cracked a grin and joined hands with us. Immediately, we began dancing in a circle in the parking lot.

"We're gonna do this when we hit a net of 10K, too," I said as I bounced along in the circle.

"That'll be the day," Bob said, clearly winded.

"We'll get there, Bobby."

"We're gonna make this thing work and make millions," Blevins said.

Bradley laughed as we stopped circling and dropped hands. "I tell you what," he said. "All I need's seven million."

"For what?" I asked.

"That's one hell of a hooker, Bobby," Blevins said.

Bob shook off the jibe. "No," he said, "to retire on. I make seven million, that's all I need. I'm done. You guys can take it from there."

We all stood around grinning at the thought of seven million dollars. It seemed so completely unattainable at the time.

So we were doing well at our new price point. The most important thing from then on was pouring our healthier margins into more radio advertising. And as far as that was concerned, the most difficult aspect involved managing the on-air talent. Many of the DJs we brought on board with the campaigns didn't grasp the idea that a story, not a canned commercial, is what sells a product. So it was a constant struggle to get them into the mode of telling their own Metabolife story rather than trying to pitch the product.

I remember one such DJ named Bill Garcia. US-99 out of Chicago. Wild Bill, they called him. Now, US-99 was a unique country station—and particularly attractive to our cause—because it went out to seven million people in the greater Chicago area. Given the incredible number of listeners, we knew we had to negotiate carefully with Bill when it came to his fees.

"Bill," I told him, "you can either take the talent fees or I can pay you a dollar per bottle sold."

Bill didn't hesitate in his response. "I'll take the talent fees."

"You're sure?" I said suggestively. "Because once we get the ball rolling, you can't change your mind. We'll be going on other stations who will be selling, too, and if we don't get your name attached to your sales, then we can't keep track."

"I'm sure," Bill said. "The talent fees are enough for me."[40]

So we had a deal in place. But to our surprise, the recording of Bill's first commercial left plenty to be desired. Completely flat. In fact, it sucked.

"Bill, I don't know," I said. "This sounds canned."

"Trust me, guys," Bill said. "I know my crowd. This will work."

Bill flashed his look of deepest certainty in our direction. He was about forty-five or fifty at the time, I would guess. Stocky (though he got a whole lot thinner on Metabolife). Great personality. Great voice. Good guy. Funny. And since his listeners really liked him, it seemed to me that taking him at his word was worth a shot.

Still, I couldn't help but feel like something was off. And as I looked over at Blevins and Bob, I could tell that they felt the same way. So none of us really bought Bill's line at the time, but we decided to let it fly.

"Alright, Bill," I said. "You have three days. If it doesn't sell, we pull the ads."

At the end of the three days, our suspicions were confirmed. The numbers weren't flying. And since this was such an expensive station, we knew we had to pull the ads.

When I told Bill about our decision, he pled for another chance. In fact, he was adamant about his ability to deliver.

"Alright," I said. "Let's get together tomorrow and work on a new ad."

Basically, during our ad meeting, I told Bill that he had to get

---

[40] Talent fees are basically just what you pay a DJ to do a standard commercial. They ran something like seventy-five dollars per spot at the time. The average DJ made about $4,000 per month in those days, depending on the size of their market. I'm sure Wild Bill, with his enormous station, did pretty well, but I wasn't sure at that moment that he realized just what he was missing out on by taking the standard fees.

into the storytelling mode and out of the selling mode—that he would do better to explain to the audience why and how Metabolife had worked for him. He agreed to do things my way this time.

The next day, I remember being by the phones at our offices on the hour that Bill's new ad went on the air. It was a good place to be standing because the success of a radio ad could be easily measured by the bursts of calls that would come in. If Bill's ad worked, we'd be inundated with callers. If not, the lines would stay dead.

Bill's ad ran. The lines stayed dead. Not a single call.

Actually, that's not true. We got one call. From Bill.

"Well," he said excitedly, "how did it go? That was perfect, right?"

I tried not to sound too disappointed. "Bill," I said, "we didn't get one call."

"I can't believe it. It can't be." Bill was clearly dejected.

"Hold on," I said. "Let me listen to the ad."

"You want us to play it over the phone?" Becky, the station's ad rep, asked.

"Yeah, go ahead," I said.

Blevins was with me at the time, so I put the call on speaker. When the recording had finished, we stood there looking at each other in confusion. The ad was absolutely perfect. I mean, dead on. Bill told the story, explained the product, and promised results. Exactly what I'd told him to do.

It just didn't add up.

"Let's hear that one more time, Becky," I said.

On second listen, Blevins and I both noticed the problem right away.

"Bill," I said, "you put out the wrong 800 number!"

"What? What do you mean?"

"I mean you said the wrong 800 number in the ad."

"Wait…that means that…"

"People aren't calling the right number!"

"Well, who are they calling?"

"I don't know."

It wouldn't be long before we'd uncover the answer to that question. Shortly after Bill hung up, Metabolife would get a call from Caterpillar Tractors. They'd been taking our calls all morning and just turning people away. I couldn't believe it.

After a great deal of apologizing and promising to fix the problem, the people at Caterpillar kindly agreed to pass along the right number to anyone who called in looking for Metabolife. That company should have signed up to be a distributor. They would have made a lot of money.

But at the time, I didn't know whether to laugh or scream. Instead, I formed a plan. I called Becky back.

"Becky," I said, "is Bill still there with you?"

"Yeah," she said. "He's here."

"Look, who's on the air right now?"

Becky gave me the name of the DJ team.

"Bill, I want you to invite yourself into the booth and tell the listeners that you made a mistake. Give them the right 800 number."

"Right," Bill said.

"And tell them that because of the mistake, your station is going to give its listeners a ten percent discount for today only."

The line fell silent for a long while.

"We can't do that, Mike," Becky finally said.

"Yes, you can," I said. "What you're going to do is you're going to give me some overnight commercials and we'll make up your losses there."

The line went silent again.

"You can't mislead these people," I urged. "You have to make it right and give the discount."

Becky sighed. "Okay, Mike."

"Get to it, Bill."

So Bill left the call and went straight in to the other DJ team's show, where he apologized to the listeners. He gave them the right 800 number this time and told them that US-99 would pay ten percent of the purchase price of any bottle of Metabolife purchased for the remainder of the day.

Instantly, our phones exploded.

From that point on, we sold 1.5 million bottles in the Chicago area on this station alone. If Bill had taken the dollar a bottle I'd originally offered him, he would've made $1.5 million.

Metabolife, meanwhile, moved on to many more markets and—thanks to ads like Bill's—was raking it in. We did so much business so quickly that it wasn't long before Bob had made his seven million dollars. I remember the day that Blevins and I first ran the numbers and realized that Bob had reached his ultimate milestone.

We went down to his office to fill him in on the issue.

"Well," I said, "it's been a pleasure working with you, Bob. We'll be sorry to see you leave."

"Yep," Blevins added. "Don't let the door hit you on the way out."

Bob looked alarmed. "What do you mean?"

"You made it, buddy," I said. "Congratulations."

Bob just shook his head, confused.

I slapped my old friend and business partner on the shoulder. "You hit your seven million."

"Your big number," Blevins said.

Bob nodded, still looking confused.

"So have a good retirement," I said, grinning. "See you later."

Bob just laughed. Of course he wasn't going to leave now. How do you leave a company whose biggest problem is figuring out how to keep up with its own sales growth?

Chapter 8

Butterfly Cookies

Good thing we'd moved into another new location in '96—this one on Santa Fe Street—because thanks to the success of our radio ads, the company continued to grow at an incredible rate. We only occupied a portion of the building when we first arrived, leasing the other half to another company, but we were growing so quickly that we ended up filling the entire building with our own staff in short order. Eventually, we even got too big for that one location, so we had to lease another across the parking lot.

We had approximately 17,000 square feet of space, all told. And by '98, we had hundreds of employees crammed into this area. Things were so cramped that some people had to work in the hallways. Meanwhile, the shipping department was a zoo. Since we didn't have enough space for them to work inside, they would have to move the entire department into the parking lot during the day. Then, at night, they'd move everything back into the building. Fortunately, it hardly ever rains in San Diego—otherwise, we might have been in trouble.

The shippers had their work cut out for them, too, because the success of our radio ads was almost unfathomable. Every day, product just flew right off our distributors' shelves. We couldn't make it fast enough. No single manufacturer could keep up with the demand.

Because of the overwhelming demand and sputtering supply, Metabolife became the first network marketing company in history (that I know of) to put a moratorium on distributors. At the time, we were getting thousands upon thousands of applications, all of them coming in with money to buy products, but we'd have no choice but to apologize for our inability to keep up with the incredible demand and explain that we would reopen our distributorships to more people as soon as we could manage. Our current distributors were already waiting as long as twenty-three days to receive their product orders—and we couldn't afford to dilute that supply chain any more. Of course it meant a great deal of money for many of our distributors—some of them were making up to a million pre-tax dollars per year, per retail location—but it also meant that we would be forced to leave a few qualified candidates out in the cold.

Our two shifts of sixty operators were taking up to 20,000 calls per day. Our sales had grown 81,000 percent from 1996 to 1998. How do you keep up with that?

By hiring as much staff as you can. I mean, we were in continuous hiring mode. It got to the point where it was difficult to find more people. Forty percent of the company at any given time had been brought in from a temp agency. Always new faces arriving. But the employees seemed to be having a good time. I guess it's easy to have fun when everyone's making money.

So we had all this success as a company. And at the same time, our millions of customers were losing weight on Metabolife. An absolute dream come true. A real Cinderella story. Rags to riches. The great American dream.

In 1998, Earnst and Young recognized our dream by naming me a finalist for Entrepreneur of the Year. A big honor. But I wound up getting beat out by Jack in the Box.

Our PR guy, Dominic Johnson, found that one particularly funny. "Hey, Mikey," he said, "how's Jack in the Box count as an entrepreneur? It's a company."

I shrugged at Dominic, a good-looking former professional baseball player now in his early thirties. At 6'5", 225 pounds, and with his engaging personality, it was no wonder everyone seemed to love him. He was incredibly committed and an extremely hard worker—two things he'd learned from his father, Deron Johnson, a former Major League Baseball player.

"Man, you got beat out by a clown," he said, laughing.

So what does the guy who got beat out by a clown do when he's not losing Entrepreneur of the Year? He acts like a clown.

We had a new receptionist at the front door. Stellita. She'd basically replaced Monica, who had gone on to doing other things for the company—namely, running the customer service department (which she did quite well). So we'd moved Stellita from the phone room to take my wife's place. And I figured she needed to be welcomed into her new position properly.

Early on in the day—before any of the regular staff even came in—I'd taken one of those stink bombs so popular amongst junior high schoolers and broken it off in the reception area. I mean it smelled terrible. Like sulfur. Like a skunk's ass. Terrible. It wafted through the small reception area like mustard gas through a foxhole. I remember feeling almost like throwing up. It got to the point where I considered tearing off through the standard glass front door that led outside from main reception. But no. If I was going to submit Stellita to such horror, I'd have to endure it myself.

Holding my hand to my mouth, I looked the place over. A small reception desk in the front. A security door to the left—Stellita had a little buzzer behind the counter that she used to buzz people through. A Metabolife sign behind the receptionist's chair. And all the standard reception equipment. So where to plant the other half of my joke?

My eyes settled on the monitor to Stellita's computer. That would do…

All morning long, I guess the staff was filing in and waving their hands in front of their faces. Stellita took it especially hard, complaining about how she had to sit in the sulfur mines all day. An attractive black woman in her thirties, our new receptionist was always a trip. Dynamite personality. Everybody liked her. And in her spare time, she also happened to sing at one of the hotels in the area. I went down to see her perform once. She was wonderful.

Anyway, I really liked Stellita. So that's why I played jokes on her all the time. Keep her on her toes.

So for this latest gag, our new receptionist might have smelled the stink bomb right away, but what she didn't know was that I also had this little machine with a remote control. When you pressed the button on the remote, the machine made a sound like a fart. I mean, it was dead-on accurate, this sound. And I'd planted this machine right behind the monitor of her computer.

I remember waiting just around the corner for someone to come in to talk to Stellita. I almost lost it when the next person to come through the door was the UPS guy. The guy's face contorted into disgust over the smell, a look so hilarious that I almost lost it right there. Almost blew my cover.

"Could you sign here, please?" the UPS guy said, pinching his nose.

"Sure can, honey," Stellita said, signing the form as if nothing were wrong. I guess by that point, she'd gotten used to the smell.

I waited for her to sit back down before letting the fart machine do its work. The second I pushed the button on the remote, the thing barreled out a huge rip.

The UPS guy seemed to be doing all he could not to laugh as he turned for the door. Stellita, meanwhile, was obviously mortified.

"Ummm...that wasn't me," she said.

The UPS guy just waved as he made for the door.

"Seriously," Stellita urged. "That wasn't me."

I started cackling from around the corner as I listened to the receptionist repeat her claim several times to the UPS guy as he plowed through the door. But it's hard to say it wasn't you when there's no one else around.

Once the UPS guy had gone, I turned the corner and stood in front of the desk, all teeth. Stellita looked up at me, frustrated and clearly embarrassed. Without a word, I let the fart machine rip a few times. The receptionist looked more and more confused with each passing rip. Then, I showed her the remote.

"Damn it, Mike," she said.

I roared with laughter.

"Now that UPS guy gonna think I got a gas problem."

"Oh, like he didn't already!"

So that was a day in the life on the ground floor, just another opportunity to keep things loose, keep morale high. In those early days—before everything started going all haywire on us—I used to take every such opportunity.

Like the day I wore the cookie suit to work...

I'd recently had a guy come in with these nutritional cookies. His was a startup company and he reminded me a little of me, so I decided to give him a chance. It seemed like a viable product, and a natural complement to our own, so I agreed to bring his line under the Metabolife wing.

The day before we launched on his cookies, I got all of our operators together and instructed them on how to up-sell the new product to the people calling in. "Tell them that with their order, they have the option to purchase twelve cookies for the special price of $19.95," I said.

"Why would people calling in for a weight loss pill want to buy cookies?" one operator asked.

"They're nutritional cookies," I explained with a chuckle. "They're good for you."

"Like, they have a lot of vitamins and stuff?"

"And they make you less hungry, too."

The operators had plenty of questions for me, and I gave them all the information they'd need. What I didn't tell them was that I'd be showing up the next morning in a mascot-style suit shaped like a cookie.[41] I mean, I looked ridiculous. The whole phone bank erupted with laughter as I walked in for the 5 a.m. shift.

---

[41] Not a typical CEO move, obviously, but I just wanted to motivate the operators and let them know that I was interested in everything they were doing.

"Remember, gang," I said, waving my arms around lamely. "Sell those cookies."

As usual that morning, calls for Metabolife began pouring in. So I listened for a while to the drone of the operators. The cookies were selling. They were selling well, in fact.

I grinned as I cookie-waddled back into my office. We already had a weight loss pill that worked. And now we were in the cookie business.

Back by my desk, I wound up taking off the cookie suit, but I kept it in the office from that day forward, just in case…

About two weeks later, I sat in my office with Dominic, who was talking on the phone. I did what I could to take care of some paperwork while Dominic did his thing, but I couldn't help but be distracted by his end of the conversation.

"Really?" he said, sounding alarmed.

I looked up at my PR man, concerned.

"*Really?*" he said again, this time with more force.

If he didn't have my full attention before, he had it now.

"Okay, ma'am," he sputtered. "Ma'am…listen. Why don't you send the cookies back and we'll go ahead and send you more cookies."

I waved my hands above Dominic's bowed head, trying and failing to get his attention.

He stared at the floor between his feet as he continued. "Yeah," he said. "I understand. Of course not."

Finally, he noticed my waving and looked up at me.

"What's going on?" I mouthed.

Dominic shrugged, holding his hand over the receiver. "This lady was eating like three of the cookies," he explained. "And when she went to bite into the third one, she found a bunch of worms in there."

I contorted my face in disgust. "You've got to be kidding."

Dominic shook his head, pressing the phone to his head again. "Ma'am?" he asked. "Are you there?"

"Offer her a free bottle of Metabolife," I interjected.

Dominic nodded. "Ma'am, we are truly sorry. We'd like to send you a free bottle of Metabolife for your trouble. Yes. That's right. And please send us those cookies."

Without another glance at me, Dominic finished the call, grabbed a pen and paper from my desk, and made a note about sending the woman a bottle of Metabolife.

"Worms?" I asked, stunned.

"Worms, man."

"In the cookies?"

Dominic nodded.

"And you offered her more cookies?" I asked with a wry smile.

"Yeah, that was pretty stupid, I guess."

"What'd she say to that one?"

"Well, she was crying," Dominic said, starting to chuckle. "She said something like, 'Fuck your cookies. I'm not eating any more of these cookies.'"

Immediately, we both broke out in laughter. But once the initial humor died down, I knew I had to investigate. If one cookie had worms in it, there was sure to be others.[42] "Go down to the operators and tell them to stop pushing the cookies," I said to Dominic.

"You got it," he said, standing quickly.

"We're officially out of the cookie business."

"No more cookies?"

"Nope...we're just a fat pill company again."

Dominic laughed as he exited.

A couple days later, the offending cookie arrived at my office. As soon as I looked at it, I knew there was something wrong. The

---

[42] I had a feeling that I knew what was going on. Almost all grain products have bugs in them when they're first formed—that's just a part of the territory with grain. What happens is that the bugs are cooked off the product when they're put into the ovens. Kind of like a barbeque in Iowa. But still, I knew we had to shut things down until I could investigate.

sealed plastic bag it had been sent over in had expanded slightly, as if some kind of gas was trying to escape. Condensation had collected in places.

Disgusted, I opened the drawer on the left side of my desk and tossed the cookie inside. I then phoned the call floor and reminded the operators never to sell the damn things again.

≈

Bob Bradley seemed pretty irritable during that period. And who could blame him? His was the responsibility of building and revising the entire accounting arm of a company that was rocketing toward the hundreds of millions in annual sales. And he had to do all of this in the cramped building space we'd leased across the parking lot from the first building on Santa Fe Street.

Even when he wasn't all moody, the distributors never much liked being around Bob because they thought he didn't appreciate them. I remember that Isaac downright hated him. But in truth, that was never the case with Bob. He might not have seen the light on how important the distributors were to the company, but he just had what he thought to be bigger fish to fry. A company that can't handle its own money won't last very long. And, lately, Bob had a whole lot of money to handle.

Anyway, Bob was always in such a rush that he hardly even had time to argue with me anymore.

"Hey, Bob," I said as we passed each other in the hallway. "What's happening, buddy?"

"Fucking phones," Bob said, charging past.

"What about the phones?" I asked as I turned.

Bob stopped and wheeled around to face me. He looked about as frustrated as he'd ever been. "The phone system's too small, Mike. Too small!"

"But we just installed it."

Bob thrust his hands to each side as if to say, "No shit."

"I thought we installed this system because the *old one* was too small."

Bob just waved me off and turned anxiously, making his way down the hall.

So we were growing so fast that we couldn't even keep up with the phone systems, let alone the phone calls.

As I mentioned, though, Bob's biggest task was creating the accounting wing. To that end, he made two really shrewd moves. First, he meticulously constructed the infrastructure of the accounting department so every single dollar, right down to the penny, would be accounted for. Bob didn't fear many things as an entrepreneur, but one of them was failing to account for all the money. And the other move: bringing in the guy whose office I passed right after my little phone confrontation with Bob.

Mike Compton. He was a good-looking guy in his early forties. Average height (though a few inches taller than me). Quiet and extremely respectful. Really likable. He was a CPA type—a little on the nerdy or awkward side, kind of numbers oriented—but he never much liked the role of the CPA type. So he compensated for it all, I guess, by doing things like buying and maintaining stock cars. He had his own car for a while and was actually a good driver on whatever circuit he participated in. He had a nice family, that Compton. A lovely, thoughtful wife and some great kids.

Anyway, I always enjoyed seeing him at work because he carried a certain calmness about him. So I stuck my head into his office as I passed.

"Hell of a day, huh, Compton?" I said.

Compton blinked in a confused sort of way as he looked up from his number-crunching. "What do you mean?"

"Bob."

The accountant smiled and shook his head. "Yeah, something about the phones."

"If only everything ran like accounting."

"No kidding," Compton agreed energetically. "Bob's really got this place in top shape. And believe me, Mike, that's not easy at the rate this company's growing."

"It's all you, buddy," I said as I ducked back out of his office. "It's all you."

The full line on Bradley and Compton is that the former had met the latter through his other business dealings. I guess stock car racing and car towing go hand in hand. Anyway, Bob had brought Compton in right about when he needed to create a new set of accounting criteria for his towing and auction company. Compton had proven his worth by bringing the whole operation up to general accounting principles (GAP) standards.

When we hired him to do the same for Metabolife, Compton would wind up doing the upper level accounting while Bob handled the deposits and more grunt-level stuff. But as the company continued to grow, just handling the deposits became a two-person job. Even the routine accounting became difficult to keep up with. Eventually, the department Bob headed was thirty people strong.

This would all get pretty difficult for anyone to bear, let alone Compton and Bradley. Plus, with all that money coming in, it's far more difficult to make sure you're keeping your accounting in pristine order. So that's probably why they were always running around with bones to pick.

Continuing down the hallway, I turned the corner into my office, where I found our company CFO, Jeff Anderman, leaning over my cigar box.[43]

"You looking for something, Jeff?" I asked.

Anderman straightened up with a start. "Nothing, Mike," he said nervously. "Nothing."

Anderman was like five feet and five inches tall. Maybe 130 or 140 pounds. So tiny, either way. Kind of weasely-looking. Short hair. Early thirties. The kind of guy who would tell you one thing, then go behind your back to ally himself with other people and torpedo your efforts. But I didn't know that part at the time.

---

[43] Our rapid expansion as a company had caused us to make the mistake of hiring consultants who proved from day one that they weren't worth a damn. The only thing we got out of the charade was a new company president, Larry Miller. Miller, in turn, had recommended and hired Anderman to serve as our CFO. The undertow of the great consulting wave, I guess.

"So what are you doing in here?" I asked.

"Oh…uh…" Anderman's eyes darted from object to object on my desk. "Just wanted to drop you a note about Wizard."

Wizard. The program our operators used for taking all the direct-order sales we had coming in. Obviously, if we had a problem with Wizard, we had a significant problem. Not exactly note-worthy. It would've been much bigger than that.

So I stared at my CFO skeptically but nevertheless in good-natured fashion. And as I came around from behind him, I realized that he'd been reaching into my cigar case. This supposedly highly qualified, educated professional, the CFO of our company, was trying to swipe my cigars. They were nice cigars, but still.

"You know, Jeff," I said, "I've got an idea."

Jeff nodded in an impish sort of way.

I pointed with my eyes at the cookie suit lumped in the corner of the room. "Any time you want one of these cigars, you have to put on the cookie suit. I catch you smoking one of my cigars without the suit on, you can never have one again."

Jeff nodded again, licking his lips.

"So what about Wizard?" I asked.

Jeff sighed, apparently coming back down from the thrill of his failed heist. "Macaulay says there's some problem with the numbering system. I don't really understand it. But he thinks it might screw up the orders."

"You're kidding."

The CFO shook his head naïvely.

I immediately bolted from the office in search of John Macaulay. Despite our agreement, I'm certain that Anderman used the opportunity to steal a cigar, anyway, but that didn't bother me. What bothered me then was getting down to the bottom of this obviously serious issue. As quickly as possible.

Macaulay was a guy who'd originally come to the company as a distributor. But we'd brought him in on a more direct level when he told us that he was one of the original guys at Microsoft. He'd presented an impressive résumé to back up his claims, so we had no reason to doubt his expertise. He proved himself almost immediately, anyway.

See, as we started growing, we began having problems with our computer systems. And Macaulay volunteered to help us sort things out. He'd done the job so well that Blevins, Bradley, and I decided to move him over to all things technical.

Anyway, in short order, I'd found Macaulay.

He stood 6′3″ at full height. Athletic. Charismatic. All the women loved him. He had brown hair and a penchant for telling stories. He did have great stories, so I couldn't blame him. I mean, the guy told us he was the center on the famous Joe Montana/Dwight Clark Hail Mary play during the '89 Super Bowl (the play simply called "The Catch"). He even had the two Super Bowl rings to back it up. Better yet, he was a licensed nurse practitioner—the ultimate jack-of-all-trades.

"What's this about Wizard?" I asked him.

In typical fashion, Macaulay replied as if he had everything under control. "The numbering and lettering system doesn't seem to be infinite."

"What do you mean?" I asked.

John began talking with his hands. "Whenever we enter an order, the order is assigned a number and a letter."

"Yeah," I said slowly, my voice lined with confusion.

"Well, the letters only go three deep. So once we hit the last number possible on triple-Z, I'm not sure what's going to happen."

My eyebrows blew back. "We could lose the orders?"

"We might even lose all of our records. The program may crash."

My heart sank. "John, this is priority one through ten right now. Call the people at Wizard and see what you can find out."

So Macaulay called the makers of Wizard and discovered that even *they* didn't know what would happen. In other words, we were selling so much product that we were in danger of outstripping the foreseen capacity of a widely used software program.

Fortunately, when we reached the last possible number, the system started replacing the letters with hieroglyphics. So, basically, the numbering was infinite after all.

I remember that it was early the next morning when we first realized that our ordering system wasn't going to take a dump on us. I'd just returned to my desk, content that my company was beginning to roar to life; content that my family was living comfortably; content that I had a product that was helping the customer every bit as much as it was helping our growing family of distributors. And as I sat down in my leathery chair, I felt completely happy.

Then, I remembered a file I was supposed to have reviewed weeks ago. Bob had called it to my attention just before closing on the previous day. According to him, it was already long overdue.

So in search of the file, I opened the drawer to my left. There, I saw the worm-cookie, still in its package. Barely. The bag had expanded to the point where it appeared ready to pop. The thing was as gassy and moist as the dankest swampland.

Curious, I popped it open.

Out flew a whole swarm of little butterflies. The worms had taken on new life.

Chapter 9

Even Monsters Cry

Despite our modest and foreboding beginnings, by 1999, we were headed to one billion dollars in retail sales throughout our distribution and network sales force.

People always ask me how it was that I could continue to believe in something so much. How it was that I could stick to a dream even when the chips were down. And I'll tell you why. I learned from my hero. I learned from my father...

I guess Dad's story actually begins with my grandfather, the man for whom I was named. Grandpa Michael was born in Lebanon. A small town called Duma. He and my grandmother, Helen, were both Orthodox Christian—and in the year of my father's birth, 1921, their faith and freedom were being challenged by the Turks. In fact, owed to a four-year blockade set up by the invading armies, even the food supply of the little town of Duma had been dried up.

So my grandfather, a hardworking and honorable man born into a family of five brothers, knew that he had to take responsibility for the wellbeing of his town, as well as that of his young family. He and Grandma had my newborn father to worry about, after all.

To that end, he called a meeting with one of his good friends: John Chalhub, my own mother's grandfather.[44]

I like to imagine them meeting in one of those small Eastern European hovels, the candlelight flickering, old records playing in the background, conspiracy in the air. And that seems appropriate since that's probably exactly the kind of environment in which they did meet.

"We have to do something about this, John," Grandpa would've said.

"I know, my friend," John would've replied. "But we risk too much. Last time, you nearly lost your head."

I picture my grandfather raising an eyebrow in challenge, an expression that's been passed down through the generations. "I'm still here, aren't I?"

A long silence would've followed as both men weighed the cost of continuing their little smuggling operation.

"John, the people are starving."

"The enemy has redoubled its efforts in securing the city."

Grandpa would've thought long and hard, running his thumb and forefinger through his short and bristly beard. "But they do not have every square meter covered by their troops. What of the pass?"

"The goat path?"

"Yes. We could go under cover of night."

"To Syria?"

"If we have to. We must feed the people."

However it actually went down, I do know that the two men would agree that, despite their recent brushes with death at the hands of the Turks, they had no choice but to continue an operation they'd run since the peak of WWI. They would sneak past the checkpoints at night and travel all the way into Syria, where they would buy food to bring back to Duma.

So that's my grandfather. A hero to the people at great personal danger.

---

[44] That was small-town Middle East in the 1920s, I guess. Everybody knew everybody.

But one man's hero is another man's smuggler and spy. Two years later, the Turks would somehow discover the fact that my grandfather was the reason the town of Duma seemed to be holding on to so much hope—and remaining so healthy and strong, despite the attrition. Word quickly reached the townspeople that my grandfather had become a wanted man. If captured, he would be executed by firing squad.

Conveniently, right around that time (1923), Grandfather received a letter from his brother Elias, who'd already settled in Calexico, California. Grandpa has told me specifically of the day he received the letter.

"That's it," he said to his wife.

Grandma Helen glided in gracefully to look over her husband's shoulder. "That's what?" she asked.

"We're getting out of this. We're going to America."

So that's why my family first deigned to escape the clutches of the Turks: a price on one man's head and an opportunity on one family's horizon. Imagine my grandparents on the slow boat to the U.S., not knowing what the future held for them—or even how they would manage to get across the vast American landscape to unite with my Uncle Elias. And imagine my father, a child of only two, leaving his homeland without ever truly knowing it.

But it was not meant to be. En route, the U.S. shut its doors to immigrants. So in the middle of the ocean, the boat turned south and carved the long, trying path to Mexico. My family wound up reaching Tijuana, where my intrepid grandfather set up shop with a street cart, selling various goods to the people without the luxury of speaking either of their languages. They had very little money at the time, I'm told, but Grandpa, ever the hard worker, wound up doing well enough to purchase a building and open his own dry goods store.

It would be another few years before the U.S. would reopen its doors to immigrants. So around that time, my grandfather received another letter from Elias, who still lived in California. Elias had agreed to sponsor my family's arrival in the U.S.

Now, there are conflicting reports on how my family came to be named Ellis. If you believe some, we were named after Elias, who had landed on Ellis Island and was given the name simply because his last name was difficult to spell and "Ellis" sounded like "Elias." If you believe others, he was granted the name of the island itself. Either way, upon arriving in the U.S., my grandfather's name was now Mike Ellis by default. And Mike Ellis would take up residence in San Ysidro, a border town in San Diego, California. He would open a dry goods business there and become quite successful. The business would even help him survive the Great Depression intact. I'm told that he made so much money because he was willing to provide lines of credit to Mexican merchants where no one else would. So they would come up to his stores, buy his goods on credit, and then cross the border into their own towns, where they would resell the items for profit.

As for my father, I'm told he was a handful to raise.

Imagine this:

Dad's only twelve and he's out with his younger brother, George. This is San Ysidro and they're walking around, shooting .22s, taking target practice on whatever they can.

"Right there, Joe," George says, looking every bit of his six years of age as he points toward the dusty horizon. A shabby old fence stands there, its wood cracked and weak. The fence leads from the middle of the open field and attaches itself to the backside of a store constructed squarely of poorly painted cement blocks.

"Right where?" Dad asks.

"That can over there by the fence. Can't you see it?"

Dad eyes up the direction in which his younger brother points. There, he sees an old beer can. Red. Rusted. And standing tenuously on the top of one of the fence posts. "Oh, yeah," he says. "I see it."

What my dad doesn't see is the men coming around the corner of the store to the right of the fence. Dad fires, missing the can and coming very close to hitting one of the men.

The group charges toward my dad and Uncle George so quickly that neither boy even thinks to run.

"Damn it, boy," the man who'd almost been shot bellows angrily. "What are you doing?" The man appears to be Mexican, as do his friends. He's hulking and furious and they're all clearly a little drunk.

"Shooting at that can," Dad says innocently, pointing toward the fence.

"Well, you almost hit me."

Dad and George look at each other and shrug anxiously.

"Sorry," Dad says, his lower lip quivering only slightly.

The man turns to one of his friends, who produces his own rifle, also a .22. "No, to hell with that," he says, checking to make sure the barrel is loaded. "That's not good enough."

My father can smell the whiskey on the man's breath, he's so close. Uncle George, meanwhile, quivers in his tiny boots, looking anxiously from side to side in search of escape. He finds none, as every man not holding a rifle has created a circle around the scene.

Dad stands proudly, looking his accuser in the eyes. Then, it dawns on him that this man intends to kill him. More importantly, he intends to kill his brother, George, as well. And he can't have that. He shrugs again and looks up at the man. "Why don't we settle this like men, then?"

All the attackers laugh drunkenly. "But you're a boy," one of them says.

"I'm no boy," Dad says.

They laugh again.

"We'll have a duel," Dad offers. "We each get a shot. One after the other."

The angry man straightens up. He's thoroughly drunk, but he looks almost sobered by what he's just heard. "Who will shoot first?"

Dad looks from man to man. "We'll flip a coin."

"A coin!" the accuser yells, glancing at each of his friends. "Who's got a coin?"

One of the men eventually produces a coin. Dad's accuser immediately flips it.

"Heads," Dad calls.

It turns up heads.

The face of the man with the gun contorts into a look of frustration. "Your shot, then, boy," he says.

George tugs on Dad's arm as if trying to get him to run. The young version of my father shakes him off.

"No, George," he says. "I have to do this."

George's eyes run moist with tears. "But why, Joe?"

"I don't know," Dad says defiantly. "Honor, I guess."

George begins to cry in earnest.

"And besides," Dad adds, "if I don't take care of this now, this guy will never leave us be."

George nods and my father clears away from him, taking his strides in the direction opposite his accuser. The midday sun beats heavily down upon his brow, which does not sweat. When he gets to about a hundred feet away, he turns. Looks his accuser over.

The man with the rifle sways from side to side drunkenly. His eyes remain open, though the way his face struggles against the sun suggests that he wants nothing more than to close them.

Dad ponders the ethics of shooting a man in the chest. Quickly, he realizes that whatever happens to him, he could never kill a man. And so he takes aim for his arm. Fires. Hits his target.

"Fuck!" the man screams.

All of his friends begin chattering in anger. "He missed, man," one of them says.

"You got him," another one urges.

"The fuck he missed," the accuser screams. "Look." He shows the others his bleeding arm.

They all tell him to shake it off and take his shot.

So the man brings his rifle to his shoulder. It's clear that he's having trouble keeping aim. He's stunned, drunk, and bleeding into the dust. It seems a long while that he sizes my father up.

"Let's go, Joe," Uncle George pleads. "Run!"

Dad shakes his head. Stands proudly, unflinching.

Finally, the man fires. He misses the target.

Honor upheld.[45]

So those were the days in San Ysidro.

In the '40s, Grandpa would open a shop in downtown San Diego and Dad would go off to fight in the War to End All Wars. Following a raid in the South Pacific, of his company of 110 Marines, Dad was one of only three men to make it out alive. He never talked about it much.

Anyway, like most men of his generation, upon Dad's return from the conflict, he seemed like a new man. His father wanted him to work in the store with his brother George and sister Mary, but Dad had other ideas.

"Dad," he said, standing in the dim yellow light of Grandpa's cluttered backroom office, "I'd like to start my own store."

"What do you mean, 'your own store'?" Grandpa asked incredulously.

"A clothing store."

After some convincing on the quality of the business venture, my grandfather agreed to go into partnership with my dad. Between the two of them, my Uncle George, and Aunt Mary, Ellis Brothers Men's Store in National City boasted a well-motivated staff.

My father proved early on to be an excellent businessman, just like his father before him. And while he lacked Grandpa's work ethic, he didn't lack for his honor or his entrepreneurial skill. Even when George and Grandpa backed out of the store to return to the warehouse business—and even when Mary went her own way— Dad managed to thrive.

Over the years, he would open several new locations. And the business would do pretty well for a while.

---

[45] Dad wasn't always honorable, though. I've been told that he would sit up in Grandpa's shop with his bb gun and take aim at fat women walking down the other side of the street. He'd plunk them in the ass and they would scream and run into the store to get my grandfather. Grandpa said he'd always spend the next few hours looking for Dad, just so he could beat his ass. But Dad would've been long gone by the time the women had waddled, steaming, into the store.

Whenever sales numbers would dip—and this would happen often because Dad had decided to open his little business right around the time that the large chain department stores had started to take hold in the U.S.—my father would call little "motivational" meetings for his staff before work. Things were different back then. Dad didn't man an army of teenage department store clerks. These were career salesmen. And he would motivate them to the point where sales would always spike tremendously on the day of his speeches.

"When a customer comes to the door," Dad would say, making the point with his hands as well as his words, "you have to greet them. You have to give them service. When they come in, you have to *up-sell* them. If they're looking for a shirt, you sell them pants, too. You sell them a tie. A suit."

And that's exactly what would happen. So, in a nutshell, that's where and how I learned to sell: in my father's clothing store.

That's not to say that I was always the perfect apprentice. I had to uphold the family tradition of giving the old man hell, after all...

When I was sixteen years old, you weren't allowed to cross the border into Mexico unless you were eighteen. That didn't stop me and my brother Joe, himself eighteen at the time. He'd throw caution to the wind, shove me into the trunk of the car, and try to make the crossing. Of course, the Mexican border guards don't care if there's a teenager in the trunk on the way down to Mexico, so we would occasionally make it. But the San Diego Police Department has a way of sticking their nose into things that concern teens in trunks. We found out the hard way that when the San Diego police set up checkpoints on the border, trunking just doesn't work.

Given that my brother was a lone teenager in a car, I guess he looked a little suspicious. So the cops immediately found me in the trunk. Then, they took me right down to the San Diego Police Department. I'm not sure where my brother went, but I remember him not being around.

So I was alone in the police station when I heard the words I'd been dreading. "We called your dad, kid," a tall, lanky cop said from the other side of the spacious processing room.

I nodded but could not find the strength to reply.

"Said he'd be down shortly," the cop added.

I nodded again, gulping through the driest throat I can ever remember having.

See, I had yet to learn one important thing about my dad: He'd only get really angry about the *little* things. "You left your shit on the table again," he'd say. "I don't like clutter." And he'd holler and yell, swearing and cussing.[46] But then, whenever I did something big and stupid, Dad would always be on my side, in my corner. The strangest and most wonderful thing.

So I sat in the holding tank in that police station. Eleven p.m. I knew that Dad was on his way over to get me. The drive would take him thirty or forty minutes, I knew, so I had time to sweat it out. I shook from head to toe at the stress, figuring I now faced the ass-kicking of a lifetime.

But what did Dad do when he arrived and they opened the cell door for him?

"You alright, Mike?" he asked.

I nodded.

"Okay, then. Let's go."

In the car on the way home, he didn't even raise his voice.

"You okay?" he asked.

"Yeah, Dad," I finally managed. "I'm okay."

Then, when we got home, he just told me to go to bed. I remember, though, on the way to my room, he capped things off in the only way my dad knew how: firmly and honorably.

"Son," he said as I stood in the hallway.

I turned at the hips, trying to look him in the eye. "Yeah, Dad?"

"Don't do that again."

I nodded eagerly and went to my room.

Those were stressful times for both of us, but not nearly as stressful as the few instances when we would both manage to get in trouble at the same time. I remember once when I was seventeen.

---

[46] Looking back, this is probably where I picked up all my colorful language.

Like most people do when they're seventeen, I'd started in with some friends who liked to smoke weed. I never bought any for myself, but I would occasionally smoke it whenever it was offered. One time, we were stupid enough to smoke in the car that my dad had loaned me.

"We've only got a little left," my friend said, the purple smoke still rolling all around us as he showed me a small, brittle nugget of weed. "Can we leave it here?"

"Sure," I said, stoned. "Just leave it in the ashtray. We'll smoke it next time."

Now, this was the car that I drove almost every day, so I figured I'd be in the clear. Felt like my own personal property at the time, after all. But of course the next day, Dad got up early, planning to go hunting in Mexico with his buddies. Whose car does he take? "My" car.

Oblivious to the fact that he was tooling around the border with weed in his ashtray, Dad and his friends nevertheless made it into Mexico without any trouble. But as I said before, dealing with cops and border agents on the way back into the U.S. is often a different story.

Immediately, they found the grass in the ashtray. So they got searched pretty hard, my dad and his friends.

"I don't know whose that is, officers," Dad said resolutely. "I swear." He watched angrily as they continued to search his car. "It's probably my damn kid's marijuana. He's the one that drives this car."

I'd catch hell when he got home. I remember that he dragged me into the hallway, his face red as I'd ever seen it. My mom, bless her heart, would wait at the kitchen table and listen in while Dad tore into me.

"We found marijuana in the ashtray," Dad said, his voice lined with accusation. "You smoking dope?"

I threw my hands up defensively and did what every seventeen-year-old does: I denied it. "It ain't mine, Dad, I swear."

"We got stopped at the border by the agents," Dad said furiously. "They searched us up and down."

"It isn't mine," I repeated. Ah, seventeen.

Dad paced away then immediately back to me. "Who would've put it in there but you? You were the one driving this car last night."

At that moment, I heard my mom stirring in the kitchen. Then, the unmistakable sound of one of the cabinets slamming shut. Shortly, I saw her wheel round the corner behind my dad. She had one of those, "Oh, yeah?" looks on her face. And in her hand, she held a condom, still in its wrapper.

My mother had dark hair and was a really attractive woman. Eight years younger than Dad. Feisty and yet warm and loving. Even at 5'1" and 105 pounds, she could look entirely threatening when she wanted to. I guess it comes from her background. Being Lebanese, English, and Irish, she'd come from families who knew how to fight. And she'd been raised old-school Syriac Orthodox Christian.

"Oh, yeah, Joe?" Mom said. "Well look what I found in *your* car."

Dad went white in the face. Instantly, he threw his hands up defensively. "It ain't mine, honey, I swear."

"Really? Well, who else would've put it there? You're the only one who drives that car."

"It ain't mine."

Mom seemed to grow a full foot as she glared at my father. "Well, then…if this thing ain't yours, then you gotta believe Mike when he says that dope ain't his."

That was it. Killed the whole deal right there. Dad was fried.

You know what the funny thing was, though? Dad wasn't lying. That condom wasn't his. That was mine, too.

So that's Dad: honorable till the end. Even if he was innocent, he knew his wife had him dead to rights. So he took the rap. Really, that's how my dad lived his life. Honorably. In more ways than one, without him, nothing about Metabolife—not any of our success— would have been possible.

And don't worry. Later, I confessed and told Mom that the condom was mine.

⌒ᴍᴍ⌒

We'd just come off a break in the deposition that proved to be painfully short. Felt like I only had enough time to straighten my tie. My lawyers had spent the ten minutes or so huddled together, Allen doing most of the talking. The question, I assumed, was whether they should continue to press Frantz off the subject of my father's medical history.

Just thinking about it made me misty. How could such a private issue matter? My father was a proud man—and it would've embarrassed him to no end to know that we were discussing his cancer and his care.

Allen sat back down as the cameraman got us rolling again. "Thank you for the opportunity to consult with my colleagues," my lawyer said. "At this time, I'll maintain my objection, but allow the witness to answer."

My heart sank. There had to be something more they could do.

Allen turned to me. "Do you want the question read back?"

"Unless…" Frantz interjected, his voice all oily. "Do you remember the question?"

"I recall the question," I said bitterly. "I do not recall how many milligrams of morphine he was taking."

Frantz's face, even through the hot light of the lamps and sunshine, went completely cold. "Other than the morphine, was there any other drug that you recall that he was taking…" the PI attorney raised his hand dismissively, as if he were having a casual conversation with his oldest friend in the world. "I'm talking about a drug that's a prescription drug—that he was taking in respect to pain control management for the cancer?"

The cancer, I remember thinking. "To my knowledge, he wasn't taking anything else for pain management."

I could hear Frantz shuffling some papers around, not sure if he was even looking at me. "When you saw that your father was so ill, did you—was it your impression that the medical doctors were not doing everything that could be done to assist him with the cancer that he had?"

That acidic lump began to form at the back of my throat again. I remember his doctors. I remember them well. "No."

"Was it your view that maybe you could give your father something else that they couldn't give him with the prescription medication?"

I tried to keep my head in the here and now. To maintain. But it wasn't working. So much anger and sadness. I feel my eyes go moist. *Fight it, Ellis,* I remember thinking. *You believe that now— believe that herbal remedies can aid prescription meds in ways that our country simply doesn't grasp—but did you believe it then?* "No, I don't believe that's correct, either."

"What would your view be—what was your view, then, in terms of how your part was going to be played in conjunction with the medical doctors that were already treating him?"

I sighed, feeling that telltale shudder in my lungs. "I was looking at his quality of life," I said. "They were looking at just, I think, drugging him for his pain."[47]

"Did you talk to the doctors about providing your father with prescription ephedrine to give him a boost?" Frantz asked.[48]

I remember feeling guilty, though there was no reason to. "No."

"Did you talk to the doctors that were treating your father for cancer about any measures in addition to what was already being done by the doctors to improve your father's quality of life?" Frantz's voice had taken on a kind of condescending tone. It was as if he was trying to make me feel like I'd been negligent in the care of my dying father.

"Yes."

"What did you discuss with the doctors in that respect?"

---

[47] There's the central difference between Eastern and Western medicine, right there. Western doctors are reactionary. They treat problems, symptoms, but only after they present themselves. Eastern doctors treat both the problems and the underlying cause of those problems. They focus on future wellness while we focus on applying band-aids, allowing the presenting problem to continue unchecked.

"It was hospice. I discussed that he had no energy. He would be going through cancer sweats." I was having a hard time even getting through the words as I thought about Dad's pain. I'm not sure if it came across on film or not, but I was struggling with these memories. "He would get out of bed, go sit on the sofa, and then he couldn't handle that and he would just go back and just lie down in bed and go to sleep."

My proud father. My proud, intrepid, improbably hardworking father. Confined to his bed. Furious with his disease, but never once complaining about it. My brave father. My proud, brave father.

I was very near losing it, just then, but I must not have been showing it because Frantz pressed on. Fortunately, he threw me a bone. Something different to think about; to grab hold of. *Focus on the herbs, on the research, Ellis.*

---

[48] In this country, we seem to be thinking more and more that doctors should be allowed to make all of our decisions regarding wellness for us; that pharmaceutical companies always know what's best and can always be counted on to supply the highest quality products. But here's the thing about pharmaceutical companies: They don't cure anything. "Curing" doesn't seem to be in their agenda. Instead, they come up with drugs that you have to take for the rest of your life. "Disease maintenance" is what I call it.

Consider the antibiotics that many of us will have to take for the rest of our lives—we all get infections from time to time. Heart disease, cancer, diabetes. Despite all the money pumped into finding a cure, there's no cure to be found. There are plenty of drugs to help you fend off the disease for a few years, though. Expensive drugs. Got cancer? They'll suck any and every cancer patient dry with medicines until the day they die. Medicines that do nothing more than prolong the illness and shrink the wallet.

The only thing bordering on a cure that big pharma has to offer is a vaccination. But for some reason, they won't make them. You've seen the reports: Every year, there's a terrible shortage of vaccinations as benign as those covering the flu. See, this is because the big pharmaceutical companies refuse to enter the game. There's just too much money to be lost in such a venture. Most of the time, the government has to give tax breaks to the smaller drug companies so they'll manufacture the vaccinations we're all clamoring for. And still, despite all this, every year, there's a shortage of vaccines. Do you think that's because we just don't have the materials to make them? No. It's because the companies so "caring" about our health don't want to spend the money.

"When you did your research," he said slowly, "did you look into herbal treatment of cancer?"

"No, I did not."

"Are there such texts out there? Do you know?"

"Yes, there are."

"When you were doing your research at the time that you started developing your product, you didn't look at any of the research to the extent that it dealt with herbal treatment of cancer. Correct?"

"No, sir."

"Why didn't you go to the herbal treatment of cancer literature?"

Something in my mind broke at that point. The lump in my throat increased tenfold. Here's Frantz—and I can't even fucking *see him*—making me feel negligent again.

Fortunately, Allen gave me a reprieve—another distraction to latch on to.

"Objection," he barked. "Relevancy. Not likely to lead to admissible evidence in any case that's currently pending." Then, to me: "You can answer."

"I believed, at the point he was at, there was no cure."

Frantz didn't skip a beat. "So you went to… I'm trying to understand how you focused your research. What was the focus of your research in the herbal area?"

I had to gather myself to speak without crying. I honestly had to pull myself together. I was in a suit and tie. Surrounded by lawyers. My company was being threatened by what we all believed to be a bogus injury claim. And all I could think about was not crying.

Through the piercing light, I caught a quick glimpse of the videographer, who looked uncomfortable when our eyes meet. I panned over to the stenographer, who still typed feverishly, but looked pained herself. It was too bright to tell if her own eyes had glazed over with tears, but I could sense her worry, her empathy. It gave me strength for a moment.

"I did not look for cancer because I did not want to give him any false hopes like his Mexican friends were doing. I was looking at giving him energy so he could start interacting with the family before he died because he wasn't doing any of that on the morphine that he was taking."

I thought about my father trying to play with my ten-year-old son, Christian—one of his favorite things in the world to do in his health. I remember him having to sit down immediately, cursing himself for not being able to keep up.

Frantz then hit me with a barrage of questions about Dad's care, each one like a blow to the head. Each one deepening a wound he'd already opened just beneath my eyes.

"So you wanted to give him something to counteract the morphine?" He said it so coldly. Heartlessly. *Who gives a shit about morphine?*

"Counteract his condition of not interacting, I think, is better put."

"Was it your view that the morphine was making him so he was nonenergetic?"

"I'm sure it was a contributing factor."

"Did you talk to his doctors about giving him an herbal product that contained ephedrine before you gave it to him?"

"I don't believe at that time there was a doctor to talk to with hospice involved."

"Your father didn't have a treating doctor when he was with hospice?"

"It was Kaiser. He did have a treating physician, but I don't think it was on an ongoing basis with him."

"Did you have much interaction with the treating physician?"

"At one point in time, I did."[49]

"Which point in time was that?"

"I believe before hospice was actually involved and they just left him at home to eventually die in the hospice program."

"What's the doctor's name that you interacted with?"

---

[49] If you've never been in this situation, it's at this point when you know it's over: when even the doctors seem to give up. When the only thing they have that will help you are more pills.

"I don't recall." Actually, I probably forced it out of my memory long ago.

"He was with Kaiser?"

"I believe, yes, he was with Kaiser."

"Which Kaiser?"

"Kaiser Permanente. I believe it was in the Mission Gorge area, whatever that was."

I was losing it. I couldn't even piece together reasonable responses now. My vision had become obscured by my tears, which still teetered on the brink of crashing down over my cheeks.

Then, Frantz hit me with the deathblow.

"How long was your father with hospice before he passed away?"

I had to pause for a long time. I turned away from the camera, attempting to hide the tears that now trickled down my face. "That whole time is kind of fuzzy," I said weakly.

Frantz continued, oblivious. "What's your best recollection?"

The heat of the sunshine and the camera's lamps had gotten to me. I wasn't sweating, but my face burned. The warmth of my tears overshadowed it all. Everyone in the room but Frantz seemed to have stopped breathing. His cologne singed my nostrils. I couldn't continue like this.

"I don't recall," I managed. Then, I collected whatever I had left and folded. "Can I take a break?"

Through the light, I caught Frantz in a nod. His eyes were wide, as if he'd just now noticed the anguish he'd exposed me to; as if he'd just now realized that he'd insulted my father's memory; as if he'd just now realized how much damage he'd wrought to his deposition. Here he'd been trying to make a monster of me. But I guess even monsters cry.

Chapter 10

Manufacturing a Product, Manufacturing a Letter

Deposition…day two. We picked up late that morning partly because Frantz had about eight stacks of papers to rifle through and partly because absolutely nobody in the room, save for the salivating PI attorneys, wanted to be there. So it was just after 10 a.m. when the usual suspects ran their introductions and the stenographer swore me in again.

Frantz was really on his game on day two: drier, shiftier, and lamer than ever. After one long, blindingly monotonous hour, he'd finally managed to get down to business with some real questions.

"When you started Metabolife," he said, "who came up with the name '356'?"

"I did," I said blandly.

"What does that mean, '356,' other than numbers?"

"Three-fifty-six is the numbers that were given to the formula when it was tested on the animal toxicity studies."

As I've mentioned already, the studies we conducted in China were exploratory in nature. But they were just the start of our overall safety agenda. Step one toward assuring ourselves and our customers that we provided a product that adhered to the highest possible safety standards. Step two was to set up the manufacturing so everything would be absolutely uniform.

From a manufacturing perspective, we did more for safety than any other company in our industry. Costly, but certainly worth it. See, with all of the money, research, and time that we poured into the agenda, we knew that at the end of our process, we could be certain that our product would be safer than any other product on the market. Here's a little background on what we did:

Since our product was a compound of natural ingredients, we had to order those ingredients from herb suppliers. The suppliers would ship the ingredients along with a certificate of analysis. Most companies, whether dietary supplement or pharmaceutical, tend to take these certificates at face value. They assume that if the sender of the herb says it's safe and standardized, then it must be safe and standardized. But we learned really quickly that these certificates weren't good enough, particularly when they came from companies in China. See, many of these Chinese companies tended to claim all-natural ingredients and extraction processes, but then would spike the shipments with pharmaceutical ephedrine or extract their ma huang with acetone instead of water (which isn't good when it comes to safety).

So we set up a manufacturing process that involved thorough examination of the ingredients before we even agreed to accept the shipments. Our manufacturers would rigorously test each shipment for contaminates, quality, active ingredient content, and much more.

When it came to ma huang, our most important ingredient, we'd run what's called an HPLC analysis. This meant that we would test the ma huang to ensure that its levels of ephedrine alkaloids fell within a specified range that we'd defined for naturally occurring ephedrine. The shipments also had to be free of any metals, contaminates or insecticides. Given all of these standards, when it came to ma huang, we had to refuse the shipments almost fifty percent of the time.[50]

Once we determined that a shipment of the ingredient was safe, we accepted it. We could then move on to manufacturing.

We manufactured only at FDA registered and certified facilities. In many of these same facilities, you could find OTC (over the counter) drugs being manufactured, as well.

Now, FDA has a standard when it comes to dietary supplements. Think about an orange. How much vitamin C is in an orange? Hard to say. See, one orange might have more vitamin C than the next. But according to FDA, as long as the product in question uses a natural orange in its manufacturing practices, then it is deemed safe.

Let's say you apply these same standards to ma huang. And say we had a batch that contained six percent ephedrine alkaloids. Then, say we had another batch that contained eight percent. Most companies—and this is well within FDA standards—would say that both batches fell within the acceptable range of naturally occurring ma huang. But we didn't think that a "naturally occurring range" was good enough. We just didn't want so much variance (particularly with our most important active ingredient). So we would blend the two batches together, testing and retesting until we reached the exact percentage that we listed on each bottle of Metabolife. Once we hit the right level, we had our ma huang.

But that was just the ma huang. We had more than twenty ingredients in our product, and we standardized the blending process for each of them in exactly the same way.

So with standards met on our twenty-plus ingredients, we could now blend everything together. Once everything was blended, we would analyze the mixture in order to ensure that one pill wouldn't be getting more of one ingredient than another. After

---

[50] Incidentally, since we were one of the biggest buyers of ma huang in the world, you have to wonder where all of the product we'd refused ended up. Most likely, it would fall into the hands of another ephedrine product manufacturer with lower testing standards. But because we were the biggest buyers, another interesting thing occurred: The Chinese companies began cleaning up their acts. I guess they just didn't like getting their shipments sent back to them.

the mixture had been approved and we had our raw caplets, we would take random and frequent samples of them for more analysis. This latest round of testing ensured that each caplet had been formulated correctly.

From there, the caplets would be moved on to the drying process. Then, they would be coated. And finally, we would take more random samples of the non-finished caplets and analyze them yet again.

All batches that were in line with our extraordinarily high standards would go to bottling. And every tablet that was put in a bottle had a batch number. We then stamped each bottle with a UPC code that would allow us to follow the batch wherever it went on Earth.[51]

From receipt of ingredients to bottled Metabolife, the process took about five weeks—longer (and at greater expense) than it took to make any other product on the market at the time.[52] But that's the way we wanted it. In this world where almost every company tries to make things as cheaply and efficiently as possible, we wanted nothing more than to produce a safe and perfect product.

"I'm going to…" Frantz stammered. "Looking at that label— you want to look at it. I direct your attention—I want to direct your attention to the suggested use and all the writing below suggested use section."

I looked down at the paper that Frantz had just passed my way. It was a photocopy of the Metabolife label. The copy was poor, so it was tough to find what Frantz was referring to, even though I knew the label like the back of my hand.

"All the way down the label?" I asked, looking up from beneath my eyebrows.

Frantz had tented his hands in front of his face. "That's correct."

I squinted through the white light as I inspected the copy. "Okay."

---

[51] Nobody does this, but we wanted to make sure that we had as much information about the product as possible, that every Metabolife tablet was as perfect as possible.

[52] So costly, in fact, that over the years, we had to turn away many companies wanting to manufacture our product because it was just too expensive for them to revise their SOPs to live up to our standards.

"Did you want to read it?"

The geniuses who'd prepared this document seemed to have copied the label while it was still on the bottle. So the copy bent and contorted on the sides to the point where I couldn't read most of the words. Just one long, narrow strip of legible font was all I had to work with. It seemed like an exercise in futility, but I figured I'd give Frantz what he'd asked for. I couldn't very well object.

"Suggested use as a dietary supplement—" I began.

"Do you want him to read it into the record?" Allen piped in.

"Yes, I do," Frantz said.

I glanced at my attorney, who signaled with his eyes that I could proceed. "Adults, one to two caplets two to three times per day." I looked up at Frantz apologetically. "It twists around."

Allen craned his neck over to examine the document in my hand. "Can you read it from the exhibit that you've been given?"

"No," I said. "I can't read the entire thing."

"Read what you can," Frantz said, sounding frustrated.

"Into the record?" Allen asked.

"Into the record."

"Let me just object. It's an incomplete recitation of the label and I'm also going to object because we haven't established in exhibit three which version of the label is on which product. Therefore, its relevance to any of the issues in the coordinated cases is unclear."

Surprisingly, we heard an unfamiliar voice enter the fray. King began speaking for the other defendant for once. "Join," she said. "The document speaks for itself."

Allen motioned my way, so I figured that meant I should read. I took a minute to look it over. This was going to be ridiculous.

Still, I did what I could. "Then I can read, 'four hours on an empty stomach one hour before meals.' In bold print, all capitalized, 'do not exceed eight caplets per,' and then I can't read the next word. Because I know the label, I believe the next word here is 'warning.'

"It's a new paragraph," I continued, glancing up for a moment, humor in my eyes. "'Not for use by persons under the age of 18. Do not use if pregnant or'—I'm assuming it's 'nursing.' I can't tell if it's a comma or not, 'consult a physician or licensed qualified health care professional.' And then there's parentheses and I believe that says, 'physician, before product use if you have or have a family history of,' and I can't read that word, 'or thyroid disease, diabetes, high blood pressure.' I can't read these two words here. 'Depression, any psychiatric condition, glaucoma, difficulty,' and I'm assuming that's 'urinating.'"

I looked briefly at Garry Pay. The expression on his face was priceless—somewhere halfway between ready-to-hurl and ready-to-break-out-laughing.

"I'm not sure," I continued. "'Enlarged prostate, seizure disorder.'"

I waited for Allen to object again. But to my surprise, he let me continue.

"If you have...if you are using a'—I can't read that word or words—'inhibitor.' Parentheses, capital 'MAO or any other dietary supplement, prescription drug, and drug containing ephedrine, pseudo ephedrine, or' and I believe that word is 'phenopropanolamine,' parenthesis, 'ingredients found in certain allergy asthma.'"

I couldn't believe it, but Allen let me continue on for the rest of the label. Everyone in the room seemed to shuffle around like penguins in heat. Papers rifling everywhere, eyes sagging, heads shaking at the spectacle of it all. Finally, I reached the end of what I could read.

"Then, I see smaller print here and I believe it says 'based on multispecies clinical laboratory testing.' Then I see a capital 'C,' an 'O' or a '044' and then I see '03/03.'"[53]

"The label that you had on the product in July 1995," Frantz said with an air of condescension, "did it warn you about taking caffeine with the product?"

"No, sir," I said.

"Did the label that you had in 1995 warn you that you could suffer heart attack or stroke if you took this product?"

---

[53] I remember thinking, *You're welcome.* No "thank you" would come.

"I don't believe so, sir."

"Did the label that you had in 1995 when you started Metabolife 356 warn you about the Ohio regulation?"

The regulation Frantz referred to here is one that called for the ban of all herbal ephedrine products in Ohio—one of the first states to enact such a ban. Incidentally, once the legislators from that state were educated on the history and safety of herbal ephedrine products, they overturned the legislation.

"No, sir," I said.

Frantz then went on to ask if there were any changes to the label between '95 and '99, which, of course, there were. The industry was under tremendous pressure from the FDA at the time. See, on the one hand, everyone wanted the safety that a warning label provides. But on the other, the FDA stated that if a dietary supplement company put a warning label on its product, it ceased to be a dietary supplement company and became a drug company. That's the strange thing about how the FDA operates: If there's a warning, then it's a drug—even if it's a product derived solely from vegetables.

So despite the fact that we were essentially in industry and regulatory limbo, we wanted warnings. In fact, we were one of the first companies to put warnings on its label.

As the years went by, the FDA continued to voice its perceived concerns. So we would have to update our label pretty consistently. And in this country, when you update a label, you get sued for not including the warning in previous years.

The FDA's a funny animal.

"Is there any particular reason that you didn't add 'the product may cause heart attack or stroke' when you put the product out in 1995?" Frantz asked.

"Yes."

"Why?"

"Because there was no evidence to show that that's true."

"You saw no evidence in your review of either literature or any personal observation of anyone taking the product that they had not suffered a heart attack or stroke from taking the product?"

"I object to the form of the question," Allen said. "You can answer."

"It assumes facts not in evidence," Bill Low added.

"That's correct," I said. *On both counts*, I thought.

"Did you read anything," Frantz added, pausing for a while to get all his gears turning in the same direction again, "do you recall reading anything from the FDA around the time period of 1994, 1995 in respect to their view of ephedrine and ma huang products that were being sold by companies such as Metabolife 356?"

"Object to the form of the question," Allen said. "You can answer."

"Yes," I said.

"What do you recall reading or reviewing?" Frantz asked.

"Articles."

"Tell me what you mean by 'articles.'"

"News article, industry article, and I may have also read their proposal, in part."

"The FDA proposal?"

"Maybe."

"What news article are you referring to?"

"I don't recall."

Silhouetted in the light from behind, Frantz shook his broad head slowly. "What's the general substance of what you recall reading, whether it be in the news article, the industry article, or the FDA proposal?"

"I think the substance of it was that they were concerned with ephedrine group alkaloids."

"What was their concern that you recall?"

"That they were dangerous."

"What is your recollection of the reason that was cited by the FDA in these news articles, industry articles, or their proposal that they may be dangerous?"

"I believe because of anecdotal reporting to the FDA."

"That's the only reason that you recall?"

"Yes."

"Do you recall whether or not the FDA discussed ma huang products when they mentioned ephedrine products when they were raising their concern?"

"Yes."

"So did they group them together?"

"Group what together?"

"Ephedrine with ma huang products."

"I'm not sure."

"Did they put the ma huang in the category of a product that they were concerned about?"

"Yes."

"Did you...do you recall what anecdotal reporting you're referring to?"

"Where the consumer apparently would call in to the FDA and report any kind of event."

So the FDA, absent of any regulation or any standards for the industry, instead asked the consumer to call its hotline to report any kind of adverse event or negative side effect experienced when taking an ephedra or ephedrine supplement. They didn't even have a real person to answer the phone. According to them, we could have been dealing with people having heart attacks after taking ephedrine products. These poor people were expected to just leave a message about their experience. And this was supposed to be a regulatory body that cared about the health of the American consumer?

"Do you recall how many events were at issue at the particular time when you heard about these news articles, industry articles and reading their proposal?" Frantz asked.

"No," I said.

"Do you recall the number 900 adverse events? Does that ring a bell?"

"Are your questions still about all ephedrine products?" Allen chimed in.

"About the FDA anecdotal reports regarding ephedrine/ma huang products," Frantz said cryptically.

"Nine hundred," I said. "Yeah, I remember 900 as ringing a bell."

"What did you do as the owner of Metabolife International, Inc., personally, to review any of those anecdotal reports?"

First of all, the notion that the CEO of an independent company should have to read and review 900 anecdotal reports regarding the industry in which it operates is ridiculous. That was supposed to be the FDA's job. They were the ones who were supposed to regulate the industry. But we did it anyway. We reviewed the reports.

"What I did was that I called for a panel of physicians that would review the reports," I said.

"When you say you called for a panel of physicians," Frantz said, "what do you mean by you 'called'? Did you call somebody?"

"Well, what it was is that I contacted ST&T and asked them if they could put together a panel of physicians that would not know why they're reviewing these reports and review all the anecdotal reporting to determine if there was a causality."

"Did the FDA have a panel of physicians that reviewed the reports?"

"I don't know."

I didn't know the answer then, but I know it today. It's "no." They did not. But Frantz wasn't interested in the FDA's lack of regulatory effort. Instead, he seemed interested in casting a shadow over the industry's attempts to do their jobs for them—to regulate *themselves*. See, several companies operating at the time (Metabolife included) wanted nothing more than appropriate labeling, manufacturing, and safety standards for the dietary supplement industry. So what we did was we set up foundations and coalitions designed to conduct research and fund studies into the safety of our products. This, we figured, would appease the FDA—and, far more importantly, keep anyone from getting hurt taking our supplements.

"You mentioned this other group," Frantz said. "The Ephedra... Can you help me with that?"

"The Ephedra Research Foundation," I said.

"That's a separate foundation from the Herb Research Foundation?"

"Yes."

"The Ephedra Research Foundation, do you know how long that's been in existence?"

"I believe for approximately three years."

"Were you one of the founders?"

"Yes."

"Is it incorporated?"

"I assume it is."

"Did you start that company just about the time that you were going to set up a panel of physicians to investigate the anecdotal reports that the FBI mentioned?"

"Objection to the form of the question," Allen said. "Do you mean the FDA or FBI?"

"I said 'FDA,'" Frantz insisted.

"Objection to the form of the question," Allen repeated. "You can answer."

"Can you please repeat that?" I asked. "I'm sorry."

The court reporter then read back the statement. Frantz did say "FBI." Call it a Freudian slip.

"Are there any other founders?" he added.

"Yes, sir," I said.

"Could you tell me who all the founders are?"

I looked up, trying to recall from the list somewhere near the back of my head. "Enrich, Shape Right and Omnitrition, Chemins Company, Star Light International. I believe it's Natural Balance. There may be some more, but I can't recall."

We would always meet in hotel convention rooms, the Ephedra Research Foundation. It would be an enormous gathering of supplement companies. Many CEOs and other industry leaders shifting around uncomfortably on folding chairs. Banquet tables arranged in a large square. All of us sitting around the circumference of the tables. Despite the fact that we would always have a room full of big egos and vastly differing opinions, remarkably we had all come to a consensus about where we needed to go with the science regarding ephedrine. We figured from the very beginning that if we spent the money on the science—demonstrated safety by providing evidence from scientific studies—the FDA would come around. How could they not? If we had verifiable proof that herbal ephedrine was safe, why wouldn't they, as a regulatory agency, move on to something that actually needed regulating? Something that might pose a true threat to the public?

"In 1996," Frantz said slowly, "did Metabolife International, Inc. receive any complaints about—from consumers that the product somehow caused a health problem for a consumer?"

"I don't know."

"Who *would* know?"

Frantz gave pause at this one. I could just barely make him out through the light. He must have thought that he could trap me in a corner, here. Honestly, though, I had no idea whether Metabolife had received any consumer complaints in 1996. I didn't know in '96 and I didn't know on May 25, 2000, day two of deposition. I wish I had known, but I didn't.

"Possibly John Macaulay," I said.

"Was he in charge of health complaints?"

"At what date?"

"You tell me," Frantz said, badgering me a little. "At what date was he in charge of health complaints?"

"I believe in '96 he was in charge of anything that would be considered a health complaint."

"You have nurses on standby at Metabolife International, Inc. right now that, if I call and I have a health complaint, they would be there ready to assist me; correct?"

"What do you mean, assist you?" I asked.

Frantz began flailing his hands again. "Answer—you know, take the call at least."

"Yes."

"How long have you had that setup?"

"Since, I believe, '96."

"Since you've had that setup, did they have a requirement that they're to write down the nature of the complaint if it's a complaint for health reasons?"

"Yes, I believe so."

"Are they to input that information into a computer?"

"Still in 1996?" Allen asked.

"Absolutely," Frantz said, his voice carrying more than just a hint of sarcasm.

"I don't know," I said.

"What was the procedure in 1996 for recording any complaints that came in to Metabolife International, Inc. for health related reasons after taking Metabolife 356?"

It's 1996. I'm sitting in my office when John Macaulay bursts in. He's carrying a clipboard, his face as sober as I'd ever seen it.

"Mike," he says as he sits down, "I've got some terrible news."

Chills run up my spine.

"A three-year-old took a bunch of our product and died," he says.

"Oh my God." I'm so devastated in that moment that I can hardly breathe. You've heard people talk about their lives flashing before their eyes just before death. The thought of a child dying because of my product.

John looks down at the complaint form on the clipboard he held. His face contorted in apparent pain. "Yeah, the customer left a bottle sitting out. The three-year-old ate a bunch of the caplets and died."

I can't find words. All the blood seems to be rushing to my feet.

All at once, John's face lights up like the sunrise. "It was a three-year-old dog," he says.

I get that sensation of relief that feels like all life evaporates from the inside out. Like you're suddenly hollow from losing all that stress. But then, that hollowness is replaced completely and instantly by raging anger. I grab the complaint off John's clipboard and crumble it up and throw it into the trashcan—something I would normally never do under any circumstances. "John," I say, "I don't see the humor in this."

John blinks, his turn to be stunned.

"This is how rumors get started," I say loudly. "If the FDA or media got wind of a rumor like that, they'd destroy us."[54]

Frantz furrowed his brow, feigning profound confusion. "What is your protocol for making the determination that the product may have caused an—may be an adverse event as a result of taking your product?"

"Anything other than a negative side effect," I said.

"What do you mean by that statement? I don't quite understand it."

"Well, adverse event, negative side effect are two different things."

"What's an adverse event?"

"An adverse event would be an event that happened that would affect a person's health."

"Alright. What's a negative event?"

"No," Allen said. "Negative side effect."

"Negative side effect."

I nod once. "Negative side effect would be a side effect that was not desired by the person taking the product."

"You have a written procedure or some sort of writing documenting these definitions at Metabolife International, Inc.?"

Allen objected again.

"I'm not sure," I said.

"Where do these definitions come from?"

---

[54] This statement would prove prophetic, as the government would indeed contort the circumstances of that call to suit its needs. But more on that later.

"The medical community."

"Is this a definition that you have talked to Mr. Macaulay about and you both agreed upon?"

Allen objected again.

"I may have," I said.

"These negative side effects," Frantz says, blasting air through his teeth. "Could you give me an example of a negative side effect?"

"The negative side effect, for example, in drinking coffee is that you might feel a little bit nervous or antsy or such or urination because it's a diuretic all pertaining to coffee. A negative side effect from drinking too much water might be a bellyache, but those are not health conditions."

"That's your opinion, correct?"

"No, sir."

"Whose opinion is that?"

"That was an opinion that was laid out at the Texas Department of Health hearing, I believe, in '95 or '96."

"Did you attend that hearing?"

"Yes, sir."

"So you were present during the entire hearing process; correct?"

"I believe so, yes."

"What is it—the adverse event? Tell me some examples of adverse events."

"Adverse event would be where a person purported to have a heart attack, a stroke, a seizure, death, infarction, and such. It affects the health."

Frantz arches one bushy eyebrow. "What about heart palpitation?"

"I don't know how Macaulay would classify that. It's been classified that all of us have heart palpitations just in the normal course of life."

"So he may have received a call about a heart palpitation—a claim of a heart palpitation after someone took the product and he may not have even reported that to you; correct?"

"When, sir?"

"In 1996."

"No. I believe John would report that to me."

"Why is that?"

"Because we were actually breaking new ice for any company to actually have a health line that a consumer taking the consumable product, which even pharmaceutical companies don't have, to my knowledge, that they could call in, get a person that was qualified to ask questions of them, give them information and direct them to a physician. So at that time we were very, very concerned by the consumers calling if anybody was going to have a condition or anything else because we wanted to evaluate that system."

This is the truth, as I know it. Part of the issue with working in the dietary supplement industry is that it remained an industry without standardization. Despite the lack of regulatory standards, we at Metabolife felt that it was important to go above and beyond the call of duty to keep our consumers safe. Even if the FDA wasn't going to tell us how to do business, we weren't going to spare any expense in ensuring the utmost in quality and health. That's the nature of a dietary supplement, after all. It's intended to *improve* health.

Consider, then, its counterpart: the Western pharmaceutical drug. Each year, thousands of people die from taking aspirin. Aspirin. If they take an aspirin and feel heart palpitations, is there a toll-free number they can call to ask questions of the company? No. Same goes for many other kinds of OTC drugs—all from proper use. See, from the pharmaceutical side of things, the FDA says that the notion of consulting a physician is enough. But how many doctors *really* know all the ins and outs of every drug?

Frantz took things in a different direction. "Did you ever tell Dr. Gwirtsian—"

"Gwirtsman," Allen corrected.

I smiled slightly. "I thought you were talking about the suicide doctor for a minute. I don't know him."

"Personal friends," Allen said jovially, raising his hand.

"He'll be visiting you next week," Frantz added darkly. Ah, Frantz. Bitter and awkward at every turn.

"Jim," Allen said, sobering up, "I think if it helps, it's Gwirtsman."

"I have trouble with that name," Frantz admits. "It looks like Gwirtsian the way it's spelled." Having sorted out his little issues, he then turned his attention back to me. "Did you ever tell Dr. Gwirtsman that you were receiving any written complaints from consumers, either to the tune of negative side effects or adverse health reports?"

"No, sir," I said.

"Dr. Gwirtsman was involved with a study that studied Metabolife 356?"

"That's correct."

"Did you have any conversation with Dr. Gwirtsman about the results of that study or—he was involved with what, one or two studies?"

"One study."

"It was at what university?"

"Vanderbilt."

"Dr. Gwirtsman, did he tell you the results of that study?"

"You mean orally?" I ask, feeling suddenly obstinate. I glance over at Pay, who's shaking his head incredulously.

"Orally or in writing."

"I believe both."

"What did he tell you orally?"

"Orally, he told me that he believed that Metabolife was very promising for a tool with the problem of obesity."

"What else did he tell you?"

"He told me it would be a shame if the FDA were to remove products like this from the market when it had so much promise."

We discussed the FDA for a while before Frantz finally got back on track.

"Did he tell you that the studies showed that your product was safe?" he asked.

Allen played along. "Again, you're including written or oral?"

"I'm talking about talking."

"Oral conversations?"

"Yeah. We'll get into the written in a minute."

"I just want to make sure."

I shook the cobwebs out of my head, feeling like I'd just fallen into an Abbot and Costello routine. "I was present when he made that statement," I said.

"He told you that the product," Frantz said, "356, Metabolife 356, was proven to be safe as a result of that study that he was involved in?"

"No. That was not my statement."

"What is your testimony?"

"My testimony is that for the acute study, Metabolife for the patients showed safety to be benign and placed no one at any health risk."

Vanderbilt was only one of many studies, but it was certainly the most thorough as it pertained to acute response to Metabolife. Between Gwirtsman and a Doctor Ming, the two physicians who would head things up, the study was in good hands.

I remember the day I went down to investigate the setup and see what this chamber was all about.

I peered through the glass into the chamber—a simple space with a chair and a bed, a TV, and medical equipment I can't even explain. "So the patients—"

"Subjects," Ming corrected. "We call them subjects in a study."

Dr. Ming was a slight man, small, but very fit. Thinning hair. Engaging. Probably forty-five at the time. And one hell of a scientist. The kind of guy who looks at everything with an unbiased eye. No preconceived notions. Checked his prejudices at the door.

"Subjects," I said. "So, the subjects take the Metabolife and then go in there for a whole day?"

"And night, yes."

"What do they do in there?"

"Read, sleep, watch TV. They're not allowed any outside stimulation."

"What do you do to study them?"

"We monitor every aspect of their existence. Everything from heart rate and blood pressure to breathing rate to the amount of energy expended when urinating. Every aspect of the subject's metabolism is recorded and tracked."

"So you'll be seeing how our product affects heart rate, that sort of thing?"

"Absolutely," Dr. Ming said, clinical right down to the last line. "We'll know exactly what's going on with each subject."

Ming would go on to explain the aspects of a scientific undertaking such as this one. He outlined the concept of what's called a double-blind crossover placebo study. As I learned, for this study, Vanderbilt would recruit a certain number of healthy adults, all of them being varying degrees of overweight. Some of the subjects would be given Metabolife and some the placebo.

The reason the study was called "double-blind" was because the scientists administering the caplets didn't even know what they were giving to the individual. They would simply hand over the caplets and send the subjects into the chambers. The reason it was called "crossover" was because each subject would be given Metabolife on one day and then the placebo on the next, or vice versa.

Despite all this secrecy, the study's findings were nothing short of astonishing. It showed that no one was at risk—that it only elevated resting heart rate by six or seven heartbeats per minute, which Ming suggested to be clinically insignificant. It did not raise anyone's blood pressure. And there were no adverse events.

"But there's something in here that's truly amazing," Dr. Ming added.

"What's that?" I asked.

"This shows that your product raises energy expenditure substantially. Not only while awake, but while sleeping, as well."

"Nice," I said, nodding.

"It's more than that, Mike," Dr. Ming said adamantly. "We didn't think that such a thing was *possible*. To raise metabolic rate without exercising…that's just remarkable."

Naturally, we were floored by the studies at Vanderbilt. But the study didn't seem absolute. I mean, we only had twenty or so subjects involved in this case. So we knew that our next step would be to conduct more studies, with much longer durations, with a lot more people, and at different universities. Hopefully, these additional studies would help reaffirm what we already knew: the high standards of safety and efficacy (effectiveness) of Metabolife.

So we contacted Harvard and Columbia. Both schools agreed to conduct efficacy and safety studies with more subjects than we'd had at Vandy. This undertaking would be a joint university study that would take six months to conduct. And at the end of those six months, we found that Metabolife showed significant weight loss over the placebo. And it demonstrated both safety and efficacy.[55]

Unfortunately, it took us two years to finish and get these studies out to the public—mostly because there was so much pressure from the FDA to discredit the studies. Here we were, conducting our science at two of the top universities in the country, and the FDA was doing all it could to discredit the studies and scientists.

Strange, I remember thinking. *Why would they do that?* It's a question that still plagues me today. The agency that's supposed to be responsible for ensuring the safety of everything we consume was doing everything it could to prove that our product was unsafe—even when the science stood squarely in our corner.

And Frantz had taken that line and run with it. "I'm going to show you what I've marked as 'exhibit six' and it's on purportedly Metabolife International, Inc. letterhead dated November 26, 1997, to the dockets management branch, Food and Drug Administration. It is purportedly executed by Michael J. Ellis.

"I'll have you review that, exhibit six, and identify it, if you can. The real question I have right now is why don't you go to the signature page and tell me if that appears to be your signature? That would be the second or third page from the end."

I flipped to the page in question. "Yes," I said.

---

[55] At Harvard, they put people on heart monitors for twenty-four hours per day, as well. The monitors showed that Metabolife didn't significantly raise blood pressure or cause any abnormal heart activity.

"Do you recall writing such a letter as set forth in exhibit number six?"

"May I see this, please?" Allen asked.

"No," I said as I passed the letter to Allen.

I saw the white of Frantz's teeth as he bared them at me. "Do you want to look at it for a minute and see if it refreshes your recollection that you wrote that letter?"

"No, I didn't write the letter," I said.

"You did," Frantz said curtly.

"No, I did not."

"Is that not your signature near the end of the letter?"

"Yes, it appears to be my signature."

"So you would have reviewed it as your custom and practice; correct?"

"Yes."

I didn't remember this letter specifically, but I had a feeling that I knew where this was going...

James Prochnow—an attorney from Patton, Boggs—and I had come to an agreement on the notion that we had a responsibility to send regular letters regarding the FDA's proposed rule on herbal ephedrine. Now, at the time, I didn't know the difference between an adverse event report (AER) and an ERA. Nobody did. And the reason nobody knew how to define AER? Because the FDA had never bothered providing the definition.

Regardless of our confusion, James recommended that we send a letter to the FDA to oppose the proposed herbal ephedrine rule. And I agreed. So every time the FDA published a proposal, we sent in a submission. Just a public comment from a representative of the industry.

James would be the one to write the letters in 1997 and 1998. The problem was that James had a deadline on the first letter. And apparently, he liked to work with his back right up to the deadline. How do I know this? I got a call.

"Mike," James breathed into the receiver, "I'm done with the letter."

"Great, buddy," I said. "Send it out."

"No, I need your signature on it."

"Alright, then," I said, oblivious. "Send the letter to me."

"But there's a problem. The deadline's tomorrow."

"James…"

"Look," the attorney interjected. "I'm going to same-day deliver it to you. I need you to sign it as soon as you can and send it off same-day to the FDA."

"Okay," I said.

"Just as long as you sign it and send it same-day, we'll be good."

"The letter's okay?" I asked.

"Of course."

I realize that the deadline isn't the greatest excuse for why I didn't read the letter that I would later be asked to read in deposition, but that's how it was. And here I was presented with the thing once more. Until this moment, I didn't realize its significance. I'd always figured that my attorney had done his research and written the letter in what I believed to be a legally accurate manner.[56] So I'd signed and sent the letter, having never read a single word of it.

"Now," Frantz said, "I'm going to direct your attention to exhibit number six, an April 17, 1998, letter that we talked about that you wrote to the dockets management branch. I'm going to direct your attention to page three and I've highlighted something for you to read into the record."

"Objection," Allen said. "The document speaks for itself. I object to reading one phrase out of context in the letter."

Frantz did his best oil-job and ignored Allen. "Can you read that into the record so we have a clear understanding of what you just reviewed that I have highlighted?"

I looked at the paper and started reading, feeling suddenly as if

---

[56] There's a tendency to trust lawyers for handling that sort of thing, after all. It's like going to the hospital. If you have a medical emergency and a doctor hands you a paper and says, "Sign this. It'll clear you for a procedure that will save your life," you don't take the time to read it. You just trust the doctor at his word and sign it. The same goes for lawyers. If they say, "This is legally sound," you trust them and sign on the dotted line.

a great weight pressed down on my shoulders. "Metabolife has never received one notice from a consumer that any serious adverse health event has occurred because of the ingestion of Metabolife 356."

It's convenient that out of this giant letter, Frantz only had me read one line from one paragraph. Not only was it completely out of context, it was also entirely inflammatory. Any unbiased observer could see that there was industry confusion on what an AER was. And this out of context quote certainly highlighted that point.

But this particular letter I did remember. I remembered this one because I'd actually made a few adjustments. Since James had provided me with enough time to review it this time around, I was able to see that he'd made a few errors concerning people calling in to the company. By 1998, see, the other founders of Metabolife and I had come to the understanding that an adverse event meant that our product had actually been the *cause* of the event in question. So I changed the verbiage of James' original letter to state, "Metabolife has never received one notice from a consumer that any serious adverse health event has occurred *because of the ingestion of Metabolife 356.*"

At the time, we'd received a number of calls from consumers who claimed that our product had given them problems. But in every case that we were able to follow up on and investigate medically, we found verifiable evidence to suggest that Metabolife had not been the direct cause of the issue. In most cases, the adverse events could be more accurately associated with the fact that most of our customers were grossly overweight. Many of them had pre-existing medical problems. In almost all the other calls, we found that the people were just using whatever excuse they could to get a refund on the product.

So the change to "because of the ingestion of Metabolife 356" had to do with our understanding that an AER had to do with causality. Since the FDA never defined specifically what an AER was, however, our understanding would soon change again.

I guess to demonstrate the fact that our thinking on AERs changed more than once, Frantz then had me read from two additional letters, marked 'exhibit seven' and 'exhibit eight.' The latter was a February 9, 1999, letter from outside counsel to Metabolife, Allen Beinke. The statement in this letter (written on his own law firm's letterhead) was similar to the one I'd read into the record during the deposition, with one clear difference: This one had been sent directly from his firm with his letterhead and his signature to the FDA in response to the World Health Organization's request for public comment.[57]

It read: "Metabolife has never *been made aware* of any adverse health events by consumers of its products. Metabolife has never received a notice from a consumer that any serious adverse health event has occurred because of ingestion of Metabolife 356. This claims-free history exists notwithstanding the widespread media attention regarding dietary supplement products containing ephedrine."

Unfortunately, unlike the other letters that Frantz had me read, I knew that this was not an accurate statement at the time that it was written.

"Do you know Allen Beinke?" Frantz asked.

"Yes," I said.

"How do you know him?"

"He's an attorney for Arter & Hadden. I'd met him once or twice in Texas."

"Will you read the highlighted portion of this letter?"

I read the sentences in question.

Frantz appeared to be beaming. "Is that a correct statement?"

"No, it is not," I said, feeling my throat dry up instantly.

"So you signed a false statement."

I flipped to the back page. "My signature is not on here," I said. "I never saw this letter. I didn't approve it."

In 1999, the FDA had provided us with yet another interpretation of what an AER was. Apparently, they believed that any and every call made to a company by a customer who alleged to have suffered some malady (however minor) was an adverse event.

---

[57] This letter wasn't even intended as a response to the FDA specifically.

Causality didn't matter. To the FDA, an AER was, by nature, a simple complaint call.[58]

Obviously, in the case of the Beinke letter, my company had made an error. It had put its trust in a lawyer who had done little more than cut and paste information from a letter that had been sent to the FDA more than a year prior—and he'd done it without our review. At the time of the letter, under what we had gradually learned to be the FDA's definition of an AER, the idea that we had never received one complaint simply wasn't true. If I had seen that statement before the letter was sent, would I, or our in-house counsel, have allowed it to be sent? Absolutely not.

But even as we closed up the deposition, even as my attorneys and I exited the conference room and the shimmering beacon of Higgs, Fletcher, & Mack, LLP, I knew that something terrible had just occurred. I knew that I'd just read into the record a letter that might be the end of my company. I knew that the fact that these PI attorneys were willing to use other people's statements to contort the image of Metabolife meant that we hadn't even begun to see the storm on the horizon.

If only I'd known then just how right I was.

---

[58] This seemed strange to us, given that when you have a billion servings of a product each year, you're going to have at least a few people who call in to complain about negative side effects. If this was the standard to which we would be held as an industry, there wouldn't be a single dietary supplement company with a clean AER record. In fact, if they had held the same standards to the OTC industry, there wouldn't be a single OTC company with a clean AER record, either.

Chapter 11

Cinderella Goes to the Ball

Our growth continued to the point where it started to seem a little ridiculous that we didn't have our own building. So we bought an empty lot near Freeway 52 and kicked off our first construction project. The first solid home for our company: a place we would come to call "Area 52." By the time the contractors laid the last brick on Area 52, we were completely happy with the building. We had more space, state-of-the-art equipment, a brand new, beautiful building, and a separate location for our gigantic shipping department.[59]

In our upgraded new digs, we truly felt like we'd arrived. Numbers were up.[60] The distributors couldn't have been happier with their profits. And morale ran high.

Together, we'd officially managed to make a fat-pill cool.

But success comes with a steep price. See, when you do as well as we were doing, greed starts to rear its ugly head almost everywhere.

---

[59] Probably the biggest upgrade, as it meant that the shipping crew wouldn't have to conduct business in the parking lot anymore.

[60] We were headed for a billion dollars in retail sales in 1999 alone.

It comes in the form of changes. *Changes*. Little changes. Big changes. Changes around the office. In the supply line. And in the retail distributor market.

With some of our distributors making a million dollars per year, per retail location, things began to get a little territorial. Naturally. Throw in the fact that many of our earliest distributors were felons and/or psych patients to begin with and you've got yourself a recipe for disaster.

Example:

I stood in my office, taking a look at some new ad copy, when I heard a knock on the door.

"Come in," I called.

In walked Mel, one of our creepier distributors—a man originally brought on board by Isaac. Mel was an older guy. Long, unkempt gray hair. A Colonel Sanders beard.[61] He tended to wear ridiculously outdated work clothes. Each pocket always seemed to be full of who-knows-what. Even from day one on the job, Mel had proven himself to be an absolute nut-bar—but his was an endearing kind of nuttiness, the kind of nuttiness that can't be faulted or controlled. So I signed him up on a down-line that made him upwards of $20,000 to $30,000 per month. Seemed a fair deal. Help a guy out and, at the same time, give him so much money that he couldn't possibly have reason to complain. Ever.

"Hey, Mel," I said uneasily. "How's it going, buddy?"

Mel raised his hands in front of his face and inspected them as if he'd never seen anything like them before. "You see these hands?" he asked darkly.

"What?"

The distributor cocked his eyebrows wildly. "You see these hands?"

I nodded.

"These are lethal weapons," he said, glaring at me through his curling fingers. "I could kill you right now."

---

[61] "Like Colonel Sanders on crack," we always said.

I chuckled, but then immediately realized that Mel wasn't joking. The crazy look in his eye suggested as much.

Before I could respond, Mel reached into the back pocket of his dingy pants, shuffling his hand around in search of something I couldn't see. In a moment, he produced a little book, handing it over to me.

Confused, I read the cover. Mel had handed me a survival guide. By the time I looked up, the distributor had already made his way out my office door.

"Well, jeez, Mel," I said to myself. "Nice talking to you." I attempted to follow him out, but by the time I reached the hallway, he was nowhere to be found.

I did find Monica, though. She stood at the end of the hallway, looking nervous. Shifty.

"Is he gone?" she asked.

"Is who gone?"

"That creepy distributor. Mel."

I grinned knowingly. "Yeah, he's gone. And look what he brought me." I showed her the book.

Monica pored over the little thing, her expression growing more and more concerned as her pretty eyes panned from top to bottom. "What the hell is this supposed to mean?"

"I'm not sure," I said, laughing.

I never really considered Mel's gesture to be a threat. He was just one of those crazy people who knew how crazy he was—and more than that, was *proud* of how crazy he was. I figured he just wanted me to share in his pride.

Not that we had a shortage on crazy at Metabolife. From what I gathered, that survival book of Mel's might have come in handy for a couple of our distributors down in Texas. I remember the day I got the call from a fire marshal whose name escapes me (we'll call him "Landis").

"Hello?" I said, pressing the receiver to my cheek.

"Mr. Ellis," came a stern voice, "this is Agent Landis, Texas fire marshal."

I practically choked on my coffee. "Okay…"

Landis didn't miss a beat. Kept up with his *Dragnet* routine. "We had an incident involving your employees down at the local flea market."

"My employees?" I asked, truly perplexed. "In Texas?"

"Yes, sir. Apparently, there were two competing Metabolife kiosks in the same market. We have evidence that, overnight, one of your employees snuck in and burned down the other employee's kiosk."

I laughed under my breath. "Those aren't employees. Those are distributors."

Landis paused for a long while. "Whatever the case, sir, we've had a fire and I thought you should know about it."

"Thank you, Agent Landis. I'm not sure what's going on here, but I'll do everything I can to help."

I took down Landis' information. Then, I set up an independent investigation into the fire. Of course, everyone involved denied any wrongdoing. But it was a little disconcerting. I mean, if they were willing to burn down each other's kiosks over territorial disputes, what would they do next? Shoot each other?

So it was all kind of frenzied. Keeping the distributors happy proved to be a constant struggle.[62] From this struggle came the term "nitwit marketing," a derivative of the more common name for our business model, "network marketing." Don't get me wrong. I loved the distributors. Even the crazy ones. Even Mel. But, sometimes, they just acted like nitwits.

Anyway, when we'd concluded our investigation, I left a message with Landis regarding all the information we'd uncovered. But I never heard back from him.

More changes:

When you sell as many units of product as we were selling, you're bound to have a few customer concerns or complaints. And what we wanted to do was we wanted to make sure we had the

---

[62] Some weren't the brightest people out there, either.

cleanest, safest product out there. So as early as 1996, we knew that we had to set up a department in the company that could take any and all medical-related or product calls and inquiries.

We would do our due diligence. Every employee in the department was instructed to take down all the information for each person calling in with a medical claim. If the claim involved an undesirable side effect like dizziness or anxiety, we would instruct the user not to take any more of the caplets (or *how* to take the caplets, in the event that they'd been taking too many). In the case of a medical issue like heart palpitations or nausea, the operators were to instruct the individual to stop taking the product completely and consult their doctor before taking it again. And in the event of a serious medical emergency like a heart attack or stroke, the operators were to do everything they could to get medical attention to the user immediately—such as alerting 911 in the caller's area code.

But even though we already had a capable call team with what we thought were reasonable instructions, we still needed someone to head up the department. Someone with a background in medicine.

That's when I remembered John Macaulay.

The day it occurred to me that we already had a licensed medical professional on staff, I went straight down to Macaulay's office. He was plugging away on his computer, as always. Doing God-knows-what.

"John," I said.

"Mike," he said.

"You say you're a nurse practitioner?"

He blinked slowly, a bland expression on his face. "That's right."

"Well, we're getting some calls coming in from customers having medical questions. Minor stuff. Mostly anxiety and dizziness. That kind of thing."

John rubbed the bridge of his nose with his thumb and forefinger, apparently taking it all in.

"Anyway," I continued, "so we're getting these inquiry calls on everything from how to take it to 'I'm not losing weight' to 'I'm losing too much weight.'"

John nodded, still giving me the silent treatment.

I thrust my hands to either side. "Would you feel comfortable heading up the department in charge of taking them? I need somebody with a medical background to investigate claims and follow up on anything that might be Metabolife-related."

Finally, John spoke. "I'd love to."

As the years went by, I felt glad that John had agreed to the position, because we began to get more and more questions on how to take the product safely and what to do in the event of a negative side effect. And I felt like we were providing an excellent (and unprecedented) service to our customers. See, *nobody* in the industry had a call center. We were pioneers in that respect. We were so cutting-edge that the FDA didn't even have regulations to tell us how we were supposed to conduct business in our call center. There were no agency-defined standard operating procedures. No instructions on what to report and what not to report. Nothing.

I guess John saw this as a problem, because he sought my advice on sorting things out sometime after taking up his new post.

He stepped into my office one day in 1998. "Mike," he said, "I'm worried."

My ears perked up. "Worried about what, bud?"

"I'm worried that we have this entire department that's supposed to be handling calls—some of them medical in nature—and we've only got a nurse practitioner on staff."

I put down whatever I was doing at the time and gave John my fullest attention. "Has it been too much for you to handle?"

"No…" He seemed uneasy. Hesitant. "It's just that I met this guy—this doctor—who I think would be good to bring in to the department."

"You think we need a doctor?"

"Well…" John said slowly, "I'm only an NP. I think it might be better to have a physician on staff."

I thought about it for a moment and couldn't come up with any reason John wasn't absolutely right. Besides, I figured he knew what he was doing. "This guy's okay, then?" I asked.

"Yeah," he said adamantly. "I met him at that medical conference in Denver that I was telling you about."

"He's a physician?"

"And a licensed psychiatrist."

"That's great![63] What's his name?" I asked.

"Doctor Randy Smith."

"Okay," I said. "Set it up."

From what I understand, John gave Smith a call that afternoon.
And in a matter of days, we'd agreed to fly Dr. Smith out to San
Diego so Bob, Blevins, and I could meet with him.

During our meeting, I found that Dr. Smith possessed considerable knowledge of both Eastern and Western medicine. Better
yet, he seemed to share our company belief that the two disciplines
should complement one another. So based on that meeting—and
John's glowing recommendation—we hired our first physician.

Early on, I found Smith to be a little odd, maybe, but since John
had vouched for him, I knew he'd be right for the job. Macaulay
was a great guy, after all. He'd done so much for the company over
the years. And I knew I could trust him.

Things weren't all so tumultuous during Metabolife's peak years.
One day, I'd just stopped into one of the break rooms for a cup of
coffee when I found a stack of those nutritional cookies we'd tried
to sell. I grabbed one up and opened the package carefully, examining the inside of the cookie. No worms. So I guess they weren't all
tainted.

Anyway, I took the cookie in my hand—it was a turd-brown

---

[63] I was happy to hear about this doctor being a psychiatrist because I knew that some
of our callers had clearly demonstrated psychological issues. So this doctor/shrink
could deliver more value to the customer. And in addition to all that, I knew it would
be good to have a doctor to consult with on the research and development of future
products, as by then I'd been considering expanding the Metabolife line for some
time.

thing—and rolled it into a log. These things were so *moldable*. Brilliant. Perfect ammunition for a classic gag.

So I was walking down the hallway, ducking in and out of all the desks and employees we had lined up in there, and I was carrying a turd in my hand. Nobody said anything. Just another day on the job with Mike Ellis. My destination: a little grassy spot near the parking lot—a spot where many of the employees often ate lunch.

Headed out the side door to the building, I passed Doc Smith. He's tall as the day is long, that Smith: 6'10". Gangly. No chin. Big nose. Knock-kneed. Jaundiced and definitely on the skinnier side, despite his strange little potbelly. So our company's in-house doctor and psychiatrist was leaning up against the wall with a greasy breakfast burrito in one hand and a cigarette in the other.

"Doc," I said, stopping for a minute, "what are you doing?"

Smith looked only mildly alarmed at the sight of the turd-cookie in my hand. "Eating breakfast," he said.

"You're gonna kill yourself with that stuff."

Smith shrugged. "You're the one walking around with a turd in his hand."

I chuckled and inspected the thing I was carrying. "It's one of those nutritional cookies."

Smith smiled distantly and took another bite of his burrito. He chased it with a drag of his cigarette, watching intently as I planted the turd in the grass near the corner of the building.

I giggled like a schoolboy as I stooped down and arranged it in a decent spot, knowing that when I came back later to do what I intended to do, it would be priceless.

But that would have to wait until the lunch hour. So after dropping off my makeshift turd, I made a few calls. Checked in with Isaac. Checked in with Monica. That sort of thing. A couple hours later, when lunch came around, I headed back out to the scene.

On the way, I passed the most unlikely sight: Jeff Anderman in the cookie suit. He was puffing away on one of my expensive cigars.

"How's that cigar, Jeff?" I asked, not terribly stunned.

"Smooth," Anderman said, exhaling slowly, blowing a nice wreath of smoke.

I did a quick double-take at my CFO—a man standing in the sunshine on a workday, wearing a cookie suit and puffing on a free cigar—before deciding that I had bigger fish to fry.

Wheeling around the corner of the building, I came to the spot where I'd planted my fake turd. It was hard to keep my composure because all of the employees eating outside on that day happened to be women. This, I realized, was going to be perfect.

Creeping up to the turd-cookie, I waited for a couple of the employees to notice me. Then, I slowly bent down and picked it up, stealing a glance at the huddle of appalled diners. Then, I took a bite of my fake turd. Almost everyone eating looked like they might throw up.

So in 1999, we were having a lot of fun and making a whole lot of money, but that didn't mean that we couldn't have made more. Especially given what I was about to discover at the neighborhood superstore...

I remember the day I walked into a Wal-Mart to do a little investigative work. See, lately, we'd been getting more and more calls from customers who explained that they'd purchased our product there—something that had proved confusing to us, given that we didn't actually *sell* to Wal-Mart. Anyway, immediately after entering the store, I saw what looked like Metabolife on one of the end-cap displays—one of those big, eye-catching arrangements that they put at the end of an aisle so the product is highly visible to the consumer.

Concerned, I went straight up to the display and grabbed one of the bottles.

The label looked like Metabolife in coloring. The ingredients were almost the same. The warnings. It was all there. Even the overall trade dress (including the logo) was close—save for a few subtle differences. The biggest difference? Instead of "Metabolife," it read, "Metabolite."

I slumped, practically dropping the bottle as I realized that this company that I'd never heard of—one that had absolutely no advertising budget (as I would later learn)—had mimicked our label so well that most people wouldn't even know that they were buying the wrong product. We had a copycat on our hands. And Wal-Mart was letting them sell in their stores...

Burning for a little confirmation, I took the bottle over to the nearest clerk, an acned kid with a greasy tussle of brown hair. "Is this that Metabolife stuff I've heard so much about?" I asked, handing him the bottle.

"Yep," he said proudly, trying to pass it back to me.

I pointed at the label. "But it says 'Metabolite.'"

The clerk squinted, giving the bottle a closer look. "Oh," he said absently. "Well...it's the same thing."

"It's Metabolife?"

"Yep." He passed the bottle back to me.

I examined the label again, continuing with my ignorance routine. "But I thought you could only buy this stuff in those kiosks at the mall."

"Well, now we're selling it at Wal-Mart."

In one moment, my whole outlook changed. I knew that if we didn't do something to fix the problem, we'd be doomed as a company. Network marketing could never keep up with the retail power of such a giant corporation. But what could we do?

As I left the store, I tried to remind myself that imitation is the highest form of flattery. Fuck that.

Chapter 12

Family

Since the day that Susan and I completed our divorce, Christian had spent half his time with her and half his time with me. This meant that I always wanted to take advantage of every moment I had with him.[64]

Back when he was fourteen or so, he and I always had a great time in the mornings when I'd drive him to school. I remember one morning in particular because it was shortly before the wave of Metabolife's success began to build.

"Mom wants me to quit," Christian said, looking down at his knees as he sat in the passenger seat.

"Quit?" I said. "Quit what, bud?"

Christian's shoulders slumped as he looked out the window. "Selling."

---

[64] Did he have a rough time with my marriage to Monica? Maybe. I suspect that Monica didn't like him very much, even though she claims to have cared for him as if he were her own son. Did he have a hard time fully accepting his new brothers? It's possible. It's tough for a kid that age. But these days, I'm proud to say that he's great around my other children, treating them as if they were his full siblings.

"Selling Metabolife?"

My son nodded, still apparently refusing to look at me.

"But you and Isaac are my best team."

Christian finally turned to face me. He was clearly upset. "I know, Dad," he said. "But Mom won't let me keep going."

I tried to keep my voice as soothing as possible. "Why not?"

"She says it'll never work. That the company won't make it. That we're all just wasting our time."

That one stung a little, so I brooded for a moment. "She might be right."

Christian, meanwhile, sounded a whole lot more reassuring. Maybe he noticed my sulky expression. "I don't want to, though," he said. "Can't you talk to her?"

I sighed. "I can try, bud. But you're signed up under her distributorship. There's not much I can do."

"Damn it."

My eyebrows blew back in shock. "What did you say?"

"Nothing," Christian said, looking morose.

"Listen," I said, "your mother's right. It's probably too dangerous for you out there on the streets, anyway."

"I can take care of myself."

I smiled proudly. "I know you can, bud. You've been one of my best distributors. Whatever happens, I'm proud of you."

After a call or two with Susan, Christian's mother would win the day. My son would be forced to quit working as a distributor for Metabolife. Eight months later, the company would explode. I remember running the math. If Christian had stayed on, he would have been making $65,000 per month by the age of fifteen.[65]

But here we were, pulling up to his middle school (he was in eighth grade at the time).

---

[65] Later on in life, after his bout with drugs had ended, Christian would confess to me that he was glad he'd gotten out when he did. "If I'd have made that money," he would say, "I'd be dead today. That kind of cash would've enabled me to do some really stupid things." And that's my son. Twenty-six years old now. Wise well beyond his years. The wisest young man I've ever known.

"You want me to stop here so you can get out?" I asked. I knew the junior high drill. Or at least I thought I did…

"What?" he said, oblivious. "Why?"

"So your friends don't see your dad dropping you off."

Christian shrugged. "I don't care. Pull up there." He pointed to a space right in front of the school.

So I drove to the space—probably the most visible in the entire lot. Hundreds of kids played and talked and hung out all around us. Everywhere. Many of them seemed to be staring in our direction.

With all these eyes on us, Christian leaned over and gave me a kiss goodbye. A kiss. In front of everyone.

I watched, stunned, as Christian climbed out of the car. "See ya, Dad," he said, closing the door behind him.

"Bye…bye," I said to myself, too slow to react out of my combination of shock and pride.

So there went my warm-hearted, caring, and lovable son. The kind of boy who already knew who he was at the ripe old age of fourteen. The kind of boy who didn't care what anyone thought. And the kind of boy who made the best of everything life ever dealt him.

For the better part of the year that would follow, Monica and I would struggle to get by. The bills had piled up, we both worked long hours, and we both wanted to spend as much time as possible with the kids. We were even borrowing money from my mother just to make ends meet. I couldn't have been more embarrassed.

But on Sundays—almost every Sunday—we had this tradition. Monica and I would pile into the car with Mikey and Nicholas and the four of us would drive around, looking for our dream home. We really enjoyed looking at houses. Pretending to be prospective buyers. Imagining what it might be like to live in those multimillion-dollar homes in the North County of San Diego.

In 1998, we would take one of our last little Sunday trips. Definitely the last one we would take for a long while, anyway.

As we pulled into the long driveway, I turned to face the kids. "Well, boys," I said, "we're here."

The boys cheered.

Monica rolled her eyes at me. "This is the biggest one yet."

I turned my attention back to the driveway. Up ahead, at a distance, was a beautiful, hilltop, single-level home. The sprawling, 7,000-square-foot place had been designed and built in the Mediterranean style. Red clay roof tiling. Palm trees. The whole bit.

Clearly, my wife was right. In this exclusive gated community in North County (Fairbanks), this place took the cake. I couldn't wipe the grin off my face as I parked in front of the house and climbed out of the car. I had a secret...

The real estate agent was waiting for us. A subtly attractive woman in her mid-thirties. Blond hair and blue eyes. That cheesy real estate agent smile. We all shook hands with her before she showed us in through the front door with a long, sweeping wave of her arm.

"And here we have the family room," she said.

"Whoa!" Nicholas yelled, wide-eyed.

"Awesome!" Mikey added, equally wide-eyed.

Both of my boys tore off into the family room, running circles in the vast space. The room was absolutely huge. Probably fifty feet by thirty feet. As I looked it over, I thought back to my days as a cop, living with Susan in a rental home that was 500 square feet in total. To save money, we used to fire up the burners on the stove just to heat the house. And it actually worked, the place was so small. But now, there I was, gawking at a family room three times bigger than that first home.

"Nice," I said, trying to sound nonchalant.

"Now, if you follow me through here," the agent said, "I'll show you the kitchen." She turned to my wife as she led us to the other end of the living room. "You're going to love this, Monica. It's Monica, right?"

Monica nodded, a little half-frown on her face. I could tell that she hated the idea that this place would never be anything more than a dream.

The kitchen was elaborate. New everything. Beautiful every-thing. All of it completely enormous. We were blown away.

The agent would then go on to show us all *five* bedrooms and all *seven* bathrooms in this giant place. All the while, Monica kept shaking her head. Even after the agent left to give us some time alone to talk things over, she looked skeptical.

"We can't afford this," my wife said immediately.

I moved in to hug her. "Yeah, we can," I said.

Monica shot me one of those "you're-full-of-shit" looks. "With what money?" she said. "What bank's going to give us a loan?"

I ran my hand through her hair. "Honey, we have the money. We can write a check for it *today*."

Monica sighed. She backed away from our embrace and looked all around the master bedroom, also enormous and well adorned. "I just don't know."

I guess I can't blame my wife. She'd gotten her hopes up about houses on our Sunday drives before. And for years, we could barely even afford the place we'd been renting in Rancho San Diego. So she'd had her share of getting jerked around.

"I don't know, honey..." she repeated.

"Monica, we can afford this," I said. "I *promise*."

My wife nodded and smiled slightly, as if still reluctant to accept me at my word. Still, I could tell that she was excited.

Immediately, I went into the kitchen, where I found the real estate agent waiting for us. I shook her hand, telling her that we could get ready to close on the place. She grinned, clearly happy with the sale, and said she'd get the paperwork started immediately.

On the day of the closing, Monica, my boys, and I returned. The agent handed us the keys, congratulated us, and left us all waving her off in the driveway. The boys roared inside the moment the agent was away.

"Let's go explore!" Mikey yelled.

"Wait for me!" Nicholas called after his brother.

Monica and I remained outside for a moment. Our arms around each other, we took a few steps away from the house then turned to look the place over. Now *I* was the one who couldn't believe it. I'd struggled for money my entire life. And now I'd just written a check for our first home. A check with more zeros on it than I ever could have imagined scrawling out.

"Let's go check the mailbox," I said excitedly.

"They don't have mailboxes here," Monica said, grinning. "Only PO boxes."

I shrugged. "So?"

"Well, we're not going to have any mail yet, anyway. Nobody even knows our new address."

I grabbed my wife's hand and began to drag her playfully away from our new house. "But it's not your house until you check the mail."

So, laughing giddily, the two of us walked down the long, winding driveway to the street. As we stood there at the foot of the driveway, several people who we assumed to be our neighbors either walked or drove by. None of them really acknowledged us, which I thought was rather strange. [66]

After pretending to check the mail, my wife and I walked back up to the house quietly. As we entered through the front door, we both examined the place, too stunned to speak. We sat down in a corner of the family room, each of us on one wall, sort of facing each other. I looked at Monica. She was crying.

"What's wrong, honey?" I asked, tears in my own eyes.

"Nothing's wrong," Monica said, sniffling. "It's just this house."

My heart skipped with sudden concern. "It's not the one you wanted?"

"No, it's perfect. I just can't believe we're here."

All at once, I started laughing and crying at the same time. "I know. It's a long way from where we've been."

Monica shook her head. "This money…"

---

[66] Coming from where we'd grown up, we were used to people being friendly enough to at least say hello. But in those early days, we didn't know any of our neighbors. Only one ever became our friend. In the early days, anyway…

I nodded, just as stunned about the whole thing as my wife. Down the hall, I could hear the patter of the boys' feet on the floor. Sounded like they were chasing each other.

"I mean…how long has it been?" Monica asked. "Two years? Three? I couldn't even afford college and now we're sitting here."

"College?" I said. "You couldn't even afford *junior* college."

Monica leaned over and hit me playfully, smiling through her tears. "You know what I mean…"

I smiled silently, gently wiping away my wife's tears with my thumb.

Then, the familiar wail of crying reached my ears. Mikey.

"Daddy!" came the call from down the hall.

Monica glanced frantically up at me as I sprang to my feet. I ran down the hall in the direction of Mikey's scream. In a minute, I was standing over him. He'd found his way into the attached bathroom of one of the smaller bedrooms in the house. Nicholas stood in the corner of this same bedroom, looking angry.

"What's wrong, Mikey?" I asked.

Mikey was one of those kids who seemed to get cuter with each passing year. He had his dark hair and big, blue, bedroom eyes. Thin. And more adorable than I can explain—even when he cried. He was sitting on the floor, his legs splayed out awkwardly. He glanced up at me only for a second, his face moist with tears.

"Nicholas threw a shoe at me and it almost broke the window," Mikey said, wiping his nose with the back of his hand as he gazed at the floor.

I looked into the bathroom, where I saw one of Nicholas' shoes laying by the wall. "Oh…" I said. "I see."

Immediately, I put on my best angry-dad face—which was difficult because I was still so happy and overwhelmed about this new house. I walked straight into the bedroom and stood over Nicholas, who'd apparently been listening in.

"Nick," I said, "is this true?"

Nicholas nodded in that way that regretful children always do.

"I think it's time for a timeout, then."

Nicholas turned and scowled at Mikey, who'd poked his head around the bathroom door, a triumphant smile plastered on his face.

"Have you picked a room yet?" I asked.

Nicholas nodded again. Reluctantly.

"Then go to your room. Don't come out until we call you."

Nicholas and I left the bedroom and headed down the long hallway in opposite directions. But before I could even get back to the family room, I heard another familiar sound: the sound of *Nicholas* crying. So I turned and walked quickly in the direction of the sound. It took some winding and weaving to locate my son, but I found him near the closet in another bedroom, this one much larger.

"What's wrong, bud?" I asked.

Nicholas did as his older brother had just done: wiped his nose with the back of his hand as he trained his eyes on the floor. "Daddy..." he said.

I crouched down and patted Nicholas' leg. "I'm here. What is it?"

My son looked strangely embarrassed. "I can't do my timeout."

"Well, you're going to have to."

His face contorted to frustration as he started crying again. "I can't."

"Why not?" I asked, confused.

His crying built in force. "Because I can't find my room."

I couldn't help myself; I laughed. There we were, in our first home. A home so large that I now stood in a bedroom I'd probably never use. A home too big for timeouts. A home so vast that my six-year-old son could get lost in it.

That was the first day that we really started to recognize how successful we'd become, how quickly Metabolife had changed our lives.

Several months later, around Thanksgiving—after a long renovation, modification, and move-in process—we'd celebrate our first true night in our new home by having our first meal at the dinner table. Since it was such a special occasion, I thought I would consult with my youngest son.

"What do you think we should have for our first dinner?" I asked Nicholas.

My son thought long and hard. "Steak and O'Doul's," he finally said.

I laughed. See, I'm not much for drinking, but I've always enjoyed the taste of beer. So whenever I felt like having one, I'd grab an O'Doul's. Nicholas was always coming up to me and asking to have a taste. Was it wrong that I would give him a sip from time to time? Maybe. I don't know, maybe I fostered in him a taste for beer. But I just couldn't resist. He was always so matter-of-fact whenever he asked for a sip.

"Okay, bud," I said. "We'll have steak. But we'll see about the O'Doul's."

See, that was Nicholas. That's *always been* Nicholas. A man's man.

Today, he's an excellent skateboarder. An excellent athlete all around, really. He could ride a two-wheel bicycle without training wheels by the time he turned two years old. By the age of five, his love of the more physical sports had already caused him to break his arm on four separate occasions. Tough kid.

But at the same time, Nicholas is maybe the most sensitive of my children—a sensitivity that would carry over into his art. From the time he could pick up a pen, he'd proven himself to be a great artist. At six years old, he could sketch Warner Brothers cartoons as if they'd been drawn by the original artists.

I'm reminded of a time, years later, when this particular talent would get him into trouble with his middle school. I remember that I'd just picked up Mikey to take him to his after-school tutor when my cell phone rang. It was Anna, the principal at Nick's school.

"Mike," she said, "we need you to come down here. It's Nicholas."

"What happened?" I asked, my heart dropping into my stomach. "What did he do?"

Anna paused for an uncomfortable moment. "I can't tell you over the phone. You'll have to come down here."

Couldn't even tell me on the phone. Naturally, I assumed that this meant that the absolute worst had happened. With all that goes on in middle schools these days, who knows what kind of trouble my son could have gotten himself into?

So I dropped Mikey off at the tutor and called Monica to tell her what had happened. [67]

"They wouldn't tell you what he did?" Monica asked, sounding even more concerned than I felt.

"No," I said, taking the onramp onto the freeway. "They want us to come down there."

"I'll meet you in Anna's office," Monica said abruptly.

By the time I walked into the principal's office, my wife was already there, speaking to my son. She drives fast, that Monica. Nick played the role of the devastated teen, holding his head in his hands. I sat down next to them, nodding hello to Anna, whose icy glare was sobering.

"So what happened, Nick?" I asked.

No response. My wife just glared at me furiously.

"Well?" I said. "What did he do?"

"Nick," Anna said softly, "why don't you wait outside for a minute?"

Sulkily, Nicholas did as he was told.

"Hey, Anna," I said jovially, trying to change the beat a little. "What's going on?"

The principal sighed and began to dig in her desk drawer. In a moment, she produced a standard notebook with a green cover. "Well," she said, "a teacher caught Nick with this notebook."

I gulped a little, getting just the slightest taste of the Skoal I'd packed in my mouth before arriving on the scene.

Anna continued before I could even get my hands on the thing.

---

[67] I guess Nicholas had asked his principal to call me instead of his mother because Monica is notorious for her temper—only I wasn't about to let him off the hook so easily.

"And she found some…inappropriate drawings inside." She then handed the notebook over.

I looked down at my son's notebook, noticing that a few of the pages had been flagged. I opened to the first flagged page. There, I saw a comically drawn, funny-looking guy clearly out for a run. "That's not so bad," I said.

"Look at the next page," Anna said dryly.

On the next page, I found some incredibly explicit drawings of two people fornicating. Unbelievably graphic. And pretty sick.

But when I first turned that page, I had problems of my own. Seeing that ridiculous drawing instantly relieved all kinds of stress. I found myself wanting to laugh, knowing damn well that I couldn't. It was kind of like thinking of something funny in church and knowing that you have to choke it back. So what I did was, I swallowed my dip to keep myself from laughing. It worked. My face contorted in disgust and the fit of laughter passed as quickly as it had come. [68]

"Turn the next page," Anna said.

The next page was even worse. But, man, I couldn't help but feel at least a tiny twinge of pride. My son could *draw*.

I felt compelled to say something, but knew that if I tried, I would only start laughing. Then I'd wind up looking like a jerk in front of my wife and my son's principal, a woman we both knew and respected immensely. So I glanced over at Monica. She sat beside me, clearly upset. Angry.

Nick hadn't been the only kid involved. I was certain of that much. Certain that some of his friends had told him what to draw then had a nice laugh over it. But my son wasn't about to snitch on his friends. And you've got to respect that.

"Now, I don't even know where to begin on how wrong all this is," Anna said. "But I'm going to leave punishment up to you. Between his embarrassment at school and whatever punishment you level at home, I'm willing to keep this off the record."

---

[68] A few things went through my mind at that moment. First, I was relieved that we were only talking about artwork, no matter how inappropriate it might have been. And second, I couldn't believe that my intelligent, capable son would be dumb enough to get caught with stuff like this.

"You won't suspend him?" Monica said with clear relief in her voice.

Anna shook her head.

"Thank you, Anna," I said, standing to shake her hand. "We'll be sure he learns his lesson. You won't see stuff like this from Nicholas ever again."

My wife and I left the office and found our son in the waiting room. When he darted his eyes up to us, he looked scared. He couldn't hold eye contact and he seemed to be shaking from the stress.

So without really looking at each other or saying anything, the three of us walked out to the parking lot, Monica chaotically angry and me just trying to size up my son.

"I'll take him with me," I said.

"You're damn right you will," Monica said, looking like she might explode from the fury.

It seemed an odd comment at the time. Seemed as if Monica had already come to blame me for the whole thing. Sure, I had a history of crude cartooning, but never in the presence of my son. I hadn't *taught* the boy his art.

So Nicholas and I climbed into the car. Immediately after igniting the engine, I turned and flicked my son in the head with my middle finger.

"Ow!" Nicholas said. He looked stunned and sort of relieved at the same time.

"We're going to have to punish you, you know," I said.

Nicholas, still rubbing his head, seemed resigned to his fate. "I know," he said.

"You can't have your skateboard for two weeks."

My son's brow furrowed so quickly I thought he might strain a muscle in his face. "Two weeks!" he howled. "You can't do that!"

"Listen, Nick," I said slowly. "I'm going to tell you something. It's two weeks because you did two things wrong." I raised one of my fingers. "You get one week for doing something stupid that got you in trouble at school."

"What's the second week for?" Nicholas asked, sulking.

I raised a second finger. "For getting caught," I said. "How could you get caught with something like this?"

After a short, contemplative silence, he smiled at me (and, boy, does this kid have the best smile). And we both started laughing. I laughed out the stress I'd carried since the original call from Anna—the stress of thinking that my son had done something truly awful. Nick laughed, I guess, because he appreciated that while I might have been angry with him about what he'd done, I could still understand why he'd done it. And from that point on, whenever I wanted to get under Nick's skin about something, I called him Rembrandt.

But back to that first night in our new house, back to eating dinner around our dining room table, boxes all around, all of us completely oblivious to just how dramatically our lives had changed. I helped Nicholas cut his steak while Monica helped Mikey with his. Nicholas had been ignoring his juice, as he kept trying to steal drinks of my O'Doul's. I gave him his one drink, but then took to fending him off after that.

"Dad?" Mikey said suddenly.

"Yeah, Mikey?"

"Johnny was telling me—"

"Johnny from school?" I asked, interrupting.

"Yeah," Mikey continued. "Johnny from school was telling me that there's this kind of elephant that can fly."

I smiled. "Oh, yeah?"

"Yeah," Mikey said, looking and sounding as deadly serious as a child can look and sound. "Is that true?"

I'd just finished cutting Nicholas' steak, so I passed his plate over to him, careful to intercept his latest grasp of my can of fake beer. I could feel my whole family's eyes on me as I prepared to answer. "No, Mikey," I said. "That's not true." [69]

"Are you sure?" Mikey stammered. "Johnny was saying that—"

---

[69] I've always been completely honest with my kids, even when they were very young. I learned that from my father.

"No, I'm sure." I smiled and extended my arm like a wing. "How could something that big fly? Its wings would have to be a hundred feet long."

Mikey grinned and nodded. "Yeah, you're right."

Mikey. Such a wonderful boy—and now a great young man. He'd always been most interested in the simpler things in life. Nature. Animals. Fishing. Camping. Later, when he'd turn thirteen years old, we'd have him tested. The tests would show that his abstract thinking would be equal to the level of a thirty-year-old. You show my son a sunset and he'll describe to you aspects of it that most people aren't conscious of. The way the rays become visible when they pass through clouds, for example.

Obviously, this kind of mind leads to an extraordinary level of creativity. And also a sense of wonder. For example, I remember another of our days of kuka fishing when he was about eight years old.

Mikey pointed to the water's edge as I strung up another hotdog for him. "Look at that, Daddy," he said.

I glanced to my left, failing to see anything out of the ordinary. "Look at what?"

"The grass."

"Yeah," I said, nodding as I tied the knot. "That's some tall grass."

"But look at how it comes out of the water," Mikey said, sounding a little frustrated with me.

"Sometimes grass grows out of the water, bud," I said obliviously.

"That's not what I mean." Mikey's frustration had really mounted now. "Look at how the grass is a different color when it's in the water."

I concentrated on the grass this time. He was right. Despite the fact that the water was as clear as could be, the grass beneath the surface did appear to be a much darker green.

Mikey waded over to the water's edge and stared down at the grass for a moment. "Why does it do that?" he asked. Then, without waiting for an answer, he pulled a handful of the grass out of the water, examining it for a long while.

"Did you figure it out?" I asked.

My son shook his head. "No," he said quizzically. "It's the same color now." He then showed his handful of grass to me. It was indeed the same color. "Why, Daddy?" he said. "Why does it do that?"

How can you answer a question like that? The only way I could, I guess: with the truth. "I don't know, Mikey," I said.

My son looked disappointed. Clearly, he was baffled. He mulled over the grass problem for a long while before returning to kuka fishing. Even though he spent the rest of the morning pulling crayfish off the line, I could see that he was still contemplating the riddle about the grass. And every once in a while, I would catch him stealing glances toward the shoreline.

But that was Mikey. As abstract and creative as they come. As curious as they come. Because of his intense curiosity, I think, nothing ever came as easily to him as it did to his little brother. But that didn't mean he lagged behind. Mikey never quit at anything. And he worked harder than any kid I've ever known.

When you're a Cinderella story, if you truly go from rags to riches, there comes a point when you start to feel guilty about all the money you have, about your ability to buy whatever car you want, the ability to buy your wife the jewelry she'd coveted since her days working in retail jewelry sales, the ability to buy anything you feel you might need to make your family "happy." You never forget those luxuries that you used to lack, never forget where you came from. You might occasionally forget who you are, but that doesn't mean you don't bear the guilt of suddenly hitting it big. And you feel somewhat guilty that not everyone in your family can experience it along with you.

What you do when you feel this way is you start to give things away. You do what you can to share the wealth as much as possible.

For Monica and me, that sharing began with the family.

That year, we decided to host the Christmas celebration at our house. Monica had cooked a wonderful Christmas dinner. Lamb, ham, and turkey. She'd been up late the night before, getting everything ready. We'd invited all of Monica's eight brothers and sisters to celebrate with us. Her mother, Martha, her stepfather, Ken, my mother, and my brother, Joe, would be joining us for the occasion, too.

Right at noon, people began to show up. My mom and brother and a few of Monica's siblings and their children all arrived bearing gifts for the many nieces and nephews in the family. Now, obviously, like with any Christmas, the children were just itching to get at those presents that everyone was leaving under the tree. By the time all of Monica's siblings had arrived, the level of excitement for the kids had reached incredible heights.

The only problem was that Monica's mother and stepfather had not yet arrived.

This came as no surprise to anyone, I think, because Martha had a tendency to be late. Not just kind of late, but *significantly* late. Like *more than two hours* late.

So everyone just sat around in the kitchen and living room, waiting for Martha because we all knew that she'd be angry if we started anything without her. For a while, I tried entertaining the kids, but when it became clear that none of them wanted to pay attention to anything but the presents under the tree, I decided to pass the time by heading into the kitchen and talking to three of Monica's siblings. My wife was there, making last-minute preparations to the meal and keeping everything warm and fresh while we all waited for her mother to arrive.

With her were her brothers, Steve and Paul Gonzalez, and her sister, Angie Evanko.

Steve was maybe ten years younger than me and three years older than Monica. At 6'5" with a kind of heavy frame (owed to a kidney transplant he'd recently had to undergo), he carved a kind of Tony Soprano figure. He even looked like Soprano. A much quieter guy and far more unassuming, though.

Angie was the oldest of the kids in Monica's family. Married to a nice guy named Jim, she had two children. She looked only vaguely like Monica, but was still a pretty woman in her own right.

Paul, meanwhile, could not have been less like his brother. He was far shorter, standing maybe 5'11", and far more engaging. A positive thinker. Happy guy. And certainly a hard worker. "Mmmm," he said in his characteristically upbeat tone. "That smells good, Monica." Then, he winked at Angie. "How come you never cooked like that at Christmas?"

Angie smirked.

"She cooks the same things I do, Paul, and you know it," Monica said wryly.

Paul chuckled.

"Never all of it at once, though!" Angie said.

We all laughed.

"It does smell good, Monica."

"Does she cook like this for you every night?" Steve asked me, elbowing my shoulder.

"I wish," I said.

Everyone broke out in derisive laughter. Then, after my wife hit me with a sarcastic glare, I changed my tune.

"Actually," I said, "she cooks a lot. And it's always perfect."

"Of course it is," Paul said. "You *have* to say that."

Everyone laughed again—and now it was Paul's turn to get the pretend glare from Monica.

"Where *is* Mom, anyway?" Angie asked.

"Where is Mom every time?" Monica said.

"Late," Steve offered.

"Probably stuck in traffic," Paul said.

"At two o'clock on Christmas?" Monica asked, clearly frustrated as she chopped hastily through a yellow onion.

Sensing my wife's mounting anger, I decided to change the subject. "How are the kids holding up out there?" I asked Paul.

"Oh, you know," Paul said. "Eyes on the presents."

Finally, the doorbell rang. Monica dropped her onion slicing and rushed to the door. I followed as closely behind as I could.

When the door swung open, there stood Martha. Ken, I guess, was parking the car. Martha Dunn. Short. No one knows her age because she'll never tell. An attractive woman (she looked a great deal like Monica, actually) with dark hair and eyes. A devoted Catholic. As she stood, grinning at me, I remember thinking about when I'd first started dating my wife. I'm not sure if it was because I was still getting over my failed marriage with Susan or not, but it definitely didn't help that Martha was trying to set her daughter up with another man at the time. [70] Whatever the case, my future mother-in-law never seemed to like me. Hardly even acknowledged me. Wouldn't talk to me.

"Martha!" I said. "So glad you could come. Where's Ken?"

Martha grinned from ear to ear. "Oh, he's parking the car," she said. "How's my favorite son-in-law?"

With a smile plastered to my face, I watched her shuffle past. Suddenly, she'd always known I'd turn out to be a great husband.

Martha made straight for the living room and announced that we could open presents now. And Ken arrived just as the kids began tearing into their gifts, everyone smiling and laughing and carrying on.

Dinner turned out to be nice. Loud, considering all the people in the room, but nice. The kids seemed to be having a good time comparing their toy hauls and we all enjoyed the great food.

When dinner had ended, Monica tapped her glass with her spoon, getting everybody's attention. "Okay, everybody," she said. "If you're finished, let's all go into the family room. Mike and I have an announcement to make."

A few excited and a few sarcastic rumblings erupted from the group. And we all filed into the family room.

Monica raised her hands a little before speaking. "Everybody," she said loudly, "in the spirit of the season, Mike and I have something we'd like to share with you."

"You're pregnant again," Angie said sarcastically.

Everyone laughed.

---

[70] See, Martha was trying to set her daughter up with one of the players from the Padres at the time. And, man, did she ever love her Padres.

"No, I'm not pregnant," my wife said. She turned and smiled at me. "We're done with all that."

More laughter.

"Honey," she continued, "do you want to take this?"

I nodded and stood, feeling nervous for the first time since I could remember. "Everybody," I said, "as you've heard, Monica and I have seen some success lately."

"You ain't kidding," Paul said.

More laughter.

Grinning, I continued. "Well, we've decided that we'd like to share some of that success with you all."

Everyone's ears seemed to perk up. All eyes were on me. You could hear a pin drop.

"We've opened up trust funds for all the children. These funds will pay for all of them to go to college."

Silence. I remember not being sure if everyone was stunned or offended. Eventually, Paul broke the lull.

"Hey, that's great, Mike," he said.

Murmurs of approval followed.

"We really appreciate it," he added. "I think we're all just reacting this way because we can't believe you're doing this."

A slightly louder rumble of agreement followed. Paul was the first to come up and hug Monica, thanking her. Then, he did the same with me.

After a minute or two, everyone began to loosen up again. They each started talking to their children excitedly, explaining that now they were going to be getting college educations. Listening in, I breathed a sigh of relief. It felt good to know that we'd be able to help the family in some small way—and, more importantly, that they would accept the gift without feeling bitter.

Without a sound, Martha had sidled up beside me. "That's a great thing you're doing, Mike," she said warmly.

"Thanks," I said. "It's the right thing to do, Martha."

She patted me on the thigh. "I always knew you were a good one. Always knew you were right for my daughter."

I'd come to learn over the years—after buying cars and houses and paying for more than twenty college educations for the family—that money changes people. Money's an enabler. It works on a person kind of like alcohol. See, people say that alcohol makes you a jerk or makes you a nice guy. But that's not what it does. All alcohol does is remove inhibition. The result varies from person to person, but basically all alcohol does is show who you are, deep down—well below those layers of insecurities that everyone tends to build up over the years. If you're an asshole when you drink, then you're probably just an asshole deep down. If you're happy and loving, then you're most likely a happy and loving person. And money does the same thing. You see some rich people who are pompous and arrogant. That's because "they can afford to be." The same goes for rich people who always feel guilty or spend their time trying to seclude themselves or hide their riches. They say that money changes people. It doesn't. It only *magnifies* them.

I recall a conversation along these lines that I had with Dad once.

"Son," he said, "you'll spend the first half of your life trying to make money, then the second half just trying to keep people from stealing it."

I remember nodding and laughing, not realizing then how serious my father was.

"When you make it, Mike," he said, adding a raised finger for emphasis, "and you will make it, there's going to be people in your life, jealous people, jealous of what you've made of yourself and what you've got. But there'll also be people who're *envious*. You know the difference between jealousy and envy, don't you?"

I shook my head.

Dad extended an upturned palm. "Say you have a '64 Shelby and you show it off to a friend. Your friend might say, 'Dang, man, that's a cool car. I wish I had a Shelby.' See…that's jealousy."

I nodded, rapt.

Dad extended his other hand, palm upturned. "But what if your friend went to the grocery store later that day and happened to see your car in the parking lot? What if your friend, as he walked past your Shelby, took out his keys and scratched a long line in the door?"

I nodded again, my mouth slightly agape.

"That's envy," Dad said.

But on the evening following Christmas, we had not yet experienced our first taste of either jealousy or envy. No, at the end of that day, we were able to go to bed happy, knowing that we'd done what we could to help provide for the whole clan. That all our success could mean something to more people than just our immediate family.

It was a good Christmas.

The high would be short-lived for my wife. See, not long after Christmas, Monica would get that first taste of jealousy and envy. For her, it would come from the people she worked with at Metabolife. She'd continued on in the customer service department even after the company had begun to take off. So she worked alongside a good number of employees who'd been with us since the early days. But while these employees continued to collect their regular paychecks, Monica was now showing up in expensive cars and wearing expensive clothing. Naturally, jealousy and envy began to take hold. Many of the employees started to resent my wife.

Now, Monica is a wonderful person, but she's always been poor with stress. She's stubborn (but then, I am, too). What this meant was that, at times, we would butt heads. Normally, whenever we argued at home, I would just get in my car and leave. See, I'm not particularly good at fights of the emotional variety. I just can't handle it. So I would leave, deciding that it would be better to just drive around and try to clear my head than face the argument head-on. Eventually, things would always cool down with Monica, too, and she would give me a call and ask me to come home. And we would always reconnect and mend things from there.

But now the stress and tension had begun to show up at work.

And all of it had started to manifest itself in more stubbornness (from both of us). I remember one instance in particular.

The two of us stood just outside Monica's office, well within earshot of the other offices and cubicles in the customer service department, very much in a public setting.

"But she sent back the bottle with one pill in it," Monica said.

"I've told you, Monica," I said calmly. "If anyone asks to speak to the president or CEO, you put them through to me. And if they want a refund, we give it to them."

"She's just trying to get a free bottle," Monica said sternly.

"If she asked for a refund, I don't care. We give her a refund."

"She's done this twice now." There was no hiding my wife's building anger as she handed me what looked like a letter.

I gave it a once-over, realizing that it was a letter from the woman, asking for a refund.

"See?" she said.

Now I started to lose my cool, as well. I could feel all the eyes of the department on the back of my neck. "It doesn't matter, honey," I said. "It's company policy."

My wife's face bent into a look of consternation. She crossed her arms in front of her chest. "I don't care if it's company policy. I'm not giving her a refund."

"Monica," I said hotly, "you're giving her a refund."

"Why should I?"

I thrust my hands to either side. "Because if this woman gets angry, she might try calling the Better Business Bureau or the FDA and try to damage our reputation. Angry customers can be dangerous."

Monica furrowed her brow. "So you're just going to let her get away with this?"

"No," I said, trying to calm myself down. "We'll give her the refund and we won't sell to her again."

My wife turned to enter her office. "She's cheating us," she said, closing the door behind her.

Now, I don't mean to give the wrong idea about my wife.

Monica is a wonderful person. A great mother. Very engaging. Incredibly loving. She just doesn't handle stress well. And as I said, she was every bit as stubborn and bullheaded as I am. So in some ways, I admire that. In other ways, it sometimes got in the way. Was I as much to blame as she was? Absolutely. But in this particular argument, I was certainly in the right. You don't deny an angry customer—I don't care who it is—a refund under *any* circumstances.

A couple of weeks later, my secretary patched a call through to my office: the woman who'd sent the letter, completely furious now because she hadn't received her refund. I confess to being surprised and extremely angry to have had to learn things this way. But I still managed to smooth things over with the irate customer by reoffering the refund and promising to take care of the error personally.

As soon as I hung up, I went straight down to the customer service department to find out why my wife hadn't processed the refund.

"Did you give that woman the refund?" I asked.

"No," Monica said haughtily.

I had to slow my breathing to keep from screaming. "Why not?"

"Because I think you're wrong."

I glanced around the room. As before, many employees were watching us. I could tell because most of them averted their eyes whenever I looked in their direction. Embarrassed, I raised my hand defensively. "At home, you know I'll concede when I'm wrong. But here at work, there's only one boss."

Monica crossed her arms in front of her chest again. "I'm not giving the refund," she said nonchalantly.

"Come with me," I said, leading my wife back to my office and shutting the door behind us. Now alone, I looked her square in the eyes. "If you don't give her that refund, I'm going to have to fire you."

"You can't fire me," she said with a half-smile. "And I'm not giving the refund."

I turned in frustration, grabbing the little stress ball off my desk. "Monica, you're not seeing the big picture here." I squeezed the ball a few times. "We have *millions* of customers. Only a few ask for refunds. This is small potatoes. It's a drop in a huge bucket."

"I won't give the ref—"

I interrupted my wife. "I'm serious, Monica. Give the refund or you're fired."

Monica stormed out of the office, raging mad. [71]

Despite how right I felt in our most recent argument, for the next few days, I would get the cold shoulder at work and at home. Still, as it always did, the whole thing eventually blew over. And I think it was a good thing, as that argument was the beginning of the end for Monica at Metabolife. Between that episode and the other employees' resentment toward her, it seemed time for her to quit.

She quit a few weeks later, deciding instead that she'd rather be a mother to her children than an employee to me. And this turned out to be probably the only argument I ever won.

---

[71] At that moment, I remember thinking about the pair of nicknames her family had given her (with my help, of course). The first was "Macha," the female form of "macho." We called her this because she never backed down and always seemed to want to fight at the drop of a hat. The other was "Devil Woman." And this one wasn't because of her personality, but because of the strange coincidence that she held with the number 666. See, Monica was the sixth child in her family, born on 6/6/66. The name "Monica" has six letters. When you dial the first three letters of her name into a telephone ("Mon"), you get "666." And when my wife got angry, you'd believe that the 666 thing was true.

Chapter 13

All the Kangaroos in Texas

Pretty much every regulatory hearing that we ever went to in Texas was troubling, but out of all of them, 1996 was the worst. But before I get into all that, let's talk about safety studies.

We'd conducted such studies on our original product back in '94 and '95, and those studies had been reviewed by Doctor Wayne Snodgrass, a well-respected man in the field. Snodgrass had been particularly helpful to the cause of demonstrating the safety of herbal ephedrine because he served as the head of the Texas Huston-Galveston Poison Center.

In '95, Snodgrass had gotten up in front of a panel of lawmakers at the Texas Department of Health (TDH) and stated that a person could take sixteen of our tablets without being at risk. According to Snodgrass, even a person with heart arrhythmia could do this and still get by safely.

Obviously, the good doctor had proven himself to be a valuable witness for our cause. So when the hearings in the summer of '96 rolled around, he was among the first people I called.

"Well, doc," I said, "it looks like we've got another trip to fabulous Austin, Texas, in store for you."

"Mike…" Snodgrass said, sighing and then pausing for a long while. "I can't go."

My heart dropped. "What? Why?"

Snodgrass sighed again. "Because the commissioner told me that if I testify on how safe these products are, the department will remove all funding to the poison control centers."

"Commissioner?"

"David Smith."

"The commissioner?"

"The commissioner."

"Well…" I said, looking up at my living room ceiling. "So what? So you won't have TDH's backing. I don't have it either and we do alright."

"Their funding accounts for almost ninety percent of our budget," Snodgrass said darkly.

I found myself speechless.

"So I'm gonna have to decline, Mike," the doctor said. "You understand."

Desperation took hold. "But you *know* we have a safe product, doc."

"You're right…" he said. "You have a safe product. But right now, I'm more concerned about the people in Texas having access to a poison control center."

In that moment, I came back down to Earth. I wracked my brain for a plan. This was blackmail. And I just couldn't let it stand. "Don't worry, doc," I said. "I don't blame you. And I'll think of…something."

Unsure of where to start, I eventually decided to contact the lawyers representing Formula One—the other Chemins Company product under scrutiny by TDH—and fill them in on the issue with Snodgrass. To that, they actually had good news, the makings of a real, live plan. These intrepid lawyers claimed to have videotape deposition featuring the administrative director of the Huston-Galveston Poison Center (who, coincidentally enough, was also named Michael Ellis; no relation). Ellis had essentially served as messenger between David Smith and Snodgrass. And here we had him on sworn videotape admitting that Smith had told him to threaten Snodgrass with pulling his funding if he testified in our corner at the hearings.

"Can you get me a copy of that tape?" I asked, pointing at my own phone as I spoke, for whatever reason.

Of course, the Formula One lawyers had no problem complying with my request. But their compliance alone wouldn't get this ball rolling down the hill, I knew. No, to keep it rolling, I needed to get the media on board. Get the wolves playing along. I figured it'd be easy since the Ellis tapes proved that we had a full-blown conspiracy on our hands. And the media eats that shit up.

So I called several of the local TV stations. The conversations went something like this:

"You've got to get down to the TDH building tomorrow morning," I'd say.

"Why?" the station rep would ask. "What's up?"

"I can't tell you right now. Just know that it's going to be big."

Regardless of the station, the rep would sound just about wet-your-pants enthralled by this point. "Some kind of scandal?" he'd ask.

"Just come down. You'll see."

So with tapes in hand and the TV media surely behind me, I went down to Austin for the hearings in August of '96, paying my latest visit to the Texas Department of Health. I knew the procedures well enough by that point to realize that I'd have to get there early if I wanted to have enough time to play my tape. [72]

The Texas Department of Health was pretty standard. A traditional government building. Multi-story. Brick. Older. It didn't look like it was a high-money operation, but there were definitely wide lawns and ample parking all around. Plenty of space in Texas, I guess. So since my lawyers, representatives, friends who were sympathetic to the cause, and I had gotten there so early, I strolled

---

[72] They had a system at these TDH hearings. A system that would need manipulating.

through the glass front door expecting that we'd be the only people in the room. My guess had been close; there was only one other guy in there. But I got in ahead of him in line.

The setup: The hearings required that everybody who wanted to speak had to take a number. The testimonials would then progress based on the numbering system. If you had number one, you got to speak first; number two would go second, etc. But the problem with this system was that it also came with a time limit. Everyone who took a number got to speak for a mere three minutes. And my tape was fourteen minutes long.

My plan: I grabbed number one off the ticker. The other guy in line got number two. But then, after him, I had everyone who'd come down with me take enough numbers so that I could keep my presentation going. The fact that we'd have to pause the tape for Number Two's turn to speak might affect the momentum, but still. I knew we had enough numbers now to get it all in.

I then found the nearest clerk.

"Hey, buddy," I said, "do you know where there's a monitor with a VCR set up?"

The clerk, a portly, uniformed man, stood up and smiled. "Sure," he said warmly, his Texas drawl about as thick and slow and endearing as I'd ever heard. "You need it for the hearing?"

I nodded and the clerk set me up with what I needed—a TV and VCR combo big enough for the whole hearing to see. Together, we wheeled it into the hearing room. The place wasn't quite as big as I'd expected. Kind of square. They'd arranged the bleachers in a theater style, all of them facing a big, bureaucratic table at the head of the room. The clerk and I set up the TV to the left of this table, in a spot that would be visible to both spectators and bureaucrats alike.

I thanked the clerk and took a seat in the bleachers, basically alone, save for my sizable entourage.

Over the next hour or so, people began filing in and filling up the seating. The TDH representatives began arriving, too. Not surprisingly, David Smith had apparently decided not to deign us with his presence. [73] More surprising: The guy chairing the entire event wasn't even a medical professional. Not for humans anyway. The guy was a veterinarian. A *veterinarian*.

Anyway, after another twenty minutes or so of milling around, the vet called the hearing to order and informed us that the person in possession of the coveted number one could take the floor. With a deep, cathartic breath, I stood up, tape in hand, and walked toward the monitor.

"My name is Michael J. Ellis," I said loudly. "And I'm here on behalf of Foslip of California, Incorporated. I have a tape here that I would like to show you."

"You may proceed," the vet said.

I slid the tape into the VCR and hit play. I then stood back and watched right along with everyone else. Ellis proved to be a soft-spoken, rather heavyset man in his fifties. Even from the beginning, the video made it clear that we were dealing with an anxious, guilt-ridden, and entirely upset go-between.

The room grew palpably silent as he began to reveal his story. By the time my three minutes neared the finish, you could hear a pin drop in the place.

During a lull in Ellis' confession, I glanced up at the vet. He looked nervous. "Mr. Ellis," he said, "your time is nearly up. How much more of this do you have?"

I paused the tape. "It's about fourteen minutes long," I said.

The vet appeared almost relieved. "Well, then you won't be allowed to finish. We'll have to go to whoever's holding number two."

At that moment, Number Two stood up from his spot near the back of the bleachers, clearing his throat. Then, without a word, he passed to the person sitting in front of him the small slip of paper

---

[73] In fact, there wasn't a single representative from applied nutrition in attendance. Not even Cynthia Culmo, the pleasant young bureaucrat most directly responsible for this whole charade. They were all hiding in their offices for the duration, I guess.

he was holding. The crowd began to pass it forward. When it reached me, I gave it a once-over even though I already knew what it was. The number two.

"Looks like I've got another three minutes," I said wryly.

The vet sulked.

I hit play and waited with baited breath for the next three minutes to unfurl. Most of this portion of the tape featured Ellis coming clean. He stated that he knew it was wrong, what Smith was doing, but that he'd had no choice but to serve as messenger. He even began crying during his confession.

The audience was rapt. And every time my latest block of three minutes neared the end, one of my people would pass their number up to the front. Number after number came up until the fourteen-minute presentation had ended. And just before closing, Ellis was even kind enough to state into the record that Dr. Wayne Snod-grass himself believed ephedrine products to be safe.

By this time, you could cut the tension and anger in the room with a knife. What had we just seen on tape? Proof that the man who should have been presiding over these very hearings had black-mailed an expert witness.

People were pissed. So pissed, in fact, that they walked out on the hearing and went directly to the governor's mansion. I'm not entirely sure of the events that unfolded because I wasn't there myself (I heard about them later from a third party). But between that third party and the stories I saw on the news, it seems like an accurate account. Here's how it apparently went down:

The governor at the time was George W. Bush, a man not known to abide controversy. See, even before he ran for president, the policy surrounding his administrations had always been to cut off or fire anyone who might be even remotely controversial. There's nothing quite like a fall guy.

So somewhere between thirty and a hundred angry people (depending on whether you believe my source or the inflated, sensa-tionalized media accounts) from the TDH hearing arrived on Bush's doorstep, virtually handing the future president his latest fall guy. The people in attendance at the impromptu protest were mostly consumers and consumer advocates, but they all had one thing in common: They were furious over the idea that a dietary supplement they counted on every day was being put through the ringers by a dishonest man. People who'd seen tremendous weight loss on ephedra, people whose children had found relief from ADD thanks to ephedra, concerned citizens who felt that they should be allowed to take a supplement without a doctor's note, industry reps, former industry opponents, everyone. They all marched outside Bush's residence, shouting and requesting his ear.

After a while, Governor Bush sent someone out to speak with the demonstrators. And they let him know their concerns in no uncertain terms.

I'm not sure what transpired behind close doors with the governor, but shortly after the protest, David Smith resigned his post as commissioner of the Texas Department of Health.

The aftermath of Smith's resignation was incredible. The media attention had kicked up quite a ruckus. As a result, many different people from the dietary supplement industry began contacting me—the man who had purportedly stirred the pot at TDH. Our calls and meetings led to significant positive change. We started setting up coalitions and focus groups designed to search for appropriate standardization and rules of governance for our products. The whole thing basically unified the industry in all the significant areas where it had been disorganized before.

In the weeks that would follow, I'd spend many random hours wondering what could motivate the man, Dr. Smith, to do what he did. In threatening Snodgrass, he'd essentially risked his job and his reputation, and even exposed himself to the potential for jail time. So with so much on the line, what would cause a man to sink to such levels?

Regardless, he'd paid the piper. And for a year, we'd ride this new wave of industry unity and agency disarray. Right up until we were forced to fight for our existence once again…

C-1fc-)

In the summer of 1997, we came armed not with a videotape, but with experts. And we also brought along everything we'd need for a roaring, Texas-style backyard barbeque.

On the lawns of the TDH building itself, we set up our little party. Behind the long table at the head of the tent we erected stood caterers, all of them ready to serve food to the many curious passersby. Regardless of whether they were distributors, customers, doctors who'd come in to dispute the changes posed by the department of health, or TDH employees, we opened the affair up to anybody who felt like passing through and enjoying some great Southern barbeque. We served chicken, roast beef, beans, cole slaw, the whole thing. And there was plenty of shady space in the large seating area we set up under and beside the tent.

We didn't mean any disrespect by the whole thing—it was just so hot and we wanted to give everyone a chance to unwind—but, obviously, TDH and our opponents weren't too happy about the way we seemed to be approaching the hearing. I will say this, though: Their supposed outrage taught us that even if a government employee takes offense to what you're doing, they'll still never refuse a free meal, no matter who's serving it. And I didn't hear any complaints about the food.

Anyway, about the hearing: When our slot to give testimony finally came up, we called Yale's own Doctor Robert Stark to provide his expert opinion. Stark was a cardiac specialist. At a fit and well-dressed 5′10″, he was the degree of "attractive" that you might see on the cover of *GQ*. If you were a casting director on a soap opera, handing this guy a part on the show would've been a no-brainer. Highly intelligent. Knowledgeable in the field. Unassuming. Well groomed.

Anyway, he stepped up onto the podium and kicked off his speech. From our industry's perspective, it peaked right about here: "It's my professional opinion that taking these herbal ephedrine products is no more harmful than taking a Sudafed," he said. "In fact, I can think of no other over-the-counter product sold today safer than these herbal ephedrine products."

It's an interesting point that Stark made, comparing ephedrine products to OTC products, and it's one worth pursuing here. The entire basis for the FDA's proposed ban on ephedrine was that the supplement was unsafe (even for a healthy adult) when taken in conjunction with the consumption of caffeine. Okay. Let's assume that this is true. Let's assume that caffeine and ephedrine, when mixed, represent a lethal cocktail for even the healthiest among us.

If we can assume this (false) notion, then the ban of either ephedrine or caffeine (or perhaps even both) seems reasonable. It seems completely justified. But how do you justify banning only certain ephedrine products and not others? Well, in 1997 (and beyond), that's exactly what the FDA tried to do.

See, Metabolife—one of the weight loss dietary supplements at risk of being banned—contained twelve milligrams of ephedrine. Your standard dose of Sudafed or Primatene, meanwhile, contains *nearly three times as much* (thirty milligrams). So we have two products, each with a given sum of the notorious active ingredient known as ephedrine.

To this day, it baffles me how the FDA could even propose a ban on a product containing twelve milligrams of ephedrine while simultaneously refusing to ban a product that contains thirty milligrams. But that's what they did. The FDA *never once* suggested that the ephedrine ban should apply to anything other than dietary supplements dedicated to energy or weight loss.

Why would the ban not apply to OTC drugs containing *significantly more* ephedrine than Metabolife? Why wouldn't the warning label requirements extend to products like Sudafed, Primatene, and the vast majority of allergy medications? Why is it that, even today, a consumer can read the label on a package of Primatene and see one thing ("30 mg of ephedrine") and not another ("Do not drink or otherwise consume caffeine in conjunction with the use of this product")?

At the same time, you've got products on the market that contain loads of caffeine. Why aren't Coke and Pepsi required to print warnings about the danger of drinking their product in conjunction with taking a cold tablet? And why aren't the two products being sued by the people who take them at the same time and are harmed as a result? Odd.

I believe that the answer to this question is simple: For a healthy adult, consuming twelve milligrams of ephedrine in conjunction with caffeine is *completely harmless.* There's plenty of scientific proof that this is the case, but just in case you're not one for science, I'd like to take a page out of the FDA's playbook and offer a little anecdotal proof, as well. Consider this: People take Sudafed and many other remedies containing ephedrine because they have a cold. And when you have a cold, what's one of the first things that you do to help alleviate the symptoms? In my house, we drink tea. A caffeinated beverage. If the combination of ephedrine and caffeine is as dangerous as the FDA would lead us all to believe, how could they continue to allow us to take Sudafed without warning us not to drink coffee or tea at the same time? And further, since they *aren't* providing this warning, *why isn't anyone dying?* Why aren't those companies being sued for hurting people? Odd.

And I think this question rang true in 1997, because with our experts backing us up, we managed to survive another year without a ban.

Unfortunately for our industry and our happy consumers, the FDA, working behind the scenes with TDH, kept pressing. In fact, during the ensuing year, political clout behind the opposition *really* started to mobilize. The engines of change began to rev the day that a new Texas health commissioner, Doctor Reyn Archer, took the top job at TDH under significant controversy. Despite all his purported political misgivings, when Archer first took office, he seemed to have a singular goal in mind: to ban dietary supplements containing herbal ephedrine.

And how did I feel about the new boss? Like I did about any politician: that while Archer's intentions were certainly pure, his *motivations* had been improperly biased by all the misinformation floating around about our industry.

Given the fact that our opposition's power was mounting, it only seemed appropriate that the herbal supplement community also be represented. And I felt obligated to lend voice to the industry. So I spoke to Texas Senator Jeff Wentworth (at the time, he was sympathetic to our cause) and asked him to arrange a meeting with the new head of TDH. [74]

The meeting would fall on July 2, 1998, which happened to coincide with the Sunset Commission hearings being conducted in Texas at the time. What happens at the Sunset Commission is this: Every seven or eight years, the state legislators review all the agencies in Texas. During the review, they approve or revise budgets, craft agendas, make sure each agency is up to task, etc. So to meet that end, the heads of every department have to go into the commission and talk to the legislators on the floor. The result: The legislators can rest comfortably for another seven or eight years "knowing" that the bureaucrats are doing what they're supposed to be doing.

So Reyn Archer, an OB/GYN, was the son of a powerful U.S. congressman named Bill Archer. He might have been portrayed in the media as a right-wing lackey for Bush, but I found him to be a bright, intelligent, and well-intentioned individual. An emotional guy—always very passionate about everything he did. My impression of his early moves in his post as commissioner was that he intended to make TDH the pinnacle of U.S. health departments. He wanted Texas to be the beacon toward which all other health services drifted. The only problem was that the self-righteous bureaucrats already in power didn't like him coming into their realm and trying to make change.

So I'm in Archer's office with Senator Wentworth, wondering what in the hell I'd be up against. Archer himself is in speaking to

---

[74] Despite what the press may have suggested, I had no dark motives for the meeting. Archer and Wentworth didn't receive any kickbacks from Metabolife. I merely wanted to educate the new head of TDH on the benefits of natural remedies.

the commission at the moment, so Wentworth and I are alone, sitting on the sofa that the new head of TDH had set up across from his desk. Plush, traditional-looking office. Nice and large. A desk and chairs constructed of clearly sturdy, dark wood. Kind of like a doctor's personal office, or maybe a lawyer's—only far bigger (at probably 300 square feet).

"Nice place, huh?" Wentworth asks.

I nod in reply, taking it all in.

Wentworth's a distinguished-looking guy. Thin. Dark hair. He took his job as a state senator seriously, always weighing both sides of the argument before making decisions. The kind of guy who always tries to do the right thing. Seriously, one of the most respectful and honest men I've ever met. And a great family man.

"So he's in there with the commission right now?" I ask.

Wentworth nods.

"When's he due in?"

Wentworth shrugs.

As if on cue, Archer comes bursting through the door. He's fuming mad.

Oblivious, I get up to introduce myself, extending my hand.

"Please sit down," Archer says, all Texas-gentlemanly, despite his clear anger.

He's soft-spoken, I notice. Well-dressed and groomed. Maybe on the smaller side, at a fit 5'7". Good-looking. And as the conversation would progress, I'd also notice that, unlike most people in positions of power, he never really raised his voice. And he certainly never cussed.

"I don't appreciate what you did to me in there," he says, scolding me now as I sit in one of the sturdy wooden chairs across from his desk.

Wentworth takes a seat next to me.

"What do you mean?" I ask, confused. "I've been in here the whole time."

Archer points at the door behind us. "No," he says. "I mean

your silk-suited lawyers. They accused me of things and I don't even know what they were talking about."

"My lawyers?" I ask, honestly wondering if I'd even brought lawyers on this trip.

"Yeah, those silk-wearing New York attorneys in there. You know, if you wanted a sympathetic ear, you could've planned things a little better."

I calmly stand and extend my hands to either side. "Look," I say slowly, "this I promise you: I don't know anything about the guys from New York. And two, I'm never going to lie to you or stab you in the back. You have my word."

This seems to calm Archer a little. "Those weren't your lawyers?"

"No."

"Then whose were they?"

I shine a little half-smile. "I have no idea."

Archer finally sits, so I join him. We all kind of size each other up for a moment.

"I know exactly how it feels to go through what you just went through," I say. "I've been fighting the wolves at hearings like these every year since '95."

Archer places both hands on his desk and takes a deep, audible breath. "Fine then," he says. "Ellis, is it?"

I nod.

"Well, Mr. Ellis. You called this meeting. What can I do for you?"

I lean forward. "Complementary medicine," I say simply.

"Complementary medicine?"

I go on to explain my belief that there is room in this country for pharmaceutical, reactionary medications as well as natural, preventative supplements. He seemed to agree with just about everything I presented.

"Yeah," he says, interrupting me on a rant about the FDA. "I'm not sure I like how the FDA is going about their business. They're refuting science without providing any science of their own."

I nod vigorously. "It's like they don't believe in dietary supplements.

They're a regulator that's regulating something they don't believe in."

Archer clucks his tongue. "Like asking a fox to guard your henhouse."

I laugh.

"Listen, Mike," he says, extending a finger to the air. "Things will change when I'm running that administration."

"What do you mean?"

"This job…" He seems unsure about how much he should reveal. He speaks slowly. "If I do it right…it's a step in that direction."

"So you think you might be tapped to head the FDA?"

He nods delicately. "I tell you what, though. If I am, I'd like to involve the dietary supplement industry and its consumers to come up with a responsible way to regulate things. Your industry's reckless right now. They need someone to implement the standards. Good manufacturing practices. That sort of thing."

"I couldn't agree more," I say. "What about labeling?"

"What about it?"

"We have to get the warnings down. Standardize them."

Archer's eyebrows blow back. "Aren't there already standards for that?"

I shake my head. "See, any product is unsafe if it's abused. You can overdose on water if you drink too much. But, here, the FDA's trying to ban ephedrine because some companies aren't following the highest standards and some consumers don't know how to take the supplement the right way."

The head of TDH nods thoughtfully, pressing his fingertips together.

"It's like, you see, a speed limit sign that says '65 mph' and you have a person who drives eighty and dies in an accident. Do you ban cars?"

Archer shakes his head slowly.

"Banning ephedrine for someone who doesn't read the label is like banning cars for someone who ignores that speed sign."

Wentworth chuckles and Archer can't seem to stop shaking his head.

"Or if someone sees a bridge, then goes and jumps from the bridge, do we ban bridges?"

Archer laughs.

So the new head of TDH *understood*. While he might have come into the room distrusting ephedrine products, by the time I finished presenting the science and history behind the supplement, he began to realize that it wasn't the supplement itself that was to blame, but the lack of industry standards. He figured there should be a law that would better suit the consumers—one that would ensure that everyone was getting safe products. He didn't care who was doing the manufacturing. He just wanted safety for the consumer.

So it was refreshing to deal with a regulator who thought that way—one who understood that you can't control reckless consumers; that every product in every industry is going to have a few customers who don't heed proper warnings or even use common sense. No, for Archer, the task at hand was not a ban on a safe product; it was an all-encompassing regulatory effort on an otherwise unregulated industry. And I couldn't have agreed with him more.

With Archer now willing to keep in mind the concerns of the legislation, the consumers, and the industry all at once, we could finally move forward with an agenda to clean up the way in which dietary supplement companies did business. To this end, Archer set up a session with key legislators, consumer advocates, and a few representatives from the industry. It wasn't a formal commission. Just an opportunity to clear the air a little.

In my first meeting in Archer's office, as part of my presentation on the safety of ephedrine, I'd fully disclosed what we at Metabolife were hearing from our consumers. Given our openness to the cause, Archer had decided that he wanted to work directly with me and ST&T on the implementation of Metabolife's customer call program for the rest of the industry.[75]

During this informal session before Reyn, I completely explicated on the call system, the kinds of calls we were getting, and what we were doing to follow up. I explained that in every case we'd investigated from a medical standpoint, we'd discovered that no claims could be directly attributed to the use of Metabolife.

Several attorneys were present during this session, and they seemed to be doing their best to keep everyone in the room completely confused. It got to the point where they responded to pretty much everything any of us said, confounding it with legal jargon and convoluted questions.

After the latest round of lawyer-speak, I glanced over at Senator Wentworth, who appeared to be almost as frustrated as I was confused. "You know, Reyn," he said suddenly, "we're not really getting anywhere with this. Why don't we consider calling a negotiated rulemaking session?"

Archer leaned back in his chair, nodding once. "That's not a bad idea, Jeff," he said. "I'll look into it."

Sometime later—several months, if memory serves—Archer did call his negotiated rulemaking session. For the session, I'd been appointed to speak on behalf of the industry while Archer would speak for the state. Together, we would come up with the most appropriate labeling to ensure consumer safety.

---

[75] Two things about this point that the media has tried to spin for years: 1) Metabolife didn't line Archer's pockets to get ourselves into some kind of favored position and 2) the fact that we so willingly granted access to all of our call records to an appointed health department official is conveniently left out of the stories alleging that we were hiding our call records from the FDA. See, as the years went by (and the crusade against ephedrine continued), the FDA would continue to say that Metabolife refused to turn over its call records. Strange logic, given that we kept records of every single call we received and shared them so willingly with every personal injury attorney who ever brought a case against us. Funny, too, how even with access to those supposedly damaging call records, those PI attorneys so rarely managed to construct even a reasonable case against us.

We held the thing in a large conference room in the Texas Department of Health building. They'd set up square tables around the perimeter of the room, with rows of chairs lined on the outside. This way, everyone could see each other. Each chair had been filled with either an industry or TDH representative. A stenographer sat in the corner, keeping track of the proceedings. And we'd make her job easier by setting the rules like so: Only Archer and I were allowed to talk.

I remember entering the room feeling unprepared. How could I even hope to prepare myself, though, really? Here I was, supposed to make decisions for an entire industry without discussing anything with anyone else. Still, it wouldn't be long before I could regain my confidence, reminding myself that no matter what happened in this room, no matter whose toes I might be stepping on with this regulation or that, in the end, all that mattered was consumer safety. And Archer and I agreed fully on the importance of that point.

The moment the session kicked off, Archer and I began negotiating back and forth on each of the agenda items. Labeling and dosage, who should be allowed to take the products, how to handle the reporting of claims. That sort of thing. By the end of the long session, we'd come to a position that we both felt comfortable with.

Was everyone in the industry happy with the results? Probably not. They now had far tighter labeling and reporting standards to adhere to, after all. And many of them would have to lower their dosages of active ingredients. Was TDH happy? Definitely not. Our agreement meant that they weren't going to get their ban on herbal ephedrine—a ban they clearly longed for, for whatever reason.

And they would still be our biggest hurdle, the bureaucrats at TDH. See, their reactions during the meeting suggested to me that they didn't care for Archer—and that Archer probably wouldn't be long for the Texas Department of Health (he'd just made too many enemies already). Unfortunately, the next step for Archer would be to present our agreement to the very people at the board of health who seemed to despise me so much. I knew they wouldn't receive it well. Unless, of course, I met with all of them individually and gave them the same speech about safety and efficacy that I'd given to Archer...

So that's what I did.

At the end of each of these face-to-face meetings, I found that everyone, once they'd been educated on the facts of herbal ephedrine—and allowed to look past the propaganda against Metabolife and others in the industry—was willing to sign the agreement and pass it into law.

But in true bureaucratic fashion, signatures behind closed doors don't count. We still had to have a formal, collective meeting so everyone could sign in front of everyone else.

I wasn't allowed to attend this meeting but, unfortunately, my likeness still managed to make its way into the building. In the worst way...

From what I've heard, during the proceedings, somebody came in at the last minute and presented a copy of a report by WCVB, a news station out of Boston. I remember the moment I first heard the news that it had been presented to the commission. I remember I was playing with one of those little stress balls that you squeeze.

"You mean the report claiming that I was a drug dealer?" I asked Dominic, falling back into my chair.

He nodded solemnly.

By 1999, for whatever reason, the media had begun a full-scale encroachment on my personal life. I'm not sure how or why they got the information on my criminal history, but at the time, I couldn't even begin to imagine how far they would take it.

"But it's more than that," Dominic said. "The reporter on the piece...this Susan Warnick...she's saying that Metabolife is *killing people.*"

I dropped the stress ball. It bounced on the floor, kicked off the toe of my shoe, and rolled under my desk and into the corner. Dominic turned and watched it roll as if rapt.

"You've got to be kidding me," I said.

Dominic shook his head.

"Oh my God," I said. "That'll ruin everything."

Dominic nodded sympathetically.

I couldn't believe what was happening. "The labeling," I breathed. "The safety standards. It'll all fly out the window."

Dominic sighed.

"So what happened after they played it?" I asked.

"The commission wanted some time to think it over, I guess."

My heart sank. "They won't sign."

"Maybe they will," Dominic said in soothing tones. "You can't know that."

I pounded my fist on my desk. "The whole industry will be allowed to go unchecked for another year!"

Dominic shook his head sadly. "I don't know what to tell you, Mike. Let's just hope they see through the bullshit."

So everyone at the commission viewed the report claiming that I was a meth dealer, a cheater and a liar, and, more importantly, that my product was killing people. Right on the day of the signing.

But my reputation wasn't what concerned me. What concerned me was that we'd finally taken the steps necessary to regulate the industry—to once and for all put the negative herbal ephedrine propaganda to bed—and in one fell swoop, the media had slammed the doors on us.

Obviously, the WCVB report put everyone in an awkward position. But you know what? Dominic was right. Archer managed to see beyond the media, keeping his focus on what was better for the consumers of ephedrine. To placate all the naysayers at TDH, he simply called for the addition of a few changes to our agreement. Appeased, the board signed.

And you know what? Archer, despite all the eleventh hour rhetoric, did the right thing.

Chapter 14

Send in the Clowns

With the Texas Department of Health now backing us, we were naïve enough to think that we could sway the FDA into realizing that they had made a mistake in their persecution of herbal ephedrine. So, operating under that (obviously misguided) notion, we ramped up our efforts to get an audience with key people at the agency.

To our delight, the FDA finally agreed to meet with us. Garry Pay's former firm, Patton Boggs, had managed to set up a meeting with several representatives from the agency. But they had two conditions for convening with us: 1) We wouldn't bring a stenographer and 2) we would agree not to record the proceedings with any other kind of recording device. I can't say as I ever understood why they would so clearly demand to remain off-the-record, but the FDA was adamant about it, claiming that they would cancel the meeting if we tried to record the dialogue in any way.

Still, we were thrilled to finally have our audience with the FDA. So despite the odd requests, we agreed to go through with the whole affair at the FDA building in Washington, D.C.

We brought Dr. Robert Stark along with us, as he was one of many the physicians we'd hired to review all of the scientific literature that the FDA had recently sent over regarding the supposed adverse event reports (AER) attributed to herbal ephedrine. Couple Stark's presence with the full-scale presentation we'd prepared on the science and history of ephedrine, and we felt confident that we would finally be able to sway opinions.

But when we arrived at the FDA building, we were a little surprised to discover that we'd be conducting the meeting in a tiny and uncomfortable meeting room. Terrible lighting. Rickety chairs. Cramped space. It kind of felt like a closet. I remember thinking that if we'd been a pharmaceutical company, we probably would have gotten slightly better treatment.

After taking my wobbly seat, I looked over at the two representatives that the FDA had sent down to greet us. They were clearly underlings. Nobody I'd ever heard of. And they had a bookish, close-minded aura about them. Everything from their expressions to the way they dressed screamed that they felt we were wasting their time.

Before we could even begin with our presentation, we were informed of the ground rules. We were to speak directly to these two reps, but should not expect them to make any comments or answer any questions. On anything. So, basically, it would be like talking to a wall.

Reluctant and confused, I began. "We have Dr. Stark here from Yale to present his findings on ephedra," I said. "Dr. Stark?"

The well-dressed doctor stood and repeated his line from the TDH hearings. "It is my opinion that it's safer to take an ephedra-containing product than to take any over-the-counter drug on the market that I'm aware of. In fact, it's safer than eating shellfish."

Of course I knew that Metabolife was a safe product—and even then, I suspected that the FDA knew it, as well. But to hear it directly from a doctor from Yale? I felt certain that the reps sitting across from us would agree, that they would finally call off the dogs and get their agency working on something that actually needed regulating. To the contrary: The bespectacled underlings seemed to be spending more time yawning and checking their watches than listening. They didn't seem impressed. Not even slightly.

And the moment Dr. Stark finished his talk, they confirmed my fears by immediately excusing themselves.

"But we have more material," I said, standing. "We put together a full scientific presentation."

"That won't be necessary," the male rep said curtly. "We have all we need here."

So that was our big meeting with the Food and Drug Administration. They didn't even have time to hear about the science. I'm telling you, it might seem strange or even unlikely, but we'd come in to give the FDA exactly what they'd been publicly asking for, and those two agency reps couldn't seem to find the door fast enough.

In the spring of 1999, things started getting even weirder. The World Health Organization (WHO), through pressure from the FDA, had recently suggested that ephedra-based products such as Metabolife were being easily and regularly converted into methamphetamine.

When we received notice of the hearing on the matter in D.C., the first thing that leapt out at me was that the proposal called for the ban of herbal ephedra, but not pharmaceutical ephedrine. Apparently, the report claimed that the herbal iteration was the only element being converted to meth. In addition to this strange dichotomy, the supervisor of Food and Applied Nutrition at the FDA, a woman named Doctor Beth Yetli, would be backing the notion that banning herbal ephedra would have no economic impact on the country.

Now, I might have been the subject of increasing media scrutiny at the time, but I knew the first proposal to be backwards and the second proposal to be completely ridiculous. 1) It was pharmaceutical ephedrine, and not herbal ephedra, that was being used to create meth and 2) pulling herbal ephedra off the shelves would have tremendous economic impact.

Naturally, I felt the need to attend the hearing. To stand up for the industry. So there I was, in Washington, D.C. once again, standing before a platform of FDA representatives and in front of a large crowd of industry supporters and customers. Behind the large table ahead of me sat the staffers for Secretary of State Madelyn Albright. I'd spent the morning sitting in a folding chair amongst the crowd. The chairs were set up in two groups with an aisle running down the center—almost like a wedding. The room probably sat 150 people, and all morning, I had gotten the impression that most of them were supporters of the industry. There was plenty of scoffing and jeering going on, anyway. And I saw many faces that I recognized.

So after a morning of waiting, my heart skipped when I realized that it was finally my turn to speak. As I stepped to the podium, I did what I could to build my confidence. I reminded myself that Hauser Labs (a facility licensed under the DEA to conduct the published street method for converting Metabolife into methamphetamine) had put our product through the ringer. They had done everything under the published street method to convert Metabolife 356 into meth. And you know what? They'd *failed*. Despite their efforts, they couldn't manufacture methamphetamine with our product. All they could create was tar. The conclusion? That it is simply not possible to convert Metabolife into methamphetamine using the street method. More than that, it didn't seem possible to convert herbal ephedra *of any kind* into meth.

I also reminded myself that the DEA agents working on the project had assured me that in all their years in the agency, they had never caught or even heard of *a single person* using Metabolife or any similar product to manufacture meth.

But my primary concern as I stood before these officials

wasn't to battle against conception. I wasn't there to refute claims that it was even possible to use my product to create illicit street drugs. I was there to discuss the potential economic impact—to put to rest the ridiculous claim that banning our product wouldn't upset the order of the American economy—and to discuss the safety of Metabolife itself.

I took a deep breath and began. "Esteemed members of the secretary of state's office," I said, "members of the FDA, thank you for allowing me the opportunity to be here today." I scanned the several people sitting on the panel. A varying array of confused, skeptical, and accusatory faces gazed back at me.

Concerned, I continued. "I'm here to address the claim that banning Metabolife and other herbal ephedra products would have no economic impact."

I noticed Yetli. She seemed to be doing what she could to avoid my eyes. Loudly shuffling through papers, she shook her head slowly, like an outraged parent. She was a woman in her fifties. Maybe 5′5″. Kind of chubby. She wore really old, out-dated, baggy clothes, I noticed. And she seemed to be having trouble clearing her throat as I spoke.

"To begin," I said, "let me just say that the claim could not be more false. Over the course of this year, Metabolife had more servings taken than the complete array of Tylenol cold, flu, cough, and sinus remedies *combined.*"

Many of the secretary of state's people seemed to react with surprise to that one. As I watched their expressions flash to shock, I felt pretty good about things. Like I'd turned the tide already.

So I hit them with the big stick. "Seventy-five thousand Metabolife tablets will be taken in the U.S. alone during the time it takes me to finish this presentation."

Stunned silence.

Feeling like I'd won them over on the economic impact, I decided to switch gears and discuss safety. I figured that maybe if Secretary Albright's people could see the light, we could finally put this whole issue to bed.

The Greatest Post-Market Survey Ever Conducted[76]	
World population (total number of living people on the planet)	6.72 billion
Total number of servings of Metabolife consumed	7 billion
Total number of people who called with health-related inquiries	14,000
Total number of so-called "sentinel events"	3
Total number of cases directly attributable to Metabolife	0

I felt pretty good about the numbers I'd presented about my company because they involved the government's own people demonstrating that herbal ephedrine was incredibly safe. *Any* company with total servings eclipsing the world population—any company who could expect a given number of people to consume its product more than seven billion times in a ten-year period—could expect at least three significant health-related events. For example, if you knew that seven billion people were going to eat a grape, how many of them would you expect to choke to death? That's a whole lot of people swallowing a whole lot of grapes. And if three of them *did* choke to death, would that mean that grapes are unsafe? Would it mean that we should pull grapes off the market entirely?

[76] These conclusions were reached in 2003 by the investigative arm for the United States Congress, the Government Accounting Office (GAO) and the RAND, a think tank that had been hired by the FDA to come up with a conclusion regarding the AER call records submitted to the FDA by Metabolife. This was actually reviewed in 2003. I never submitted this at the hearing.

Now…what if you could offer certifiable scientific proof that the grapes themselves weren't the cause of the choking deaths?

Let's move away from grapes for a moment and examine a product a little more similar to Metabolife: aspirin. Out of every 5,000 people who take aspirin—only 5,000 people—at least *one* will have an adverse event. So if you have seven billion servings of aspirin, you might be able to expect as many as 1.4 *million* significant health concerns. That's a slightly higher number than three. Should we ban aspirin? Should we eliminate a product that has saved countless lives?

So my ten-minute speech went off without a hitch. As I concluded, I felt confident that I had won over the crowd of doubters—or at least all of those on the fence. Yetli confirmed my suspicion by continuing to avoid eye contact.

Anyway, the chairperson thanked me and I took my seat. Then, we all waited for the other reps, some from the FDA and some from the industry, to present their arguments.

When the meeting had concluded, many of us kind of milled around as we waited for people to leave. As I stood from my folding chair, I was approached by a man who I knew to be with the FDA. I'd seen him before at industry meetings, anyway. To respect his privacy, we'll call him "Phil." Like everyone else in the room, Phil wore a suit. And he carried a deep look of surprise as he approached me.

"That was quite a speech," Phil said. "I had no idea."

"You're with the FDA, right?" I asked.

Phil nodded.

"Yeah," I said. "Before today, it seemed like you guys didn't even know that I existed." I tapped Phil on the shoulder. Nice suit. Suede. "But listen, now that you know, we need to work together on the problem."

Phil shook his head distantly, his eyes darting all around the room. "Christ," he said bluntly. "I had no idea." He finally looked me in the eye. "You guys are bigger than some pharmaceutical companies."

I noticed Yetli out of the corner of my eye. She seemed to be approaching, so I waited with baited breath for her to join in on the conversation. But she just kept walking on by.

I nodded to Phil. "We are."

The FDA rep began to get all blustery. "I mean, that's a lot of clout you've got behind you. You're no drop in the bucket."

"This is ridiculous, you know," I said. "Banning herbal ephedra and allowing pharmaceutical ephedrine."

My new best friend nodded mournfully. "I think the FDA's just concerned that there aren't enough regulations behind supplements."

I brightened up, patting Phil's suede-clad shoulder again. "So let's work together. Let's figure out how to regulate the industry."

"Not a bad idea," Phil said.

"I mean, we shouldn't be fighting about product viability. We should be working on ways to make everything safer. We've got to standardize harvesting, manufacturing, labeling, everything."

I heard no disagreement there.

So I left feeling good about how everything had gone down. If Albright's people were nodding in agreement—and if one of the FDA's own people seemed to be on board with our regulation agenda—then I *knew* that saner times lay ahead.

On my first morning back from this latest trip to D.C., I learned that no matter what we did or how we performed in front of representatives of state, we wouldn't be free from continued encroachment by the media. For whatever reason, the media had gotten itself under the impression that ephedra was just a natural iteration of meth, that it was entirely unsafe for everyone, and that Blevins, Bradley, and I were the kinds of corporate leaders that America just couldn't trust.

So I'm sitting over a cup of coffee on a Monday morning. My wife sits at the head of the table, diagonal from me. Monica, now a stay-at-home mom, eats her bowl of cereal, knowing the kids will wake up soon. I'm letting my coffee cool because I'm too busy poring over the latest *San Diego Union Tribune* article on my company.

"What's with this Crabtree?" I ask.

"Crabtree?" Monica says obliviously. "What crabtree?"

"Penny Crabtree. That writer from the paper who seems to have it in for us."

Monica shrugs.

"She keeps calling me a meth dealer in here. Says the product is causing deaths."

Monica suddenly looks and sounds completely aggravated. "I can't believe that woman. What's she got against us, anyway?"

"I don't know," I say. "But she might as well have said I eat babies."

"Why do we buy this rag newspaper, anyway?"

I grin cathartically and take a drink of my coffee. It's so cold by now that I spit it back out. I've suddenly lost my need for caffeine, anyway. So I get up and dump the contents of my mug into the sink.

Despite my demeanor, I'm furious. I decide that the only thing I can do to take my mind off Crabtree's vendetta is to go to work. So I grab my shoes and head for the door. "I'm gonna go," I say back over my shoulder.

"Have a great day at work," Monica says from the kitchen.

I reach for the door, forcing some air through my teeth, seething. Without another word, I hop in the car (a Mercedes SL 500) and head down the driveway. By the time I reach the end, I notice that I'm running on empty. So I take it to the nearest gas station.

As I'm standing by my car, filling up, I hear a voice from over my shoulder.

"Hey, Mike! Mike Ellis!"

I turn and see a face I recognize from the neighborhood. But I've never talked to this man before.

"Hey…neighbor," I say.

My neighbor introduces himself. I shake his hand.

"Ugly morning, eh?" he says.

I take a quick look around. "What? What do you mean? It's beautiful out here."

The neighbor chuckles uncomfortably. "No," he says. "I mean the papers. I read that story about you."

"Oh," I say. The level of awkwardness between us suddenly peaks.

"You're famous," my neighbor says.

I nod my head back. "You mean infamous."

This straightens my neighbor up. He doesn't seem to get dark humor. "Well," he says seriously, "you know that none of us in the neighborhood believe a word of it. We all know you're a great guy."

My gas pump clicks off. Full tank. And it's all so surreal, standing here with this grinning and genuflecting best friend I've never met. Like I've walked into an entirely new life. *How could the neighborhood know I'm a great guy?* I think. None of them had ever even made an effort to get to know me. Now, suddenly, I'm the king of the neighborhood.

Confused, I thank my neighbor and say goodbye.

By this point, I wanted to be at work so badly that I couldn't even think of anything else. So I hopped into the Mercedes and let its German engine roar down I-5 to the Metabolife offices.

Traffic remained light because it was still so early. The parking lot was basically empty, too, except for a media van near the corner, as far away from the front entrance as possible. I shook my head as I parked in my assigned space, knowing that, somewhere, some reporter would be waiting to pounce.

I slammed the door of my car and stepped out, looking from side to side like some kind of casually dressed secret agent. Then, I made straight for the door.

Just before I got to the handle, a figure leapt from the bushes next to the entryway. The *bushes*. Stunned, I stepped back and took a moment to gather myself. Clearly, another reporter. This one stood, wobbling in place as she rifled around for her tape recorder. Her hair was disheveled and her clothes a mess. She'd been hiding in the freaking *bushes*.

"How long do you think your company can hide the fact that it's a dealer of legal methamphetamine?" she asked.

I waved my hand defensively and brushed her aside. "Are you serious?" I said. "No comment."

The reporter tried to get my attention again, but I pushed through the door, leaving her in my wake. For her part, she stayed outside. I guess she figured I had security guards inside who would toss her out if she followed. If only that had been true.

As I sat behind my desk, my frustrated head in my hands, I thought about all the reasons the industry had gotten to this point. All the reasons the walls seemed to be closing in on our dietary supplement company...

In the middle to late '90s, all kinds of strange misinformation began to surface about herbal ephedrine. That it caused heart attacks, stroke, and arrhythmia. The smear campaign was so effective that it actually managed to convince many politicians to ignore the piles of contradictory science and the 5,000 years of evidence of ephedrine safety. See, ephedra is one of the only herbal elements to be found in the gravesites of Neanderthal man. So in other words, even back when we were living in caves, people saw the value in it. Strange, then, that such a powerful regulatory industry didn't see the value in it now. But the FDA, for the ten-year period between 1994 and 2004, made any negative allegation it could about ephedra or ma huang.

Anyway, still steamed, I got up to search the filing cabinet in the corner of my office—the place where I kept all my personal copies of white paper on the industry. What was I looking for? Something to distract me: the latest report from the FDA on the so-called adverse event reports attributed to ephedrine products.

But when I found the paper, I discovered that it only made me angrier. See, these adverse event reports (AER) cut straight to the heart of the matter. What makes for an adverse event? Even though the FDA was using the concept in the media—in the hopes of discrediting the entire industry, apparently—they never managed to define the answer to that question. So we were told that we had to report these adverse events to the FDA, but never told what an adverse event was in the first place.

Basically, all of us in the industry were sort of feeling around in the dark—very few companies even carrying the same understanding of an AER. We at Metabolife always believed that an adverse event meant that your product had *caused* a medical issue, not just that someone had called in and made an anecdotal claim. But the FDA would eventually evolve their opinion on the matter to the point where *any* call that your company received (for anything as simple as a mild headache) amounted to an AER. In other words, their eventual definition of an AER was *any* anecdotal report claiming an adverse event.

So what's the trouble with anecdotal reporting? For one thing, by nature, it doesn't prove (or even imply) causality. For example, imagine that someone you know gets into a car accident. They claim that it wasn't their fault because their tires blew out and they lost control. Now, you might believe their story. You might take their anecdotal claim at face value. But anecdotal claims often have a weakness: They aren't supported with hard evidence. What do I mean by this? Imagine that you don't take your friend's story at face value. Imagine that you decide to go and investigate the crash site— and that, when you get there, you discover that all four tires are in perfect condition. Do you still believe your friend's story? Of course not. It's lost all credibility.

This is obviously just one simplified example, but make no mistake, anecdotal reporting *as a practice* carries almost zero credibility. If we consider an anecdote to be an AER—the ultimate black mark on a company's record (from the FDA's perspective)—then an AER could amount to a concerned caller with heart palpitations, or it could be little more than a bored individual who just wants to cause some trouble for the FDA.

Let's look at this kind of reporting from another angle. Typically, whatever reports the FDA receives on a given product, it considers them to be little more than static. Normal feedback from people anxious to blame an adverse event on something they took. Don't believe me? Get online and take a look at the FDA's anecdotal reporting system (they publish the reports they receive on every product). If you pull up vitamin C—a supplement that I think most of us can agree to be completely innocuous and beneficial to our health—you find numerous calls from people claiming to have had a stroke, seizure, or heart attack *because of vitamin C*. So if we are to believe the practice of anecdotal reporting, vitamin C is at least as "dangerous" as herbal ephedrine. If all these people are "suffering strokes, seizures, and heart attacks," shouldn't we ban vitamin C, as well?

And therein lies the problem. Almost any product on the market bears anecdotal reports regarding the exact same "events."

How can we explain such a phenomenon? By chalking it up to natural human behavior. Consider this: Recall the last time you talked to somebody and they said, "Gosh, I don't feel good."

"What's wrong?" you probably said.

What do they almost always say? They almost always say, "I guess it's something I ate last night."

You look this person over. They're green, clammy, obviously shivering, clearly ill. They have the flu—and the funny thing is that their *first instinct* is to blame the food they've eaten.

Almost all of us have a tendency to blame our ills on the things that we consume. How many times have you thought you had food poisoning, only to discover later that you had the flu? The same common mistake applies to the combination of virtually any ailment and any consumable. If someone with poor eating habits has a stroke on the day that they take a vitamin C supplement for the first time, they might well blame the vitamin C.

So that's what's wrong with anecdotal reporting. And as expected, without any effort to prove or disprove the callers' claims, the FDA's number of "adverse events" in our industry grew pretty quickly.

Anyway, I took the latest FDA report back to my desk and had a seat. After running through the numbers, I eyed up the phone, feeling the urge to call someone at the agency to set up another meeting. Anything to get the ball rolling again. But I knew it would be a waste of time. Even after our first ridiculous meeting in D.C., we were always trying to create dialogue with the FDA. But they would refuse.

During the period between 1994 and 2004, our industry associations bent over backwards to set up the very same scientific studies that the FDA claimed we were lacking. Those studies, in turn, showed that herbal ephedrine is safe when used as directed.

Completely safe. What did FDA do in response? They *attacked the credibility of the scientists.*

So in summary, here is the playbook on how the FDA achieved and maintained its leverage against herbal ephedrine:

- Claimed that the product was causing innumerable adverse events to American consumers
- Refused to even define what an adverse event was
- Used anecdotal reporting to "demonstrate" the dangers that the product posed to the people
- Failed to set up scientific studies of their own to prove their case against the product
- Harped on the industry for not putting together "sufficient scientific evidence" in support of the safety and efficacy of its product
- Put all their weight behind a campaign to discredit the scientists involved in any and all safety and efficacy studies sponsored by the industry

That last point always gets to me. I'd like to know how much money the FDA spent on their campaigns to discredit our safety studies. And in the end, these campaigns were essentially pointing at doctors and scientists from Yale, Harvard, Columbia, and many more of our country's most distinguished and credible universities and calling them quacks.[77]

---

[77] And all of this for what, exactly? A playbook like this might make sense if you assume that the FDA had some working knowledge of the supposed dangers of ephedrine. If what they were after truly was a ban on ephedrine, then you can forgive their aggressiveness. Hell, you could even condone it. The only problem is that recent history shows us that they weren't after a ban on ephedrine. They weren't out to bring down a supposedly dangerous product. The only thing they banned was ephedrine in its herbal form. To this day—even after the ephedrine ban—you can still buy ephedrine weight loss products (all with larger doses of ephedrine than Metabolife ever had). The only difference is that you have to buy it from a pharmaceutical company. Don't believe me? Check out www.buyvasoproephedrine.com/metabodrene356.html.

Obviously, since this whole drama was just beginning to unfold before my eyes on that morning, I remained pretty upset. So I picked up the phone and dialed Dominic's cell, hoping like hell that he'd answer.

In three rings, he picked up, sounding a little winded. "Dominic Johnson," he said.

"Dominic, it's me." Given all the media scrutiny, my PR man and I were on an "it's me" basis by then.

"Hey, Mike."

"Yeah, listen," I said, "I'm having a media meltdown here. I need to talk to you right away."

"I'll be right down. Hey, Mike?"

"Yeah?"

"Everything okay?"

I sighed. "Just get down here, Dominic. We'll sort it out."

As I waited for my PR man, I thought about the many articles I'd read about myself and my product in recent years. My favorite media quote involved the FDA pointing out that ephedrine was only one molecule away from being methamphetamine. Full disclosure: This is true. But it's also true that molecular comparisons are completely ridiculous. See, it's true that if you remove or alter one molecule of ephedrine, you get methamphetamine; but it's also true that if you remove or alter only one molecule of the air we breathe, you die. Additionally, it's true that humans and chimpanzees share ninety-seven percent of their genetic makeup. So we're only three percent different from a chimp.

From a scientific basis, claiming a one-molecule difference is pretty lame. The process of changing, removing, or adding a single molecule from a substance is incredibly elaborate. And it's crazy to suggest otherwise. But, well, the media picked up on it. The idea sold copy, after all.

Anyway, Dominic came bursting in without knocking, which was pretty customary by then. He had the office next to mine, but I'm sure by this point, my office felt as much like his office as anything.

"Hey, buddy," he said. "Sorry I wasn't in earlier. Still tired from D.C."

"That's fine," I said. "You think we got Albright in our corner?"

"I think so."

"Alright. Well, now I'm more worried about getting the media in our corner."

Dominic shook his head mournfully. "Not easy."

"Some reporter was waiting for me in the bushes this morning."

Dominic scoffed. "Must have learned that one from Warnick."

"Susan Warnick?"

My PR man nodded.

"The one from WCVB?"

"Yep. Caught her waiting in the bushes a week or so back."

"You gotta be kidding me."

Dominic playfully thrusted his hands to either side. "See? We should have dogs."

I shook my head, having heard this one before. "But Warnick would bite the dogs," I offered.

Dominic laughed. "So another one in the fucking bushes, huh?"

"The bushes."

My PR man smiled, apparently still trying to lighten the mood. "You should've seen Warnick last week. Trying to interview employees. Looking like some kind of cracked-out secret agent."

"Yeah, only with eight gallons of makeup."

Dominic laughed again.

"What's her deal, anyway?" I asked. "Why's she got it in for us? Did you find out?"

"I think she used to be the anchor out there in Boston." Dominic raised his eyebrows for emphasis. "Used to be. Sounds like she fell out of favor there. So she's a has-been reporter just trying to get back on top. Seems like she's on her way out."

"She's been talking about meth, man."

Dominic leaned forward. "And so has every other reporter for the past few weeks." He's got this calming sense about him. "And we've gotten through that, right?"

I blew some air through my teeth. "Doesn't feel like we've

gotten through anything, Dominic. Feels like we're still fighting the same battles."

Dominic stood, brushing off the gravity of it all. "Trust me, buddy," he said. "The tide's turning. Texas is coming around. Isn't TDH supposed to sign that new labeling legislation this week?"

"Yeah."

"See, that should put everything to bed. You've just got to weather this little shitstorm this week, and then it all goes away."

I truly wanted to feel better, but I couldn't bring myself to come around. "What if it doesn't go away, Dominic?"

Dominic turned to leave, pointing back at me as he did so. "Then we'll fight back."

Given that in the days to come, Dominic kept getting calls from distributors in Boston about Susan Warnick and her increasingly combative news reports, we would decide that we needed to start fighting back sooner rather than later. So we would hire a PR firm called Sitrick and Company. Mike Sitrick and his associate, Tony Night, would agree to come on board to help us fight the PR issues that we saw looming on the horizon.

But even with our new troops on board, the fight would soon take a serious turn against us. Right around this time, we would learn about TDH's private screening of WCVB's stories on Metabolife. The collective reaction to the screening would lead to one important addition to the labeling standards: All companies would now have to print the FDA's 800 number on their labels (something that the FDA, in all its concern for consumer safety, opposed vehemently, for some reason). I had no problem with the addition of the 800 number. In fact, I welcomed it, since it would give consumers an additional number to call if they ever needed advice on how to safely take the product.

The WCVB report being aired in Texas represented that first point where the media began getting its footing in the misguided vendetta against us. And day in and day out for two weeks, Warnick would use this solid footing to run even more damaging stories on Metabolife. With each installment, things got dirtier and more outrageous. And with each installment, media attention across the country began to build.

I remember a night during this hellish two weeks when Blevins, Bradley, and I were all sitting out in the courtyard outside the Metabolife offices. We had just closed up the building and were enjoying a rare moment of peace.

"Listen," I said, "we have to do whatever we can to keep the media's attention on me."

"But they'll bury you," Bob said.

"I don't care about that," I said. "As long as they stay on top of my personal life, none of our customers will really care, either. They'll keep buying the product."

"So the idea, Bob, is to keep the focus off Metabolife," Blevins offered.

"Exactly," I said.

Bob, never really a PR man, seemed confused. "But how do we keep them off the product?" he asked. "They're going to report whatever they want, anyway."

"We defend the product," I said, pounding my fist into my hand for emphasis. "Whenever they write a story about Metabolife, we send in corrections and ask for retractions. Whenever they attack me personally, we just let it slide."

That night, we all agreed that this would work. The media would eventually give up on the story we kept fighting and would most likely assume that they had something to run with on the story we didn't fight. But in order to pull it off, we knew we would need help.

So we did two things:

First, we took the fight to them. To do this, we brought in Akin, Gump and had their reps review everything that was being aired about us in the public eye. Steve Mansfield's own review would suggest that stories like Warnick's were false and misleading—and that these were the kinds of stories we could call for retractions on. In response to our requests for retractions, Warnick would call me out on the air, asking why I continued to refuse to give interviews. From our perspective, it all came across as some kind of childish game. Predictably, the game would only end when we took out a successful lawsuit against WCVB. So despite their certitude on the air (and a tremendous outpouring of support for WCVB on the part of the national media), we'd won the battle against irresponsible and sensationalized journalism. But you didn't hear about *that* in the news.

And, second, we began using their own weaknesses against them. Under the recommendation of Steve Horn and California Creative, the company that was doing all our media buying, we would periodically create and submit our own news segments. To this end, we would get a real doctor and film him caring for a patient he'd put on Metabolife. We would show the patient's before-and-after pictures, show the doctor talking about the product (and discussing warnings and directives), and then cap it all off with an interviewer asking him questions. Basically, we filmed a three-minute commercial regarding the benefits and safety of Metabolife.

See, the reason this strategy was brilliant is because media outlets around the nation have to manage time on their newscasts. Sometimes, they don't have enough news to fill their entire block of time. So they pick up filler and do the "lighter side of the news." Lo and behold, we would have this three-minute broadcast to offer to the stations that couldn't fill all their airtime.

At 2 p.m. a few days each month, we would inform the stations all around the country that we would be bouncing the story via satellite. The stations never knew the source of the story; they only knew what it was about. On any given day, twenty to 100 TV stations would pick up our piece. Many of them would just slice out our interviewer and replace him with their own interviewer. So they were basically running a Metabolife commercial for their broadcasts and presenting it as locally produced news.

Now, were the stories we provided true and accurate? Absolutely. But it just goes to show you the level of research that television media employs. They didn't even check on the source of the story. They just gobbled it up and ran with it, desperate to fill airtime.

So, basically, our two strategies amounted to taking the fight to the media while simultaneously exploiting their own laziness. Whenever we did this, two things would happen: The negative press would cease for a while and sales would explode in the areas that picked up our puff stories.

While we were all happy to be gaining some ground, little did I know then that our strategy would eventually awaken a sleeping giant. It wouldn't take this giant long to strike, either. And there I was, too busy putting out smaller fires to see it coming.

⌐ℳ⌐

Mother's Day, 1999. We've invited Monica's family over to celebrate the occasion with us. With our sprawling home and comfortable digs, we've come a long way from kuka fishing in the streams down in National City. The weather's nice, and so we're all out by the pool, splashing around, soaking up the sun, and enjoying each other's company.

Then, a strange noise from above. The wind picks up as the sound moves closer. It roars now overhead.

Nicholas looks terrified as he paddles to the edge of the pool and pulls himself onto the deck. "What's that, Daddy?" he asks frantically.

I squint through the sun, cupping a hand over my eyes. "It's a helicopter," I say.

"But what's it doing here?" Mikey asks as he comes up beside me.

"It's a news chopper," Monica yells angrily.

A wave of helpless fury washes over me as I continue to shield my eyes from the sun and stare up at the helicopter, trying to make out its call letters. But the chopper's at the wrong angle. Instead, what I see is this: the cameraman leaning out the door, his giant camera lens beaming down on us like some kind of cold, alien face.

"Everybody in the house," I yell.

A mixed response ripples from Monica's family—some of them linger in curiosity while others bolt inside. My children, so used to this kind of media attention by now, waste no time in taking cover. I follow Monica into the house. There in the kitchen, soaking wet and shivering, stand Mikey and Nicholas. The two of them seem frightened out of their wits.

"Don't worry, guys," I say. "They'll go away now that we're inside."

"I wish it would *all* just go away," Mikey says wistfully.

"I know, Mikey. Me, too."

"No," he says, his voice more forceful now. Furious. "You don't understand. I wish all the *money* would go away. I want things to go back to how they were before."

I choke up, unable to think of anything to say.

"No one bothered us when we were poor," my son adds softly.

My eyes brim with tears as a part of me realizes that I feel the same way. On Mother's Day not three years prior, we could only afford hotdogs. How simple life had been. And now we had this giant house and all these luxuries, and what did we have to show for it? An air raid roaring outside.

Chapter 15

Hindsight's 20/20

Thanks to the lawsuit we'd filed against WCVB, we were in the midst of a standstill on the increasingly ridiculous media assaults being leveled against us. This period of sanity proved to be prolonged thanks to Steve Mansfield. See, Steve had had the foresight to keep the claim against WCVB vague. The genius of the tactic was that we'd claimed slander without specifically stating what had been slanderous about the report. So with the country's many media outlets operating in the dark as to what was and wasn't slander, none of them could proceed without fearing a lawsuit of their own. We'd effectively tied their hands.

But our moment of peace would be broken one day when Dominic picked up the phone in my office.

"Dominic Johnson," he said.

I looked up, concerned. Phone calls in those days rarely meant good news.

"Yeah," he said impatiently. "Media relations director for Metabolife and Michael Ellis."

My heart began to pound.

Dominic spent about forever listening to the caller. "What kind of story?"

"Oh, no," I said, my voice cracking under the weight of the constant stress.

"Okay. I'll ask him." He put down the phone. "That was Mary van Horn, producer of *20/20*."

I spit my Skaol into a Styrofoam coffee cup on the corner of my desk.

"She wants *20/20* to do a story on you and Metabolife."

I felt like gagging. "What kind of story?"

Dominic smirked. "She says it's more of a *special interest* story."

I failed to match my PR man's lighthearted mood. "I don't like it."

"Then neither do I."

"Let's call Sitrick first."

Dominic nodded and then dialed Mike Sitrick. Sitrick had already weathered a number of media storms since we'd brought him and his company on to help us. When he answered, Dominic immediately put him on speaker.

"Mike," I said, "it's Ellis and Dominic."

"Hey, Mike. Dominic." He sounded hesitant. Concerned.

"I'm gonna let Dom take over."

"We got a call from Mary van Horn," Dominic chimed in.

"Of *20/20*?" Sitrick asked. This time, he sounded a little more along the lines of "alarmed."

"Yeah," Dominic said.

Sitrick fell noticeably silent. "Who's going to be the reporter?" he finally asked.

Dominic looked at me questioningly. "I don't know," he said. "I'll find out."

We hung up with Sitrick and called Mary at *20/20*, who made no bones about the fact that it would be a guy named Arnold Diaz who would interview me. I listened in on the speakerphone while Dominic talked to Mary. As soon as I heard the name, I logged onto my computer and looked up Diaz on the Internet. I was immediately directed to his website: something called "Shams, Scams, and Save a Buck."

I furrowed my brow. This would be no "special interest story."

"This is no special interest story," I whispered to Dominic, still holding court with Mary. I pointed to the monitor.

Dominic nodded.

"I mean…whose interest?" I said, louder this time.

Dominic smiled wryly. He said his goodbyes and thank you's with van Horn and then immediately hit the speed dial for Sitrick. Pay and Mansfield happened to stroll in just in time for the call.

"Arnold Diaz," Dominic said to Sitrick.

Sitrick groaned loudly over the speaker.

"This doesn't sound too good, Mike," I said naïvely. "Diaz does these *stories*. These…these…*smear campaigns*."

"I don't think we should do it," Sitrick said dryly. "Obviously."

"Me neither," Pay said.

"Second," Mansfield added.

I listened for a while as my attorneys patted each other on the backs about why it would be a good idea to avoid the interview. But while I might have agreed with them at first, I couldn't shake the sinking feeling that we couldn't just ignore the problem and hope it would go away. It felt like maybe if we turned our back on *20/20*, they'd run some kind of sham story, anyway. And if we allowed that to happen, we'd essentially be forfeiting my and my company's right to defend ourselves.

"We can't just cut them off," I said suddenly.

"No, of course not," Sitrick said. "No one's suggesting that."

A potentially great idea suddenly hit me. "Let's send them whatever company information they ask for in connection with the story," I said. "Copies of studies. Info on people taking the product. That kind of thing. Then we'll see what they do with it."

We all agreed. It would be best to string them along and see what would come of things.

So we would send them stuff whenever they asked for it. And they would keep calling back and insisting that they'd gotten conflicting reports—stories like our product had been discovered in the apartment belonging to a meth cook. That sort of thing. But whenever we'd do our research into the matter, we'd find that stories like the one about the meth cook had actually been a matter of the police finding a bottle of Metabolife in the medicine cabinet of the cook's home (nowhere near the site where he'd produced his product). Basically, *20/20* just seemed to be attempting to twist Metabolife into a juicy story. And the more they did this, the more aggravated I became.

So I called Pay, Mansfield, Sitrick, and his associate, Tony Night, into my office. Sitrick strolled in, looking very much in control. An intelligent, attractive, forty-something with thinning hair, Sitrick definitely knew the lay of the land with the national media. And he kept a company with plenty of knowledge, as well. All his employees had once held positions as editors or other positions of high rank in the industry. Snappy dresser, that Sitrick. And a good family man. Committed and passionate about everything he did.

He was followed by Tony Night—all 6′2″ of his large self. Night was the studious type. The kind of guy who does all the research he can for his clients (and in this case, that meant Night learning a whole lot about ephedrine). Non-confrontational. A career PR man who understood that, for whatever reason, our product was getting hosed by the media. But he was no stranger to the concept, after all. See, he and Sitrick had once worked for a company called Food Lion—one of *20/20*'s former marks in their great struggle against "inappropriate business practice."

"Food Lion," Night said, glancing knowingly at Sitrick as he took his seat.

"Food Lion?" Dominic asked.

"Yeah," Sitrick said. "They're that grocery chain in the Southeast. I represented them during their own little *20/20* fiasco."

"What happened?" I asked.

Sitrick nodded at Night, giving him the go-ahead to share the anecdote.

"*20/20* wanted to run a story about Food Lion keeping and selling tainted food, but they couldn't find anything. So they waited for the head of the company to leave, then had one of the workers plant rotten meat in the deli. They did the segment with the planted meat and ran it on the air as if these were Food Lion's standards."

"You've got to be kidding," Mansfield said.

"Nope," Sitrick said solemnly. "There's the Ford Pinto, too."

"You mean that one where they showed the Pinto blowing up?" Pay asked.

"Garry," I said with a smirk, "I didn't know you watched *20/20*."

Garry shrugged it off.

"Yeah, Garry," Sitrick said. "That's the one. The thing about that is that they wanted to show the Pinto blowing up, but couldn't make it blow. So they planted charges in the trunk and fired them off on camera."

We all mulled that one over for a while, shaking our heads in disgust.

"So this is a barbeque and I'm the guest of honor," I said.

"More or less," Night said, extending his hand to demonstrate calm. "But don't worry. We'll take care of it."

"I don't mean to give the wrong impression, here," Sitrick added. "*20/20* is pretty sophisticated. It's just that they're not actually news. They're an entertainment show that portrays itself as news."

"They don't report the news—they *make* the news," I said.

"Exactly."

"And they're trying to *create* news on Metabolife," Pay offered.

Sitrick and Night both nodded.

"That's so unfair to the viewer." Pay looked ready to pound the table with one of his giant fists.

"Do you think they're coming after us because of WCVB?" I asked.

"It's possible," Night said. "They're an ABC affiliate."

More silence for a while. Nobody seemed sure of what to say or do.

"I've got to give the interview," I finally said.

"Mike…" Mansfield said, raising his hands defensively. "The hell you do."

"Don't give the interview," Pay said forcefully.

"No," I said. "Listen. Hear me out."

Pay and Mansfield's faces took on a kind of intense expression.

"If I don't give an interview," I said slowly, "they'll be able to do and say whatever they want about us. I've got to get up there and defend the company."

"You know that's exactly what they want you to think," Night said.

"Of course. They need me in the story because they need to make me the villain."

"They'll do that anyway," Sitrick said matter-of-factly. "They just know that it would be a better ratings grab if they embarrassed the villain on TV."

"Don't do it, Mike," Pay said adamantly. "I don't like it."

"Yeah, Mike," Mansfield chimed in. "We'll have no control over what they put out."

I motioned for silence so I could run something through my head. Mansfield had given me an idea. "But we can control the *environment!*"

"What do you mean?" Sitrick asked.

"We can control what they get on film. We could have the interview at a neutral location. And we could bring our own camera crew so they can't slice and dice it to make us look bad."

Night's eyes lit up. He glanced from face to face around the room, apparently sizing up the support I'd gotten for my concept. "That's a good idea," he said. "But they'll still run their story...and no one will see yours."

"Couldn't hurt," I said. "And we can't just stand on the sidelines while they tear us up."

It took some time, but everyone finally came around on this interview idea. So we contacted van Horn and told her we were in, but only on a few conditions: First, they would have to allow us to record the entire interview with our own camera crew. She had no problem with that. Second, they would have to allow all of our employees—all of the people who would potentially be affected by the interview—to be present at the taping. She seemed confused as to the reason for this second stipulation, but eventually agreed. And finally, we wanted to be able to pick the venue. Again, she agreed. While these might not have been ideal conditions for *20/20,* I guess they just wanted the interview badly enough to do just about anything we asked.

So we needed a venue. And for that, I called Ed Brand—the superintendent of Sweet Water Union High School and a friend with whom I'd help set up a scholarship program for inner city kids. Ed agreed to allow us to use the auditorium at his school, a space plenty big enough to accommodate any and all of Metabolife's employees that might want to come down.

Funny to look back at this story now because Sweet Water was the same high school that my father had attended growing up. Seemed appropriate, even then. Dad was the beginning of my company, and it was only fitting that his former high school would potentially serve as the location where it'd finally come to an end.

On the day of the interview, between me, my lawyers, my PR guys, and some of the Sweet Water Union High School maintenance staff, we set up a great viewing area in the auditorium. The room itself was actually really nice. Carpeted. Acoustically sound. Brown paneled walls decorated with student photos and art. The only thing that was missing when we got there was the seating. And by the time we got all of the rows of chairs we needed ready, evening had set in.

I'd expected a healthy turnout of our employees, but I'm not exaggerating when I say that it felt like every single one of them had turned out for the event. Many of them were filing in and taking their seats—and it already looked like we wouldn't have enough chairs. Outside, about a hundred or so employees stood in front of the gym's main doors, waiting for the arrival of the media contingent. Some of them had made signs that said things like, "Welcome 20/20" and "We love you, Mike." This wasn't my idea (they'd done it all on their own), but I loved it. I couldn't help but laugh in appreciation as I went out to greet and thank all of them for coming down.

It's funny, the high school's marching band was practicing nearby at the time, too. So by the time 20/20 arrived, we even had a marching band to greet them.

When Diaz, van Horn, and their crew arrived, I was sitting in one of the school's offices with Garry Pay, Steve Mansfield, Mike Sitrick, Tony Night, and Dr. Randy Smith. Pay's huge frame seemed to be taking up the entire room. He wore a classic suit on that day, I remember, and he looked terribly nervous. In fact, glancing around, everyone was clearly nervous. Especially Doc Smith.

"Doc," I said with a grin, "what's the deal, man? You okay?"

Smith's brow poured sweat. He was covered in it. He nodded.

I elbowed him playfully. "You're sweating like crazy and we haven't even gone on yet."

"I'm just nervous, I guess," he said.

"You'll go on, though?"

Smith nodded reluctantly.

"Good," I said. "Because I need you up there with me. It'll look better on camera if I have a doctor to back me up when I start talking about the science."

Smith nodded again, but it didn't do anything to put me at ease. Something was bothering him. Something bigger than stage fright.

Hoping to settle my nerves, I stepped out to take a look at the auditorium. The place looked far more intimate with all the people filing in. Plenty of the school's kids had hung around after school to see what all the fuss was about. They huddled up behind Metabolife employees and distributors alike. Standing room only in this place, this cozy little auditorium in National City. In front of the rows of chairs we'd arranged, on the far wall, *20/20* had set up the interview space—three chairs in total: one for me, one for Doc Smith, and one across from us for Diaz. On one side of the chairs, we'd arranged a space for our camera. On the other side, *20/20* had theirs up and ready.

I watched as Arnold Diaz, his crew, and Mary van Horn scurried around, looking anxious and, it seemed, almost as nervous as my lawyers. Van Horn was probably thirty. Reddish hair and fair skin, if memory serves—but I don't remember much else about her. I'd met so many other people on that day. And besides, at that moment, looking over the auditorium, it was Diaz who captured the majority of my attention.

At 5'10" and 175 pounds, Diaz was a pretty average guy. If not for his waxy, fish-like face, you might not pick him out of a crowd. His was the kind of greased-up arrogance that leads a man to grow a 1970s Burt Reynolds mustache. Dark hair that looked glued on. Big, blindingly white, fake-looking teeth. And as I would soon find out, rude as all hell.

The second that Diaz took his seat, I turned back to my representation. "Looks like we're on," I said.

Everyone stood and straightened out their suits. Sitrick suddenly had the look of a man in charge.

"You ready to go, Doc?" I asked Smith.

Smith nodded nervously again.

With me in the lead, we all headed into the auditorium. Before taking my seat, I waited for words of advice from my PR guys, but nothing came. Sitrick just nodded and Dominic gave me a thumbs up. All the confidence I needed.

Dr. Smith went immediately to his seat and sat down. He kind of slouched, his eyes darting everywhere but at Diaz, who sat proudly in his chair as a makeup girl applied about a pound of foundation to his face.

I sat down. "It's nice to meet you, Mr. Diaz," I said.

He didn't reply.

"Listen," I added, "do you have someone here to get me in to makeup?"

"No," Diaz said dismissively.

I get it, I thought. *He's Kennedy and I'm Nixon.*[78]

Frustrated, I turned to my PR and legal team and waved for help. But they were all too busy taking things in and talking to each other to notice. So I got up.

---

[78] I'm referring, of course, to the debate that many historians believed to have cost Nixon the 1960 elections. In the famous debate, Kennedy had chosen to wear makeup for the televised broadcast. Nixon, on the other hand, must have thought that makeup would make him look like a sissy. What he didn't realize, though, was that makeup is critical when you go on TV. Otherwise, you come off just as sickly and inhuman as Nixon wound up appearing during the broadcast of the debate. So with Nixon looking like a wax statue sitting across from the handsome and well-made-up Kennedy, his poll ratings took a huge nosedive.

Van Horn swooped in out of nowhere, intercepting me. "Where are you going?" she asked. "We're about to start."

"I just need one minute," I said, hatching a plan on the fly.

The basis for my plan: my underactive sweat glands. See, I don't sweat. Not because of heat, anyway. Not ever. The only time I sweat is when I'm at the gym. So I figured that, if Diaz was going to play hardball about the makeup, I'd just level the playing field by cranking up the heat. Way up.

I remembered seeing a temperature control dial next to the door when I'd first entered the gym, so I made straight for the thing. With a quick turn of the dial, I had the heater working full blast. I felt bad for the many supporters who turned out for the event, but I figured they'd be able to stick it out for an hour or so.

As soon as I got back around the chairs, van Horn was there to grab me. "Are you ready, Mr. Ellis?" she asked.

"Sure," I said. "I'll be right over."

I waved to a few people in the stands and took my seat in the phony little carpeted "room" set up for the taping. I saw Sitrick motion for our camera crew to fire things up, but it seemed a long while before we began the actual interview. Diaz sat there, not making eye contact with me, pretending to shuffle through notes.

"Out of curiosity, have you ever tried Metabolife?" I asked him softly.

"No," he said dismissively.

For a long, uncomfortable stretch, we all shifted around, taking sips from water bottles and glancing at anything but each other. Smith sat like a statue—I mean an absolute statue—to my left.

Then, with almost no circumstance, Diaz put on his "nice guy" face and started the interview. He stammered slightly. "Why don't you start out telling me how the Metabolife diet supplement was developed? Who developed it? Why? And what is it made out of?"

I told him the story of my father as calmly and smoothly as I could. My father was my best friend, I explained, and I was only interested in making him feel better.

"So you had no background in herbal medicine, and yet you came up with this pill," he said.

I provided him with as many details about my trial and error period and all the expert advice I received as I could. He was clearly trying to make me look like I had no idea what I was talking about. What he hadn't bargained for was that talking about ephedrine itself was probably the worst thing he could have done. If I know one thing, it's ephedrine. And there just wasn't any way he was going to beat me on the topic. I think I came across as quite knowledgeable in the field.

Not even the obvious drug angle seemed to go well for Diaz. His attempt to connect Mike Blevins' past to Metabolife's present fizzled out entirely. And his initial prying into our safety studies blew up in his face. Right before my eyes, his arrogant demeanor began to melt away.

But then, for the briefest moment, the tide turned in his favor. He accused our company of using Vanderbilt on its website to promote the idea that our product had been "proven" safe. Now, as I explained, there were two things wrong with that statement. First, it's not possible to *prove* that something is safe. As I've already mentioned, not even water is safe at high doses. Second, I honestly believed that we no longer printed this quote on our main website.

"That's not true," I said.

"Should I read you your own literature?" he snapped, suddenly seeming a little unnatural in his anger.

"Yes, please."

He riffled through papers, finally coming to what he was looking for in the giant stack on his lap. "'The unique formula of Metabolife 356 has been clinically tested for efficacy at two major universities. These studies have also concluded our product to be safe.'"

Quickly, I pointed out the fact that the paper he was reading—the supposed home page of our website—had the words "Metabolife Independent Distributor" printed at the top. "That website belongs to one of our distributors," I said, pointing out that we did everything in our power to control what our distributors claimed and didn't claim, but that there were tens of thousands of them, and that their sheer numbers sometimes made policing the documentation a little difficult.

He then claimed that the statement was also on our main webpage. That he'd seen it himself. I found myself immediately confused because I knew that Vanderbilt was no longer mentioned on our website. At least, that's what I'd assumed at that moment. Why had I assumed this? Because a year prior, I'd told Larry Miller to remove all reference to Vanderbilt from our site. And he'd told me that he would take care of it.

Later, I would discover that Miller had let me down on this one. That he didn't take care of it. We *had* conducted energy expenditure and safety studies at Vanderbilt, of course, but Vandy was denying it because we had agreed not to use their name in any marketing material. I'm sure that once they were told that we had them up on "our" website, they denied the whole thing even happened.

With Diaz looking snarky and me feeling confused and cornered, the two of us began arguing in full about the logistics of the study and those involved. It all seemed so irrelevant to me because I knew that the doctors Diaz was quoting—the ones he claimed had denied the safety considerations of our lab research—had already submitted formal papers and articles to various medical journals following the study. I knew that I could prove that safety had been a part of our protocol if only Diaz would let me see the publications (publications he claimed to have on hand). But he wouldn't give me the paper.

It's a funny thing, the disadvantage they put you in when they're filming an interview. Diaz had a ream of paper with "damning evidence" against my company. But he wouldn't even let me look at any of it without my having to argue. For him, resources were acceptable. For me, as far as Diaz was trying to make it seem, if I didn't have all the resources logged in my head, then I was obviously lying.

Funnier still: When he finally produced what he claimed to be the publication on the study (and I had to beg him for it), it wasn't actually the publication. It was just a paper carrying another out-of-context quote from one of the study's doctors.

So we continued to argue semantics, Diaz claiming that our marketing literature suggested that our product had been proven safe and me reminding him that proving something safe for everyone on the planet is impossible (and that that's why we have warnings on the label).

Finally, Diaz lost steam. "Okay," he said, sounding frustrated. "We need to change tapes." Then, he yelled for Mary.

The audience thundered with applause as I stood and strolled into the corner, just behind Diaz's chair. I watched as Diaz began barking in frustration at Mary van Horn. With the clapping still ringing in my ears, I couldn't hear exactly what he was yelling about, but I felt pretty bad for Mary.

20/20's techs changed the tape quickly, so I didn't have much time to speak to anyone from my group. But when I sat down to get going again, we had some trouble calming the crowd. They cheered loudly and boisterously. Diaz was clearly pretty aggravated about it, and he seemed completely willing to let everyone know that his patience wore thin.

I remember asking him how much longer we would be filming because Monica and I had to go pick up the kids from the babysitter. He couldn't even give me a reasonable response for that. Instead, he accused me of trying to rush the interview "after he'd come all this way" and his company had "jumped through so many hoops" to get things in line with us. I had the sinking feeling that the rest of the interview would be a nightmare. My interviewer had already started looking at me like I was something stuck on the bottom of his shoe.

Finally, we began again. Diaz kicked it off subtly, trying to lead me into a corner that I honestly didn't see coming.

"What's the website for Metabolife?" he asked. "What's the web address?"

The moment I gave him the address, he showed me a white paper that he claimed to be a copy of our website's homepage. The document suggested that we were making safety claims, something Diaz had been trying to get me to refute for the whole of the interview.

"C'mon," he said, "you just told me that that statement was made by your distributors in error and you couldn't control what they were saying and that it wasn't on your company website."

Even though I felt terrible about the fact that I'd obviously failed to follow up on Miller's promise to remove the safety claim, I tried to answer Diaz's accusations. But he wouldn't let me get a word in edgewise.

"Now I'm showing you your company website and it says the same thing."

I took a deep breath, making sure he'd finished his rant. Satisfied, I gave the best answer I could under the circumstances. "What I'm saying is in all fairness to both of us, I don't know my company website. I honestly don't."

"Are you saying that this is not from your company website?"

I feel confident in suggesting that Diaz didn't really misunderstand me. He just wanted to get a sound bite for the telecast. Wanted to get me on film lying about the contents of my website. Truthfully, my interviewer's demeanor and approach were starting to seem entirely juvenile. Even if he did manage to pry that false sound bite, I couldn't wait to see whether it would even be possible to make Diaz look like anything less than a prodding and childish asshole on the resultant broadcast.

By this point, if I hadn't been so annoyed, I might have found it difficult to avoid smiling or laughing. Diaz was pouring sweat. Melting like the Wicked Witch of the West. His makeup ran like streams of brown mud down his cheeks. Between questions, he would wipe his face with napkins—leaving them as gunky brown wads—and toss them on the floor like he expected someone else to pick them up.

My heart raced as I realized that Diaz's sweat didn't just mean that he had finally succumbed to the unreasonable temperature in the room. It also meant that the interview wasn't going the way he apparently wanted it to go. In fact, his tone and posture suddenly made it seem as if he was losing the thing badly. The truth presented itself on film: that I'm not a monster driven by greed and a lack of conscience—that I am merely a man who developed a product to help his father feel better. And one who did everything in his power and then some to ensure its safety.

The latter point made itself apparent when Diaz finally allowed me the time to summarize our unprecedented corporate efforts on safety.

"Metabolife was not mandated by any regulatory agency by any laws to do any studies," I explained. "But Metabolife has taken the high road on this issue. We've done animal studies, we have done clinical trials, we have done post-market surveys with our consumers. Those are things that have never been done by the dietary supplement industry. And I think that's very valuable information to the Food and Drug Administration and the entire industry if we could pull together and do more of those things."

I could feel it even then. With my explanation—clunky as it may have been—the momentum had shifted again. And when Diaz began accusing us of distributing a dangerous product (when he followed the line of comparing ma huang to synthetic ephedrine, claiming the latter to be safer than the former) he pretty much drove the last nail into his own coffin. Dr. Smith and I essentially buried him on the topic.

When he'd finished asking his prepared questions, the look on the interviewer's makeup-run face confirmed the sentiment. Especially when Doc Smith finally made a detailed contribution and hit him with a long, well-spoken monologue on the historical safety of ephedrine.

"I think one thing I'd like to add," Smith said, "there's been a lot of talk about wondering if it's safe, but I think there's a lot of reasons to say that it is. We have over sixty years of experience with pharmaceutical ephedrine to look at; we have over twenty studies with the FDA showing pharmaceutical ephedrine being safe up to a hundred fifty milligrams a day; we've got centuries of experience with the Chinese; we've got over four years of experience with our product, millions of people taking billions of servings. If there was a significant health problem, I think we'd know it."

I nodded. In one fell swoop, the doctor had destroyed the whole interview. Pity it would never see the air.

"Okay," Diaz said. "Thank you for your time."

The crowd erupted again as we all stood.

The first person I wanted to talk to after the interview was my mother. And when I found her in the roaring crowd, she seemed to be glowing. So proud of her son who would be on TV. See, Mom was a big fan of *20/20*—in particular, of Arnold Diaz's segments on the show. And I could see in her eyes that she wanted badly to meet him.

As I hugged her, Sitrick came up beside us.

"Mike, that was perfect," he said happily. "You *killed* it."

I smiled and gazed down at my mother. "Mom, do you want to meet Arnold Diaz?"

Mom looked frail. By then, she was an old woman. But as she nodded, she seemed about as eager as I'd seen her in years.

"I'll get Mary," Sitrick offered. "Mary?"

Van Horn, wide-eyed and maybe a little troubled, came right over.

"My mom here would like to meet Mr. Diaz, if she could," I said.

"Oh, sure," van Horn said cheerily. "Let me ask him."

It only took Mary about two steps to find Diaz, who stood with his back to us, well within earshot. As he loosened his tie with one hand, he continued to run napkins over his makeup-caked face with the other.

"Mr. Diaz," we heard van Horn say, "would you like to meet Mr. Ellis' mother?"

Diaz turned around to glare at me. "Fuck Mrs. Ellis," he said. And without another word, he stalked away.

In one microscopic instant, my mood changed from triumphant to enraged. Today, I have a harder time blaming Diaz for losing it (he obviously felt stupid, after all, like he'd been set up), but in the moment, it took every ounce of my effort not to chase him down, grab him, and beat the hell out of him. I mean, who in his right mind would say something like that to an old woman? To a man's *mother*?

For me, Diaz's slight was the turning point. The point when I decided that the media had harmed my family for long enough. From that moment on, I would remain on the offensive. I'd had enough rolling over.

"I'm sorry about that, Mom," I said as soon as Diaz was out of sight.

My mother nodded, looking dejected and a little startled. I led her back to Garry Pay, who took her over to the first row of chairs to sit down again.

"Garry?" I called to my lawyer.

Garry looked back at me, wide-eyed.

"Could you turn the heat down?" I asked. "The control's by the door."

Garry nodded eagerly, wiping the sweat from his brow with a handkerchief. The cloth appeared to be sopping wet already.

As I shook my head at Garry, Monica came up and kissed me on the cheek.

"You did a really good job," she said.

I couldn't tear my eyes away from my mom. She seemed so upset. "Thanks, honey," I said distantly.

"I'm proud of you."

Despite my trepidation, I smiled at my wife.

Mike Sitrick had hatched another plan before we'd even left the high school, but I was too busy being angry at Diaz to give it too much thought that night. The only thing I'd managed to do was contact our company's head of IT and arrange a meeting with him on the following morning.

I sat now in that meeting, Sitrick, Night, Dominic, Mansfield, and Pay huddled all around and my head of IT staring us down in what looked like relative confusion.

"We've got this video of the unedited interview, right?" Sitrick said to no one in particular.

"Yeah..." I said slowly.

"I want a copy."

"No problem," Dominic said. "Why?"

"We need to figure out a way to get it on the Internet," Sitrick said excitedly. "If *20/20* is going to slice and dice Mike, we should make sure that the public has access to the full interview."

We all sat in stunned but delighted silence. I could hear the analog clock ticking from its spot on the far wall.

"That's brilliant," I said.

"I don't know, Mike," Mansfield said hesitantly. "You should think about the legal—"

"I don't know," I said, interrupting. "Is it even possible to put this up on the Internet?"

"Absolutely," Dominic said eagerly. "You can put the entire streaming video on the Internet!"

This was 1999. I didn't know that such technology existed. So I did what I always did in that situation. I looked to my head of IT.

"See if you can set up some streaming video," I said to him. "And register the web address 'newsinterview.com.'"

My IT guy bolted from the room, clearly on a mission. In about two hours, he returned and confirmed that we could run the streaming video. It would be a considerable undertaking, but we could do it.

"Will everyone in the country be able to view it?" I asked him.

"Well…not everyone," he said. "Not everyone has an Internet connection fast enough to stream video."

"That's okay," I said dismissively. "Will we get enough people?"

My IT guy shrugged.

Sitrick practically jumped out of his chair. "We will if we ran an ad campaign!"

Pay leaned forward and thrust his hand out to slow down the flow. "Hold on a minute," he said. "We're just going to slam *20/20* here?"

"Why not?" Sitrick asked. "They intend to slam us."

"I'm not sure we've got any legal footing here," Mansfield said.

I sighed, not feeling much in the mood to deal with overcautious lawyers. "Let's see what Bob and Blevins think," I offered.

With everyone nodding, I dialed up my partners and put them on speaker. Blevins first. Then, Bob.

"Bob," I said, "I've got Blevins on speaker and I'm here with my entourage."

Bob chuckled. "Okay. What've you got?"

"Sitrick wants to put this video from *20/20* on the Internet and so do I. IT says we can do it."

"Why?" Blevins asked.

"Because it'll give us a chance to show the country that *20/20*'s version of the interview isn't exactly accurate."

"Might help us save face, too," Bob said, sounding as if he was on board already.

"Exactly," I said. "And if we play our cards right, it could save the company."

"That's certainly interesting," Bob said.

I started talking rapidly, like a kid discussing his haul of Christmas presents. "We could get it all up on the Internet in streaming video. IT says it'll work. Sitrick thinks we could have a whole website with links to the transcripts, the science, our label, the studies, everything. And we could show the total unedited version before *20/20* airs."

I could sense that my attorneys had moved to the edge of their seats. They were clearly uncomfortable.

"Let's do it," Blevins said.

"I agree," Bob added. "Let's take the fight to them."

Three days later, I'm in my office at 8 p.m. Pay's there with me and we've got Mansfield on speakerphone. Despite the fact that we've already got the ball rolling on the website, both of my attorneys continue to drag their heels.

"Garry and I both agree," Mansfield says. "You really shouldn't do this."

"It's just too dangerous to launch a campaign against a news outlet," Pay says.

I'm angry as hell. "I already told you I'm going to do it," I bark.

"But, Mike," Mansfield whines, "we could get sued. This could bring more problems down on us than we've already got."

Furious, I stand up and get as close to the speaker as I can, looking back and forth between the phone and Pay. "Do you guys think I'm fucking deaf?" I say. "I've heard these same complaints for three days. I *know* this is risky."

Pay seems to be avoiding my eyes.

"But it's what we're going to do," I continue. Then, I level the boom. "Either do what I need you to do as my lawyers—mitigate the damages—or I'll find attorneys who will."

Now, do I like Mansfield? Yes. Do I love Pay? Yes. But I lost it on them a little in that moment. Why? Because I was going into battle—and taking my entire company along with me. And since we were risking so much, bringing in troops who weren't willing to fight seemed like a bad idea. Call it my Patton moment.

As soon as I drop my ultimatum, Garry stands. I say my uncomfortable goodbyes to Mansfield and watch as the big man makes for the door.

"So are you in or out?" I ask just as his hand comes to rest on the handle.

Pay turns, his expression as serious as I've ever seen. "I guess I'm in," he says.

"You *guess*?" I say. "You can't guess. Either you're in or you're out."

Pay sighs, and the whole room seems to sigh with him. "I tell you, Mike…working on this case is like getting a drink of water from a fire hose."

I grin through my frustration.

An hour after my favorite lawyer crawled his way onto our bandwagon, I decided that I couldn't have a grumpy attorney. So what

I did was I waited for about an hour—long enough for Pay to get back to, situated, and comfortable in his office in the building across the parking lot. Then, I picked up the phone and dialed his number.

"Garry," I said frantically, "I think you need to come down here."

"Why?" Pay said, sounding appropriately concerned. "What is it?"

I laid the feigned anger on thick. "Look," I hollered, "I can't tell you over the phone. But I need you down here right away."

Garry slammed down his receiver. The force of it rang in my ear.

Giggling, I watched through my window, which overlooked the spacious parking lot between Pay's building and my own. I knew that in a matter of minutes, my lawyer would come lumbering out of his building and make the long, sunny trek across the lot.

I burst out laughing when he came into sight. He wasn't lumbering; he was jogging. In full business attire. I laughed right up until he was out of sight again. Then, I did what I could to put on a straight face and wait for him to knock on my office door. Focusing on a little paperwork did the trick.

Then, at last, a knock.

"Come in," I said, standing and walking around to the front of my desk.

Pay was sweating profusely and panting. "I came as fast as I could," he said.

"Good," I said calmly. "Thank you."

Pay (still panting): "Well, what is it?"

I turned sideways and smoothed my hand down the back of my pants, craning my neck to take a look at my own ass. "Do these pants make my butt look big?" I asked nonchalantly.

For a second, it looked almost like Garry would scream. Then, all at once, he began to chuckle. His chuckle quickly roiled into a laugh.

"You with me now, buddy?" I asked with a grin.

Pay (still laughing): "You're out of your mind, you know that."

"Brought you out of it, didn't I?"

Pay (still laughing): "You know you did."

"So you're with me on this."

"I'm with you," Pay said through his grinning teeth. "It's still crazy. But I'm with you."

Now that everyone was on board for the streaming video idea, the next step would be to set up our advertising campaign. We knew that if *20/20* was going to screw us, we would have to beat them to the punch. More importantly, we would have to drive more traffic to our full version of the interview than they would get for the creatively edited version of theirs. But we knew we had a good shot—mostly because we were getting as many as 20,000 calls per day at Metabolife and an unbelievable amount of Internet activity. Everyone who called in or visited the website would be informed about newsinterview.com.

Meanwhile, Sitrick began putting his efforts in to taking out full-page ads in traditional media. He began with the *Washington Post* and the *Wall Street Journal*, who he believed to be the most credible paper in the country. I also put our media buying company, California Creative—headed by Steve Horn, an old friend of mine—on the task of contacting all 1,500 radio stations already carrying Metabolife advertising. We requested that the stations make mention of the website and to direct people to "watch the unedited interview with Metabolife's CEO prior to the airing of *20/20*."

"You know what we should do, Mikey?" Sitrick asked me one day.

I raised my eyebrows.

"We should rent out that giant TV in the middle of Times Square. We'll loop an ad with Diaz wiping all that makeup off his face."

I cracked a smile.

"The tag-line could be, 'Why is Arnold Diaz sweating so much? Go to newsinterview.com to find out.'"

We both had a good laugh at that one.

Then, I turned it around. "No, bud," I said. "We're victims here, not smartasses."

We wouldn't need the Times Square TV, anyway. We quickly discovered that print media didn't much care for *20/20*. Who could blame them? In the papers, you're supposed to report the news. *20/20*, on the other hand, had a habit of *creating* the news. Not many people in the industry respected what they did to Food Lion or the Ford Pinto—or the way they did business, for that matter. But that was *20/20*. Entertainment first. News second. And here was the print media's chance to take a swing at them.

So the story kept building and building. Slowly but surely, it turned away from being about this supposedly dangerous product and untrustworthy CEO to being about scrutinizing *20/20* and the way they do business.

The day we first fired up the site, something extraordinary happened: It exploded with viewers. So many viewers that we found ourselves ill prepared for the volume. By noon on day one, we'd already gotten approximately a million hits. We had to rush to install five more T-1 lines just to handle all of the traffic.

I heard through the grapevine that one of the media outlets carrying our newsinterview.com ads contacted one of *20/20*'s lawyers and asked her what she thought about what was happening with Metabolife. Apparently, she said, "More people will view *20/20* than will go to their website."

The media outlet basically said, "We've talked to Metabolife. They've already had over a million hits. They're adding five more T-1 lines as we speak."

So *20/20* knew they were in trouble.

Back at Metabolife, with our confidence renewed, we really cranked up the bombardment. We were constantly on the radio, in print, on TV, everything. Our efforts drove so many hits to the website that it was absolutely astounding.

There came a point where it looked almost as if *20/20*, if they could have gotten away with it, would have thrown that story away. But here we were, advertising everywhere about the upcoming interview. They couldn't very well not air the thing. How would that look?

Just as we thought they would delay the airing forever, they announced the date it would run. The announcement immediately took me to DEFCON 1: My final plan, my last kill stroke on *20/20*. I had Steve Horn call up the ad rep from ABC and look into buying some commercial time on the day of the story.

"I'd like to buy some ad time," Horn told him.

"What date and time?" the ad man asked.

"I'd like to get as close to the start of the Metabolife *20/20* episode as possible."

"You've got the ad ready?"

"Yep."

"Send us a copy."

Horn same-day'd a copy of the ad to ABC. The commercial was pretty basic. It featured script scrolling down the screen—kind of like the introduction to *Star Wars*. Steve Horn's voice read the script, which invited people to go to newsinterview.com and watch the unedited interview. Then, they were told that they could vote on whether *20/20*'s version had seemed fair and balanced.

Early the next morning, Horn got a call from the ad man.

"Yeah," he said. "We can't air this."

"We'll bump any commercial," Horn said. "Whatever you've got. We'll pay a bigger price."

The ad man kind of chuckled. "No…look, I'm sorry. We can't run this thing."

Frustrated, I decided to do a little Internet research on the story. So I plugged "ABC *20/20*" into my search engine. When I hit the "search" button, I immediately saw a banner ad about the *20/20* story. The thing that struck me as strange about the ad was the description of the episode. According to ABC's website, the *20/20* story would lead with the idea that we claimed to have done safety studies at Columbia—but that we were lying about that fact.

My heart raced. We *did* do safety studies at Columbia. Basically, *20/20* and, by extension, ABC were lying in bold-faced print.

So I called Mansfield and told him to check out the website. Later, Mansfield, with me standing over him, called *20/20*.

"I'm looking at your website as we speak," he said. "This statement about Columbia. That's a false statement. This is false advertising, libel, and inflammatory."

The lead counsel of *ABC News*—the woman who answered the call—sounded defensive. "Well, if you guys wouldn't have attacked us, this never would have happened."

Mansfield cocked his head to one side. "Attacked you? What do you mean attacked you?"

"Posting that unedited interview was like attacking us. We're the media. You can't attack us like that."

Mansfield scoffed. "So you're the only one with First Amendment rights?"

ABC's lawyer fell silent for a long time. "No, no, I don't mean that…" she said. Another long pause. "Please don't sue us."

I thought Mansfield's face would split in half, he was grinning so widely. And over the next half-hour, he used his new leverage to negotiate our way into that commercial we wanted. In exchange for the prime commercial slot right before the show, we would agree not to file a lawsuit about the false statements regarding Columbia.

The funny thing about the commercial is that it didn't identify who had sponsored it. As far as any of the viewers would know, it could have been *20/20* itself that was airing the commercial.

The airdate finally came—right at the same time as a World Series game. I'm convinced that *20/20* did this on purpose. With one of the biggest sporting events of the year going on at the same time, this would minimize viewership.

On the morning that we first put the story on the Internet,

Sitrick put a reporter at the *Wall Street Journal* on the trail of Arnold Diaz. From what I understand, the reporter went to Diaz's house at 6 a.m., and asked him what he thought about Metabolife's actions regarding the complete unedited version of the interview. According to Sitrick, Diaz just closed the door in the reporter's face. That's poetic justice if I ever heard it.

As the commercial and then the show hit the East Coast, millions of votes started pouring into the site. *20/20* had cut the 72-minute interview of me all the way down to one minute. The one minute was basically just about the Internet site mix-up that Diaz and I had argued about. I guess everything else just made me look too good to air. The entire segment ran for fourteen minutes.

At first, fifty-two percent of the voters on our site said that the *20/20* story was unfair. It bounced back and forth, back and forth as the show traveled across the time zones. Fifty-one percent in favor of us, forty-nine percent against. For a while, a 50/50 split.

Meanwhile, many members of the print media wanted a blow by blow. They called almost continuously. "What's the vote at now?" they would ask. "What's the tally?"

By the time the entire country had seen the segment, fifty-one percent of voters agreed that *20/20*'s version of the story had been unfair.

It might have been a narrow margin, but we had won. In fact, as far as I was concerned, even if we had only gotten twenty-five percent of the vote, we would have won. But as it stood, we had the majority.

In the process, we had done something to the media that had never been done before. We'd challenged their tactics—turned the story inward. They'd attacked our product, so we attacked their product. And what did we learn? We learned that the media has a great offense, but no defense.

We all sat around the computer proudly, knowing that we had just circumvented their offense with the Internet.

Over the next two or three days, I kept getting emails and letters from CEOs from all around the world. Congressmen. Senators. All of them congratulating me on a job well done. None of them could believe that we had managed to beat *20/20*. Many expressed their longing to be able to do exactly what we had done (I guess it's more difficult to challenge the media so outwardly when you have stock-holders and political alliances to think about). I was completely shocked at the response.

Later, a magazine reporter (who I won't name) did an inter-view with some of the decision makers at *20/20*. This reporter informed me that he'd never had to go off the record for a story so many times in his entire life.

"They said they wished they'd never heard of Mike Ellis or Metabolife," he told me.

I recently visited *20/20*'s website. And you know what I noticed? They now have links to allow their viewers to watch both the edited and unedited versions of their stories.

Van Horn and Diaz would soon leave the outfit. Did they get fired because of Metabolife? I don't know. I like to think that they did (for all I know, they just moved on to different things). I can't say as I've lost any sleep over the matter, but I do know this for certain: As little as I think of Arnold Diaz, and as much as I enjoyed burying his underhanded story, I would never insult his mother.

Chapter 16

Cinderella Does the Mopping

In 2000, despite our win over *20/20*, we had a real storm brewing. Wal-Mart had continued to sell the knockoff known as Metabolite, and as a result, we were losing a significant amount of revenue. Metabolite's estimated sales at Wal-Mart had reached $300 million, and as far as we were concerned, without the deliberate deception of the customer, those sales would have been *our* sales.

So there we were, hemorrhaging $300 million a year to a single knockoff product[79], our distributors taking big hits and the company slumping considerably below the profitability line. We fought for a long time to get Wal-Mart to take the phony product off the shelves, but they resisted. And as the year wore on, it became

---

[79] There were more than seventy Metabolife knockoffs on the market at one point, Metabolite being far and away the most profitable of the group. Any manufacturer of a product will tell you that knockoffs aren't necessarily a problem (people will always buy the real thing). But when a knockoff comes along *designed* to trick the consumer into believing that they actually *are* buying the real thing, you run into problems—especially when the phony iteration sells for twenty dollars cheaper than your own.

increasingly apparent that we had only one choice as a company: adapt to this new threat or go bankrupt.

It killed me to even think about it, but the only adaptation that presented itself was the possibility of converting to a retail sales model—which meant that our network marketing model would have to be abandoned, which in turn meant that our distributors would be forced to move on to other things.

As heavy as it made my heart to think about such a change, I knew we needed help. We *all* knew we needed help. That's why we were having weekly board meetings over our declining sales.

At the latest such meeting, we all sat around the board room— a twenty-foot by thirty-foot space featuring one very long, well-finished, wooden table that stretched from one end to the other. Along each side of the table, there ran sixteen to twenty reclining chairs made of plush leather. A working boardroom. Grease boards and projection screens and notepads all around.

I sat staring at Larry Miller, the Keebler-Elf-looking president of our company. He stood about 5'8" and sat even shorter. Kind of dumpy. The kind of man who would never make a decision on his own—the kind of man who would always just agree with the safest position leveled at any meeting. Predictably, he kicked the event off in the usual fashion.

"So what's the damage this week?" he asked.

"That's not funny, Larry," Blevins said, his tired eyes like daggers.

Miller just shook his head. "Well, what is it, then?"

"We're at a point where we have to do somewhere between thirteen and fourteen million per month, just to break even," I said.

"In sales?" Bradley asked.

"In sales."

"Just to break even," Blevins said. It felt strange having to bring my two oldest business partners up to speed. But as I've said, they'd moved on to more peripheral work with the company, leaving their regular posts for more charitable ventures.

"How do we do that?" Miller asked.

I blinked at him for a while. He honestly didn't have a clue. "Well," I said, "the distributors are claiming that we need to do more ads. And that we need to do something about Wal-Mart."

"Hands are tied, there," Miller said.

Long silence.

"Well we have to do *something*," Blevins offered.

Of course, I already had the idea in mind, but I wasn't sure at that time whether it would be good to share it with the rest of the group. I knew that first I would have to do some research. So after our rather fruitless meeting, I paid a visit to a trusted employee, my head of marketing, David Gumner. I asked the energetic David to check in with every major retail store in the country (save for Wal-Mart, of course) and see if they would be willing to sell Metabolife on their shelves.

"Don't worry about why just yet," I said. "Just see if they'd be interested."

David agreed to the task. And on the next day, when he got back to me, he came bearing great news. "They all said that if we're serious about it, they'll sell our product immediately."

I think a part of me was disappointed. If my plan to go retail had proven impossible after all, then I wouldn't have had to suggest that we bail on the distributors—all those people who helped make our company such a roaring success. Obviously, converting to retail would have been catastrophic for these people. But then, if the company truly wasn't going to survive into 2001 (and it truly wasn't), then it would have been catastrophic for the distributors, anyway. We'd have *all* been out of a job.

So with David's news in mind, I knew that the only viable solution to our Metabolite problem would be to convert to a retail model—something that had never been done before in the history of network marketing (as far as I know). Assuming that the rest of the board would approve the plan, we would drop the suggested retail price per bottle to $29.95, sell it at every major retail chain (save for Wal-Mart), and watch our sales rise back to the point where the company could be sustainable again.

When I presented the idea to the board, Blevins, Bradley, and our new crack team of executive nitwits agreed. So after getting clearance from Garry Pay about any potential contractual issues with the distributors (there were none, as he explained), I put David on the job of calling the retailers again. This time, he would actually be setting up the sales.

And I also got together with Blevins, because I knew that we couldn't trust Larry Miller to handle the conversion. [80]

"So what do you need from me?" Blevins asked eagerly. I could sense that he missed working regularly with Metabolife.

"We have to change *everything*," I said. "Everything from our computers to our department protocol to our supply lines to our shipping. I mean everything. UPC codes, everything. Retail's a completely different animal from network marketing."

Blevins smirked. "Sounds like it."

I reached up and placed my hands on my much taller friend's shoulders. "You're the only one I can trust to get this done," I said.

Blevins said he'd be up to the task.

In the days and weeks to come, he would work with David. The two of them reorganized everything with the heads of sales, IT, and marketing departments. Basically, they had to revise everything

---

[80] Several years earlier, I'd set in motion plans to diversify our product base. We already had our incredibly successful weight loss supplement, but as far as I was concerned, that was only the beginning. In my time in China, I'd discovered a number of herbal remedies that we had turned into prototype supplements that I knew would be every bit as successful. We had pills that would eliminate indigestion in five minutes. We had pills to completely wipe out PMS pains, replacing them with a sense of wellness and happiness. We had pills that could cure migraine headaches in ten minutes. And maybe the best one: instantaneous cold relief. We called the whole line of products "Chinac." The distributors expressed the feeling that the Chinac line would sell right off the shelves. My only mistake on the agenda: leaving Miller in charge of getting all the staff working on the transition to a diversified product line. He would bark things like, "Now that we've got all these products in place, we're going to launch in January!" But come December, during a meeting with all of the vice presidents of our various departments, I learned the hard way that Larry Miller had yet to push anything through. The whole line flopped—in my opinion, thanks in no small part to Larry's inadequacy as a business leader.

from front to back on how we fulfilled a sale (UPC codes, shipping, points of purchase, etc.).

Meanwhile, David continued checking in with retailers. True to their word, they all agreed to jump in. We deliberately didn't sell to Wal-Mart, preferring to give all other drug stores and grocery stores the first shot before we even considered the corporate giant who'd we felt screwed us into this situation in the first place. True or untrue, Wal-Mart seemed to have participated in the knockoff of our product—and we weren't going to sell to a company that seemed to be deliberately subverting our sales. Once we'd determined that the retailers would work with us diligently,[81] we knew that we'd be alright without Wal-Mart, anyway.

Our biggest problem was that we already had this retail conversion machine rolling (Blevins was doing an unbelievable job putting things together) and we didn't have anyone to lead us once the process was finished. I was out as CEO—partly because of all the media attention, but mostly because of the fact that I'd completely lost desire to lead the company now that we weren't going to be running a network marketing model anymore. And company president Larry Miller wasn't even close to qualified for the job. So we had to have another board meeting in search of a suitable new leader. The most difficult meeting I've ever been a part of.

"None of us are qualified to run a retail operation," I said, glancing from face to face around the long table.

"I'm qualified," Miller said defiantly.

"No, you're not. But neither am I."

"So what are you saying, Mike?" Bradley asked.

"I'm saying it's time I stepped down."

Silence.

"If this retail thing is going to work," I said, "we need to bring in somebody who's qualified to run it."

"Got anyone in mind?" Blevins asked.

"David Brown." I filled the board in on David's credentials,

---

[81] This meant that they would have to launch the product, sell it at the new retail price of $29.95, and place it in standalone displays on the store floor.

explaining why I thought he would make for a good CEO in my stead. [82] When I finished, I looked around. Everybody seemed surprised and a little perplexed. "Anybody object?"

No objections.

"Garry," I said, glancing over at the big man, who was scribbling notes, as usual, "could you give David a call and have him come see me?"

Garry nodded. And it wasn't long before I found myself face to face with David Brown. In my first meeting with our potential new CEO, I explained what we'd already begun doing—explained the pains that Blevins had gone to, along with his remarkable results. And then I asked him if he thought he was qualified. [83]

"Sure," he said. And he was on board. From that day forward, he would be the president of Metabolife International, and by January 2001, I would step down and David would be CEO.

Blevins continued to coordinate every aspect of the transition. He pulled everything off in an unreasonably short timeframe—everything from reformatting computers to reassigning bar codes to reconfiguring shipping routes to revising points of purchase with all the staff. In just forty-five days, he pulled off this monumental task (a feat that had never been accomplished before, as far as we knew). [84]

So we were a retail sales company now. And even early on, the

---

[82] I'd met Brown a few times at industry conferences. Brown was the head of a company called Natural Balance at the time—a smaller herbal supplement company that already operated on a retail model. So in other words, he had the experience.

[83] Now I asked about David's qualifications because the difference between Natural Balance and Metabolife (as almost everyone in the industry would have said at the time), is that Metabolife was the elite, a monster. This isn't to say that Natural Balance was a poor company. Quite the opposite. It's just that they weren't the Lamborghini that Metabolife was. So, anyway, faced with the offer to drive an Italian sports car of a company, David naturally agreed to hop in the driver's seat. Poor David just didn't know at the time that this Lamborghini would soon be stolen…

[84] To this day, I still marvel at everything that Blevins and our staff managed to achieve. What they did should have been impossible. But they did it. And they did it well.

sales turned out to be far better than we could have hoped. The retailers were happy because they had this giant new product to sell (and better yet, they knew that they weren't going to have to compete with Wal-Mart).

Wal-Mart, on the other hand, was pissed.[85] We gave the megastore the cold shoulder for a while, but they persisted. Finally, having tired of their almost childish demands, we explained to them that we planned on selling our product to the other retailers for a period of ninety days before we would even entertain the idea of selling to Wal-Mart. Naturally, the biggest retail chain in the world was absolutely angry.

Anyway, we had just kicked off our retail sales model. By the beginning of August, we were finally on the verge of having our legs back under us financially. Only then did we call for all the distributors to come to San Diego to talk to us. Since we had been forced to cut off their line of income, we knew that we had the obligation to compensate them somehow.

Originally, we wanted to cut every one of our distributors in to the company (give each of them a piece of the profits we'd generated through retail sales), but our legal team pointed out that there are FCC regulations against that sort of thing. So the only thing we could do was offer to pay them for their "consulting services." In other words, we would divide a lump sum amongst each of them in exchange for their efforts in visiting their local retail sites and inspecting the Metabolife displays. They would basically just have to visit a site or two and fill out a form to send back to the company. And for this job, we would pay the group of distributors $20 million

---

[85] Immediately after we launched the retail stream, Wal-Mart called us three times. We always made sure to avoid these calls. But, eventually, the retail giant insisted that we have a meeting with them. So this is what we did: We sent out one of our people who knew absolutely nothing about retail sales. I guess Wal-Mart wined and dined our guy, explaining to him that we could expect to do $200 million in sales with our product in the first year alone. Seriously, this is what our guy said in response to that claim: "Then maybe we shouldn't do that move. We make a whole lot more than that now." Back at Metabolife, we all pretty much rolled on the ground laughing when we heard that story.

in the first year (with the option to renew for a second year). Essentially, we pledged the immediate future of the company to the people who'd helped make us a company in the first place.

By the time the second year rolled around—and even though we (Blevins, Bradley, and myself) didn't make much money at all in the first year—we decided to exercise the option and give the distributors another $20 million. Our attorneys were fully against it, but we did it anyway. Bob, Mike, and I knew that we legally didn't have to give the distributors anything (our attorneys kept reminding us of that) but from a moral standpoint, we knew that there was only one choice: We paid our distributors the extra $20 million.

Unfortunately, despite the fact that we'd almost crippled the company again upon renewing the contract, we still garnered a few lawsuits from disgruntled distributors. Did I agree with the logic behind these lawsuits? No. Did I understand it? Yes. I assumed that the distributors who would come after us never really saw the big picture: that if we hadn't converted to retail, they wouldn't have had a product to sell, anyway.

"We got a couple more, Mike," David Brown said in another of our board meetings.

"Oh, no," I said. "Who is it this time?"

"Mel." [86]

"You've got to be kidding me," I said with a cathartic smirk. I turned to Bradley, making claws of my hands. "The guy with the lethal weapons for hands."

Bradley smiled and rolled his head back.

"How much did we pay him again?" I asked.

"I'd have to check the numbers," Bradley said. "But he made plenty."

---

[86] Mel, along with a small group of distributors, would sue us for millions instead of taking the hundreds of thousands they would have gotten through our consulting contract. Mel's suit actually claimed that he was "instrumental in making our company a success." He seemed to have forgotten that I did him a favor by signing him up on a downline that would make him tens of thousands of dollars per month. I guess no good deed goes unpunished.

"And now he's suing us?"

"Yep." Brown said. Then, he shuffled through the stack of papers in the leather portfolio in front of him on the table. "And I've got another one here..." He gave up on his shuffling, shaking his head. "I don't have the sheet in front of me...but it's some guy who claims that you betrayed him when you went to retail."

"That we betrayed him?" I asked, crestfallen. "Look, we weren't going to survive!"

Brown shrugged in agreement. Our hands had been tied. But still, we had lawsuits to face. [87]

From that day forward, we would win every suit that went to arbitration. Most of the other cases settled out of court for very little money—many for less than we had originally agreed to pay through our $40 million consulting contract. I felt bad for them. Truly, I did. If I'd had things my way, we would still be a network marketing company to this day. And even those people who made legal claims against us would still be making hundreds of thousands of dollars per year at their distribution sites.

Meanwhile, thanks to the continuously abrasive media coverage, consumers were really starting to come out of the woodwork to sue the company, as well. A new consumer lawsuit would be heaped on our plates every ninety days or so. The plaintiffs would piggyback

---

[87] David Brown was the one who kept us all together during all this turmoil. His job at the time involved three things:

    1) Overseeing our retail model

    2) Cleaning up our employee infrastructure

    3) Preparing us for sale

These three things would in turn ensure a couple of things. First, the company that Bob, Mike, and I had worked so hard to build would survive. And second, our families and we would remain financially secure for the future. And David proved himself perfectly capable at handling this job. Under his guidance, the company got to where it was running more smoothly than it had ever run before.

on one another, all of them apparently wanting to cash in on the ATM machine that Metabolife had become.[88]

It's funny, though, when you think about the demographics of the people who tried suing us. Almost exactly fifty percent of Metabolife's customers were affluent. They had plenty of money to get by. The other fifty percent, meanwhile, were low-income, and many lived near or below the poverty line. Now, out of all the lawsuits we faced—out of all the people who claimed to have been somehow injured by our product—I'm not aware of a single one of them that came from an affluent background. So out of the millions of Metabolife customers, the only ones leveling claims against us were the less affluent of our customers. In other words, the only people getting "hurt" by Metabolife were people in need of money. Strange...[89]

It got to the point where we were seeing so many suits that it became clear that we had to fight back.[90] It was Garry Pay who finally managed to convince the insurance company that it would be a good idea to allow one of these cases to make it to court. It took some time, but they eventually realized that Garry was right.

All that we had to do was wait for the perfect case to come along...

We wouldn't have to wait too long. A plaintiff in California soon

---

[88] For the most part, each case would involve a pre-trial deposition, followed by the insurance company settling out of court, cutting the plaintiffs a check. Simple as that. See, insurance companies have strange policies: Rather than spend millions fighting a lawsuit, they just settle with the claimants out of court. So since we had all these piggybacked suits coming up, it started to feel a little like we'd become a kind of get-rich-quick ATM. Many plaintiffs would file for millions and then wind up taking only $5,000 or so in settlements.

[89] Stranger still, many of the plaintiffs in these suits were linked somehow to the medical field (most of them working as nurses' assistants or hospital reception staff.)

[90] The funny thing is that, later on, during our company's bankruptcy proceedings, Mike, Bob, and I would pay out of our own pockets to have many of the plaintiffs in these cases watched under constant surveillance. We hired private investigators, former FBI agents, to follow our claimants all around the country. Now, in their lawsuits, many if not most of these plaintiffs had claimed to be a hundred percent disabled because of Metabolife. But our surveillance revealed that none of them appeared to have any injury at all. In fact, when they weren't headed to the doctor's office, they were working, partying, and barbequing just fine.

claimed that he'd had a heart attack because of taking Metabolife. Pretty common for these lawsuits. What separated this case from the pack, though, was that we discovered that the claimant also happened to be a heavy smoker, alcohol abuser, and *illicit drug user.*

In the beginning, this one seemed like a slamdunk. In addition to our research into the plaintiff's not-so-healthy lifestyle, we also had the deposition of his doctor (in this deposition, the doctor explained that he didn't believe Metabolife had contributed to the claimant's injuries, suggesting that he had instead instructed him on many occasions to quit smoking, drinking, and doing drugs). So, basically, our evidence pointed to the idea that this guy was a walking heart attack waiting to happen.

Unfortunately, the judge wouldn't let us use any of said evidence. He tossed out the doctor's testimony because of doctor/patient privilege. The drug abuse claim? The judge felt it might *unduly influence the jury.*[91]

Even without the evidence, we knew that to claim that Metabolife was solely (or even partly) responsible for this plaintiff's maladies seemed ridiculous at best and idiotic at worst. But that didn't change the fact that omitting the plaintiff's drug history basically meant that this one wouldn't be the sure winner we'd hoped it would be.

As the case progressed (with Garry Pay and a young attorney named Sam Baxter handling the majority of the proceedings from our end), we attempted to present the science and history behind ephedrine. The plaintiff's side, meanwhile, attempted to compare Metabolife to phenopropanolamine, a component formerly found in cold tablets, and one that the FDA had banned.[92]

---

[91] I honestly couldn't believe the news when Garry informed me of the judge's decision. Basically, he'd allowed the plaintiff's attorneys to influence the jury with every piece of inflammatory nonsense about Metabolife that they could get their hands on. Meanwhile, we had verifiable proof that this particular plaintiff wasn't exactly kind to his heart even when he wasn't taking Metabolife. But our proof that this man was a significant heart attack risk wasn't admissible.

[92] It's funny, when phenopropanolamine was taken down, most OTC companies went to ephedrine as a replacement, claiming that it "had a longer history, was safer, and more proven." Interesting...

During the suit, Pay made sure to update me on a daily basis (sometimes twice daily, whenever I felt a little anxious about the whole thing). With every passing call, he tried to reassure me. But with every passing call, it became clearer in his voice that Pay needed a little reassuring himself.

Finally, the day for the jury to deliberate came. We were all on pins and needles—and I mean all of us. Imagine working for a company that the media claims to be irresponsible, a company that promotes a potentially deadly product. I don't care who you are (founding CEO or front desk receptionist)—when you're tied to a notorious company, you yourself become notorious. Friends begin to alienate you. Family starts asking prodding questions they'd gleaned from the media. It's pretty much hell. So we all had a whole lot riding on the outcome of that suit.

I remember waiting by the phone for a call. All day. Finally, it came.

"Mike," said the familiar voice of Sam Baxter, "the results are in."

My heart raced. "And?"

"We won the case."

I pounded my fist on my desk in celebration.

Baxter continued. "The only thing they found us to be deficient on was the old label. They felt that we could have had more on our label in the early days."

"Well…" I said slowly. "We knew that. That's why we *changed* the labels."

Baxter chuckled slightly. "I know that, Mike. But the jury claims that we probably didn't provide the most thorough warning label back on the date in question."

"But I thought you said we won."

"We did."

My heart started pounding again. "Doesn't sound like a win to me."

"We won because the jury didn't award the plaintiff anything."

"They gave him *nothing?*"

"Nothing."

"That's great. But why?"

"They said that he was equally to blame. That he should have consulted a doctor about his medical condition before taking anything for weight loss. That even though our warning label didn't specifically say 'heart attack and stroke,' it was sufficient enough to clue him in to the idea that it would be dangerous to take in his condition."

I pounded my fist again. An enormous amount of stress forced its way out through my teeth. An unbelievable feeling. And all at once, euphoric, I realized that everyone else should share in it. So I called the front desk receptionist and asked her to pass the word over the intercom.

Almost immediately after I hung up the phone, I heard the receptionist's voice over the speakers in the hallway: "The plaintiff was found to be partly responsible for his injuries," she said. "He was awarded no money. We won the case!"

A wide smile crossed my face as I heard cheering and hollering reverberate from down the hallways. All afternoon, the entire staff celebrated. You could see this extra bounce in their step, hear extra vigor in their voices. It was like the whole building had just lifted a huge collective weight off its shoulders. And who could blame them? In this country, if the media even reports that you're being sued, you're automatically assumed to be guilty of wrongdoing. So each and every employee had this perception of guilt—this unfair tag as the "peddler of a dangerous product."

You know what's funny about the media, though? Even if you manage to win the lawsuit, even if you're found to be innocent where they had spent weeks calling you guilty, they don't run the story about your victory. Either they don't run it or they distort it. See, in this country, *the media is always right.* And if you're branded the villain, you're *always* the villain.

So we'd finally reached a point where we had our financial and legal feet on the ground. And now that we were a retail company, we had a firmer case against Metabolite (and we seemed to be winning it). When we filed the suit, for the purposes of researching our case, we were allowed access to Metabolite company records. These records revealed many things. Among them:

1. As a part of their marketing plan, Metabolite had specifically designed their product to confuse the consumer.
2. Wal-Mart had agreed to place this unproven product on an end-cap in every store.

Now, do I believe that Wal-Mart directly participated in confusing the consumer? I don't know. That's not for me to decide. But it certainly is odd that they would use an end-cap…

Anyway, in the end, Metabolite (the knockoff product) wound up settling the matter with us out of court—and needless to say, for a large sum of money.

Momentum. That's how it felt at the time. We were making money again. We were winning lawsuits. And for once, it seemed almost like we might be able to outlast the media. We had Dr. Smith and John Macaulay as our witnesses in every case. And they made great witnesses, seemed credible, and were always well-spoken and direct in deposition.

But then, as quickly as it had turned in our favor, the momentum shifted once again.

I'm standing with Mansfield in the hall outside my office. Mansfield's just come from a meeting with Pay and the counsel for our insurance company. As Steve and I talk, Pay lumbers up, looking like his foot's just been run over.

"You won't believe what just happened," he says.

"What?" I ask, feeling my face run white.

"Macaulay…" Pay says distantly.

"What?" I say frantically. "What about him?"

Pay sighs. "All these years, he's been lying to us about being an NP."

"What?" Mansfield asks, shaking his head aggressively.

Pay nods. "One of the PI attorneys we're up against researched his background and found that he hasn't even been *educated* in medicine."

I feel all the wind leave me. With Macaulay's testimony, we've been crushing cases. But if he really isn't who he says he is, we now have almost nothing to go on.

Mansfield looks floored. And why not? For as long as we've known John Macaulay, we've had no reason to disbelieve him about his background. [93] For example, during his effort to revise our computer systems, Macaulay had claimed that he was one of the first six people to help Microsoft get started. We had no reason to disbelieve him because he proved himself completely talented on our computer systems.[94]

But this most significant lie—this lie under sworn deposition about being a medical professional—now stands as the biggest setback for our company. We'd all been misled. And Macaulay had been caught this time.

After the news settles in, I immediately call Bob and Blevins. We set up a meeting with Macaulay in Bob's office, a fifteen- by twenty-foot space with no windows. Well organized, but still cluttered with plenty of work-related reading material.

"John," I say with a sigh, "do you know why you're in here?"

---

[93]   Later, I would begin to think about all the other things that Macaulay had told me over the years. Now that I'd thought about it, he did seem to have lived a pretty fantastic life. For example, he claimed to have played with the 49ers—and even to have been part of the famous Joe Montana/Dwight Clarke play in the 1982 NFC Championship Game, the play known simply as "The Catch." He had the Super Bowl rings to prove it, so we never questioned him about it. But later, in looking into NFL records, I discovered that Macaulay had earned his rings as a center on the practice squad. He never once saw the field for the 49ers.

[94]   Obviously, in retrospect, it wouldn't have taken a genius to figure out that Macaulay couldn't possibly have told the truth about Microsoft. He'd have been a billionaire.

John nods. His face is white as a sheet.

"Garry told us that you were caught lying under oath," I continue. "He says that you're not a nurse practitioner at all. That you've been lying to us all this time."

John shudders and shifts in his chair. "It's true."

I glance over at Blevins, who wears the expression of a man who's just caught his wife cheating on him. "How could you do that, John? We trusted you."

"The drugs," John says plainly.

"Drugs?" Bradley asks, his head cocking to one side in confusion.

"I've been using drugs for years," John explains. "I'm addicted. It's the drugs that caused me to lie."

We all sit in stunned silence.

"I don't know why I did it," John adds. "I'm so sorry."

I shake my head mournfully. "You understand the position you're putting us in here, John?"

"I know…I'm so sorry."

So that was that. John would wind up going on disability for his drug use and we would begin our research into his history. Our attorneys would discover that almost everything John had ever told us just wasn't true. Blevins, Bradley, and I remained (and remain) devastated over the betrayal of John Macaulay. We'd always trusted him, believed in him, and thought that he was the greatest, most trustworthy guy.

Having purged ourselves of one lying expert witness, we were obviously down. But not out. Our position then became, "Well, okay…we still have Dr. Smith." But in questioning further, we discovered that Dr. Smith was also a drug user. In fact, he had first met John Macaulay at a *rehab clinic*. [95]

---

[95] This little fact was most shocking to us given that we knew that our human resources team had done a complete background check on Smith before we'd originally hired him. Apparently, rehab isn't the sort of thing that shows up in background checks.

Given that all this new information had come to light, Doc Smith refused to testify in court. So in one fell swoop, we'd lost all of our medical staff.

In spite of it all, we continued to win our lawsuits. The reason? In the end, no matter what evidence is presented, it all comes down to the product. Even today, there's not *one shred* of evidence that Metabolife is dangerous if you take it as directed and heed the warnings.

We could prove all of this in court, of course, but we had yet to prove it on a grand scale. But in the period that followed, we would be given the opportunity to do just that. On the *grandest* of scales...

Chapter 17

The IRS Sticks Its Foot in the Door

In July of 2002, I had just returned from a multi-week vacation with my family. A much needed one. But I'd cut the vacation short because I'd finally received the green light from acting FDA Commissioner Lester Crawford to have a face-to-face meeting in Washington. Something I'd been waiting for for a long time.

Naturally, I was floored and excited to know that I would finally get the chance to put to bed this ridiculous issue about the safety of herbal ephedrine. I figured that an appointed official like Crawford might be more apt to listen to reason than the low-level bureaucrats I'd been dealing with up to that point.

So Garry Pay and I boarded a plane for D.C. I remember sitting near the front of the plane, waiting for passengers to board, when I noticed a man in a suit and dark glasses. Why did I notice him in particular? He seemed to be holding an unnatural level of interest in me. Every time I glanced over at him, he would look away. It seemed odd, but eventually, I just shook it off, chalking it up to paranoia.

Anyway, when our flight touched down in D.C., and we'd all filed out of the plane, I immediately turned on my cell phone. I had five unheard messages. All from Monica. Each one more frantic than the last.

Pay must have noticed my increasingly downtrodden expression, because he couldn't help but cut in.

"What is it, Mike?" he asked, his lips curling into a pained sort of frown. "What's wrong?"

"It's Monica," I said softly. "She's crying." I had a hard time deciphering her words as recorded and an even harder time repeating them. "Talking about our house being raided by 'agents.'" I covered my free ear with my hand, drowning out the dull lull of the bustling airport. "Says she could barely even slip away to make…this call."

"Agents?"

"I don't know. I think we've been hit with a warrant."

"What for?" Pay asked, sounding almost as confused as I felt.

I shrugged, my heart already in my shoes. Generally, I got the sense from the message that the agents were ordering my family around, tearing my house apart, and that my wife had no idea what to do.

The second I hung up the phone, my nerves went through the roof. I felt helpless. My family was obviously in trouble and there I was, all the way on the other side of the country.

Gary and I stood on one of those trams they have at the airport in D.C.—the ones that shuttle you from terminal to terminal—he awkwardly trying to assess my mood and I trying to figure out what the hell I was going to do. Regardless, I knew that I would have to cancel my long-awaited meeting with the FDA commissioner. I had no choice but to return home.

"What are you going to do?" Pay asked.

"I have to go back."

My attorney nodded agreeably.

"We'll buy a ticket home as soon as we get off this thing," I said, rattling the grimy silver pole designed to keep me from tumbling to the ground.

As soon as the words passed my lips, I noticed out of the corner of my eye the man from the plane. He stood behind us, apparently trying to look as inconspicuous as possible—but how inconspicuous can you be when you're wearing a suit and sunglasses (indoors) and always seem to be attempting to find space just behind someone, just within earshot? I shook him off again, deciding in one quick moment that both my problems could be solved simultaneously.

I dialed Monica. In three rings, she answered.

"What do I do?" she pleaded. "They're tearing the whole house apart."

"What are they doing?" I asked, having trouble hearing my wife over the roar of the tram.

"They're hitting Blevins' house, Metabolife, and Bob's warehouse or something." My wife sounded frantic.

"Okay," I said, as calmly as I could. "We'll figure this out. Don't worry, honey."

Monica began to cry. "They threw me out of the house and wouldn't let Yvonne leave."

Yvonne is Monica's youngest sister and our personal assistant.

I sighed and pinched the bridge of my nose. "Monica, listen…I want you to call an attorney right away."

"Uh-huh," Monica said through her sobs.

"Call an attorney, okay?"

This seemed to calm her some. "Yeah…yeah…I'll call."

So my wife held it all together. Really, I don't know what I would have done if she hadn't been home. If she hadn't been able to call an attorney. And if I'd known that a raid was going on and hadn't been able to talk to my wife, I might have lost my mind.

Anyway, the only attorney that Monica could get on such short notice was Blevins' attorney, a man named Mike Lipman. Since Lipman had apparently been called to represent Blevins during his portion of the search, he had to leave Blevins' residence to help out Monica.

Mike Lipman is a tall, thin, well-dressed[96] former assistant U.S. attorney. And given that he specialized in tax cases, I was thankful that Blevins proved willing to let him go for the morning. I also

---

[96] I always called Lipman "Farmer" because he once came to a meeting dressed in an outfit that looked kind of hayseed. He looked ridiculous. And with me, you never live down ridiculous.

knew that his special brand of smart-ass directness would help out when it came to getting on the level with a band of overly aggressive raiding agents. And, honestly, he's a great attorney.

The moment that the doors to the tram opened up at our destination, Blevins called to inform me that his attorney would be heading over to my house. Pay and I immediately bolted for the ticketing counter, where we bought tickets back home to San Diego. We were fortunate to get a flight at all—the only one left had a connection in Denver, and the Denver to San Diego leg only had two seats left.

Here's where things got interesting: As we were standing in line to buy tickets, I noticed that the guy in the suit had come up behind us. I figured at that moment that he was tailing me. I mean, who buys a ticket to D.C. then immediately buys a ticket back to San Diego? But we didn't have time to wait around and confirm my suspicions because we had to rush to get back to the other terminal, where we would immediately catch our flight to Denver.

But to get back to the other terminal, we had to take the tram again. And before the shuttle arrived, the guy in the suit was standing near us once again. Suspicions confirmed.

The tail boarded the flight to Denver just after we did. Suspicions further confirmed. Still, I knew that we would lose him in Denver because Pay and I had gotten the last seats on that connecting flight. [97]

No matter. Once the plane landed in Denver, I had bigger fish to fry: calling Mike Lipman to set up a meeting.

"Garry and I are on the next flight to San Diego," I said. "We'll be there in three hours. Where can we meet?"

"Let's meet at my office," Lipman offered. "I'll have everything ready by the time you arrive."

"Good. See you then."

I hung up the phone. And there Garry and I were, in some rotten terminal in Denver, coldly playing the waiting game. I sat there silently, brooding, knowing that my whole family was getting

---

[97] We would indeed lose the suspicious guy in Denver.

bullied around, knowing that everything I owned was getting tossed upside down, and not having any clue why it was all happening. For anyone who's never been in such a situation, it leaves you feeling a whole different brand of helpless.

It was David Brown's wife's birthday. To celebrate the occasion, he'd taken his family out to breakfast, with the plan that he would head in to work a little later than usual. So he was sitting in this restaurant when his phone started ringing. Garry Pay. Calling from D.C.

"David," Pay said, "you gotta get down to the office."

"What? Why?"

"Mike heard and Baxter confirms that there are agents down there. It's a raid."

David's head started swimming. "What? What do you mean it's a raid?"

"They have guns!" Pay howled, sounding like something out of *Bonanza*. "David, Baxter says they have guns!"

Naturally, Brown had to excuse himself from breakfast a little early. After apologizing profusely to his wife and kids, he made his way down to the Metabolife offices in haste. By the time he showed up, news helicopters had already begun circling the building. [98]

Brown examined the scene. Dozens, maybe hundreds, of agents scurried around, some of them checking cars and hassling employees, some of them darting in and out of the office buildings, some of them talking into two-way radios with "we-got-this-guy" smirks draped all over their faces. The CEO immediately made for the nearest such agent, tapping him on the shoulder and clearing his throat. "What's going on?" he asked.

"Mr. Brown," the agent said, "we're here to search the premises."

The fact that this agent knew his name without having to ask for it immediately struck Brown as odd. In fact, by all appearances,

---

[98] Strange that the media would know about an IRS raid long before the company's CEO.

every one of these agents seemed to have done his homework on the company and its personnel.

"What for?" Brown asked.

"I can't say, sir."

"You have a warrant?"

"Yes."

"May I see it?"

The agent waved his hand dismissively. "Martinez has it."

"Take me to him."

David was escorted by the agent over to one of those standard police-type vans. The man standing beside the van wore t-shades and a black bulletproof vest.

"This is Agent Martinez," the escorting agent said.

Martinez did not look up from whatever he was scrawling across the clipboard he held. At maybe 5′8″ and a little chubby, here was a man with a less than average appearance. Early to middle forties. Hispanic. Clearly the kind of man who looked like both an accountant and an idiot in his SWAT-style uniform. But I suppose both David Brown and I should have given him the benefit of the doubt from the beginning, given that he's reportedly handled many major investigations for the IRS. But, honestly, how can you respect the lead agent on the circus that was about to go down? Especially when the guy's such a wet rag to begin with.

"Mr. Brown," Martinez said, an air of condescension in his voice. "How are you?"

"I'd be better if you told me what this was all about."

"Don't worry." Martinez shook his head, grinning. "It has nothing to do with you."

"I know it has nothing to do with me." Brown glanced over at the Metabolife building. Several agents went barreling inside. "But I'm the CEO of the company you're tearing apart."

Martinez finally gave Brown his full attention, looking at him over the rim of his t-shades. "I'm well aware of that, Mr. Brown. And as I said, this has nothing to do with you. It has everything to do with the shareholders of Metabolife."

Brown began to lose patience. "Why would you raid us? Why

didn't you just give me a subpoena? We would've given you *anything* you asked for."

Martinez clucked the roof of his mouth. "Just doing what we were told to do."

The CEO of Metabolife International looked over the scene, feeling utterly powerless. He watched as one small battalion of agents carted away a trolley full of computers and what looked like hard drives and company records. They immediately began tossing it all into a truck similar to the one beside Martinez.[99] Standard search and seizure protocol didn't seem terribly high on their list of priorities.

Inside the office, things were just as cheerful. It was 8 a.m. when the IRS agents first busted through the door. Since Garry was with me in D.C., Sam Baxter, one of our newer lawyers at Metabolife, was the only legal counsel in the office at the time. Baxter was a lean young man in his middle twenties. An excellent attorney. Highly committed to Metabolife—which was a good thing, given that he would eventually end up being somewhat in charge of our civil litigation concerns. Sam sat at his computer, typing away, when, suddenly, a figure dressed in black appeared at his doorway.

"Can I help you?" Sam asked, confused.

"We're agents," the man in black said cryptically. "We need to talk to you right away."

Sam nodded and stood. But before he turned to leave, he leaned back down to shut off his computer.

"Don't! Touch! The! Computer!" the man in black shouted.

---

[99] It's interesting to note the IRS' apparent fixation with computers and company records. In fact, to our knowledge, seizing computer and paper files is the *only* thing the agents did on the day of the raid. David Brown feels particularly strongly about this point, given that as the CEO, he would have expected to be interviewed by an agent or two. Consider that point for a moment: On the day of an unannounced raid on Metabolife, the CEO of Metabolife *wasn't even interviewed*. They just took his computer, scanned his hard drive, and then returned it to him later.

The young lawyer backed away with both hands in the air. As he did so, he noticed the gun holstered conspicuously at the agent's side. Why did he notice it? Because the agent made a gesture to draw attention to the gun—as if he wanted Sam to know that, while he might not have drawn the thing on him, he still had it. And would use it, if need be.

"What's going on?" Sam asked, his voice quivering more from confusion than fear.

"We're here to seize all computer records."

"What?" Sam said, stunned. "Why?"

"You let us worry about that." The man in black backed in to a crowd of other agents, all of them charging down the hallway outside of Sam's office. Many of them were engaged in scanning the many computer terminals set up in the bullpens and offices everywhere. Some of them were engaged in the hassling of employees who'd had the misfortune to be at work so early in the morning.

Garry Pay. The name exploded in Sam's mind like a gunshot. *He'll need to know about this.*

At that moment, the attorney's phone rang. Garry. Apparently, the raiding agents were too busy sacking the place and scaring the employees to notice when Sam pressed the phone to his ear.

"Garry," Sam whispered, "there's a bunch of agents here. They won't say where they're from or what they're doing."

"I know," Pay said mournfully. "I heard."

"What should I do?"

Pay sighed. "Just keep cool. Ask to see the warrant."

Sam looked around the room nervously. Everyone seemed to be focusing on everyone and everything but him. Bodies everywhere, all dressed in black. Loads of yelling and running. "They aren't talking to me," he said.

"Well…" Pay said slowly. "Did you tell them that you're a lawyer?"

"No."

Long silence.

"I'll call David," Pay offered. "They'll listen to him."

Sam felt a wave of anxiety wash over him. "Please hurry, Garry," he said. "They're tearing the place apart."

"Hey!" came a voice. "Get off the phone! You can't make calls right now."

Sam looked to his right and saw the man in black who had shown him his gun. The man pointed his finger threateningly as he approached.

Sam hung up with Pay, quivering now with fear, not confusion. "I'm an attorney," he said. "Counsel to Metabolife. I'd like to see the search warrant."

Immediately, the approaching agent tensed up. When he continued his line, he seemed a little more willing to treat Sam humanely. "I'll see what I can do about that warrant," he said, sounding almost apologetic. "Follow me."

He escorted Sam to one of the corner employee lounges—an area where he wouldn't be bothered by all the yelling and running around. The two of them stood in this space for several minutes without talking. Sam tried to occupy himself by listening to all the crashing and banging going on around him. Then, a whole other concern hit him. All at once.

"Sir?" he said sheepishly.

The agent turned mechanically to look at his charge. He nodded.

"Can I use the bathroom?"

The agent smirked and turned to leave the lounge, motioning for Sam to follow. He actually escorted him to the bathroom and waited for him outside the door.

Sam could only watch for the next hour as the agents barked orders at the petrified staff. They would make each employee stand in the corner of his/her office while they accessed his/her computers. Much like with the attorney, they were only allowed bathroom breaks under the supervision of one of the raiding officers. And none of the employees were allowed to work or to leave. They all looked terrified.

Sam, meanwhile, did what he could to buddy up to the new pair of agents watching over him. They were young guys, these agents. Maybe twenty-one or twenty-two. And they, too, were dressed in those thick, black, bulletproof vests. Eventually, they loosened up to the point where they began sharing a little too much information with the young lawyer.

"So, are you ever going to tell me why you're here?" Sam asked, grinning in a brotherly sort of way. "What're you looking for?"

"Our supervisor thinks your bosses cheated on their taxes," Agent Number One said.

"And who's your supervisor?"

"Martinez," Agent Number Two said.

Sam tells me that he remembers sitting there and thinking, *You guys are fucking crazy.* "Hey listen," he said. "If this is only about Bob and Mike, then why don't you just let the employees go home?"

"They might take off with evidence," Agent Number One said flatly.

Baxter shook his head incredulously. "You could escort each of them out, if you want. But look at them, man." He pointed into the hallway. "They're terrified."

Agent Number One looked through the door leading out of the employee lounge. He must have gotten the point, because his face was much more sympathetic when he turned back inside. He nodded at Sam before picking up his thick, heavy two-way radio. "Is there any reason for all these people to be here?" he squawked into the box.

Silence—only static—from the other end.

Agent Number One depressed the button on his two-way once more. "I mean…we could just let them leave," he said. "They're not doing anything right now."

"Copy that," said a tinny voice from the other end of the line. "I'll look into it."

So in the end, it was Sam who managed to convince the agents to let all the employees go home. Everyone in the building and everyone in the parking lot[100] would finally be granted their right to leave.

After granting Sam's request, Agent Number One apparently felt a little chummier. "How can you work for those goons?" he asked.

"You mean Ellis, Bradley, and Blevins?" Sam asked, his eyebrow raised.

The agent nodded.

"They're great guys," Sam explained. "Great to work for."

Agent Number Two chuffed.

"You don't agree?" Sam asked, wheeling around to face the other agent.

"We don't necessarily think that Metabolife is bad," Agent Number Two explained. "But as long as you're associated with those owners of yours, we have good reason to be here."

Now it was Sam's turn to chuff. "But they're the *owners*," he said. "They made this company."

Both agents just shook their heads. A long, awkward silence followed.

"So what are you looking for, anyway?" Sam asked eventually.

"Don't know," Agent Number One said. "We're just supposed to copy everything on everyone's hard drives."

And now it was Sam's turn to shake his head.

At that moment, a big ruckus erupted from the lobby. Loads of hooting and hollering. It brought both agents guarding Sam to attention. Agent Number Two bolted for the door.

"Come with us," Agent Number One said, following his partner.

Sam got in line behind the two uniformed men and tailed them into the lobby. There, gathered around the fountain, were a few other uniformed men, most of them laughing, one of them soaking wet.

---

[100] See, when the agents raided the office, they found a few random employees coming and going in the parking lot. So what they did was order all of them back into their cars, where they were held and interrogated. Imagine sitting in your car, roasting in the early morning sun, and being grilled for reasons you don't even understand. That's how it went down for many of our employees. From what I've gathered, they were all getting a full dose of the good cop/bad cop treatment.

"What happened?" Agent Number Two asked.

"He fell in the fountain!" barked one of the agents on the scene, pointing at the dripping wet agent (who we'll call "Drippy").

I guess Drippy had been so excited about the idea that he'd "found something" (he hadn't) that he wasn't paying attention when he came down the stairs. In fairness to Drippy, the fountain was more like a circular pool of water in the center of the lobby—the whole thing surrounded by all these fake bamboo plants. I guess Drippy just didn't see it. And it wasn't the first time this had happened, either…

Back when we first moved into the building, we had an insurance broker investigate the place for any potential hazards. During the investigation, he fell into the fountain.

I'll never forget his reaction: "Um…you might want to take care of that," he said, soaking from head to toe.

So the thing had proved hazardous enough to get the best of our insurance broker, even. That's when we put in the bamboo— as a visual cue to avoid the edge of the pool. I guess it didn't work. Later, when I heard the story about Drippy, I made it a point to check on getting some glass put over it or something.

Anyway, the whole scene seemed to loosen everybody up. The agents even started to let Sam wander around the offices on his own. Now free to roam, the first person the young lawyer sought out was Steve Mansfield. He found him down the hall, talking heatedly with an agent.

"Steve," he said, "I'm glad you're here."

"Just got here," Steve explained. "What the hell's going on?"

"I don't know. Something about tax fraud."

Steve shook his head incredulously. "What was all that commotion in the lobby?"

Sam chuckled. "One of the agents fell in the fountain."

Steve flashed a wry grin. "I get it. He was looking for laundered money."

They both laughed.

"Listen," Steve said ominously. "Somebody needs to get over to the warehouse. They're searching there, too."

Sam volunteered for the job, figuring it might be good experience to oversee the execution of a search warrant. But when he got
down to the warehouse, he found everyone standing around
outside the gate.

He tapped the nearest agent on one of his broad shoulders.
"What's going on?" he asked.

"We're just waiting to go inside," Shoulders said.

"Waiting on what?"

Shoulders seemed uninterested in making eye contact with the
young lawyer. "They're getting someone to kill the security
cameras."

"Why?"

Shoulders shrugged.

Sam found himself a little confused. "What do you mean? Do
you mean you don't want to search with the cameras on?"

"Just doing what we're told."

The lawyer, frustrated and confused, turned around to take a
look at the small gathering of Metabolife employees standing
behind him. "What about all these people?"

"Can't let them inside," Shoulders said coldly.

Sam looked to his left and saw Jean Smith, an employee he
knew. She stood with her hands flat on the hood of her car as several
agents searched the trunk. I guess she'd arrived early that morning
to pick up some distributor files to bring back to the office. And
she'd had the misfortune of timing her departure from the warehouse right when the agents executed the warrant. So here they were,
having stopped her, putting her through an extensive search.

The lawyer shook his head in disgust. Jean never hurt a soul.
And here she was, being treated like a common criminal, being made
to hunch over her car while they tossed it, like some kind of mid-
level drug dealer in the streets of National City. It occurred to Sam
suddenly that if they'd been willing to go to such lengths with a
departing employee, they would certainly plan to go to such lengths
in the warehouse. And it almost made him laugh to think about
what a monumental undertaking that would be. We had hundreds

of six-foot-tall file cabinets in the warehouse, all of them containing detailed files on each of our thousands of distributors. I mean, that warehouse was wall-to-wall file cabinets.

"So what are you going to do once you're inside?" Sam asked.

"We're going to seize all of your records," Shoulders explained.

Sam chuffed. "Where are you going to put all of it? We've got hundreds of file cabinets in there."

"We're going to take 'em down to the federal building."

A smile began to form on the young lawyer's lips. "You think you have room down there?"

"Well...I don't know," Shoulders said slowly. "We'll put it in the parking lot."

Sam smirked now in full.

"Look," Shoulders explained, "you just caught us all a little off-guard here. We didn't know how much information we'd be dealing with."

I guess they finally managed to short the security cameras so they could feel comfortable enough to break into the warehouse. [101] And they did wind up having to rent trucks to take all the cabinets down to the federal building. I guess it literally took them all day to load everything up.

By the time Pay and I touched down back in San Diego, the whole scene at my house had blown over. Monica was home—picking up and trying to figure out what had just happened—and my kids were with a family friend. So since we knew that all of them were now safe, Pay and I went straight from the airport to Lipman's office. There, I found Lipman, Steve Mansfield, Bob Bradley, and

---

[101] And let's examine that strange point for a moment. If you're executing a perfectly legal search and seizure, why would security cameras matter? If they were confident that they were in the right with their warrant and that their agents would act accordingly, wouldn't they *want* to capture all of that on tape? I've heard of people cutting security cameras before charging into places. They're called thieves.

Mike Blevins. All they knew at the time was that we'd just been the victim of an IRS raid and that the agents were searching everything. Warehouses, homes, everything. I remember laughing when I heard that the reason for the raid was a so-called "tax issue."

"What tax issue?" I asked, chuckling. "We don't *have* a tax issue."

"Well, they think you do," Steve explained.

"This is ridiculous," Blevins said.

"Who's the prosecuting attorney on this?" Pay asked.

"Phil Halprin," Steve said dryly. "Assistant U.S. attorney."

"Steve," Lipman said, pinching the bridge of his nose, "one of us needs to go talk to Halprin and figure out what this is all about."

"I'll see what I can do tomorrow," Steve said. "First, I think Mike and I should go back to his place and talk to his wife about what went on today."

I agreed and we adjourned.

Back at home, Steve and I sat down with Monica to get the whole story. The following is how she related it to me:

She was having coffee with her sister, Yvonne, and her sister-in-law, Flo. So they were all sitting at the kitchen counter, chatting away over a little caffeine. The three of them were laughing over a joke Yvonne had just cracked when Monica looked out the window. There, she saw several cars come squealing up the driveway.

Her heart raced.

Men in black uniforms sprang from every door of every car. My wife bolted for the front entrance, getting there just as the men were preparing to knock it down with one of those handheld battering rams.

"What are you guys doing?" Monica asked frantically.

Two of the agents shoved my wife out of the way. Many more poured into the house behind them.

"Who are you?" Monica asked desperately.

"Move aside!" the agent holding the battering ram said (we'll call him "Rammy"). "Do you have any guns?"

"No," Monica said, confused. "Why?"

"Is there anyone else in the house?" Rammy asked.

"My two children are in bed," Monica said reluctantly. Then, she pointed back to the kitchen. "And then there's us three."

"Where are the children?"

"Down in bed."

Rammy signaled for two of his comrades to grab Yvonne and Flo. The men then led the women outside.

"Who are you?" Monica asked.

"Stand back!" Rammy howled.

My wife was shoved out of the way once more. "Wait," she pleaded. "I want to go down there with you. You can't just grab my kids."

Another agent shoved past Monica, staggering down the hallway. We'll call this agent "Drunky," for reasons that should soon become obvious.

En route, Rammy, Drunky, and another agent ran into Mikey, who had woken from all the ruckus and now walked down the hallway in his underwear.

"What's going on?" my son asked sleepily.

He received a terse reply. "Where's your brother?"

"In the room," Mikey said, confused as he pointed to the bedroom behind him.

Monica explained that her heart practically leapt from her chest as she watched the three men burst into her youngest son's bedroom. See, Nicholas had been awake all through the previous night due to an asthma issue. It had gotten so bad that he'd had to lie down with a nebulizer on his face. He still rested under the nebulizer when the agents burst in.

Drunky pulled the nebulizer off my son, waking the boy up. In the confusion, Nicholas must have thought that the agent pulling him out of bed was me, because he went to give him a hug. The moment he realized that it wasn't me, fear overwhelmed him, triggering another asthma attack.

"Get his nebulizer!" Monica wailed as the three agents escorted my sons past her. "He can't breathe!"

The agents ignored my wife. Instead, they took my children onto the driveway, both of them still in their underwear, Nicholas gasping for air. Monica followed them out. She lunged for her children, but the agents held her back. Then they led her back into the family room.

"Who are you people?" Monica asked, tears pouring down her face.

"Ma'am," Rammy said, "are there any guns in the house?"

"No, I told you that. Who are you people?"

"Is there anyone else in the house?"

"You have all of us out here. *Who are you people?*"

"Would you look at all this nice furniture?" Drunky said, kicking his booted foot at the sofa. "I wonder how they could afford all of it."

Several of the other agents laughed uncomfortably.

Drunky got right up next to my wife, bending down to speak right into her ear—so close that she could smell the alcohol on his breath. "Wonder what everything costs here?"

More derisive laughter.

This sort of thing went on for another ten minutes. [102] They continued to hold Monica in the family room and my children in the driveway. Monica's sister and sister-in-law were arguing with several of the agents in the yard.

Finally, a supervisor came to Monica. She was a woman, and carried an air of compassion about her that brought just a little warmth to the increasingly cold environment.

"Who are you people?" my wife repeated softly.

"Ma'am," the supervisor said, "we're IRS agents."

"Do you have a warrant?" Monica asked, crying softly.

She handed over the warrant.

Monica would later explain that the raiding agents must have had a blueprint of the house before they'd raided, because they

---

[102] And keep in mind that the agents still hadn't identified themselves. For all my wife knew, we were being robbed in broad daylight by men in bulletproof vests.

seemed to know exactly where everything was. Once they had my entire family "secured," they made straight for the walk-in closet in the master bedroom. I had put a safe room in this closet, which must have been included in the blueprints, because the agents knew it was there. The only problem was that they couldn't find it (which, of course, meant that my safe room had worked out exactly as I'd hoped it would in the event of emergency). See, this safe room was designed to hold my family. If we'd ever been attacked, I would have had to remove the clothing rack on the end of the closet, let my family inside the room, lock it up, and then replace the rack. This meant that I would've been left outside to take whatever danger was coming. Fair trade.

In any case, the IRS escorted my wife into the bedroom, demanding that she help them uncover the entrance.

"Where's the safe room?" Rammy asked.

Monica pointed to the clothing rack and explained that it would need to be removed. Rammy and another agent grabbed the rack and tossed all the clothing onto the floor.

"Look at all your clothes," Drunky said. "Who needs this much...this much clothes?"

Monica turned her head away as several of the agents cackled.

At that moment, Rammy and his pal burst through the safety door and into the safe room. Inside, in addition to a small space to hold my family, they found two safes: a large one and a smaller one. [103]

"Whose safe is that?" Rammy asked, pointing at the larger of the two.

"It's ours," Monica said nervously.

Rammy pointed at the smaller safe. "And whose is that?"

My wife began to quiver anxiously. "It's not mine."

"That's not your safe?"

"It's not my safe."

---

[103] The large one I'd purchased specifically for the safe room, but the smaller one Monica had for years.

Rammy stepped aside and waved his hand dramatically. "Open them."

Monica would later explain that she immediately knew she'd slipped up. Why? Because the smaller safe *was* hers. There's a story behind why this point is so important:

At the time of my conviction back in 1991, I knew that I could no longer possess firearms. So I asked a federal agent friend of mine what I should do with the two handguns that I already had.

"Just give them to your girlfriend," he said.

I agreed. "She might need the protection, anyway." See, since I had cooperated so willingly with the government, I was always worried about potential backlash from my police department shooting and my drug arrest. I figured that there were plenty of people out there who might want to get even with me by hurting the ones I loved.

So I gave my guns to Monica, my girlfriend at the time, explaining to her that I couldn't have access to them, no matter what. She promised that she would keep them away from me—and to that end, she bought a safe that only she would know the combination to. She put several things in there with the guns, including her paper copy of the safe's combination. [104] Long story short, for the three or four years leading up to the raid, we couldn't access that safe, even if we wanted to.

But now we were faced with two problems. First, Monica had accidentally told the agents that the small safe didn't belong to her. Who could blame her? Here she was, getting shoved around so threateningly, and she knew that there were guns inside. I would

---

[104] I know that Monica put her only copy of the combination in the safe because she also put one other item in there: the pink slip to a Mercedes SL that I would buy a few years later. See, by the time I went to sell the Mercedes, my wife had forgotten the combination to the safe. So with the only paper copy of the combination inside, I couldn't sell my Mercedes. Instead, I had to fill out a form at the DMV, indicating that I'd lost the pink slip to my car. There are records of this. There are records, also, of the fact that we once called a locksmith to help us with the safe (but that locksmith never showed up).

have been nervous, too. And second, she couldn't exactly help the agents get into that safe because she still didn't remember the combination.

"What's wrong?" Rammy asked coldly.

Monica trembled with fear and frustration as she tried the lock once more.

"Why aren't you opening the safe?"

"She's doing it on purpose," the supervisor suggested, all compassion suddenly leaving her voice.

"Are you stalling for time?" Rammy asked.

Monica shook her head silently as tears streamed down her face. She moved over to the larger safe—the one whose combination she did remember—but was so anxious that she couldn't get it open.

"Why won't you open these safes?" Rammy asked.

"I can't," Monica explained, quivering.

"Why not?"

"I just...can't."

"Why don't you just give us the combination?" the supervisor suggested.

My wife did as she was told. The agents quickly opened the large safe.

"What's the combination to this one?" Rammy asked, pointing to the smaller safe.

Monica shook her head as she cried. "I don't remember."

"You don't remember?" Rammy asked skeptically.

"No," Monica said softly.

Sarcasm now: "*Right.*"

A few minutes later, the supervisor called in a safe cracker, who had little trouble forcing his way inside. They all practically drooled, I'm sure, as they looked over the safe's contents. Hand guns. Monica would later say that they couldn't seem to wipe the grins off their faces as they impounded my old gifted guns.

When they had finished with the safe room, they searched every other room in the house, beginning with the bedroom, where

Drunky immediately started rifling through Monica's underwear drawer, holding each piece up and laughing.

"Oooh," he would say, "look at this one. I wonder what it cost."

Laughter. All of this happening right in front of my wife.

They searched the children's rooms, turning everything upside down. They searched my home office, where they copied my hard drive and took all of my white papers. They rendered the family room in such a way that it didn't look like the same room anymore once they'd finished.

By the time they started in on their search of Flo and Yvonne's cars, Lipman finally arrived.

"What are you doing?" the lawyer asked sharply.

"Searching the cars," one of the agents said.

Lipman made a motion to shoo the agent away. "You can't search these cars. That's ridiculous."

"Who are you?"

"I'm this woman's attorney," Lipman said, pointing at my wife (who had finally been allowed outside to comfort her crying children). "May I see the warrant, please?"

Monica, on her knees, a sobbing son under each arm, looked up at Lipman and thanked him. "Is there any way I can get these two out of here?" she asked.

"Certainly," Lipman said, suggesting that Monica should call a friend to come pick up the kids.

So my wife called Quinn Early, a family friend and former NFL player with the Jets, Chargers, Bills, and Saints. Quinn said that he would be over right away.

The moment Monica hung up the phone, a younger agent came up to her, looking dejected and apologetic.

"Ma'am," he said softly, "I'm really sorry for all of this. It shouldn't have happened this way."

Monica nodded, too frustrated to speak.

A few minutes later, just as the agents were yanking Yvonne back into the house for more questioning, Quinn Early delivered on his promise. He pulled up and quickly ushered the kids into his car.

Monica sighed in desperate relief as she waved the three of them off.

The agents remained for hours, still playing with Monica's clothing while searching and seizing who-knows-how-many documents. By the time I arrived home, they'd been gone for maybe an hour. And our house was in shambles.

Later that night, once the IRS had finished raiding the warehouse, Sam Baxter secured the building. Feeling bad for all the agents who had had to remain at the Metabolife offices all day, the young lawyer went to a local taco stand and picked up a bunch of tacos to bring back to the main building.

When he returned, box of tacos in hand, he found only two agents left in the building. The two of them slouched in their chairs by a bank of computers, guarding them, I guess. Sound asleep.

Confused and a little amused, Sam called me from his cell phone.

"Mike," he said, "where are you?"

"Home now," I said. "Finally."

"You're never going to believe this."

"What now?"

"I'm back at the office and there are these two agents here."

"Yeah? So?"

Sam laughed under his breath. "So they're sleeping. They're sort of hunched over in these computer chairs. Sleeping."

Despite all that had gone wrong on that day, I laughed. "Sam, here's what you do."

I could hear Sam breathing as he listened closely.

"You go down to the liquor store and buy a bottle of Jim Beam."

"Mike…" Sam interrupted.

"No, no," I said. "Hear me out. You take the bottle and you pour half of it out. Get some of it on the agents."

"Mike…"

"And then you put the half-empty bottle on the table next to them and take pictures."

Sam stood silently for a long while, I guess mulling it over. For a minute, it almost seemed like he'd go through with it. "Mike," he said finally, "I can't do that."

I couldn't blame him for shooting me down. I was half-kidding with him anyway. And, of course, I understood. He's a lawyer. Ethics wouldn't allow him to do something like that.

It's funny to think how ethics can drive one man and not another. Later, I would learn that the Department of Justice tends to check its ethics at the door. And today, when I think about the opportunity that literally lay before Sam Baxter, I can't help but wish he'd bought that bourbon. I mean, how's a man to play a fair game when the rules are completely stacked against him?

At my request, Steve Mansfield's first stop after the raid was Phil Halprin's office. He went in maybe a little biased about what to expect (we'd heard a great deal from several of Halprin's former coworkers about the assistant U.S. attorney's reputation). Word had it that he was jovial and gregarious—a real fun guy to have around the office. A talker. A chatter. A divulger. [105]

As he stood now in his office, Steve thought about how Halprin was purportedly a good attorney, but only when he actually felt like working. The rap on him was that he usually took the lazy way out, [106] preferring instead to train for one of his many bicycle races. That was Halprin: an avid competitive cyclist (despite his bad hip and

---

[105] Word also had it that defense attorneys loved squaring off against Phil Halprin because he wouldn't shut up. They'd get more support from their cases from his mouth than from anywhere else.

[106] Threatening witnesses with incarceration if they didn't confess to things they didn't actually do, cutting backhanded deals, pawning off the toughest work on his junior colleagues, etc.

rather pudgy frame). The kind of guy who would put a federal case on the backburner so he could train for the Hell's Kitchen 503. [107]

Don't get me wrong; Halprin had a reputation of being a highly competitive and powerful advocate…when he put his mind to it. Mostly, though, he would string along single cases (for years) with exorbitant subpoenas and unnecessary warrants, just so he could keep his workload light. Give him credit: He knew how to take advantage of the system. But what else could you expect from a seventeen-year bureaucrat with a family and a time-consuming hobby?

"Why all this for an IRS investigation?" my lawyer asked him. "Why didn't you just subpoena everything?"

Halprin's tone and posture (throughout the whole ordeal, really) couldn't have been more condescending. "Because I don't trust the owners that they wouldn't destroy everything," he said, sneering through his Van Dyke mustache. "In fact…I'm really…*concerned.*"

"About what?"

Halprin thrust one finger down onto the surface of his desk. "I want to know who in the FBI tipped you guys off about our raid."

Steve (a former U.S. attorney himself) stood in shock. "What are you talking about?"

Halprin shook his head as if trying to remove cobwebs. "I know there were agents who tipped them off."

My attorney smiled in utter disbelief. "Why would you think that?"

"Because all the stuff we were looking for wasn't there."

Steve chuckled cathartically. "Listen to yourself, Phil," he said. "That's *crazy.*"

"You tell Ellis, Blevins, and Bradley that if they tell me who tipped them off, I'll go easier on them."

Steve left Halprin's office feeling entirely beside himself. Strange and unproductive as the whole meeting had been, his next stop

---

[107] Even during the Metabolife investigations, it was a standing joke that you'd never be able to reach Halprin after noon because he'd be out training on his bike. I wanted to have him followed by private investigators and filmed squandering his tax-funded salary on extracurriculars, but my attorneys claimed that such an act could be construed as an obstruction of justice.

would be the Metabolife offices, where he would meet with Pay, Lipman, Bradley, Blevins, and me. He still seemed to be having trouble believing it himself as he told us the story about what Halprin had said.

We all had a good laugh about it.

"Why would he say that?" Bob asked. "Why would the FBI even want to call us?" [108]

Nobody knew. We only had stories about Halprin's ridiculous behavior to draw from. For example, there was a case he'd once prosecuted—long before Metabolife—and he'd done something that would likely get him in trouble. A concerned agent wrote a letter to the judge presiding over the case, hoping to clear the air about Halprin's supposedly unethical behavior. Apparently, Phil got wind of the letter. So he took it upon himself to remove the damaging document from the judge's chambers so the judge wouldn't read it. Imagine an attorney stealing a judge's mail.

Phil did get caught for his theft, which landed him in trouble with the judge and the U.S. Attorney's Office. I don't know what happened to him as far as his conduct was concerned, but if you or I were ever caught stealing a letter from a federal judge's chambers, I can't help but believe we'd be in prison.

So, yeah, that was Phil: a man who, on little more than a whim, would authorize one of the biggest IRS raids in the history of the Southern district. A man who could very well have been responsible for alerting the media about the raid before the agents even arrived at Metabolife to serve their warrant. A man for whom the end always justified the means. Soon, we would discover that this point also extended to his desire for the spotlight. See, Phil Halprin loved seeing his name in the headlines…

---

[108] Now this is all hearsay, but I heard sometime later that the director of the FBI got wind of Halprin's allegations. What I heard secondhand was that the director went into the U.S. attorney's office and yelled at Halprin about even accusing the FBI of interfering with an investigation. But that's Phil Halprin in a nutshell. If you believe the word on the street, he'd pissed off so many people that the only government agencies who would work with him anymore were the FDA and the IRS.

Chapter 18

Guns, Or
"The $93 Million Farce"

Three days following the raid on Metabolife and my home, we would get the pleasure of the IRS' company at our family's ranch, a piece of property that we'd purchased near the end of 1997. The 165-acre ranch rested near San Diego in a town called Julian. A nice place, this ranch—and one that we had turned into a kind of playground for the family. We had a ballfield out there. A lake. Plenty of wide-open space.

We had two houses on the property: one of them a duplex and the other a smaller home where Louis, our groundskeeper, took residence. Monica's sister, Charity, and her husband, Guillermo (who everyone called "Memo") lived in one half of the duplex with their children, five-year-old Alejandro (who we all called "Alex") and three-year-old Alicia. Memo and his family stayed on one side of the duplex, year round. Monica, the kids, and I would stay in the other side whenever we came up to visit. Since we didn't get up to the ranch nearly as often as we would have liked, my family's side of the house was basically empty. There were some clothes up there, basic furnishings, but not much else. The two sides of the duplex were completely divided. You had to go outside to get from one to the other.

Memo was in his late twenties. Good-looking, fairly tall, and in great shape. As an incredibly nice and engaging former member of the U.S, Army, everybody seemed to like him. And with his background in the military and his current job working for the border patrol, he was certainly no stranger to guns or even police action. So three days following the raid on our house, when Memo looked out his window and saw dozens of black cars coming up the long driveway from the road, I'm sure he wasn't terribly surprised.

He would later tell me that there were many agents in the approaching unit, many cars. And one solitary sheriff's department car bringing up the rear. The sun beat down heavily from the sky, glinting from their black hoods and dying on their tinted windows.

Charity, curious as to what her husband was looking at so intently, took a look out through the other kitchen window. "What's going on?" she asked frantically.

"I don't know," Memo said calmly. "You stay here with Alicia." He then turned to his son, who looked up at him with excited eyes. "Come with me, boy."

Memo walked out through the front door, five-year-old Alex in tow. He flatted his hand and placed it over his brow, shielding his eyes from the sun. With his son by his side, he waited for the long line of cars to draw up beside the house.

The instant the caravan stopped, every door of every car flung open, agents pouring out all over the place. Memo explained that, before he could even process what was going on, there were agents all around him, all of them dressed in black, some of them with guns drawn. A few of the officers wore black, bulletproof vests (with no shirt on beneath). IRS desk-jockey Rambos.

As Memo tells it, the agent who appeared to be in charge—the one wearing aviator shades with a nice mirror-shine—stalked up to him with his gun drawn.

"Freeze, motherfucker!" he barked.

Memo raised both hands in the air, high above his head. "Hey, I'm not going anywhere," he said. "I'm a vet."

Alex tugged on his dad's shirt, silently curios, silently petrified.

"I don't care what the fuck you are," the agent howled. "Get on the ground or I'll shoot you."

The young boy broke instantly into tears. "Don't shoot my daddy!" he wailed.

"Get the fuck down!" the agent repeated.

Aviator Shades pulled Alex away from his father while another of his cohorts thrust his gun in Memo's face. My brother-in-law slowly lowered himself to the ground, where he was quickly cuffed, his hands behind his back.

So with Memo lying on the ground in handcuffs, his children crying and pleading, and his wife hysterical, the agents charged into the house, strafing around in search of more people. Memo tells me that the way they were acting, you would've thought it was another Waco.

Finally, after about a half-hour of searching, the agents came back outside and removed Memo's cuffs. Only then did they present him with a search warrant. My brother-in-law looked it over with a skeptical eye—but here's a man trained for combat, not for legal matters. He grumbled and nodded, which immediately sent the agents scrambling into groups. One group would search Memo's side of the duplex, another would search the garage we had on the property, and still another would search the home of Louis, our groundskeeper. [109]

"Where are the guns?" Aviator Shades asked my brother-in-law.

"They're in the closet," Memo said, smirking at the comedic value of the whole scene. *Who the hell were these guys? And what did they think they'd gotten themselves into?*

"Take us there!"

Memo calmly led the agents through the house and to the closet in question. As the officers stood behind my brother-in-law, many of them still holding the jumpy posture of attack-mode, one of the sharper-minded agents noticed that the door was padlocked.

---

[109] They found a .22 rifle at Louis', but it should be pointed out that the search warrant did not cover our groundskeeper's home. They searched it anyway...

"Where's the key?" Aviator Shades asked.

"In the bedroom," Memo explained. "I'll get it."

One of the agents escorted Memo into the bedroom, where he retrieved the key and brought it back into the hall.

"Give it to me," Aviator Shades demanded. The agent flailed for the key, inserting it into the lock as soon as it was in his hand. He unlocked the closet.

Inside, they found Memo's guns. Not exactly Ruby Ridge grade material (just a few rifles he used for his hobby: range shooting). But guns are guns, I guess, and it seemed increasingly likely that guns were exactly what these agents were after. [110] The suspicion was confirmed when one of the agents, we'll call him "Camera Eye," swooped in and started snapping pictures of everything.

"We have to impound these," Aviator Shades explained.

"Why?" Memo asked.

"You let us worry about that."

"Have I done something wrong?"

"No." Aviator Shades turned to smile hungrily at a few of the other officers. "We're here about Mike Ellis."

Memo scoffed. "Well, I can save you some time, then. He's never been in this closet. Never touched those guns."

Aviator Shades dropped his aviator shades a little lower on his nose, glaring over the top of them with his piercingly serious eyes. "How do *you* know?"

My brother-in-law had a hard time keeping from laughing in frustration. "You saw it, man!" he said. "It was *locked*. Those are *my* guns, not his."

Aviator Shades waved his hand in a dismissive sort of way. "Get him out of here," he said, obviously exasperated. "We've got work to do."

One of the agents, we'll call him "Grabby," led Memo out of the bedroom and into the hallway. Grabby, apparently eager to get his hands dirty, left my brother-in-law under the watchful eye of

---

[110] Despite the fact that many (if not most) of the agents seemed to be wearing the insignia of the Internal Revenue Service: with the acronym "IRS" printed in giant white letters across the backs of their bulletproof vests.

the lone deputy from the sheriff's department. The deputy, in turn, led Memo down into the kitchen, away from all the ruckus.

"I'm really sorry about all this, Memo," he said softly. "The way they're acting. What they're doing. It's all bullshit."

"I appreciate that, officer," Memo said resolutely. "Not your fault."

The two men stood in uncomfortable silence for a moment, the kind of awkwardness that comes from recognizing but not really knowing another man from your small town.

"Who are these guys, anyway?" Memo finally asked.

"Well," the deputy said, making a list with his fingers, "we've got guys from the IRS and guys from the ATF. I think that's everybody."

"Who are the ones running around in the black vests with no shirts?"

The deputy clucked his teeth. "That's the IRS."

"Who do they think they are?" Memo asked, chuckling.

The deputy shrugged. [111]

Memo looked through the kitchen window and into the yard, where an agent was standing beside his wife and two children. Charity was in tears as she pressed her children's faces to her side, trying to shield them from all the frightening things going on. The kids cried, too. My brother-in-law's heart leapt into his throat. Anger began to spread.

At that moment, a loud crashing noise came from another room. That did it for Memo. He'd seen enough of this ridiculousness. But what could he do? He couldn't go back into the rooms. Instead, he glanced at the deputy. The deputy gave him a knowing nod, signaling that it would be okay for him to leave, if that's what he wanted to do. So Memo walked straight out the front door.

He quickly checked on his family. Charity and her children

---

[111] It should be mentioned here that the ATF actually searched the ranch appropriately, conducting themselves in a professional manner—a manner befitting an officer of the law. It was the IRS agents who were acting like idiots, pointing their guns everywhere, swearing in front of the children, turning the place upside down.

were being held in the yard by a few of the ATF agents, who seemed to be treating them well, despite their obvious fears. The three of them cried silently.

Memo sized up the ATF agents. They appeared to be accommodating. And the looks they gave him suggested he was welcome to talk to his family.

"Are you okay?" Memo asked his wife softly.

Charity nodded.

"You're sure?"

She nodded again.

"I'm going down to the garage, then."

She nodded again.

Memo turned slowly, lending one last appraising glance at the agents. The two of them seemed more interested in talking quietly to one another than terrorizing his family.

So my brother-in-law headed for the garage. As he approached, he noticed that many agents darted in and out of the doors to the building, hustling between their cars and the site of their apparently frantic search.

By the time he reached the garage, Memo could see that the IRS agents were indeed having a field day. He wasn't surprised, given that this is where he and Louis kept all of their ammunition and even a couple of extra guns. See, in addition to Memo's range shooting hobby, Louis kept his .22 rifle on site in order to kill the rattlesnakes that occasionally slithered a little too close to the house.

Anyway, I guess because of the fact that all of these guns were seized on a ranch that I owned, the agents assumed that they all belonged to me. Either way, they continued taking pictures of everything—hundreds of pictures.

Now, here's how the chain of evidence is supposed to go:

Step one: Uncover incriminating material.
Step two: Take a picture of the item exactly where you found it.

Step three: Remove the item from its original location
              and take a picture of it on its own.
Step four: Tag and bag the item for evidence processing
              (such as fingerprinting and/or DNA swabbing).
Step five: Take a picture of the original location without
              the item in it (to demonstrate that the item
              has been properly seized).

Now, this is all normal protocol when executing a search warrant—
and Memo couldn't exactly keep an eye on everything that was
going on (there was just so much going on)—but my brother-in-
law felt certain that a few of the agents weren't exactly following
everything to the letter.

"That's all mine, too," Memo said, pointing at a few items that
some of the agents were sifting through.

"I'm sorry," one of the agents said (and we'll call him "Sifty").
"But we need to seize it all, anyway."

"That's fine," Memo said, shaking his head. "Just be careful."

"We've got your brother-in-law dead to rights on this shit," Sifty
said.

"I told you that stuff is mine." Memo's voice was slightly more
emphatic this time.

"His ranch, his guns," Sifty explained.

I guess Memo got a little nervous upon hearing that. And the
fact that the agents were basically just throwing his things around
didn't help him any with his anxiety.

As my brother-in-law left—still feeling fairly confident that
the agents just might wind up burning the place to the ground in
their overeager states—he noticed that several of them had laid
out a few things on the work table at the head of the garage. What
he saw was a gun that belonged to him, a blue duffle bag, and a
couple of boxes of ammunition. They took a picture of the pile
just as he turned the corner and headed back up toward the
house.

As he approached the house, he overheard a conversation between the two ATF agents who had been watching his family.

"This isn't possession for Ellis," the first agent said.

"You ain't kidding," the second agent said.

"I mean, they've only found stuff in the other house and the garage. There's no way they can prove Ellis even knew it was there, let alone had access to it."

"I know! It was all locked up!"

The first agent shook his head. "Fucking IRS."

After overhearing this conversation, Memo decided that it was time to just let the officers do their thing. If they were going to behave like idiots, there was nothing he could do about it. And besides, he had a frightened family to attend to.

So considering the fact that Memo spent most of the remainder of the raid huddled in the yard with his crying wife and children, the majority of the information that I am about to reveal came to me not from a person on the scene, but from my lawyers. I learned most of the following information after the fact, once my legal team had had the opportunity to examine the so-called evidence produced by the raid.

Now, we aren't sure when the search began on my end of the duplex (it could have been after the garage or it could have occurred simultaneously), but at some point, the IRS agents began to search the closet in my bedroom. Inside, they found a scant array of clothing, some shoes, and, reportedly, a blue duffel bag full of ammunition, assorted fishing gear, and a knife. [112]

When I first examined the docket of seized items, it was the duffle bag that confused me the most. Not only had I never seen a blue bag that met that description, but I knew that I didn't even have any fishing

---

[112] It should be mentioned that Memo was in fact present when the agents first searched my closet. He'd taken momentary reprieve from watching over his family when the agents began tearing up my end of the duplex. According to him, when they first searched the closet, they found only clothing and some shoes. There was no duffel bag uncovered in the initial search. Only after Memo left the bedroom did the blue duffel bag magically appear. Memo testified to this under oath in front of a grand jury.

gear in my house, let alone bullets and a knife. I honestly don't know how a bag such as the one seized could have ended up in my closet.

But there it was, in living color: The investigating agents claimed to have found in my possession a blue bag full of ammunition. And under the statutes of the law, the act of possessing ammunition as an ex-felon is known as "constructive possession of firearms or ammunition," a felony. Conveniently, Phil Halprin and the U.S. Attorney's Office would now have something they could use to leverage a plea in their pending IRS case against me. [113] And it was substantial leverage: If they could prove that that bag did in fact belong to me (it didn't), it would come with a sentence of five years.

Even though my legal team and I were still a little confused as to why the IRS would investigate Metabolife and its founders at all, we could rest easily because we knew that we hadn't committed tax fraud of any kind, let alone the kind of tax fraud that would trigger such a significant raid. But the question still remained about who had pointed the dogs in our direction in the first place. And why?

We would have to wait approximately a year to receive an answer to this question. It would come in the form of the affidavit that led to the search, which was unsealed for the media.

In a nutshell, the following points would be covered in the affidavit:

- That Ken Dix, by far our weaseliest attorney, had made incriminating statements against Metabolife— completely in violation of attorney/client privilege. [114]

---

[113] And would it surprise you to learn that, within a short period of time, this also became an FDA investigation? Well, it did. See, once the IRS had executed their warrants on Metabolife, the FDA was legally free to waltz in with its own warrant, seeking the call records we had on site.

[114] Not that we would have needed to invoke privilege, anyway. See, statements that Dix provided to the government were later proven to be completely untrue.

- That Jeff Anderman, our cookie-suit-wearing CFO, had made false statements about Blevins, Bradley, and me, indicating that the three of us had been regularly engaged in the siphoning off of company funds into an offshore bank account.[115]
- That the IRS claimed to have evidence backing up Anderman's claims about offshore accounts—also proven (upon subsequent government investigation) to be flatly false.
- That the IRS claimed to have reason to believe that the founders of Metabolife had defrauded the government of *$93.7 million* in taxes.[116]
- That John Macaulay had flatly lied about me and Metabolife's call records.

In retrospect, it seems logical to infer that this final point on the list is the reason that the investigation quickly became an FDA investigation. The more I reviewed Macaulay's story, though, the less sense it made to me. In his statement, he claimed that he'd once walked into my office to tell me about a valid injury suffered by one of Metabolife's customers. He claimed that I furiously grabbed the record of the incident out of his hand, crumbled it up, and threw it into the garbage can, saying, "Don't ever bring this stuff in to me

---

[115] These claims were such blatant lies that, later, when asked to testify, Anderman would invoke the Fifth Amendment, refusing to repeat his accusations on the grounds that it would incriminate him.

[116] The formula used to arrive at this completely asinine figure was cooked up by one Agent Martinez. Later research into the matter would prove that Martinez had essentially invented his own calculation to arrive at the number—all without even examining our tax records in order to validate it. In a nutshell, Martinez essentially looked at our reported deposits and compared them with our reported sales. And without paying attention to tax codes or tax records, this enterprising CPA concocted a rudimentary and backwards mathematical formula that arrived at a staggeringly large number: $93.7 million. An impossible number (as you'll see later), but certainly one that would warrant a massive, massive raid.

again. The government would stomp a bloody hole in my chest if they knew about this." Seriously.

Two things seemed a little off about this story. The first was that I would never say something like that. A bloody hole in my chest? That's ridiculous. But the second is more remarkable: John Macaulay hadn't necessarily lied. He'd just stretched the truth (much like he'd done with the story of his instrumental involvement in "The Catch" play for the 49ers). He'd stretched the truth for *miles*, mind you, but the scene itself wasn't exactly a lie. See, Macaulay had stretched the story of the three-year-old dog into the story of a human consumer.

So, in summary, over time, every single allegation in the affidavit would be proven completely and utterly untrue. But of course the media didn't wait for approval to run with it. And who could blame them? The charges and claims by the government were so shocking to the conscience, who could resist reporting it? The affidavits made by two of our more disgruntled former employees suggested that Blevins, Bradley, and I were funneling company money into offshore accounts. And here we had our former "nurse practitioner" claiming that I had directly refused to follow up on a supposedly devastating AER claim. And best yet, we'd defrauded the government of $93.7 million—*$93.7 million!*

Nevermind that the IRS had done absolutely nothing (to our knowledge) to substantiate any of the claims by Dix or Anderman. Nevermind that the FDA had no real reason to believe the shamed and drug addicted John Macaulay. Nevermind that the blindingly huge tax evasion figure had been arrived at by a bored pencil jockey using fourth grade math. Nevermind that absolutely none of it was true.

The media just *took off* with it. They found their story and they hammered it right into the ground. And you know what? Many people in the government—even former allies of ours—began to believe the bullshit.

But none of that is even close to the scariest point about that damning affidavit. Here's the scariest point: Because the government was so ready and willing to raid us based on "evidence" that they didn't even bother validating, what's to stop them from doing it again? What's to stop anybody (from anywhere and for whatever reason) from making a false allegation about anyone else in this country? What if the government didn't even need *proof* of wrongdoing before stepping in and systematically dismantling your bank account, your job, your family, your reputation, your livelihood? What if all it took was a lie from someone who hated you? [117]

So these were the things facing my attorneys and me as we began to pore over a defense for everything in the affidavit and everything that was seized from my houses and place of business.

The first things to address were the statements made in the affidavit. And we approached this task with a slight advantage: We knew that there wasn't even a shred of truth to the allegations and that the government would be facing an uphill battle in the effort to show otherwise.

The second things to address were the guns seized from the ranch. But we knew we would beat that charge, as well, given that I'd never even touched a gun since my 1991 conviction, let alone the guns in question. Remember, these particular rifles had been locked up or stored in areas of the ranch that I'd never even visited.

The only connection that could possibly be made between me and the guns was that they were once my father's guns. See, when Dad died, Mom found all these rifles in his safe. Obviously, she didn't have any use for them (and it made her kind of nervous to have them around the house, anyway), so she asked me if I would like to take them off her hands. I knew that, because of my felony conviction, I couldn't accept the gift. So I told her to give them to

---

[117] "He's a communist!"
   "He's a terrorist!"
   "He's a *tax cheat!*"

Memo—an idea that she was thrilled with because she absolutely loved my brother-in-law.

So basically, considering that we were dealing with guns I'd never even touched (guns that were locked in a closet whose only key belonged to Memo), I figured I was clear on that one. Not even Louis' .22 could come back to me. Unless Louis was shooting snakes outside my house, I'd never been within 200 yards of that gun, as Louis' place was 200 yards away from my own. [118]

And as for the accusations made directly by the IRS, consider the conduct of their agents. See, Julian's a small town. And neighbors talk...

Sometime following the raid on the ranch, Memo would later hear a story about a bunch of the agents. The group had visited the local diner to have breakfast early on the morning of the raid. Apparently, many of them were laughing and bragging about how they'd already been to the ranch. They joked about how they'd looked into the windows at Memo and his wife; joked about how one of the agents had gotten drunk the previous night and wasn't looking so good; joked about everything they'd done while partying the night before; joked about the quality of the diner and its food. Basically, they were loud and obnoxious enough for the other patrons at the diner to overhear it all and then relay the story to Memo later.

But even without such embarrassing behavior to lean on, there was still the final and strangest point of the affidavit to consider: the $93.7 million in tax fraud.

Let's break that point down a little. Even if Blevins, Bradley, and I *were* tax cheats—and I was certain at the time that none of us were—how could someone possibly cheat on his taxes by such a wide margin? Martinez, the brains of the operation, had come up with a calculation to suggest that we had committed truly monu-

---

[118] Both Louis and Memo supported these assertions with statements of their own to the government. They both confirmed that they (and only they) owned and possessed the guns.

Grade-School Math	
Total cost per bottle of Metabolife (retail)	$29.95
Percentage of total cost taken as profit	25%
Total profit per bottle of Metabolife	$12.49
Rough tax percentage	23.25%
Total profits necessary to account for $93 million in tax evasion	$372 million
Number of bottles sold to account for $372 million	12.42 million

mental tax fraud. How about a little grade-school math to prove how ludicrous this claim truly was?

Now, as a network marketing company, you always talk about your numbers at the retail level (so if you're on your way to doing a billion in sales, then you're actually only making $500 million). So according to Martinez, we not only would have had to hide the sales of many, many, many warehouses full of our product. Just to *produce* 12.4 million bottles in a given year, we would have had to keep three full-scale factories churning out product twenty-four hours per day, seven days per week. That's nearly a physical impossibility. [119]

But that's not even the fun part. The fun part is that we also would have had to hide almost seventy-five percent of our profits. That's one hell of a skillful tax cheat. And consider the fact that in order to avoid the paper trail of stealing that much money, we would have had to keep it all in cash. That cash couldn't have been stored in anything other than twenty-dollar-bill form, either, since the movement of hundreds of thousands of hundreds probably would've tripped the IRS' radar. So let's consider the logistics of

[119] And, by the way, our factories were already running at full capacity. It wouldn't have been possible to produce more than twelve million units off the record. We were too busy creating our millions of on-the-record units.

Hiding $372 Million in Twenties	
Number of twenties in $93 million	4,650,000
The height of a stack of 4.65 million twenties	508 m (1/3 of a mile)
The weight of a stack of 4.65 million twenties	4650 kg (10,230 pounds)
The length of 4.65 million twenties (end to end)	72.54 km (45 miles)

hiding $372 million in twenty-dollar bills.

So, all things considered, for a company that did $2.5 billion over its entire lifetime, that's a lot of tax fraud.

But that's just it. It's not possible. Mike Blevins, Bob Bradley, and I had just become victims of one of the biggest rat-fucks ever perpetrated. And there are two different ways to get rat-fucked:

- Somebody does something and their actions come back to affect you. Since their intention wasn't to harm you, this kind of rat-fuck you can usually forgive.
- Somebody *deliberately* does something to you that leads to harm. This one, you can't forgive.

Dix, Anderman, and Macaulay had given us rat-fuck number two. So we couldn't forgive any of them.

Regardless of who was responsible, by the time the dust settled, it was our understanding that we'd just been the victims of one of the biggest IRS search warrants in the history of the Southern district.

There's some good news, though. During the IRS investigation, Blevins and I did some investigations on our own with our CPAs.

Guess what? As it turned out, the IRS actually owed *us* money. So during their investigation into whether we'd shorted them $93.7 million, they actually had to pay both of us millions of dollars in refunds. Essentially, not only had the government wasted countless millions in tax dollars over the course of their misguided investigation, but they wound up having to pay us money in the end, as well.

No wonder Martinez isn't in private practice…

Chapter 19

Mr. Ellis Goes
to Washington

In early July of 2003, we received a letter from Congress. A call to come testify on the safety of herbal ephedrine. It was exactly the kind of letter I'd been hoping to receive for years, but because of all of our legal trouble, it came at the worst possible time.

It was Garry Pay who'd first received the letter and brought it to my attention. It had gotten to the point that I needed a huge room just to accommodate all of our legal teams, so Pay and I took out the conference room at Area 52 so we could all talk about what we were going to do.

To protect the attorney/client privilege as well as the individuals involved, I will omit my attorneys' names in the following dialogue.

"I want to testify," I explained. "I've wanted this for years."

"They'll only make you look bad," one of my lawyers said.

"What do you mean?"

"You'll have to invoke the fifth on all of their questions because of what's going on. You'll look guilty as hell." [120]

I felt trapped. Raped. My hands were tied. "So what do we do?"

"We'll have to decline."

"We can do that?"

"Yes. This is just a request to attend. Until they hit you with a subpoena—"

"Which they might do," another of my attorneys added.

"Which they might do—until they hit you with a subpoena, you don't have to attend."

I sighed. "Then let's decline."

It killed me to have to decline that letter. I'd been waiting for it for years. Here I was, with my first real opportunity to offer the truth about herbal ephedrine on a grand stage, and I couldn't do it. I had to stand on the sidelines.

Anyway, in our return letter, we advised Congress of the fact that, if called, we would have to invoke the fifth for every question due to ongoing federal investigations. Chuck LaBella[121] informed me that Congress has a policy—and it is their own policy—that they will not call citizens before them if they know that it will only embarrass. They have this policy in order to avoid witch hunting, I guess. Besides, if a citizen is only going to go up there and invoke the fifth to all of their questions, what's the point? So in our letter, we reminded them of their policy and explained that we would have to decline their invitation.

The turnaround on the second letter from Congress was quick. Within the week, we had it in hand.

"What's this one say?" I asked.

---

[120] In addition to the Fifth Amendment issue, we also had the motives behind the congressional hearing to worry about. See, Congress calls these kinds of oversight gatherings all the time, but whenever they do, they always have an agenda in mind going in. It's more like posturing. Or grandstanding. What they do is formulate an opinion on something, then they have their investigators go out and find all the people who support that opinion. If these people refuse to testify, then they're threatened. Not exactly a non-biased investigation.

[121] Chuck LaBella was fifty-eight years old. Had salt-and-pepper hair. He was my attorney, whom I'd hired to represent me with the federal investigation. Chuck used to work as an assistant U.S. attorney and later became acting U.S. attorney in San Diego before going into private practice. Very bright guy.

"They want you to come out and talk to the panel in private before the hearing," one of my attorneys said.

"I don't like it. Sounds like a setup."

My attorney nodded. "You're right. It is a setup. They know you're under investigation."

"Decline."

In response to our second return letter, Congress hit me with a subpoena, saying that I would be in obstruction if I didn't comply. So much for their policy of not calling witnesses just to embarrass them.

They also subpoenaed David Brown and Dan Rodriguez, the head Metabolife nurse from our call center. We knew that, given the nature of our investigation—that it had somehow become an IRS, Department of Justice (which is the agency that the U.S. Attorney's Office falls under), and FDA investigation simultaneously—neither one of these two men would be able to say anything at the hearing, either. So we had to do something. Otherwise, Congress would put us in their little dog and pony show and completely incriminate us.

So I called together my attorneys once again.

"I want to testify," I explained.

"No, no," one of my attorneys said ardently. "You can't!"

"Why? I'll just be telling the truth. The truth can't hurt us."

Downturned gazes all around the room. Nobody seemed to want to look me in the eye. "Because it would put you and Metabolife at risk."

"What do you mean?"

"Everything you say in Congress they can use against you in a court of law. Metabolife's insurance company could even come and sue *you* for what you say."

"I'd get sued by my own insurance company?"

Everyone nodded solemnly.

"Well…" I said desperately. "We've got to do *something*."

At the time, we were in the process of selling the company to a venture capital group called Russel Schreck and Company. Schreck had insisted that he become CEO of Metabolife because he felt it would help him finance the acquisition. Only trouble was that the acting board at Metabolife didn't like the idea of replacing David Brown, who'd served us so incredibly well as CEO, with basically an unknown commodity. So as much as we disliked the idea, the timing actually worked out really well. We could move Brown to the board and install Schreck as CEO. This way, we'd be sending a CEO who truly didn't know anything about the company to speak to Congress. He wouldn't have to invoke the fifth. Given that he would only have been head of the company for about three days, he just wouldn't know how to answer.

It pained us all to ask David to step down. And I'm sure he was confused at what was going through our heads. But he understood once I explained that I just didn't want him to get wrapped up in this whole incrimination game with Congress.

When we told Schreck, meanwhile, he just seemed to be excited about being named CEO. The tall, rather heavyset man in his sixties had finally reached his life's goal, I guess. He didn't even consider our other motives—or what he'd gotten himself into by agreeing to accompany me to Washington.

We arrived in Washington on the day before the hearing. And immediately, we began to suspect that this thing was going to be a bloodbath. When we received the list of people who would be testifying and attending the hearing, our suspicions were confirmed. They were obviously trying to stack the deck against the advocates of ephedrine. How did we know this? The other "captains of the industry" they'd invited had come from companies that were basically marketing their products as legal street drugs—the companies that marketed to children who wanted to get high or use ephedrine for sports enhancement. These products had names like "Black Beauties" and "Yellow Jackets," things like that. And then the only responsible dietary supplement company they invited was Metabolife—the most popular herbal weight loss supplement in the world, but, conveniently, also a company currently under criminal investigation for $93.7 million in tax fraud and lying to the FDA.

In addition to that, they had invited PI attorneys running suits against the companies, disgruntled employees who had been fired from the companies, and scientists whose studies Congress and the FDA had spent a great deal of time discrediting.

So this is the picture they were trying to paint of the entire industry.

We knew that many of the others involved would have been sent letters requesting that they meet with many of the congressmen and investigators in the weeks leading up to the hearing. We knew, also, that these meetings would have been really heavy-handed. Our counterparts would have heard things like, "You know, if you say that, it's possible that you could be held in contempt of Congress. You'll be found obstructing justice. And you could go to jail for that." Naturally, this would have scared the life out of just about everyone involved. And the cards would obviously fall right into line.

So with all of that in mind, we knew that the hearing would wind up being little more than a circus to put on TV for the viewer. For the *voter*.

On the day I'm to testify, my attorneys, Schreck, David Brown, Dan Rodriguez, and I all sit around in the plush, conservative meeting room of the Patton, Boggs building in D.C. [122] We're joined by an assortment of Patton, Boggs attorneys that I've never met before. There's a TV set up on a little stand and we're all watching the start of the hearings.

The table at the head of the hearing room looks improbably tall, even on TV. It's covered in white cloth and seems to tower over the proceedings. Sitting at this table is a whole slew of congressmen and women. The man who'd called the meeting—the chair of the congressional committee in question—W.J. "Billy" Tauzin of Louisiana, is nowhere among them. Instead, James Greenwood, Republican of Pennsylvania, presides over the matter. The first thing

---

[122] Patton, Boggs would be serving as our primary counsel on this thing, as they had worked a great deal as lobbyists in Congress.

I notice about Greenwood is his high forehead. He's got graying hair. His big, round glasses sit high atop his pointed nose. And the hungry smile he flashes for the camera looks carved out of his face with a shovel. He is every bit as no-necked as I remembered Tauzin being, and he carries the same sense of entitlement about him.

At the feet of Greenwood's towering table rests a set of wooden witness tables buffed to a high shine and scattered over with microphones. Behind these tables sits the audience—in a large collection of wedding-aisle seats designed to hold the press, people waiting to testify, and anyone who might have enough time in their day to come down and spectate this sort of thing.

"This morning," Greenwood begins slowly, "we will hear from two families who have witnessed firsthand the risks associated with ephedra. We will hear from Steve Bechler's mother and father[123] and from Sean Riggins' dad. And let me thank you all for coming here today to share with us your tragic and personal experiences."

Greenwood seems to be relishing every moment of this little power trip. "On the first panel," he continues, "we will also hear from Michael Vasquez, a nurse who worked for Metabolife in 1999 and who will discuss how the company handled complaints of serious adverse health events. [124] We also are fortunate to have five independent experts on issues relating to ephedra safety."

The congressman clears his throat and keeps on. "Our second panel will be appearing before us only briefly. Michael Ellis, David Brown, and Daniel Rodriguez, all of Metabolife, have appeared before us this morning pursuant to subpoena. All three are expected to assert their constitutional right against self-incrimination and will not provide any evidence or testimony to the subcommittee today." [125]

Greenwood then goes on to describe the third panel, a conglomeration of other ephedrine companies—some of which I'm familiar with and some of which I'm not. Then he raps up his speech. "I would like to thank all of our witnesses for attending. And now recognize the ranking member of the subcommittee, Mr. Deutsch, for his opening statement."

"Mr. Chairman," Congressman Peter Deutsch says, his Herman Munster head bending into a placating nod, "I'd like to yield to the ranking Democrat of the full committee to make his opening statement."

"The chair recognizes the ranking member, Mr. Dingell," Greenwood offers.

More back-scratching ensues from Congressman John Dingell, a round-headed and bald old congressional minion with glasses that make him look like an owl at hunt. "Mr. Chairman, I thank the distinguished ranking member of the subcommittee for his courtesy to me. And I am very appreciative. I thank you, also, Mr. Chairman, for convening these two days of hearings on a very important topic: the failure of the United States to properly regulate the use of the herbal form of a stimulate drug that has caused death and other serious health problems. I repeat, it kills."

So there it is. Spelled out in black and white. This would indeed be a bloodbath.

---

[123] The parents of Bechler and Riggins had been the victims of terrible tragedies. The only problem with having them at this hearing was that their sons did not actually die from ephedrine use, as the media and many other sources suggested. In the case of Bechler, the young pitcher for the Baltimore Orioles had died in spring training because he'd come to camp overweight and had been made to run around in a rubber suit. Without drinking water. He was under tremendous pressure from his team and his teammates to lose weight, so there he was, doing something in that Florida heat that nobody should be asked to do, overweight or otherwise. When he died, the team, of course, pointed the finger elsewhere, claiming that Bechler had succumbed to the dangers of taking herbal ephedrine. And, of course, the media ran with the story. The only trouble with this claim is that when the autopsy results came back on Bechler, they showed that absolutely no ephedrine had been found in his system. But the ball club kept harping on about ephedrine. Why wouldn't they? They didn't want to get sued by Bechler's widow or parents.

[124] We hadn't invited Vasquez to the party. His invitation had come from Congress. See, as a disgruntled former employee currently locked in a financial dispute with Metabolife (I believe we were even engaged in civil litigation with him at the time), he would obviously make for the perfect government witness.

[125] Good thing they mentioned the subpoena. The viewers of this circus weren't biased against us enough already.

We watch the story unfold for what feels like hours. Things don't seem to be going well. Eventually, it comes time for us to head up to the hearing to take our seats in the crowd and await our turn to go on. And so we walk.

On the way over from Patton, Boggs, I notice a corner drugstore. The store window boasts ads for Metabolife 356's new "EZ Tabs," a product with a more concentrated formulation that allows the consumer to take a much smaller pill. Our original pills were more than a gram in weight, so this new EZ Tab had proven pretty popular. I smile at the irony of seeing the ad on my way to get turned into mincemeat on national TV. But my reverie is broken by one of the lawyers from Chuck LaBella's firm, an attorney named Andrew Robertson. Maybe in his fifties, Robertson's a tall and thin guy in a cheapish suit that makes him look more like a schoolteacher than an attorney.

"Hey, Mike," he says. "Remember, don't say a word. If you say anything at all, they could construe that as you're waiving your Fifth Amendment rights. If they do that, they can make you talk."

"Fine," I say dismissively. Call it the culmination of my frustration. For years, I've wanted to tell the story of Metabolife in front of Congress, but now that's the only thing I can't do.

With Robertson still counseling me, we make our way into the building and take our seats in the audience. The stage looks even bigger in person than it did on camera. It's hot as hell in here, and with everyone in suits, it reeks of sweat. My attorneys, David Brown, and Dan Rodriguez all take their seats next to one another. I take a seat in the row just ahead of them. Sitting alone, I've got time to think. And here's what I come up with:

I recall that the maximum safe daily dose of ephedrine for a healthy adult published by Goodman & Gilman is two hundred milligrams—significantly more than the twelve milligrams found in a single caplet of Metabolife. I run the math, deciding that if I can't speak before the panel, at least I could act.

Here's my idea: I would ask one of the Patton, Boggs attorneys to run down to the corner drugstore we'd passed and bring back a bottle of Metabolife's EZ Tabs. Then, as soon as the panel called me to speak, I would pull out the bottle of Metabolife, open it, splay the contents on the table, count out twenty caplets, and take them all, right in front of Congress. Right in front of the entire country.

Now, this would be a dose of 240 milligrams, a little above the Goodman & Gilman recommended daily dosage. But what would taking this many tabs accomplish? A few things:

- I would be taking a supposedly dangerous dosage of my own product on national television.
- I would be doing this during a congressional event designed to show the world that products like Metabolife, even at their recommended dosages, were unsafe for even a healthy individual.
- I would sit there calmly during my portion of the hearing and then spend the rest of the day in the audience.
- I wouldn't die.

I sit there knowing that I'd wind up being uncomfortable but okay because our earlier studies had shown that such a dose wouldn't harm me—instead, it would make me feel a little like I was sitting on an electric fence. So I turn back and motion to an unknown Patton, Boggs attorney.

"Yes, Mr. Ellis?" the attorney says, stooping down next to me.

"I want you to go down to that corner drugstore we passed and pick up a bottle of Metabolife EZ Tabs."

"What for?"

I fill the young attorney in on the plan. As I explain myself, he grows greener and greener.

"Okay," he says.

But then I watch as he heads back and starts talking to the senior attorneys from Patton, Boggs. Quickly, they fall into what seems to be a rather heated discussion—lots of frantic hand motions. Still, the young attorney leaves the building.

I wait patiently in my seat, thinking about how brilliant my plan would be. It would completely subvert the whole proceeding. Instead of burying us further, the media would have to run with the story about why Mike Ellis didn't die. And everyone watching would learn that Metabolife wasn't *nearly* as unsafe as everyone was saying.

But the young attorney doesn't return for a long time. I've just begun worrying about where he's gone to when I hear my name called by the panel. As I stand, I turn back and watch as prodigal attorney finally walks through the doors. Perfect timing. Only he's holding his hands out and shaking his head. Motioning that he couldn't find what I'd asked him for.

My blood begins to boil.

"And I will call forward our second panel," Greenwood says ominously. "Mr. Michael Ellis, Mr. David Brown, and Mr. Daniel Rodriguez. Please come to the witness table, gentlemen."

I glare at the young attorney one last time before making my strides toward the witness table.

"Michael Ellis is the founder and director of Metabolife International," Greenwood continues. "David Brown is a former president of Metabolife. And Daniel Rodriguez is the head nurse working at Metabolife handling consumer complaints. They are all here with us today pursuant to a subpoena."

Just in case the viewers didn't get the point about the subpoena, Greenwood rubs their noses in it a little more.

"On July 3, 2003," he says, "the committee invited these three individuals to voluntarily testify at this hearing, but they declined. On July 10 of this year, the subcommittee authorized subpoenas to be issued to compel their appearance, which were subsequently issued by Chairman Tauzin and served. My understanding is that these witnesses will rely on their constitutional right not to testify at today's hearing and will not provide any evidence or testimony to this subcommittee."

I remember thinking, *Yeah, so why are we here?*

"I believe that this privilege," Greenwood says, "which is the only basis upon which a witness may refuse to cooperate with an inquiry by this house, the people's House of Representatives, should be personally exercised before the members as is our standard practice in such cases. That is why we have insisted on the appearances of Mr. Ellis, Mr. Brown and Mr. Rodriguez today.

"Given the importance of their testimony to this subcommittee's fact-finding processes, I would hope that these men might reconsider their decisions to invoke their Fifth Amendment rights today and decide to cooperate with this critically important investigation."

He then turns his beady eyes down upon us. "Mr. Ellis, Mr. Brown, Mr. Rodriguez, I know that each of you is represented by counsel today who will advise you with respect to your appearance, as is your right under the rules of the house and the rules of the committee.

"Mr. Ellis is represented by Andrew Robertson of the law firm LaBella & McNamara. Mr. Brown is represented by Gordon Greenberg of the law firm McDermott, Will & Emery. And Mr. Rodriguez is represented by Lee Blalack of the law firm O'Melvaney & Myers."

I begin to wonder if he'll ever stop pontificating. I'm anxious to get to swearing in my silence.

"As such," he says, "I understand that each of you is aware that the subcommittee is holding an investigation hearing today and in doing so, has the practice of taking testimony under oath. At this time, please stand, raise your right hand, and I will swear you in."

As we get sworn in, I can't help but think about how I'd been screwed by the young attorney and his cohorts. Taking those tablets would have changed everything. Instead of presenting their biased opinions against the supplement, the scientists who would come up after me would have had to admit that even 240 milligrams of ephedrine won't kill a normal healthy adult. And everyone—even the panel—would have had concrete evidence to believe them. The sham of these hearings would have been exposed. Congress would have been embarrassed in much the same way I'm about to be embarrassed as I lower my right hand and lean toward the microphone. The hype game, the smoke and mirrors game, all that smoke would have been brushed away. And we would've all gone home happy, knowing that we had exposed the truth.

Greenwood finally gets things going. Greenwood-style. "The chairman then will recognize himself for questioning of the witness. My first question is for Mr. Ellis."

I tense up.

"As the one-time president of a company selling supplement products ingested by millions of consumers, could you tell us if Metabolife ever conducted any studies on the risks associated with use of its product Metabolife 356, or did you put sales above safety?"

"I respectfully decline," I say. Only I'd forgotten to push the button on the mic in front of me.

"Would you please push the button on your microphone?" Greenwood asks.

Embarrassed, I push the button this time. "Thank you. I am sorry."

"That is quite alright."

"I respectfully decline to answer that question in these proceedings based upon my privilege against self-incrimination, sir."

Greenwood's eyes light up with just a hint of excitement. "Okay. Let me be clear. Are you refusing to answer the question on the basis of the protections afforded to you under the Fifth Amendment to the United States Constitution?"

"Yes, sir," I say.

He starts feigning like he's offended and maybe even surprised. "And will you invoke your Fifth Amendment rights in response to all of our questions today?"

I feel like standing up and shouting, "You know damn well that I will," but I know that I can't. So I take the easy road: "Yes, sir."

"Then you are excused from the witness table at this time," Greenwood says. All that circumstance for nothing. "But I advise you that you remain subject to the process of the committee and that if the need is such, then we may recall you."

"Thank you, sir."

"You may be excused."

I stand and stride back to my seat amongst the audience, listening all the way.

"My next question is for Mr. Brown," Greenwood says. "Mr. Brown, welcome. As the one-time president of a company selling supplement products ingested by millions of consumers, could you tell us why it took several years for Metabolife to send in to the FDA the 14,000 customer complaint call records, many of them involving serious adverse medical events, after years of insisting that Metabolife had received no such complaints?"

David remembers to depress the button on his mic. "Mr. Chairman," he says cordially, "members of the committee, under normal circumstances I would be happy to be here with the committee and answer all of your questions. Unfortunately, due to an investigation by the Justice Department in California, I think it would be inappropriate for me to answer your questions today. And, therefore, I am going to follow the advice of my attorney and out of prudence decline to answer the committee's questions today based upon my rights under the Fifth Amendment of the Constitution."

"Very well said," Greenwood says, sounding slightly belittling. "And that is indeed your right. But let me be clear: Are you refusing to answer the question on the basis of the protections afforded to you under the Fifth Amendment to the United States Constitution?"

"Yes, sir."

"Okay. And will you invoke your Fifth Amendment rights in response to all of our questions today?"

"Yes."

"Then you are excused from the witness table at this time. But I advise you that you remain subject to the process of the committee and that if the committee's need is such, then we may recall you."

So that was that. Embarrassment over.

How did it feel to testify in front of Congress? Like a shitty setup. Like a classic no-win situation. I felt like I was in a shooting gallery just waiting for someone to shoot me.

It all could and should have been avoided, though. If only I'd had those tablets. But much later, when I talked to my advisors about those tablets, I heard that Patton, Boggs would have been publicly embarrassed by the scene because they work with many of these people in Washington. So did they shoot down the stunt to save face or was it legitimate that the young attorney couldn't find the tablets? I don't know. Why don't I know? Because right after the hearing, I shuffled off to meet my wife, who'd been kind enough to take the family on a vacation to Hawaii during the circus. From there, the issue about the tablets on camera simply died.

But even after we left, the proceedings weren't over. I did my best not to watch any of them, but my attorneys filled me in on the details later. The scientists who'd come up to speak on behalf of the industry got absolutely railed, from what I understand.

Doctor Boozer from Harvard was there and it sounds like they treated her unfairly in trying to discredit her studies. Greenwood just laid into her, I guess. But the most remarkable turn of events came during Doctor Carlon Colker's time on the stand. As the CEO and medical director of a company called Peak Wellness, Inc., his job was to do independent safety reviews of various companies' drugs or supplements, Metabolife among them. He'd sat up there with Robert Chinery, the president of Cytodyne Technologies, and Kelly Conklin, also of Cytodyne. The three of them were getting the BS piled on them thick by Greenwood and Greg Walden, a congressman from Oregon and vice chair of the congressional subcommittee on oversight and investigations.

When questioned, Conklin attempted to explain who Dr. Colker was. "This is Dr. Colker who, as he has on several other occasions, has spoken as an independent researcher, not on behalf of the company."

"Okay," Congressman Walden said. "But if I read this right, I thought you referred this to the reporter so that she could hear from an independent research scientist. Yet, did not Dr. Colker do work for your company? Was he not on a retainer?"

"Yes, sir, he was," Conklin said. "But he was not an employee. And—"

"Well," Walden interrupted, "what's the difference between somebody on a retainer and somebody who is an employee? Is that...it seems to me that if I am on a retainer, I am not as independent as if I am not either an employee or on a retainer."

"Well," Conklin explained, "he has done consulting and he still may for companies other than Cytodyne."

"But he was on Cytodyne's cost of doing business, right? How much were you paying him, Mr. Chinery, do you know at that time, 2001?"

"I believe at that time it was in the range of around $5,000 per month," Chinery replied.

"Five thousand a month?" Walden asked, really pouring on the phony shock. "On a retainer? And yet Mr. Conklin, I guess, tells the press here that he is independent. Do you believe him to have been independent?" [126]

"This will have to be the gentleman's last question," Greenwood piped in.

"Oh, I am sorry," Walden said.

"In a certain capacity, yes," Chinery offered. "Because Dr. Colker has done a lot of research for a lot of other companies and other products, and we do consider him an expert on the subject of dietary supplements."

"Mr. Chairman," Walden pleaded, "could I just ask one question of Dr. Colker?"

"Quickly," Greenwood said.

Walden turned to glare at Dr. Colker. "Do you consider yourself independent when you are paid $5,000 a month by a company?"

"I did," Colker said.

---

[126] Funny—at the time, Greenwood and Tauzin were both enjoying significant contributions from pharmaceutical companies, apparently the mortal enemies of our industry. I guess the congressmen themselves were cost of operations, as well. And they got a whole lot more than $5,000. Yet no one questions their independence.

"It is all the independence money can buy," Greenwood quipped.

So here's the kind of showmanship and posturing we were dealing with: Congress called a long list of scientists and doctors to support their theory that ephedrine wasn't safe. Likewise, the people in the industry hired scientists and doctors to run fair studies that would prove that our products were safe when taken as directed by healthy adults. But Greenwood and Walden were trying to make it seem like their end was conducting science while our end was running bribes. I guess it's okay for pharmaceutical companies to pay for science, but when the dietary supplement industry does it, it's tantamount to putting scientists in our pocket. [127]

So in a nutshell, Congress treated all our people like they were tainted. And the best part is that Greenwood and Tauzin themselves were receiving more money than Dr. Colker could have ever dreamed of making. There aren't many congressmen who have ever received more contributions from pharmaceutical companies. [128]

But then, we weren't there for truth. We were there for grandstanding. Here was the game plan, as I see it:

- The FDA strikes out at attacking Metabolife directly, so the IRS, DOJ, and now Congress had stepped in, rendering us ineffective at defending ourselves against their claims.
- Now Congress holds hearings that give the FDA the green light to do whatever it wants to with herbal ephedrine.

Supporting this game plan theory is what happened in late 2003. In the months following the hearing, not coincidentally, the FDA announced the ban of herbal ephedrine, claiming that it is a dangerous and imminent hazard to the public. But the funny thing is that they gave every company—every peddler of this supposedly dangerous and imminently hazardous product—sixty whole days to sell out of their inventory before the ban went into effect.

Let's back up for a second. Does that even make sense? The FDA is supposed to be responsible for keeping the American consumer safe. And here they've "proven" that ephedrine is a deadly product—one that would kill even healthy adults left and right. And yet they gave the public sixty more days to buy all the ephedrine they wanted.

But that's the Washington game, I guess. We just got a firsthand taste of it. Actually, we got the firsthand and then the backhand.

---

[127] The notion that Greenwood alluded to with his "all the independence money can buy" line is even more ridiculous when you consider the logistics of the matter. What kind of scientist is going to do his work for free? That's the nature of the game. You have to pay scientists to run studies or they won't have the funding to actually run them. To imply that what Colker was receiving from the industry was a bribe is pretty much ludicrous. He was just doing his job. And for that, he got publicly embarrassed.

[128] In the year following these proceedings, Greenwood would go to work for a pharmaceutical company. And in the same year of the hearings, Tauzin would be instrumental in the Medicare Prescription Drug and Modernization Act that wound up screwing Americans out of at least $200 billion. Soon after, he became one of the highest paid pharmaceutical lobbyists in history. What do you think of that independence?

Chapter 20

The Win-Win...Win?

The fallout of the great search and seizure of Metabolife was severe for almost everyone concerned—but no one got it worse than the people involved in the three stories I'm about to tell. We'll start with Bob Bradley, because at least he earned his ticket...

The only significant tax dirt that the giant IRS investigation turned up happened to be in Bob's column. [129] See, in any investigation, there has to be a fall guy. Otherwise, the investigators wind up looking stupid. And I guess Bob fit the bill.

The crux of what Bob wound up pleading to was borrowing money from his own charitable foundation to fund a real estate deal. Basically, he'd borrowed $4 million from his foundation, done the real estate deal, and then paid the foundation back with interest. Despite the fact that nobody got hurt on this move—in fact, the foundation actually *made* money due to Bob's actions—the government pushed it through as a fraud case. Apparently, even

---

[129] Blevins and I were both found to have clean taxes in the end. We even received unpublicized letters from the U.S. Attorney's Office stating their investigation of taxes was concluded and there would be no charges against Blevins or me.

though the money in question was paid back with interest, borrowing in such a way is still a violation of the tax code.

But as the numbers and accusations unfurled, it became clear that Bob, as the former head of the accounting department, had made one other error in the early days of Metabolife. For years, we'd been paying our taxes as if Metabolife were an S-corp, which meant that the owners would pay taxes on all of the company's earnings. As Bob would later discover, Metabolife was in fact a C-corp, meaning that we should have been paying corporate tax instead of personal tax on the profits.[130] When Bob discovered the error, he immediately and legally converted Metabolife into an S-corp. The only problem was that while we were a C, we were behaving like an S. Like so:

We'd established one particular wing of our business in Nevada (because of the tax advantages there). Basically, this outfit was set up to handle consumer refunds. When we set up the account, I think we assumed we'd be getting more refund requests than we actually did, because we dropped a half-million dollars into the account. In addition to that, we had a second half-million-dollar account set up to purchase media on behalf of the company. So a million dollars in total was allocated to the branch in Nevada.

Ultimately, we didn't have many refund requests at all. And we quickly discovered that our media buying opportunities were easier handled at Metabolife, as well. So we never really used the accounts. And I guess, as a result, the accounting department kind of forgot about them. They just sat there in Nevada, collecting dust.

After converting to an S-corp, we discovered that we still had our dusty million dollars resting in Nevada. So on Mike Compton's advice, we decided to close the accounts in Nevada and roll the money back into Metabolife. Mike, Bob, and I all personally paid the taxes on that money. This was wrong. Given our new corporation status, it should have been Metabolife, and not its founders, who had paid the taxes on that million (which amounted to approximately $300,000).

---

[130] You CPAs will know what I'm talking about

In any other circumstance, this kind of mistake would've amounted to a simple penalty by the IRS. Essentially, it would've been considered to be a $300,000 accounting error. But no. Not for Metabolife. They'd spent loads of tax dollars trying to prove that we had stolen $93.7 million. And even though they could only find a $300,000 accounting error, they *had* to move on it. Forget the fact that we had actually *paid* that $300,000 (it had just come from our pockets instead of Metabolife's); they were grasping at straws.

So our big, bad accounting mistake became a *crime*. And it was Bob who would serve as the fall guy. He pled out to it as a crime, even though none of us ever saw any actual financial benefit from the error.

Over a two-year period, Bob's attorneys and the U.S. Attorney's Office negotiated on a plea that would ultimately release the IRS from their jam of not finding any real Metabolife tax issues. Can I blame Bob for what he did? No. If you were threatened with twenty years and $30 million in fines, wouldn't you take whatever deal was offered? [131]

So Bob was guilty of doing what we all did: He trusted his CPA. And ultimately, this trust (along with a few oversights and silly mistakes) cost Bob six months in prison and $7 million.

Now, the next question becomes, considering the fact that he was originally facing far greater penalties, why did Bob get such a comparatively sweet deal? I have a theory: Because the IRS and the

---

[131] Besides, Bob was also just a victim of circumstance. Of trust. See, when you're dealing with so much taxable income coming from so many different streams, it becomes virtually impossible to personally do your own tax returns. The returns are so complex that they wind up being two inches thick. So in other words, Metabolife's erroneous taxes were prepared by a hired CPA. Now, why wouldn't Bob review his taxes and spot the error? Two reasons: One, it's a two-inch-thick tax file—good luck reading something like that without falling asleep; and two, we were paying our CPAs $75,000 per year each for personal taxes—and for that kind of bread, you should be able to trust that they did a perfectly accurate job. You just take note of the CPA's impressive credentials, examine the bottom page of the stack (the one that says how much you owe), and sign your name. Show me a person who wouldn't handle things that way and I'll show you a guy with way too much time on his hands.

U.S. Attorney's Office were so embarrassed about the $93.7 million, they had to get Metabolife on something. *Anything.* So they put Bob in a place where he had no choice but to incriminate the company.

I remember the day of Bob's plea…

They had the courtroom packed with people that my longtime partner had done charity work with. Many, many people who used to depend on his and Metabolife's foundation—everyone there to support him in overwhelming fashion—would get to see big, bad Bob Bradley go down. It was all kind of a sad scene. A courtroom packed with ardent supporters from the very pool that Bob supposedly defrauded: The irony was lost on no one.

So, even though they could never find anything substantial on Metabolife, counting the indictment that the DOJ would eventually get of me, this would be the first of the triple win that the DOJ would seek. But they wouldn't get there without breaking a few eggs…

As I've mentioned several times, I've been friends with Mike Blevins since I was thirteen or fourteen years old. So for forty-one years now. Gosh, that's hard to believe. Our friendship had come to be because Blevins had been abandoned by his parents at a young age. And so, essentially living under the same roof, we became fast friends. More like brothers, really. And given all that, I feel confident that I can say better than anyone that Mike Blevins is a great human being, despite all that's happened to him in his life.

A great business partner, that Blevins. The kind of carefree guy who kept Bob and me in balance. The kind of carefree guy who would wear a Hawaiian shirt and shorts to work every day if he could get away with it. The kind of guy who got tired of cigarettes, so he switched to cigars. The kind of guy with a large frame, sandy blonde hair, and a deep, commanding voice who still managed to lighten the mood with his remarkable sense of humor. The kind of guy who always knows the score. Who makes snap decisions (and good ones). Who can't help but occasionally fall victim to his uncommon level of sensitivity.

But that's Mike Blevins. His M.O. is to save everyone else before he even thinks about saving himself. All this from a man once abandoned at the age of sixteen, from a man forced into being a survivor during his formative years, to a man who would be more caring than anyone I've ever known. What are the odds of that?

Mike eventually married a sweet, middle-class, all-American girl named Danica. I'm not sure what Danica saw in Blevins, but what will be will be. [132] Anyway, I mention Danica because the story of Blevins' fall begins with his (then) girlfriend's fear following the events of September 11, 2001. A natural fear. The kind of fear we all felt. In any case, she did what many Americans did in that time of crisis: She convinced herself that it might be a good idea to own a gun. And her father felt the same way. The two of them agreed that they should buy guns to protect their families from the kinds of threats that none of us had ever even imagined before. Only trouble was, when it came to guns, Danica and her father didn't have the slightest clue about what they were doing. So she asked her boyfriend for help.

Now, Blevins was in the same boat that I was—he couldn't own or even handle guns—so he explained to his future wife that all he could do was go down to the sporting goods store with her and point to a rifle or two that might suit her. So this is what he did. And under her boyfriend's advice, Danica and her father bought two guns, signed up for the NRA, and made plans to go down to the range to practice regularly.

It's important to note that Blevins never handled the guns and never went down to the range with Danica and her father. He remained true to his vow to never break the law again (and handling guns seemed like a pretty stupid way to break that vow). Later, even when Mike and Danica got married, Blevins was sure to

---

[133] Just kidding, Mike!

keep the guns out of his possession, asking his wife to promise him that she would always keep her gun and ammunition at her father's house. Obviously, despite the fact that not having the gun nearby essentially made her gun ownership moot to begin with, she agreed.

And so begins our story:

One day, Danica went out shooting with her dad. When she was finished, she put all of her gear into the trunk of her car. But I guess when she was unloading the stuff back at her dad's house, she didn't notice the box of bullets that she'd left behind—because later, when she went out grocery shopping, she found the bullets amongst the bags of produce. Anyway, as she unloaded the food into the house she shared with Mike, I guess she decided that she didn't want to keep bullets in her trunk, so she took them out and put them in her closet.

Now, the Blevins' house was very large. Large enough to support his and her walk-in closets. So Mike had no clue that the bullets were in his wife's closet. Obviously, this would set the stage for disaster on the day the raid came.

When the IRS and ATF hit Mike with a search warrant, they hit him hard and they hit him comically bad.

"So how long's this going to be?" Mike asked, agents charging past him into the house.

"Don't worry about it," the agent presenting the warrant said gruffly (and we'll call him "McGruff"). "It'll take all day if it has to."

The two men stood quietly for a while. Then, the silence was broken by a scratching sound from above Mike's head. Like the sound of rats running through the attic. Blevins backed away from the source of the noise.

"Are they searching the attic?" he asked.

McGruff shrugged. "Don't worry about it."

"What do they think they're going to find up there?"

As soon as the words passed Mike's lips, a loud crash came from above. When my old friend looked up at the ceiling, he saw that a portion of it had splintered and broken. Through the hole came two legs, clad in black pants. They fell fantastically then stopped with a thud. A loud yelp followed.

Many of the agents up in Mike's bedroom could be heard to roar to life. Several of them came barreling down the stairs with their guns drawn, pointing them everywhere.

"What the fuck happened here?" one of the agents said.

Blevins began laughing hysterically when he realized what had happened. He pointed up at the flailing legs. "I think genius here doesn't know that plaster breaks!"

I guess that the agent searching the attic, in all his wisdom, forgot that you have to walk on the wooden beams when you're in an attic. Apparently, he was walking along on the drywall when it caved in on him. His legs came down on either side of a support beam, cracking him right where he didn't want to be cracked. And his wailing made it sound as if he was in fantastic pain. I guess IRS agents do have nuts.

McGruff crackled his two-way radio to life. "We need a medical team in here right away," he barked.

It wasn't long after Genius was carted away to the hospital that his comrades reconvened the search of the bedroom and found something of note: the bullets in Danica's closet. Immediately, they ushered poor Danica in. She was a wreck. Nervous. Frightened. Confused.

"Where are the guns?" an agent asked, showing Danica the bullets and pointing right in her face with his free hand.

"At my father's house," Danica said meekly.

As a result, the agents hit Danica's father's house with a warrant. They seized the guns and ammunition, took pictures, and later lifted prints. Only problem? Blevins' prints weren't on the guns. Or the bullets. Or anything weapons-related, really. So what did they do? What the U.S. Attorney's Office does best. They picked out the weak link and leaned on it. Hard.

They charged Danica, this sweet little all-American girl who had never done anything wrong in her life, with eight counts of aiding, abetting, and supplying firearms to an ex-felon. Simultaneously, they charged Mike with multiple counts of a felon in possession of a firearm.

At first, the idea from Mike's corner was that there was no way that Danica would be convicted. But the word of a few lawyers wasn't enough for Mike. He had his attorney hire a company that puts on mock trials. The company took the whole case of big, bad Danica through a mock trial. They brought up Mike's past, Metabolife, and everything that was going on at the time with the IRS and DOJ. In the end, to everyone's great surprise, the mock jury convicted Danica.

That's when Blevins decided that he had no choice. He had to take the deal offered by the DOJ—had to plead to a crime he didn't commit—in order to protect his wife.

"I'm going to take the deal, Danica," he said.

"No, this is wrong," Danica said defiantly. "None of this is your stuff. I'll fight this to the end."

Blevins sighed. "I can't let you do that."

If it were your wife, what would you do? Probably exactly what Blevins did. Even though the guns being linked to him had never even been in his house—and even though there was no fingerprint evidence to suggest otherwise (and absolutely no real case against him)—he pleaded guilty in order to protect his wife. [133]

The following details of the plea represent my own interpretation. Mike Blevins never speaks of this, so the blame is all on me if I've misinterpreted the details. But here's how I believe it went down:

Mike couldn't let his wife go to jail, so he had his attorney contact Phil Halprin to cut a deal. Essentially, the deal would require that Mike lie and claim that Danica's guns had been in his house for a period of two weeks before being moved to Danica's dad's. [134]

So that was that. After all these investigations, after all this

---

[133] I'm sure that Mike was angry and maybe even a little afraid of returning to prison, but how could he let this poor girl (who he loved) take the rap just because the government was tying to put pressure on him?

[134] I suspect that this lie was necessary because the DOJ felt that it wouldn't have had a case against Blevins based solely on the bullets they actually *did* find in his home.

wasted tax funding, Mike Blevins pled out to a crime he didn't commit. [135]

About a month before Mike's sentencing, I went against my attorneys' advice and met with Phil Halprin, IRS Agent Martinez, and my counsel, Chuck LaBella. We all met on the sixth floor of the federal building in San Diego. After Chuck and I had passed through security, Halprin came out to greet us, walking us over to a small room outfitted with folding tables and chairs. Martinez sat across from me. LaBella across from Halprin. Halprin to my right. Halprin wore a shirt that made him look like a farmer. [136]

"You look like a farmer," I said. "You want to come work for me on my ranch?"

"Ha," Halprin said.

"I'm not here for me," I quickly explained. "I'm here for Mike Blevins."

I plea with the assistant U.S. attorney not to give Mike any time, that he was a good man, and that the only reason he got Blevins' plea was because my old friend couldn't allow Danica to be prosecuted.

"That was really chickenshit, by the way, Phil," I added.

"This is very disconcerting," Halprin said—as if this was the first time any of this had occurred to him.

---

[135] Notice that there were no IRS convictions in his case. In fact, as I mentioned, during these proceedings, Mike and I both got letters saying that the investigation was over and that the IRS wouldn't be prosecuting us. After all this search and seizure, all this media frenzy, we actually wound up getting *refund checks* (for several million dollars). But you didn't see any of that in the papers. As far as the public is concerned, we're still colossal tax frauds.

[136] He also seemed to be terribly concerned with the time (he kept checking his watch). I would later learn that this is because the assistant U.S. attorney has three sons, and that he'd never missed a soccer game in ten years. Very family-oriented. In many ways, it's commendable. But even though he was meeting with a man he intended to bury, he seemed more concerned about making a three-thirty soccer game than hammering out the details of a failed IRS raid. Your tax dollars at work, folks.

"It should be. We can't fight dishonesty. If you were all going up there telling the truth, we would win."

Halprin didn't seem to know what to say.

"And you know that $93.7 million was bullshit."

Halprin looked over at Martinez, then at me. "Yeah," he said slowly. "We were a little embarrassed about that."

"Embarrassed?" I barked. "What about *me*? *You're* embarrassed?"

Halprin threw his hands to either side defensively. "Hey, don't blame us for what the media did. We just said we were investigating you."

I chuckled darkly. "C'mon, Phil. You know that's the kiss of death. And don't tell me you didn't spur the media along. You released an affidavit!"

He had no response. Martinez just sat there, looking stupid.

"This wasn't an IRS investigation," I said. "This was an FDA investigation from the beginning."

Halprin denied the claim.

I pressed on. "You saw it, I saw it, it was all wrong."

Halprin ducked the issue. "Well, that's grand jury stuff," he said. "You know we can't talk about it."

So LaBella and I left angrily, knowing we wouldn't have another opportunity to point the finger at Phil Halprin and his minions until the day of Mike's sentencing.

When the day finally arrived, I had a hard time containing my anger. In fact, there are very few times in my life when I've been angrier or more upset. See, word had it that Halprin was going to request eighteen months in prison for Blevins.

I remember that I was walking down the hall from the hearing room (I had to use the bathroom) when I saw Phil Halprin. He sat like the idiot version of the Thinker on a little wooden bench in the hallway, probably fifty feet from where Blevins' hearing would soon be taking place.

I went straight up to him, looking him in the eyes, though it infuriated me. "You know you basically extorted Mike into pleading to this," I said. "He's fifty-seven years old. He's not going to harm anyone. But you're going to send him to jail until he's almost sixty. How is that justice?"

Halprin grinned. "Justice? You don't get justice *here*."

I scoffed. "How do you live with that?"

The assistant U.S. attorney just shook his head. "I've got a job to do."

"Your job is to convict a guy who did nothing?"

Halprin turned away. "Well, that's just how it is."

As much as I hate to do it, I have to give credit to Phil Halprin. When he went into court that day, he told the judge that Blevins was a completely rehabilitated criminal who would not break the law again. And I have to credit the judge, as well, for seeing through the bullshit. He explained that he believed that the charge against Blevins had been used as a pressure point to get information on Metabolife. And as a result, he sentenced my friend to three years of probation and a thousand hours of community service.

Out of all the years I've known Mike Blevins, the first time I cried in front of him was when I heard that gavel come down. Tears streamed down my cheeks. When my oldest friend turned to be escorted out of the court, I saw that he had tears in his eyes, as well.

Could Halprin have been harder on him? Yes. Did he throw softballs at him in court? I think so. But fair's fair.

The agents who'd investigated Mike didn't seem to agree. Many of them scoffed and made lewd comments to Blevins as he passed down the aisle after the sentencing. I remember laughing through my tears at the irony. What did they have to be angry about? Sure, Mike didn't get prison time. But the investigation had been bullshit to begin with—a smokescreen designed to cover the asses of these same outraged men.

I remember wondering then if these scoffing agents had ever gotten wind of the story of Mike Compton—the ultimate and most painful fruit of their farcical investigation.

As I mentioned, Bob Bradley had met Mike Compton through his auction company. And Compton had been brought on board with Metabolife to help revamp and dramatically improve our entire accounting department. Compton had proven himself more than capable at this task but, eventually, the job simply outgrew him. When you're dealing with the kinds of money we were bringing in, accounting becomes the job of a team, not just one man.

Either way, by the time Mike Compton left Metabolife, he was in a unique position. He knew just about everything about the company's accounting department and its practices. He knew almost better than anyone that tax fraud, within the walls of Metabolife International, was even less *possible* than it was likely.

When the government came into play in 2002, they ran a search of all the Metabolife buildings and the homes of anyone who had ever been directly involved with the company's accounting. This included Mike Compton's house. In seizing Compton's financial records, the IRS ultimately discovered that he had lied on his stated income on the purchase of a home. *Leverage.* And that's all they would need to launch their great $93.7 million witch hunt: just one person with a little dirt, just one person they could seriously lean on to testify against Metabolife in whatever tax proceedings would ensue.

So the IRS threatened to suspend Mike's accounting license and send him to jail for bank fraud if he didn't cooperate with the investigation.

Now, it's important to note that Mike was a happy-go-lucky kind of guy. Not a strong individual. He was a great man—one of the greatest—but he just didn't have the intestinal fortitude to deal with the level of threat or intimidation that our government can dish out. Just about everyone involved with Metabolife can now speak from experience: When you've got agents showing up in bulletproof vests, all dressed in black, pouring into your house...it's pretty intimidating.

Essentially, the hollow threats led Compton, under all this duress, to say things about Bob Bradley[137] as if they were fact. In

---

[137] That he was embezzling money from Metabolife, his towing company, and the auction company.

exchange for lying on the stand, Mike Compton would get a walk on his bank fraud case.

So here's Mike Compton: He's lost his house; thanks to all this undue legal trouble, his marriage is over; he's lost his kids in the divorce; he's dead broke after months of fighting the charges against him; he's been threatened with five years in prison; and now he's presented with a get-out-of-jail-free card, the answer to all of his problems.

All he had to do was lie...

All he had to do was provide false information that incriminated the founders of Metabolife...

All he had to do was shed his morality and sense of honor...

So the day before he was to lie on the stand, Compton called Bob Bradley. "Bob," he said sadly, "they're asking me to lie about you."

"What do they want you to say?" Bob asked.

"That you embezzled money from Metabolife."

"Ninety-three million?"

Compton emitted a shuddery sigh. "Not exactly, no. They just want me to testify against you."

"So what are you going to do?"

Compton chuffed. "I think I'm just going to shoot the motherfuckers the next time I see them."

Bob's fingers began to tingle uneasily. "Mike," he said slowly, "you don't mean that. And you have to be careful what you say. We're under investigation. You never know who's listening in on these phone calls."

Compton sounded near tears. "So what should I do?"

"Tell them whatever you need to tell them, Mike. You got yourself into trouble because of your house loan."

"But, Bob—"

"You can lie if you want to," Bob interrupted. "I've got records that'll prove that whatever you say isn't true."

"But, Bob, they want me to lie about you and Metabolife."

"I don't know what to tell you."

Compton fell silent for a long while—perhaps mulling over how the whole thing had brought an end to life as he knew it. His family, his money, his career. "Well, then…" he finally said. "I'm not going to lie."

"Do whatever you have to do."

So Mike Compton hung up the phone, apparently knowing that he had to tell the truth. But he also knew that if he told the truth, he would be prosecuted for bank fraud. Imagine feeling trapped in such a way. Imagine knowing that a lie would spare you while the truth would ruin you, get you tossed in jail, and eliminate your ability to even make a living.

The day that Compton was supposed to testify was a Thursday, I remember. We were all sitting around in another of our all-too-frequent board meetings when a call came through on my cell phone.

"Hello?"

"Mike?"

"Yeah, this is Mike Ellis."

"There's no good way to say this, so I'll just say it…" I didn't recognize the voice, but how do you interrupt someone who says something like that? "Mike Compton put a gun to his head and killed himself last night."

I set my phone down on the table in front of me, too stunned to speak. I must have lost all the color in my face, because it wasn't long before someone noticed.

"What's wrong, Mike?" Garry Pay asked.

"Mike Compton shot himself," I said, having trouble getting the wind to speak.

Every face staring back at me looked stunned. Liked we'd all fallen into some kind of big, unbelievable dream. [138]

Still, Compton's family was angry at us. Specifically at Bob. And who could blame them? Right or wrong, Mike's death was the result of an investigation into our company. We all felt sorry about it, but there was nothing we could do. The load that the IRS had brought upon us had proven heavy enough to break a man completely. A kind man. An honest man. Just an easygoing CPA who loved stockcar racing.

In all this madness, people had lost their jobs, people were sent to jail, people were forced to plead to crimes they didn't commit. But ultimately, the most devastating part of it all was that a great man lost his life.

---

[138] For days, I couldn't stop thinking about poor Compton. About how terrible and help-less things must have been for him. I couldn't imagine reaching a state like that. Couldn't imagine getting so close to the end of the rope that I would want to kill myself...

Chapter 21

Modern Law with the U.S. Attorney's Office

With my partners essentially erased from the map, the U.S. Attorney's Office could now turn its attention toward me. The first indictment they hit me with concerned a letter to the FDA[139] and a few bogus obstruction of justice charges. Each count of the indictment carried a five-year sentence.

Now, I had two different judges working on my two cases. For the gun case, it was a judge named Miller. For the FDA case: Judge Napoleon Jones. Fortunately, Judge Jones, during a motion to dismiss presented by Steve Mansfield, saw through the smoke and mirrors and threw out all of the obstruction charges. So this brought my demise down to two counts of submitting false statements to the FDA. [140]

In the weeks that would follow, Phil Halprin—a man who'd

---

[130] The Beinke letter first presented to me at Frantz and Keegan's deposition.

[140] This proved to be a significant blow to the federal government, having their obstruction charges completely dismissed. And it must have come as a shock to just about everyone involved. See, federal charges aren't normally thrown out in court, not unless there's something flagrantly wrong with them to begin with, anyway.

certainly picked the right profession, given that he absolutely refused to lose at anything—formally asked the judge to reconsider his ruling on two separate occasions. [141] Obviously, Judge Jones declined. Vehemently.

Despite our little victories in court, the *San Diego Union Tribune* continued to beat up on us. Penny Crabtree seemed to be all over us, 24/7. She ran stories about the FDA charges, about Blevins' firearms conviction, and about any and all IRS-related crap she could wrap her hands around. Naturally, she would always twist the story to suit her sensationalist needs. Funny, though. To my knowledge, she never wrote an article about the dismissal of the obstruction charges. [142]

I remember that this new wave of assaults occurred right around the time that we'd all begun to wonder what in the hell Penny Crabtree had against us. Then, completely out of the blue, the answer to the question basically fell into our laps. Dr. Carlon Colker (of congressional hearings fame) had been invited to guest on the Rodger Hedgecock talk radio show in San Diego. Since we'd done business with Colker before, we were all obviously intrigued by the interview. The interview was supposed to cover Colker's stance on basic health and medication issues, but it eventually evolved into a conversation on the hot-button topic of the day: Metabolife.

"But what do you say to people like Penny Crabtree who claim that Metabolife is dangerous?" Hedgecock asked on the air.

"I'm not sure where Penny's coming from," Dr. Colker explained. "But I can tell you that there's no basis for the claims she's making."

A soft little cheer rang out among those of us listening.

"I understand that we have a caller on the line," Hedgecock said. "Go ahead, caller. You're on the Rodger Hedgecock Show."

---

[141] This sort of thing doesn't happen very often, either, given that judges don't particularly like to have their rulings second-guessed.

[142] There was a small mention of the dismissal in another article by a different writer. That's the best I ever got.

"I'll tell you why Penny Crabtree is always writing dirt about Metabolife," the caller said. "Because her husband is associated with a pharmaceutical company in San Diego that's working on its own weight loss product."

"No!" Hedgecock exclaimed.

"No kidding," the caller said adamantly. "They've got the product ready to launch and everything."

"So what about that, listeners? Is there anything to this theory that Crabtree's discrediting Metabolife for her husband's own financial gain?"

We later researched the caller's claim and found that Crabtree's husband was in fact an executive for an R&D company in San Diego. So the accusation seemed reasonable. So did she attack Metabolife for personal gain? I don't know. But it sure seems like she might have had good reason.

Regardless, soon, she would get her day in the sun. The media's villain would soon get what he "deserved."

On the day of my indictment on FDA charges, there were all kinds of camera crews milling around in front of the courthouse. See, in San Diego, the federal court building does not allow cameras inside, so the media contingent had assembled on the stone steps out front. It was one giant circus. People with cameras and tape recorders and microphones, all of them jockeying for position outside the courthouse, all of them pining to get the best footage of me coming out of my hearing. From what I understand, all of the major news stations were in attendance.

Unfortunately, I didn't get to see any of this go down, as I was busy inside the building, preparing for my hearing. I heard about it all from Jan Strode, a PR officer employed by Metabolife. As we waited for the proceedings to begin, she would drop in regularly to update us on the conditions with the media outside. Jan was a kind and capable PR woman. She was pretty, and I'd say middle-aged. She'd gotten used to normal PR work, I think, because she wasn't quite as adept at crisis-management—and, boy, did we ever have a lot of crisis management work in those days.

Following my appearance before the courts, I was walking out to the lobby with my lawyers when Jan walked up, looking frantic. "Mike," she said, "it's gotten too bad out there."

"What are they saying?" I asked.

Jan blustered. "That they won't leave until you talk to them."

I nodded. "Listen," I said, "I have to go downstairs to get booked by the marshal's office. I'll be back up."

"Hurry, please," Jan said. "They're about to tear my head off out there."

Trying to accommodate Jan, I hurried down to and through the standard booking process. I had my fingerprints and picture taken, answered all of the obligatory questions about tattoos and everything, and filled out the paperwork. It was kind of funny because the marshals didn't have any idea how to classify the charges of my indictment (that I had made false statements to the FDA). I guess it was such a rare charge that they didn't have a standard code in their book of infractions to match up with my paperwork. Eventually, I guess they found something that worked because I was soon signing on the dotted line and being released to my own recognizance.

When I came back up from booking, LaBella and Mansfield joined up with me, LaBella on my behalf and Mansfield on behalf of the company. Jan, clearly frazzled, immediately made her way in our direction. The media had continued to harass her about when I would be coming out—just hungry for the story, I guess. [143]

As she stalked up to us, a gallows smile crossed my face—all at once, a plan had occurred to me. One last little "screw you" to the media. See, the media had never been fair to me, so I didn't see any reason to oblige them now. They had harassed my family, defamed me entirely, and had always failed to tell both sides of the story.

---

[143] It was later in the afternoon, by that point, and I'm sure they needed to get the shots so they could put me on the six o'clock news.

I didn't wait for Jan to speak. "This is what you do," I said. "You go out there and say to them, 'Gee, I don't know where Mike is…must be taking longer than usual at booking.'"

"But they're really mad at me," Jan said desperately.

"Hear me out. Just tell them, 'When he comes up, he comes up.'"

She nodded reluctantly, not meeting my eyes.

I put my hand on her shoulder. "Just go out there and tell them that. Can you do that?"

She nodded again.

"But I want you to keep leading them on," I explained. "I'm going to sneak out through the other end of the building, through the U.S. Attorney's Office."

Jan's eyes widened in shock and fear. "You're going to *what?*"

"Just hear me out, Jan," I said. "Keep leading them on that I'm gonna be coming up and you don't know why it's taking so long. Then, when I'm clear of the building, I'll call you on your cell phone."

"Okay…" Jan said slowly.

"Here's what you're going to do: Call your husband. Have him come around to the front of the building to pick you up."

"What's my husband got to do with anything?"

"Listen, Jan," I said calmly. "This is important. Have him waiting for you, okay?"

She nodded.

"When your husband gets here, you're going to tell the media, 'Jeez, I don't know where Mr. Ellis is, but I have a dinner appointment, so I'll talk to you all later.' And you're gonna walk right through the crowd, go out to your husband's car, and leave."

Jan nodded, furrowing her brow. "And where are you going to be?"

"Gone. Out the back."

Jan reluctantly agreed to do as I asked of her. And I guess it went off without a hitch. Needless to say, this upset the media greatly. They yelled at her terribly as she got into the car and drove away.

Everyone but Jan had a great laugh at that one. I guess Jan didn't think it was so funny because she felt like she'd been thrown to the wolves. But isn't that what PR people are for? To take the hit? And who cares, anyway? The media finally got what was coming to them.

Since charges about supposedly lying to the FDA certainly weren't enough to get me to plead out, I was later charged and indicted on federal firearms violations. The DOJ called it "constructive possession of firearms." But I knew going in that we had a good case against this charge, too. I hadn't done anything wrong, after all. Chuck LaBella sat now in my home office, running through everything with a fine-toothed comb.

The office was pretty much dominated by wood. Monica decorated it personally[144] with an antique desk and a credenza built in behind. It was a comfortable setup, plenty of windows overlooking the backyard and the pool.

Chuck stared in the direction of these windows as he briefed me. "They say they've got this bag from your closet," he said, tracing his pen down a list he'd made on a legal pad. "This blue bag that was full of ammunition, fishing gear, a knife."

"Chuck," I interrupted, "that bag is bullshit. I've never seen that bag. There's no way they found it in my closet. I mean, I don't even have any fishing gear in my house! Memo's got it all in his garage!" Even Memo, who went in the closet with the agents at the time of the search, testified in front of a grand jury that there was no blue bag in my closet.

"Well, that's where they said they got it," Chuck reminded me.

An idea suddenly occurred to me. "You know what?" I said. "I want to see all the photographs the government took from that day

---

[144] And she'd done a hell of a job. My wife was always an excellent interior decorator.

at my ranch." I just knew that something was amiss, and I figured that photographic evidence might be the best place to start searching for exactly what that something was.

Eventually, Chuck managed to get me copies of the photographs taken on the two cameras from the raid of the ranch. [145] There were hundreds of them. Some came from a traditional camera with negatives. Some on a digital.

I began my search by going through the pictures of the infamous blue bag they'd reportedly taken from my closet. When examining the photos, it quickly became clear to me that this wasn't my bag—in fact, I'd never seen anything inside that bag (or even the bag itself). In addition to that, the first picture on the negatives depicted the bag sitting in the garage. Then, several shots later, there was a picture of the bag in my closet. And later still, a photo with the bag's contents splayed out on the bathroom counter, near the sink.

Confused, I showed the negatives to Chuck, who noticed a detail that had escaped me: a small tear in the bag pictured in the garage. Together, we looked at the before-and-after photos from the garage, then compared them to the one supposedly found in my closet. Each bag had the same tear. It appeared as if we were dealing with not two bags, but one.

Our suspicions were confirmed when we examined the list of items seized from the ranch. The agents hadn't listed the bag as being part of the items seized from the garage. The bag only showed up on the list of evidence confiscated from my closet. But if the picture of the bag in the garage were to be believed, what happened to that bag? Why hadn't it been added to the list of items seized? Its picture sat right there in front of us.

"I can't believe this," Chuck said, his eyes as wide as I'd ever seen them. "I hate to say it. But it appears that someone planted that bag in your room."

"That's what I've been trying to tell you," I said.

---

[145] After several bitter appeals for information from the U.S. Attorney's Office, appeals that they didn't seem too eager to meet.

Chuck shook his head slowly, clearly trying to reason things out. "We should hire an expert...just to make sure."

So we hired a forensic photographic expert. We even took him out to the ranch so he could get a sense of the lighting, the angles, the layout, everything.

When we handed him the negatives and photographs we'd gotten from the Department of Justice, the expert informed us that he could help us out with the negatives, but that he couldn't make a clear determination about the digital photos until he had the original disks to examine (obviously, it's harder to determine the order in which a group of photographs was taken unless you can see them in a string in their original format). And even before he could help with the negatives, he needed to know the exact models of the camera they had come from.

So we took the fight for this information to the courts—and what a fight it was. The DOJ kept giving us the runaround. At first, the only thing we could get out of them was the makes and models of the cameras used in the search.

Despite this scant information, the forensic expert managed to confirm everything we already knew about the negatives. But we couldn't fully confirm our story until he could link the digital photos.

In search of these elusive original disks, we had to file several motions in court. Halprin and his cronies kept heehawing around, claiming that they had misplaced the original disks and had to look for them. [146] Only after a few more motions and several different stories on the part of the government would the DOJ finally explain that they customarily just recorded over the original evidence with pictures from new crime scenes. [147]

Still, we had the evidence from the negatives. And our expert confirmed that the pictures showed a bag in the garage, then (at

---

[146] It felt like the classic, "The dog ate my homework" excuse.

[147] Let me just say this on the record: This is complete and absolute bullshit. I was once a cop. I know the drill. You *never* destroy or otherwise alter original evidence.

least) a very similar bag in my closet, and then that bag opened up on my bathroom counter. It certainly seemed to all of us that the bag had been moved from the garage and then purposely dropped into a place that I clearly had access to.

If it can be believed that the agents followed the normal chain of evidence (and assuming that each picture depicts the same torn blue bag), then what we had was indisputable, absolute fact. Given the order of the pictures from the negatives, first, the agents had taken a picture of the bag on the garage counter. Then, they had moved the bag to the counter in the bathroom connected to my bedroom (where they removed its contents and took photos of the incriminating evidence). And finally, they packed all the contents back in the bag and placed it on the shelf in my closet.

The government's own negative photos prove this to be true. Further, the government's own time logs prove that a blue bag was found in the garage before its apparent twin was found in my closet. Meanwhile, no one can seem to explain what happened to the bag supposedly seized from the garage.

Because we couldn't get the original disk from the digital camera, we couldn't prove conclusively that the "two" bags in question were actually the same bag—and that that bag had been planted in my bedroom. [148]

But you know what's craziest to think about these days? The fact that that wasn't even the worst sin committed by the U.S. Attorney's Office. No, the worst involved their handling of the supposed fingerprint evidence in the case. See, we'd spent fifteen months fighting just to get a crack at the evidence, and Halprin's corner had hemmed and hawed about giving it to us. Eventually, after all this fighting, they informed us that all of the evidence had been *lost*. In a *fire*.

---

[148] And isn't it remarkable to think that the burden of proof in this case was on *our* shoulders? We were the defense. "Reasonable doubt" should have been all that we needed to raise—and I believe we raised it quite well. But that's not the federal court game. On that stage, it's all about *winning*. Justice be damned.

Here's how things apparently transpired. Instead of using a federal employee to handle the evidence (which would have been normal protocol), Halprin's investigators had employed the services of a forensic evidence expert in San Diego. [149] This expert, a man named Torrez, was basically a contractor who worked for many different agencies in the area, including the San Diego Police Department.

Now, Torrez made several significant blunders in the case of Metabolife. The one that concerned us initially was the way he had handled the fingerprint evidence. See, Torrez had lifted prints from the guns seized from the ranch. He'd then checked to see if the prints matched my own. They didn't. But strangely, he didn't take the investigation to its next logical step: cross-checking the prints on the guns with the prints taken from Memo and Louis, the two men ardently claiming that the guns belonged to them (and only them).

Since that evidence would effectively exonerate me from the gun charges, my attorneys and I naturally felt like it would be important for us to do the DOJ's job for them. But when we finally got the guns from the government, [150] all the prints were smeared. Our own forensic expert determined that they'd been smeared on *purpose*. It appeared as if someone had intentionally wiped the guns clean. But only the guns that had prints on them that would clear me. Odd.

In the weeks that would follow this little revelation, we would claw and scratch with Halprin to release all of the evidence so we could investigate everything and make our case. [151] Halprin would stall. So we would send a formal written request to the DOJ. The DOJ, in turn, would stall.

Eventually, we brought the matter before the courts. There, the truth finally came out: As we would finally discover, Torrez's second major blunder was that he'd stored all of the evidence in the

---

[149] Why the divergence from the norm? Who knows?

[150] Again, after much pleading in court.

[151] Providing the defense with a chance to examine evidence is a matter of law.

Metabolife case not in a federal building, but in his *home* (effectively violating all federal and state policies regarding the handling of evidence). But this little point of embarrassment wasn't why they were stalling. Why were they stalling? Because Torrez's home (and all the evidence in it) had subsequently been destroyed in the wildfires that had swept through Southern California in 2003, fifteen months after the government seized the evidence from my home and ranch.

Finally, we understood the reason for all the stalling. It wasn't a matter of embarrassment. It was a matter of *leverage*. See, as long as my attorneys and I didn't know that the evidence had been destroyed, we would continue to believe that they had us dead to rights—and we would be that much more likely to cut a deal. [152]

So for weeks, we'd requested access to evidence. And for weeks, they kept stringing us along, all the while knowing that the evidence in question had been burned up.

Fortunately, we would later discover that some of the evidence, including the infamous blue bag, hadn't been destroyed. But when we requested access to the bag so we could have everything fingerprinted (the knife, boxes, ammo, everything), Halprin tried stonewalling us again. It took a court order to finally get the evidence released—and by the time we received it, it was in such a state that our (government approved) fingerprint expert found numerous prints. None were mine, so we suspected them to be the agents'. When we asked to obtain prints from all the agents, the government refused.

So every single aspect of this evidence was dirty. Tainted. We'd seen the destruction of original photographic evidence, the (probable) removal of fingerprint evidence, the improper storage of evidence, and the loss of evidence in a wildfire. And the impropriety had been all but confirmed by the fact that Halprin and

---

[152] I still lose sleep at night knowing that our own government wouldn't just try to prosecute me with "artfully interpreted" evidence, but would try to do so even after that evidence was *lost.*

friends had strung us along about access to the evidence for fifteen months. For more than a year, the evidence sat in Torrez's house. For nearly a year, they'd known that most of the evidence had been destroyed in a fire. And for more than a year, they'd stonewalled us about gaining access.

And you know what the craziest part was? We couldn't even subpoena Torrez about our claims because he was under *California state indictment* at the time. He'd been accused of committing something called "employee retirement fraud" in San Diego. So even if we'd subpoenaed the government's expert witness, he would have had to invoke the Fifth Amendment for all of our questions, so as not to incriminate himself.

So by February of 2006, between the misconduct of the agents and the destruction of evidence, getting the gun charges dismissed seemed like a virtual guarantee. So we filed a motion to dismiss in camera. [153]

During the many years of fighting the government, Monica and I grew further and further apart. I guess the stress became too much for all of us. It got to the point that Monica appeared to not be interested in what was happening. It was probably better because, of all the wonderful things about Monica, she was very bad at stress.

Miller ruled that our accusations of tainted evidence would be a matter for the jury to weigh. In short, our motion was denied.

Naturally, I was devastated. I wanted nothing more than to vent to my wife. But even when Monica came home, all she seemed to want to talk about was other things. She completely avoided the issue of the hearing, I don't know. Maybe it was Monica's way of dealing with the pain of everything that was going on.

---

[153] For those not familiar with the legal vernacular, "in camera" means that we submitted the motion to the judge behind closed doors, where neither the U.S. attorney nor the public would be privileged to the contents of the motion.

$\sim\!\!\mathcal{M}\!\!\sim$

Many months later, we were preparing to fight the gun case in court. We felt good about everything that had been taken from the ranch, given that we had the planted evidence, the destruction of evidence, and the indicted expert witness to lean on. The only thing we were nervous about was the pair of guns seized from Monica's safe. The only thing that could clear me on this charge would be the testimony of my wife—but given the way that she had been acting about the whole thing lately, I was a little anxious about asking her to testify. [154]

I remember that she stood in the bedroom (near the window) when I approached her this time. "Monica," I said, "it looks like we're going to court on the gun case."

She nodded vaguely, not looking me in the eye.

"But if we're going to beat this thing," I continued, placing my hands on her shoulders, "then I need you to tell them your end of the story about the guns in your safe—how you made a mistake when you said the safe wasn't yours."

Monica immediately pulled away, looking furious. "You know, this is all your fault," she yelled. "All of it."

My head swam and my heart raced.

"If I say anything wrong," she yelled, "you'll blame me."

I tried to remain calm. "No, I won't, Monica," I said.

She shook her head furiously. "I can't do this. I just can't do this."[155]

It was that moment when I first realized that I would lose. That

---

[154] Given her kind of aloof nature about the whole thing, I'd begun to suspect that my wife was in denial about all my legal trouble. Can I blame her? Absolutely not. In many ways, I was in denial, too.

[155] Sometime later, my wife would recant her statements about testifying. But by that time, both LaBella and I felt Monica was not up to the stress of testifying and would be a dangerous gamble to take. I mean, the penalty against me was five years. And, see, if you plead out, you get leniency. But if you fight the charges and lose, you get the maximum.

no matter what I said or did, I was cooked. There was plenty of evidence to suggest that I didn't have access to the safe (the combo locked in, locksmith never showing up, the DMV papers, the lack of my fingerprints, etc.), but without my wife corroborating that evidence, it wouldn't hold up in court.

So the government had its leverage against me. And they used it to force the issue on the FDA case. I was cornered. Finished. A man without a choice.

That's when I called Chuck to ask him the most difficult question I've ever had to ask. "Under a federal indictment like this," I said, "if I were to die, would I be found guilty?"

"No," Chuck said slowly. "The case would be over."

"So...say I got hit by a car. I wouldn't be found guilty for making false statements to the FDA?"

"No."

"And the PI attorneys couldn't come after my family's estate?"

"They could go after Metabolife, but it would be far more difficult to go after your wife's estate."

"Thanks, Chuck."

"Mike...are you alright?"

I sighed. "Sure I am, Chuck. I'll see you tomorrow."

Of course, that was a lie. Knowing what I'd just learned from my lawyer, I could now begin contemplating suicide in earnest.

It all seemed so clear. If I were gone, Monica would be set, my family wouldn't be harassed by the DOJ anymore, and everything else would simply disappear. The media would eventually back off and my family could go back to leading a normal life. And I wouldn't have to worry about them having to struggle to get by after the PI attorneys took all our money away. I wouldn't have to worry about making them go back to living in a rented house and eating hotdogs. See, if I pled out to giving a false statement to the FDA, the PI attorneys could come after everything I ever earned, and potentially everything Bob and Mike earned also.

But if it were going to be suicide, I realized, I would have to make it look like something other than suicide. I honestly just didn't want my family to have to live with the idea that I killed myself to secure their future, so I'd have to make it look like an accident.

To that end, every time I'd drive somewhere (which was more in those days, given that that's how I dealt with stress), I would look for places to stage my accident. It's funny the things you notice when you're trying to kill yourself. For example, the freeways are constructed in such a way that they're actually incredibly safe. Even if you wanted to ram into the concrete pillar under an overpass, the state has set up deflection and barrels designed to cause your car to glance back onto the road. But the freeways were out, anyway, because I didn't want to hurt anyone else in the accident. If it were to be a car accident, I would have to find a more secluded area.

All this time—all these days and nights of driving around in search of a lone tree or an unguarded precipice—I thought about Mike Compton and what he must have gone through before he shot himself. More and more, I began to understand the man. Maybe suicide wasn't the coward's way out. Maybe he'd done it just to protect the ones he loved. Like I intended to do.

About a week into my journey—right about when I'd worked myself into the kind of frenzy a man needs to punch his own ticket—I found my location. Del Dios Highway. Over by Lake Hodges. They have a dam there. There's a spot where the two-lane highway bends. Right there, there's a little gravel turnabout just off the edge of the pavement. The turnabout opens up to a cliff, a drop-off to the freedom represented by the countryside below.

I pulled onto this turnabout and stepped out of the car, examining the precipice. "This is perfect," I whispered. "I'll drop a long ways." I began to pace, reasoning it out. "I'll take my seatbelt off…and I'll do it late at night so it looks like I fell asleep."

I returned home, deciding that I would need a chance to see my family one last time before I did the deed. I would plan to return on the following night.

I don't remember much about the next day or the next evening, but I do remember reaching for the door to leave. For the last time.

"What's wrong?" Monica asked me when she heard my hand on the door handle.

"Nothing," I lied. "I'm just going for a drive." Hesitantly, I left.

By the time I reached the site of my death, it was late enough that nobody was on the road. So I unbuckled my seatbelt and backed far enough down the highway to give myself the kind of momentum it would take to launch me into oblivion. Breathing slowly, I slammed on the pedal, sending the car reeling toward the precipice. I roared around the turn, careening toward the edge.

But when the end came in sight, all I could think about was my kids. Who would be there to provide for them? Who would be there for Isabella, my new two-year-old daughter, the one who had essentially saved my sanity years earlier? For Mikey? For Nick? For Christian?

Obviously, we're all afraid to die. But fear wasn't what kept me from driving over that cliff. It was *love*.

As I slammed on the brakes, my perspective instantly changed. "I'll just keep fighting this thing as long as I can," I breathed. "Just keep fighting." I thought about how I'd have at least sixty days to surrender, should I in fact be convicted for the gun charge. "You'll know when the right time to do this will be," I said.

When you get to a position like this one, it's funny how drastically your perspective changes. I sat there on that cliffside for an hour, trying to reason out how things could have fallen this far.

By the time I'd come back down to Earth, I might have been depressed, but I had certainly returned to the mindset where I felt we could beat both of the cases against me. The government didn't want the gun case—they just used it as leverage to get what they needed to get: the FDA case.

Several weeks after my aborted suicide attempt, Halprin contacted Chuck LaBella, wanting to cut a deal. I guess he finally figured that he was, in fact, in trouble on a whole lot of his evidence. On the call, Halprin explained that he couldn't drop the FDA case [156]—that this was the one plea he needed if he was ever going to back down. But Chuck reminded Halprin that I'd flatly refused to lie in court. [157]

Eventually, the two of them came to an agreement on what I would plead to: in a nutshell, knowing about the Beinke letter, and "aiding and abetting after the fact."

Later, it would be determined that what Halprin wanted me to plead to was not, in fact, a crime. Apparently, you're not obligated to inform the FDA of misinformation. So both attorneys worked diligently on the verbiage of the eventual plea.

It would be Halprin who would write the final draft. Word for word, here is the plea agreement that I would come to sign:

- Defendant has fully discussed the facts of this case with defense counsel. Defendant has committed each of the elements of the crimes, and admits that there is a factual basis for this guilty plea. The parties agree that the factual basis includes the following and Defendant specifically admits the following facts to which he has personal knowledge:

- In or about early February of 1999, within the Southern District of California, Defendant knowingly and will-fully caused the law firm of Arter & Hadden, LLP, and attorney Allen P. Beinke of that firm to be retained by Metabolife International, Inc., to communicate with the FDA; [158]

- On or about February 9, 1999, Allen P. Beinke sent a letter to the FDA, which stated that Metabolife had a "claims-free" history. Defendant was aware that at

---

[156] The FDA just wouldn't let him.

[157] Even after all that had happened, I was adamant about that point.

[158] True, I did hire the law firm in question. And according to grand jury testimony, Beinke did in fact write that letter.

the time this letter was sent, Metabolife did not have a "claims-free" history; [159]

- Defendant had reason to believe that the FDA may have relied upon the false statement contained in the February 9, 1999, letter relating to consumer allegations of health complaints; [160] and

- The false statement was in a matter within the jurisdiction of the FDA, which is a department or agency of the United States. [161]

If you read this plea carefully, it's absolutely accurate. The only trouble is that it's missing one key element of the crime—the one that holds the whole thing up, the one that makes or breaks it as a crime to begin with: whether or not I even *knew about* Beinke's writing of the letter at the time it was written. And that's the thing. I *didn't* know that Beinke had written that letter and sent it to the FDA.

But forget the fact that the central element of the crime is missing. Forget that I hadn't actually knowingly committed an illegal act. The plea served the purpose of the U.S. Attorney's Office and the FDA. Meanwhile, I could finally put this whole ordeal behind me. My family and friends could finally be allowed to breathe into something other than a media microphone. Everything would return to relatively normal—and, no matter what happened, my family would be financially secure. [162]

---

[159] This is a true statement. The letter did in fact claim that Metabolife had a claims-free history. And, yes, at the time it was written, I knew that statement to be untrue. I was just unaware the letter was written and sent until two years later when I learned of its existence in the Franz deposition.

[160] Because the FDA said under sworn affidavit that it relied upon the information in that letter, I'll assume that this is a true statement.

[161] Any idiot knows this.

[162] I would only sign the plea under the condition that Phil Halprin wouldn't release it until Metabolife's bankruptcy proceedings had reached the point where the PI attorneys couldn't come after my personal finances. Halprin knew that was the only way I would agree to plea—and he followed through on his end of the bargain, holding on to my plea for almost a year.

I was very nervous on the day of my pleading because I worried that Judge Napoleon Jones would realize that the plea didn't meet the element of the crime. If he caught this little point, he would have to ask me the damning question: whether I actually knew about the letter when it was written. And if he asked the damning question, I would have to answer with the truth: that I didn't know about it. This would have completely unwound the deal with the U.S. Attorney's Office. And frankly, if such a thing transpired, none of us knew where the case would go from there.

As I stood behind the defense table, staring up at the bench, things began rather ominously.

"Mr. Ellis," Judge Jones said, "if you lie to me, I will seek perjury penalties against you. Do you understand that?"

"Yes," I said.

He asked if I would like to read my plea or if I would like my attorney to read it.

"I'd like my attorney to read the plea."

Chuck read the statement.

"Mr. LaBella," the judge said, nodding his head knowingly, "do you believe that this is a true statement?"

"Judge Jones," Chuck said, "*in the way that it is written*, this is a true statement."

Halprin glared over at our table. Fortunately for all of us, the judge let it slide. He adjourned the hearing, informing me that I would have to reappear for sentencing. I later received a sentence of six months in federal prison. I shook Chuck's hand, breathing a sigh of relief for the first time in six years. The two of us turned to file out of the courtroom. But apparently, Halprin wasn't done with us.

"Chuck," he said angrily, "why did you answer that way?"

Chuck threw his head back. "Because you know I don't agree with the way this all went down."

I can't say as I disagreed. The overarching logic is pretty interesting, when you think about it: If you believe everything that the government had accused me of and that the media had said about me—mainly, that they purportedly had me dead to rights on tax evasion, gun possession, and the purveyance of a deadly product—then why did they have to manipulate the system just to get a plea they could make stick? Why did they push so hard for a plea in the first place? In fact, if everything they accused me of were true, they should have just taken me to court and buried me for decades. But, instead, they settled for an agreement that called for zero to six months of prison time.

All those tax dollars wasted; all those trumped up charges and resultant pleas; all those marriages and families ruined; the systematic destruction of a weight loss supplement that actually worked; the loss of one man's life. Compton's suicide. And for what?

Epilogue

Believe it or not, my goal in writing this book wasn't simply to influence what you think of me. I'm obviously not a saint. But given all that I've been through, I'm no longer interested in vindication. Only truth. I just wanted to tell the story of what happened to Metabolife from the inside out.

Whenever I tell my stories, people always have the same question for me: "Why do you think all of this happened?" They all seem to want to know *why*—assuming that I'm truly *not* the villain (that I'm truly *not* a tax fraud and a gun nut and an irresponsible business owner)—I was made out to be one. What were the motives behind the systematic destruction of Metabolife?

I have my theories:

If it hasn't become clear already, let it be known that we at Metabolife tried very hard to get an audience with the FDA. And we tried for many years. No matter what we did, it seemed like they would avoid us. At first, we assumed that the bureaucracy was refusing our advances because they just didn't get it—that they just weren't seeing that the science and history behind ma huang proved that our product was safe and that we weren't doing anything irresponsible. But as the years went by, we slowly discovered that the problem was that they *did* see the truth. They *did* understand the safety and efficacy of herbal ephedrine. And you know what? The evidence *frightened* them.

See, right around the turn of this century, as an industry—with our newly formed coalitions and associations and connections—dietary supplements were growing in political clout. Congressmen and senators began to examine the science instead of the smear campaigns. And for a short while, it seemed as if the powers that be had finally seen the light.

Now, the FDA had been saying for years that ephedrine couldn't be trusted because there just wasn't enough known science on herbal preparation. The crazy (and confusing) thing is that we all believed that if we got them their scientific proof, then the agency would back off their rather misguided stance. But we were naïve. Once we ran the studies, the FDA did everything it could to discredit them. In the end, it's hard to deny the idea that the FDA didn't *really* want to prove that ephedrine was effective and safe.

Today, it's my belief that the FDA simply wanted to help a single special interest group to corner the market on ephedrine. As long as it was being sold by dietary supplement companies, they would continue to spout about how unsafe it was. But take it out of the hands of dietary supplement companies...

The process was subtle at first. The media kept raising the AER counts associated with the supplement industry. First, it was 400. Then, it was 700. Eventually, over several years, it swelled all the way to 900 supposed cases reported to the Food and Drug Administration.

So I know what you're thinking: If ephedrine is so safe, then how could this happen? It helped that the FDA launched an advertising campaign asking for people to call in and report their adverse events. They advertised on *Oprah*, on television, in print—whatever avenues they could use to get the word out nationwide. And you know what's funniest about this big, expensive effort to collect dirt on the industry? Even with all their national advertising, out of millions of Metabolife consumers, the FDA only received 800 total calls. A full year of advertising and only 800 calls!

Let's think about the significance of this for a minute. If I were a news anchor and I went on the air and said, "If you have ever driven on I-5 over the past five years and gotten sick, or if you know someone who got sick, we would like you to call in and report it," how many calls do you think my station would get? Thousands?

And the FDA only got *800* calls?

Still, a call is a call. And the agency could use these calls (regardless of their level of medical seriousness or believability) to keep pumping the American people with the idea that dietary supplements containing ephedrine were dangerously unsafe.

Okay, so now we've established opportunity. What about motive?

Since the early '90s, the FDA has been working with the World Health Organization (WHO) on the harmonization of dietary supplements worldwide. Basically, what this means is that these two organizations have been attempting to create a dietary supplement market in which all nutritional supplements come from a single source. When they say "harmonize," they pretend to be talking about the ability to ensure consumer safety. What they're really talking about is harmonizing the revenue streams.

See, in 1994, several years after the FDA first began working publicly and diligently with the WHO, millions of consumers began writing in to Congress with objections to the FDA's apparent attempt to eliminate free access to all nutritional supplements. To more and more Americans, it seemed almost as if the FDA wouldn't rest until the consumer couldn't get a dose of something as benign as vitamin C without a doctor's prescription (and only if that dose came straight from the coffers of big pharmacy). The WHO had already succeeded in bringing this nightmare to reality in many other countries. The U.S. was just the latest to climb into the money boat.

In response to this public outcry, Congress implemented something called the Dietary Supplement Health and Education Act (DSHEA). What DSHEA did was ensure that dietary supplements would remain freely accessible to the American population. And the tide was stemmed. For a while...

DSHEA clearly upset the FDA. They openly objected to the legislation. And I'm sure it really razzed them when its passing led to the ability of companies like Metabolife to grow into wildly profitable and increasingly politically powerful organizations. In a few short years following the legislation, the industry (and the companies within it) would reach the point where they could begin funding the science necessary to legitimize its products. [163] And, in turn, we became a nice little obstruction to the FDA's efforts to undo DSHEA.

Make no mistake, the FDA did in fact continue its efforts to get that legislation overturned. And it is my belief that they viewed Metabolife as their coverboy. As far as they were concerned, if you discredit Metabolife, you discredit the entire industry. Don't believe me? Consider the following:

The FDA worked directly with many of the personal injury attorneys attempting to sue us. Why would a regulatory agency want to trouble itself with funding lawsuits? They funded PR campaigns in the media in order to poison public opinion and even circumvent the state court systems. Why would a regulatory agency use tactics most often reserved for political smear campaigns? Even today, you'll never hear the FDA say that an herb of any kind is safe and effective. Why would a regulatory agency spend more money discrediting natural supplements than on scientific studies into those same supplements?

When the FDA finally found the chink in my company's armor (the IRS investigation), they immediately charged in and seized every piece of information they could get their hands on—information that we would have gladly given to them (no search necessary!) if they had just gone through the proper legal channels.

---

[163] The fact that we had to "legitimize" anything is still one of the great ironies of this story. Not one of the dietary supplement companies that existed then or now sold a product that hadn't been used safely and effectively for thousands of years (in China).

But obtaining information legally and privately just doesn't get press. And it sure doesn't discredit a company and industry. No, if you want to bring someone down, you have to publically humiliate them with a search. And then, as they stand there with their pants down, you tell everyone who will listen that they were *hiding information from the FDA*.

But that's just it. It seems as if, from the FDA's perspective, Metabolife *had* to fall. We were the biggest and most organized machine standing in their way. We were part of a driving force that finally turned the corner on bringing credibility to the dietary supplement industry.

But I digress. Let's get back to the FDA and its questionable relationship with the WHO. See, in 1963, the World Health Organization established a commission known as the Codex Alimentarius Commission. The motivation behind this commission seems harmless (and even beneficial) at first glance: Their stated goal is to develop food standards and practices in order to ensure safety for the consumer. But for decades, it has become clearer and clearer that, to the Codex Commission, safety goes hand in hand with *harmonization*. In other words, as far as they're concerned, you can only ensure safety if everything comes from a single source.

So what does this mean? This means that, if the FDA and WHO had their way, the American consumer would have only *one choice* when it came to their dietary supplement needs. They might tell you that this monopoly is necessary in order to ensure your safety as a consumer, but what about the money? Who stands to benefit most from the harmonization of dietary supplements?

If the answer isn't obvious already, let me give you a hint: Today, in most European countries, you need a *prescription* for all dietary supplements. Even if you want some vitamin C, you have to get a note from your doctor. Essentially, what this means is that all dietary supplements are in the hands of pharmaceutical companies.

Now, back up for a minute. Here's a scary thought: Do you have any prescriptions right now? What do you pay for those prescriptions? The price is astronomical, I'm sure. Imagine paying ten dollars for a single dose of vitamin C. Now extend that expense to any and all dietary supplements you might currently take. Ginkgo biloba? Fifteen dollars per dose. Valerian root? Two hundred dollars per bottle. Fish oil? Eight dollars per pill. And all of that money going straight into the pockets of big pharmacy.

Obviously, I can't just say something like that without backing it up with a little evidence. For the most compelling evidence, look no further than the timeline of the FDA's actions since Metabolife's raid in 2002:

Timeline of FDA Action Since 2002

2002	The search of Metabolife offices by the IRS and FDA
2003	The congressional hearing on the safety of herbal ephedrine (spearheaded by Congressmen Greenwood and Tauzin, giving the FDA the go-ahead to ban herbal ephedrine)
2004	Herbal ephedrine is banned.
Late 2004	Congressmen Greenwood and Tauzin leave Congress to begin working as lobbyists for pharmaceutical companies.
2005	The launch of Alli, a new pharmaceutical over-the-counter weight loss product[164]
2008	GlaxoSmithKlein posts a petition that asks the FDA to make all weight loss claims equivalent to drug claims.[165]

---

[164] A drug that, due to its tendency to cause anal leakage, never could have competed with an ephedrine-based product.

[165] If this petition is heeded, you will never again be able to buy dietary supplements (of any kind) for weight loss or weight management. Your only choice will be to take a pharmaceutical drug.

By 2010, the United States will be at a pivotal point when it comes to dietary supplements. If DSHEA is overturned (and it seems as if we're a matter of years from this actually happening), Codex will be able to step in and circumvent U.S. law. We will see the harmonization of all nutritional supplements. Americans, for the first time in history, will lose almost all free access to dietary supplements. More importantly, they'll be stripped of their rights to govern their own health (a foreign entity will regulate what is safe or unsafe for you to ingest). And Americans will lose free access to alternative medicine and nutritional supplements.

But how can the FDA do this, you might ask? Aren't there voters writing in to their congressmen and women? Isn't the will of the people still sacrosanct?

Good questions. In search of the answers, let's examine how the FDA wields its power:

Let's imagine a politician who publicly pledges to keep his/her constituency in charge of its own nutritional choices—a politician who promises to do everything he/she can in order to ensure that you will always be able to make your own healthcare decisions. Now, this politician, having the rights of his/her voters in mind, is rightfully elected to office. That politician is now in a position to help implement regulation that influences how the FDA approaches the dietary supplement industry. And the voters win. Another triumph for democracy.

But there's the flaw in the plan. See, the FDA is the ultimate bureaucracy. They've demonstrated an incredibly long track record of beginning regulation proposed by Congress, but then never seeing it through. So basically, if they don't agree with the legislation in question, they get things started in order to save face, but there's nothing compelling them to *finish* that legislation. They can stall and stall and stall until the whole thing loses steam. If they'd rather not deal with a new law, they just wait for the lawmakers to get voted out of office. In other words, the FDA can do whatever it wants simply because it *outlives its bosses*. The legislative process is thus circumvented. And *bureaucracy* wins.

It's enough to make a man wonder why he even votes to begin

with. The bureaucrats in power will just do whatever they want to do, anyway. [166]

Millions of lives have been adversely affected by this clear and dangerous agenda. At Metabolife, thousands of people lost their jobs. For the rest of the country, millions of Americans lost a safe and cost-effective weight loss product (that worked exceptionally well). Mike Compton lost his life.

In Mike Blevins, Bob Bradley, and me, the FDA, IRS, and DOJ got their Chinese straight. They managed to secure jail time or probation for all of us. But if you examine the charges eventually leveled against us, none of them match their overarching claim that we were tax cheaters peddling an unsafe product. The straight doesn't connect.

And what about everyone else who was involved in this bizarre series of events? What about all those people who either helped or hurt us during those dark times? How about a kind of "where are they now" for the story you've just read?

Mike Blevins: My oldest friend has moved to Florida in the hopes of getting away from it all. Who could blame him? In the papers, they made it look like Mike was a dealer of illegal guns. They even seemed to suggest that he was responsible for the death of Mike Compton. To this day, we still sometimes jokingly call him "Machine Gun Blevins."

Down in Florida, Mike managed to complete his thousand hours of community service in what must be record time. But you know what? He hasn't stopped serving his community. These days, he's dedicated his life to helping the elderly—not because he's mandated by the courts or because he's receiving compensation, but because he genuinely cares about these people and wants to

---

[166] That's not even the scariest thing. The scariest thing is this: If legislation and regulations aren't being followed or implemented by the FDA as they pertain to dietary supplements, what else isn't being followed or implemented? What else is the FDA letting slide just so it can meet its own agendas?

help them lead a better life. His driving motivation is to help all those people cast aside or forgotten.

Bob Bradley: Bob has served his time in prison and concluded his mandated charitable services. But he still works closely with children and the less fortunate, providing them with the things they need to get by. He now considers himself semi-retired (the "semi" coming from the fact that he still helps with charities and dabbles in real estate).

Our lawyers: Steve Mansfield now works in San Francisco as a partner at Akin, Gump. He manages the entire office, from what I understand. Bill Low is still cracking away at Higgs, Fletcher, & Mack, LLP. Garry Pay has moved on to the employ of Ideasphere, the company that acquired Metabolife's assets following the bankruptcy. David Allen still practices law at Akin, Gump. Sam Baxter now works for Bill Low's firm. And Mike Lipman hasn't changed his scenery—he still works for the same firm. Chuck LaBella is still a partner in LaBella and MacNamara, LLP, and is practicing law in San Diego, California. Thank you, Chuck, for your hard work and dedication and believing in me throughout all the trying years.

Dominic Johnson: Apparently exhausted with the life of the PR man, Dominic now works with kids as a baseball coach at Poway High School in San Diego County.

David Brown: David has moved on to become the CEO of a publicly traded nutritional supplement company known as Life Vantage, based in San Diego.

Jim Weaver: Jim has recently retired from the FBI. He now owns a company that provides personal security for executives who travel abroad.

Jim and Diane Cameron: The Camerons have sold the Chemins Company and retired. They're both still happily married and living in Colorado Springs.

Isaac MacLamore: The famous Isaac now lives and works (in sales, of course) in Florida. Apart from that, he's very happy with the wonderful woman he met. He and I have remained in contact through the years—and we still love each other like brothers.

Steve Horn: Steve has retired from California Creative and now lives happily with his family in San Diego.

Ron Sanculli: Ron still lives in Iowa with his family and has remained a close friend for many years.

Joe Ellis, Jr.: Living happily in San Diego with his three children, Jacob, Jackie, and Justine.

Carmen Ellis: Still living in San Diego and enjoying her grandchildren. She no longer watches ABC's *20/20*.

Susan: My first wife now lives happily with her boyfriend of twenty years. The two of them own a restaurant called the Baja Rock 'n Lobster. She and I remain friends.

Monica: My second wife and I are now divorced. She lives happily in San Diego. And the two of us share fifty percent custody of Mikey, Nick, and Isabella.

My children: Christian lives in San Diego, where he works as a partner with me in several companies. Mikey is now going to college in pursuit of a profession in the film industry. He's incredibly talented. Nicholas is a sophomore in high school. He still skateboards like a champion. Little Isabella is four years old, unfortunate enough to have been born during this entire crisis. Still, as an avid crayon artist who has more joy for life than seems possible, she's about as perfect a four-year-old as you'll ever meet. She ended up being the best surprise that I could have ever asked for. In many ways, she saved me. Her presence and love were some of the only things that helped get me through many of the hard times. And I thank her dearly for it.

Dr. William Reynolds ("Reyn") Archer III: Reyn is now the managing director of an organization known as Global Healthcare Practice based in Washington, D.C.

Jeff Wentworth: Jeff remains in his post as a Texas senator. He continues to fight for the good of the people. And he remains completely committed to the causes of the citizens of Texas.

Patrick Keegan: Keegan still practices the good law. At some point during these events, he filed a lawsuit against another dietary supplement company. In this suit, his plaintiff was another *attorney*. Unfortunately for the both of them, the company they were suing filed a SLAP motion against them, effectively quashing the suit. The best part is that Keegan's lawyer client wound up having to pay all the legal expenses (all six figures of them) accrued by the company they were suing. So for once, the litigators had to pay the defendants, instead of the other way around.

Jim Frantz: Still Jim Frantz.

Larry Miller: I'm not sure what happened to Larry. We've since lost contact.

Jeff Anderman: Same with Jeff. I hope that whatever he's doing, he's not doing it in a cookie suit.

Ken Dix: Ken's bounced around from company to company, never staying at any one place for too long. I guess that's what happens when you're a lawyer who likes to talk a little too much.

John Macaulay: The last thing any of us ever heard about John was that he was still representing himself as a doctor and claiming that he was an integral player on the 49ers championship teams.

Dr. Randy Smith: The good doctor now lives and works in Atlanta, where he peddles an "aging process management" system called Cenegenics. Basically, it's a wellness program designed to help a person age better, but it's marketed as if it were some kind of fountain of youth.

Dr. Carlon Colker: Dr. Colker is practicing medicine, working with patients, and living with his family in Greenwich, Connecticut. He's still a strong advocate of holistic and natural supplements.

Cynthia Culmo: Hearsay is that Culmo was fired or removed by the Texas Department of Health. Reasons unknown. Regardless, she now holds down a position for a company called Abbott Laboratories in Abbott Park, Illinois (which is interesting because Abbott Laboratories is one of the biggest contributors to the pharmaceutical drug lobby).

Dr. Beth Yetli: To my knowledge, Dr. Beth still works for the FDA, where she serves as a champion of Codex.

Penny Crabtree: Last I heard, the intrepid reporter was being sued for blurring the line of ethics with one of her articles. As far as I know, she still works for the *San Diego Union Tribune.* I wouldn't know for sure, though, because I don't buy that rag anymore.

Susan Warnick: I'm not sure if Warnick can even find work anymore.

Arnold Diaz: Arnold who?

Agent Martinez: Still acting as an IRS agent for the U.S. government. Acting.

Phil Halprin: Phil Halprin is still busy being Phil Halprin. He continues to work for the U.S. Attorney's Office. I wonder if anyone ever asked him what happened with Metabolife. I wonder if anyone ever questioned him about how he could commit so much of the taxpayers' money to an investigation based on accusations that were ultimately disproven. Where's the oversight committee on this one?

Carol Lam: Carol was removed from her post by the Bush administration.

Billy Tauzin and Jim Greenwood: Ah, my favorite two former congressmen to talk about. In 2004, Tauzin and Greenwood left their posts with the government to go work for big pharmacy. Tauzin enjoys one of the largest annual lobbyist fees in U.S. history.

At one point, Congress began an inquiry into the exorbitant funding that Tauzin was receiving. Conveniently (and mysteriously), during the investigation, old Billy came down with a rare form of intestinal cancer. Capitol Hill backed off their old buddy, not wanting to belabor his pain, given his cancer and all. But lo and behold, as soon as the smoke cleared on the inquiry, Billy was cured by an experimental drug—one developed by a pharmaceutical company.

So now, Tauzin seems to be using his little miracle as political leverage, as a kind of mandate for his mission to keep citizens from going into Canada to buy "unsafe products." It's a strange mission to uphold, though, given that these so-called "unsafe products" are manufactured in the exact same FDA-certified locations as are the drugs in the U.S. So you have to ask yourself, what does Billy's agenda actually protect? The American people or big pharmacy's bottom line?

Greenwood enjoys similar benefits for all his hard work to protect the American public. He also works for a pharmaceutical company. And he ain't exactly having a hard time making ends meet.

You could make the argument that the ultimate fruit of Tauzin and Greenwood's labors was a pharmaceutical drug known as Alli, which was approved by the FDA for release in 2005. Given that all the viable dietary weight loss supplements had recently been stripped from the market, the company behind Alli projected three to four billion dollars in sales. Unfortunately, Alli's many side effects included anal leakage and the depletion of vital nutrients. So the consumer had to take an expensive vitamin with it, just so they wouldn't die. This being the case, sales didn't go exactly like the company thought they would.

So good job, boys. Keep enjoying your fat working retirements while Americans foot the bill with their diseases.

Michael J. Ellis: I'm currently serving six months at Taft Federal Prison. I'm due to be released in February of 2009. Six months. So after one of the biggest IRS sting operations in the history of the Southern district, I received six months for presiding over a company that employed a man who in error wrote a false statement and submitted it to the FDA. I never even knew about that statement when it was written—and never would have authorized it, had I known—but I guess that's beside the point.

My lawyers and I would later discover that during this supposed IRS investigation, not a single financial account was seized. My accountants and investment brokers were never interviewed. Now why would the IRS not do that? I'm not sure of the answer to that, but I will tell you this: The FDA got its hands on everything it needed to trump up some charges against us—charges just significant enough to bring about the death of the company.

So the IRS never brought charges against Mike Blevins and me. In fact, as I've already mentioned, we even received refund checks (totaling several million dollars) during the farcical investigation into tax fraud. And now I sit in jail, waiting for my release over an attorney error that I was unaware of for several years until the Frantz deposition. And even better, it's not even technically a crime to begin with—but they saved face and got their win.

This is my story. Whether or not you choose to believe it is entirely up to you. I know that, at times, in a country full of CEO scandals and the misuse of power, many of my claims might seem a little difficult to swallow. But for the more skeptical of my readers: I invite you to visit the accompanying website. There, you'll find legally irrefutable evidence that supports everything I've said.

You'll find proof that they never found a gun in Mike Blevins' house, that they never found a single print of Blevins' or mine on anything they seized. (Not one thing. Ever. Not even from the guns they seized from Monica's safe). You'll find that by the end of the whole six-year charade, my case involved a minimum of twelve search warrants—which my attorneys tell me almost never happens in a fraud case—evidence burning in a fire, a government witness under indictment, a dismissal of obstruction charges, and a plea to something that doesn't even amount to a true crime. Still, from day one to the present day, no one from the government ever gave up. No one ever apologized.

As I sit here with all this time on my hands, I can't help but wonder why the government couldn't simply back away from the investigation once they saw that there was no real tax fraud. My theory is that they were just trying to save face. By the time Blevins' and my refund checks went out, the IRS and DOJ had already committed themselves to a five-year investigation. One hundred and thirty agents had been involved, all told. So Halprin and his cronies had committed all this time, energy, and tax funding to find something, *anything*, on Mike Ellis and Metabolife.

But that's just human nature, I guess. You can't just turn away with your tail between your legs. You have to *win*.

So, in the end, I'm a tax fraud, a gun nut, and an irresponsible business owner who doesn't care about the health of his customers. Being called all of those things without apology isn't what keeps me up at night as I lay awake in federal prison. No, what keeps me up is that everyone was informed of my supposed wrongdoings, but no one was informed when everything was *dropped*. The government tried to convict me on irresponsible business practices, on distributing a "dangerous" product, on owning guns, and on defrauding the government for $93.7 million. And you know what conclusions they came to? That I was *innocent on all charges*.

Does anyone know about that fact? No.

But not anymore. I told myself that I would use all this newfound free time to write a book on the truth. I told myself that now it was my turn.

To this day, there is still no valid, credible, scientific evidence to show that ma huang or its derivative ephedrine is unsafe when used as directed by healthy adults. Still, under this inaccurate claim promoted by the FDA, dietary supplements took a huge hit. Make no mistake, if the FDA has its way, in the very near future, all dietary supplements will wind up in the hands of pharmaceutical companies and regulated by the World Health Organization. You'll have only one choice for your dietary or weight loss needs. And it'll probably cause anal leakage.

Do I believe that most people in the FDA think that they're doing the right thing? Yes. Absolutely. I'm sure that there are many who honestly believe that a person should not have the right to choose their own agenda when it comes to his or her health. They likely believe that doctors, as trained professionals, are the only people who can be trusted to make healthy decisions for the consumer.

Still, if the American people fall in line with this logic, then everything that we do will eventually be harmonized by the WHO. And who is the WHO? They're not a country. They're a coalition. They're big money. Everything we eat, every supplement we take, everything we wear, everything—it will all be controlled by big money companies. We'll have no control over what we can buy or eat. And we won't have free access to many of the things that we so take for granted today.

Don't believe me? Then let's back up for a minute and see exactly what's been accomplished by this huge hostile takeover of herbal ephedrine. Herbal ephedrine provided by dietary supplement companies is now illegal. The reason? Ephedrine was deemed by the FDA to be unsafe for healthy adults. So it stands to reason that a healthy adult wouldn't be able to buy ephedrine in any form. Wrong. You can still buy ephedrine today. And, in fact, you can buy it in higher doses than you would have ever found in the supposedly dangerous Metabolife. The only difference? You have to buy it from a pharmaceutical company. Over-the-counter. You don't even need a prescription. Just Google "Vasopro" and see for yourself.

So take heart, reader. You didn't truly lose your ability to purchase a supplement that will supposedly give you a stroke. You just have to buy it from a mega-corporation now.

In closing, I would like to thank Senator Tom Harkin, Senator Orrin G. Hatch, and Congressman Dan Burton for fighting the good cause for Americans. Whatever you may think about them politically, Hatch and Harkin spearheaded DSHEA legislation and worked to protect consumers' free access. And Dan Burton fought the good fight for free access and free choice. Without these men and others like them, we would have lost our access to dietary supplements a long time ago.

Reader, you might think that you've just finished a story about what happened to Metabolife. But it's more than that. What happened to Bob Bradley, Mike Blevins, Mike Compton, and me could happen to *anyone* in this country. In fact, it *is* happening to many people *right now*. Every day, people are wrongly accused of federal crimes. Every day, guilty or otherwise, people plead out to minor (or even major) crimes just so they can end the nightmare. Every day, people are wrongfully defamed by the media. Every day, public opinion swings toward guilty until proven innocent.

But you don't hear about many of these cases. Why? Because they can be conveniently and quietly swept under the rug. See, most defendants in federal cases don't have the profile or the ability to fight against wrongful charges. They just don't have the money it takes to battle the giant government, law, and media machine that works so hard to discredit people. Metabolife had enough money to fight the FDA. They had good enough recordkeeping to discredit the IRS. They had enough money to go head to head with the DOJ.

Was it a battle that we could win? Not alone, no. Even if we'd kept going, we would've run out of money and political clout eventually.

But it *is* a battle that the citizens of this country, working together, can win easily.

Reader, if you are a voter who wants to maintain your access to supplements, if you are a voter who would rather hold on to your right to make choices about your own healthcare, then you still have control. Your vote *matters*. Your letters to Congress *matter*. The FDA and big pharmaceutical agenda was beaten in the middle '90s by DSHEA—a largely voter-driven initiative that was pushed rapidly through Congress and the Senate. And that agenda can be beaten again. We simply need to band together and put a stop to all this fear mongering and misrepresentation.

As for me, I've been on both sides of the fence for my entire life. I was a crook and I was a cop. I've been the hero and I've played the villain. I don't know how I will eventually be perceived. I don't even know how to perceive myself. But in the end, none of that matters. The only thing that matters is the story.

The events that you have just read about are true. They all happened. And if you take anything from this book, just remember that if it could happen to me, there is no reason to believe that it couldn't happen to you. The abuse of power and money in this country continues to spiral dangerously out of control. And the task of balancing the scales once more lies squarely in our hands.